# Undimmed Lustre

Portrait of Tudor. *Source unknown*

# Undimmed Lustre

## *The Life of Antony Tudor*

Muriel Topaz

The Scarecrow Press, Inc.
Lanham, Maryland, and London
2002

SCARECROW PRESS, INC.

Published in the United States of America
by Scarecrow Press, Inc.
4720 Boston Way, Lanham, Maryland 20706
www.scarecrowpress.com

4 Pleydell Gardens, Folkestone
Kent CT20 2DN, England

Copyright © 2002 by Muriel Topaz

British Library Cataloguing-in-Publication Information Available

**Library of Congress Cataloging-in-Publication Data Available**

ISBN 0-8108-4128-2 (alk. paper)

The paper used in this publication meets the minimum requirements of
American National Standard for Information Sciences—Permanence of
Paper for Printed Library Materials, ANSI/NISO Z39.48-1992.
Manufactured in the United States of America.

# Contents

# List of Photographs

Frontispiece: Portrait of Antony Tudor. Source unknown

Page xiii: Marie Rambert and Antony Tudor. Ballet Rambert Archive, Arthur Todd, Photographer

Page 5: Alfred and Florence Cook, Tudor's parents. Courtesy of Isabel Brown

Page 8: William Cook (later Antony Tudor). Courtesy of Isabel Brown

Page 16: Tudor and Eugene Loring in Loring's *The Great American Goof.* Courtesy of Nancy Zeckendorf

Page 22: Tudor practicing a lift with Helena Dukes, one of the Rambert children. Ballet Rambert Archive

Page 27: Maude Lloyd. Courtesy of Maude Lloyd

Page 34: Cavorting on the beach. Top: Hugh Laing and Antony Tudor. Bottom from left: Nigel Gosling, Tudor, and Laing lifting Maude Lloyd. Courtesy of Maude Lloyd

Page 36: *Lysistrata.* Victoria and Albert Museum and Ballet Rambert Archives

Page 46: *The Planets:* Hugh Laing as Mars. Ballet Rambert Archives

Arts, Astor, Lenox, and Tilden Foundations. Photograph by
Serge Le Blanc.

Page 184: Sally Brayley (Bliss) and Lance Westergard in
*Concerning Oracles*. Courtesy of Sally Brayley Bliss

Page 190: *Judgment of Paris*. From left to right: Maria Karnilova, Agnes de Mille, Lucia Chase. Courtesy of Sallie Wilson. Photograph by Fred Fehl

Page 202: *Britannia Triumphans:* The "Cat" Section. From
left to right: Charles Wadsworth, Bruce (Kevin) Carlisle, unidentified, Rena Gluck. The Juilliard School Archives. Photograph by Frank Donato, Impact Photo, Inc.

Page 205: *A Choreographer Comments:* "Arabesque" Section.
From left to right: Virginia Klein (?), unidentified (either Jerry
King or Benjamin "Buck" Heller), Michal Imber, Chieko
Kikuchi, Myron Howard Nadel, Jennifer Masley (?). The Juil-
liard Archives. Impact Photo, Inc.

Page 213: Tudor choreographing *Dance Studies: Less Orthodox*. Photograph by Elizabeth Sawyer. Courtesy of Isabel
Brown

Page 219: *Echoing of Trumpets*. Courtesy of Sally Brayley
Bliss

Page 224: Tudor rehearsing in Japan. Courtesy of Tomoji
Tsutsui

Page 229: Anthony Dowell in *Shadowplay*. Jerome Robbins
Dance Division, New York Public Library for the Performing
Arts, Astor, Lenox, and Tilden Foundations. Photograph by
Donald Southern

Page 237: Heather Macrae and Karl Welander of the Australian Ballet in *The Divine Horseman*. Courtesy of the Australian Ballet

# Acknowledgments

The genesis of this book can be traced to a conversation I had quite a few years ago with Nancy Zeckendorf. She urged me to consider writing about our mutual teacher, Antony Tudor, and proceeded to introduce me to Isabel Brown. Isabel was the person to whom Hugh Laing, Tudor's lifelong companion, left his own effects upon his death. While she had turned over to the New York Public Library for the Performing Arts (NYPL) many of the documents, Isabel still had quite a collection stored in shopping bags in her closet. She very generously offered to allow me access to them, access which had not been afforded to anyone before that. I was highly honored. As I perused the material over a yearlong period, I felt very obligated to do something to address the lacunae of information about this man whom I so respected and who had had such a profound influence on my life.

A second incident furthered that sense of opportunity and obligation. Tudor's first ballerina, Maude Lloyd, was aging and, more out of curiosity that conviction, I asked to interview her on one of my trips to London. We spent a charming and informative afternoon together. As I was leaving, Maude told me that since her eyesight was beginning to fail, she could no longer read the many letters that Tudor had written to her. Then, she handed them to me, and gave me permission to copy them before turning them over to the Tudor collection at NYPL. It was an amazingly generous gesture for which I am very grateful.

A third occurrence sealed my fate. I knew that the only way a proper biography could be written was to embark on the same sort of odyssey as had Tudor himself. This meant extensive travel, which was beyond my means. Without much hope for success because I was neither a creative artist nor a scholar with academic *bonafides*, I applied for a Guggenheim grant. It was, indeed, granted!

To Nancy, Isabel, Maude, and the Guggenheim Foundation I say a rousing thank you.

The number of other people who have been so generous in sharing their time, information and resources with me is quite astounding. I wish to thank Judith Chazin-Bennahum for sharing the tapes of the many interviews she did in preparation for her wonderful book *The Ballets of Anthony Tudor*. Jane Pritchard, archivist for the Rambert Dance Company and the English National Ballet, was particulary helpful in providing information, introductions, and clues for further research.

There were many other achivists who were most helpful: the staff of the NYPL, the Department of Special Collections at Boston University, the Dance Notation Bureau, the Australian Ballet, the Carina Ari Library, and Inger Mattsson of the Kungliga Teatramas Arkiv (Archives of the Royal Theaters) in Stockholm, archivist Pennino of the Metropolitan Opera, Florence Pettan at American Ballet Theatre, Norton Owen at Jacob's Pillow, Chris Jones of the Dance Resource Centre at the University of Surrey in Guilford, the libraries of the Laban Centre in London, the University of California at Irvine, the Paris Opera, and Jane Gottlieb, chief librarian at the Juilliard School.

Sally Brayley Bliss of the Tudor Trust has been both helpful and encouraging to the point of hosting my stay in St. Louis to facilitate my study of the archives of the Trust.

My stay in New Zealand with the Cook/Palmer clan could not have been more delightful nor more informative. Their hospitality was more than one could hope for. I am particularly indebted to Ian and Connaught Palmer for all of their efforts on my behalf.

I thank all of the many people whom I interviewed; I appreciate their willingness to devote considerable time and effort to my quest, and to share their very precious memories with me. Others who have been most helpful include Meg Denton, Selma Jeanne Cohen, Harry Haythorne, Barbara Horgan, Bruce MacCombie, Madeline Nichols, Gaileen Stock, Anna-Karin Stahle-Varney and Anna-Greta Stahle, Mauricio Wainrot, Carl Wolz, and a host of others who, I hope, will forgive me for not mentioning them by name.

Finally, I thank my loyal and patient friends Judith Norell and Richard Philp for their insightful suggestions on the manuscript, and especially Claire Brook for her professional expertise and immaculate editing of the work.

Marie Rambert and Antony Tudor. *Photograph by Arthur Todd*

# 1

# Growing Up: 1908–1928

The ballet ended, the curtain closed. Absolute silence. "They are not clapping. It's a disaster," ballerina Nora Kaye whispered. Then the sound pierced the silence. The applause had started; it rose and swelled. As the crescendo began to wane, the choreographer signaled, "Now!" The dancers emerged from the wings to a burst of shouting "Bravo! Bravo" from all over the theater. The uproar continued for about thirty curtain calls, an unheard-of tribute. The debut of Antony Tudor's great ballet *Pillar of Fire*, the first of several astonishing works he created in the United States, had taken place.[1]

When Tudor emigrated from his native Britain to the United States in 1940, at the start of World War II, he had already choreographed a series of iconoclastic ballet masterpieces. The man's genius was a known fact, known, that is, by English critics, intellectual cognoscenti, and a small coterie of that country's balletomanes. In the United States, however, he was an unknown quantity.

Although Tudor's fame has grown greatly both in America and throughout the world in the years that followed those first triumphs of the 1930s and 1940s, and although he became an icon for his most avid fans, he is still a vastly underrated choreographer. Even in the ballet world his extraordinary gifts have never achieved the celebrity of his contemporaries George Balanchine (1904–1983) or Frederick Ashton (1904–1988).

Misconceptions about the man and his work abound. His public commonly believes that he never had his own company, but, in fact, he founded and, for a year, directed the tiny London Ballet. He was an all-important force, a prime mover, in the early years of Ballet Theatre. One of several apocryphal legends speaks of his miniscule body of works, but he created more than fifty ballets, choreographed more than a dozen operas and created many dances for theater, film, and television. Although by reputation he was universally hated by dancers, in actuality those who worked closely with him regard the man with great affection and respect.

Tudor's enigmatic personality, his English propriety mixed with his rapier-sharp, often vulgar wit, his overwhelming need for personal privacy, his insecurities, his total inability to compromise artistically, and his Zen Buddhism all made him a lonesome figure in the very communal dance world. While his work is subtle, detailed, and passionate, it eschews star turns and bravura displays of virtuosity. It demands great emotional and technical skills not always immediately obvious to the audience. He imbued the simplest gesture with profound meaning, bringing drama into "academic" ballet. He mixed everyday gesture with the classical vocabulary and incorporated the ideas of Freud and Stanislavsky into his dances. He adapted cinematic techniques to the ballet medium.

This biography reveals some of the reasons behind the series of misconceptions and contradictions that have attached themselves to Antony Tudor, one of the most creative forces of the twentieth century.

## The Background

"Britannia rules the waves" and "the pound sterling is as good as gold." These catch words reveal the conventional wisdom of 1902. Edward had been crowned king, ushering in a genteel, if short-lived, time of peace and prosperity.

The Boer War, the last of Britain's imperialist adventures, had ended. India was still under the fist of its English viceroy Lord Curzon, but the British Empire had begun to crumble. In a city like York, in 1900, it was estimated that 40 percent of the population lived in poverty, while the aristocracy continued in full power and the merchant class was amassing great wealth. The House of Lords had full veto power over legislation; only in 1911 could the House of Commons override the veto by voting to pass a bill in three consecutive years. Even so, the transition from an aristocratic to a democratic society would soon begin.

Class distinction held (and in some smaller ways still holds) an important status in the life of every English man, woman, and child. As soon as a person speaks he or she reveals a pedigree, by the lilt of an educated or a regional accent. In the early days of the twentieth century, however, there were already signs of change. The Education Act of 1902 made schooling children up to the age of fourteen compulsory. A narrow first rung in the ladder of opportunity was opening; publicly educated children could now begin to gain academic qualifications. In the next decade, up until the advent of the Great War (1914–1918) when the war effort usurped all focus, social reform laws began to be discussed and a few reforms finally implemented. The ratio of wages to cost of living began to improve, reducing infant mortality and the number of women who died in childbirth. Better nutrition meant a taller, stronger populace and fewer deaths from tuberculosis.

The most famous writers of the period were George Bernard Shaw, H. G. Wells, and the aging Rudyard Kipling. (Kipling was born in 1865 and probably fit more comfortably into Victorian rather than Edwardian England, although he won the Pulitzer Prize for literature in 1907).

Every town with a population of over 50,000 had its football (soccer) league. Youngsters also played rugby and the national sport, cricket. Only in England could there be a sport that took time out for tea.

Music Hall became the popular form of entertainment at the turn of the century. Originally based in pubs, it featured comedy and popular songs with a cynical undertone of sharp social criticism. The audience participated often and loudly. Music Hall finally became somewhat respectable when it later moved into theaters; Harry Lauder, one of the most well-known singers, was knighted in 1919. Popular pastimes included a wide range of social activities, many of them based in the churches: friendly societies for girls, boys clubs, choirs, and amateur theater groups. There was a strong tradition of self-help, middle-class self-improvement, as well as an avid reading public for works of literary merit.The audience flocked to hear the Savoy Opera present Gilbert and Sullivan. Other professional theater was another matter. The law insisted that the Lord Chamberlain grant a license for all public performances on stage. To avoid problems, many of Shaw's plays, for example, were mounted by the Stage Society in so-called private performances.

Homosexuality was a criminal offense until 1960. Some of the poet Wilfred Owen's homoerotic work had to wait fifty years before publication, not only to satisfy the sensibilities of his surviving family but also to get past the censor.

A revolution brewed in the ballet world. In 1907 Mikhail Fokine (1880–1942) choreographed the first "abstract ballet," *Chopiniana (Les Sylphides)*. Two years later the Diaghilev Ballets Russes astonished the public with its glamorous Paris debut; in 1911 the company repeated its astounding success in its London debut.

## Beginnings

On 4 April, 1908, William John Cook, the man we now know as Antony Tudor, was born into this social climate. He lived at 105 Cen-

tral Street in the Finsbury section of London, a stone's throw from the
famous Smithfield meat market in Islington. His family belonged to
the working class: his father, Alfred Robert Cook, a butcher; and his
mother, Florence Ann Cook, née Summers, a housewife and helper to
his father. There were two boys, the eldest, Robert, and, three years
younger, William (Antony). Mrs. Cook had French forebears while Mr.
Cook came from a line of hardworking butchers. Alfred headed the
household, of course, but Tudor's mother functioned, perhaps more
effectively, as the family breadwinner. Often she ran the shop while his
gregarious father was off visiting with other shopkeepers.

A short walk from the family store brought one to the renowned
Sadler's Wells Theatre and, less than two miles farther, London's
Royal Opera House at Covent Garden. Central Street was dreary. Brick
houses, originally yellow, gray, or red, sported soot-darkened facades
as a result of the coal fires used for heating. While Finsbury was not
exactly a slum, it was clearly a working-class neighborhood, full of
vitality and subject to stereotypical working-class values and toughness.

Tudor's family lived above the store. The butcher shop occupied
the ground floor; the floor below contained the freezer where the meat
was stored. The top two floors housed the living quarters.

My parents had a little butcher shop and two doors away was a
retail fish shop. The fish shop had marble slabs for counters . . .
When we played we'd get up and dance on the marble slabs with
lace curtains and use a little hole cut in them for the spotlight. I
was already inventing dances at six or seven.

When I was still a toddler my father kept a horse in a stable in a
nearby mews. There was a photograph taken with my brother
and myself perched on its back. One day at the shop on Central
Street the horse slipped and broke its leg. To my horror my father went indoors and came back with a heavy revolver in his
hand. It was doubtless absolutely necessary but the sight of all
the bubbling blood pouring forth into the gutter was an intimation of mortality that could never be forgotten. And of firearms
that can so quickly destroy the life force in us.

My earliest memories are roughly what could have been expected: visits to my grandparents on high days and holidays,
coming home on the train from Forest Gate to Liverpool Street
Station curled up in my father's lap, or going to a neighbor's
party at Xmas and being envious of all the presents they re
ceived. I do not think we even had an Xmas tree until many,
many years later.[2]

Alfred and Florence Cook. *Photograph courtesy of Isabel Brown*

Perhaps this early memory shaped Tudor's life-long pacifist inclinations as well as his brother Robert's career as an environmentalist. Neither one of them ever wanted to have anything to do with killing.

During Tudor's childhood, Music Hall, the nearest British equivalent to American vaudeville, featured "toe dances," short variations performed by young ladies. These attractions had more to do with the length and shape of the ladies' legs than with how they got up on their pointe shoes. True ballet was a high art form no working-class child would sit through. Thus Tudor never saw Nijinsky dance, nor was he aware as a young boy of what was happening in the world of Diaghilev. That came later.

But, by the age of four, Cook (Tudor) had already been captivated by the enchantments of the theater.

Before the old Sadler's Wells Theatre had closed down for a period of some years, I had been taken to a Xmas pantomime there and succumbed to the chorus dancing to the song *Follow the Footsteps in the Snow.* (A corps de ballet of eight girls danced in the manner of the Rockettes—they were bad. Even so, the audience liked it.) I enjoyed the spectacle of a comedian climbing up a flight of stairs that collapsed into a slope, down which he precipitately tumbled to the total hilarity of the audience.[3]

My other theatre memory from an early age is of being taken to a performance of a variety program. A dancer stayed centre stage on a small raised platform, and, with the use of veils, gave the impression first of sea green waters, then of an evocation of fire. Then came a golden light with a shower of glittering gold particles descending from above the waving of the gauze scarves.[4] This was part of a program at the big variety theatre on Holloway Road, the Marlborough. . . . It seemed I had been privileged to see Loie Fuller[5] in action.

My father was inordinately fond of variety programmes and almost weekly we would go to one of the many "Empire" music halls, the Islington or the Shoreditch or the Holborn. I saw most of the stars of the English music halls of that time from Vesta Tilley [Professional name of Lady De Frece, the most celebrated of male impersonators in English Music Hall] to Harry Lauder [popular singer of sentimental songs] to Gracie Fields [the famed comedienne]. As part of these programmes we would have Tableaux Vivantes presented by the Lorraine sisters, Irma and Violet. They used a small false proscenium centre stage. Whenever the curtains were opened a ravishing and presumably seductive posing was presented. By this time I was completely stage-struck. Forever and ever.[6]

Tudor attended the Hugh Myddleton School, about a twenty-minute walk from his home. He had to cross several large roads on which streetcars ran. Although he was only four years old, his parents trusted him to make the crossings safely each day. And, each day he would spend his penny pocket money on little fairy tale books rather than on candy.

Tudor, always a good student, devoted time to his school work, while his brother Bob's interests lay elsewhere. Both boys agreed on one thing: they were not going to be butchers, nor were they going to stay in Finsbury. Robert eventually emigrated to New Zealand where he did environmental work, while Tudor spent most of his adult life as a resident of the United States and a restless traveler.

Tudor's childhood experiences remained a rich source of material for many of the incidents in his ballets. As a small child he went to dances at the local town hall. On occasion his mother told him about the "balls" that she attended, small gatherings no doubt. She reminisced about the little cards on which one signed up for each dance of the evening. And, he remembered being taught etiquette, manners, and the correct way to speak, even in kindergarten. Expressing one's feelings in public was indiscreet and impolite, not acceptable Edwardian behavior. A child had to be "nice" and did what he was expected to do.

A voracious reader, in his childhood Tudor used the Skinner Street library as a source. Throughout his life he continued reading an eclectic diet of plays, poetry, novels, history, and anything else he could come by. He read in both English and self-taught French. Later he became a collector of fine editions. Inspiration for many of his ballets came from literary sources.

Literary evocations of an Edwardian garden party as portrayed in Sigried Sassoon's Memoirs of a Fox Hunting Man (1928) and L. P. Huntley's The Go-Between stayed with Tudor throughout his early years. He confessed to loving the Edwardian period for its dress and manners, and several of his ballets take place in that context.

Another example of the influence of Tudor's early life on his work occurs in *Undertow*. There is a moment in the ballet when three drink–sodden ladies wander across the stage, barely able to stand. One of them walks to a corner and lifts her skirt, presumably to urinate. It is an incident that Tudor remembered witnessing as a child.

Making music was not an unusual pursuit for the sons of a proper, upwardly mobile, blue-collar family. Music pervaded the Cook family household. Tudor's father played the violin and his grandfather,

William Cook (later known as Antony Tudor). *Photograph courtesy of Isabel Brown*

the cello. His mother played the piano and gave both boys lessons; Tudor's began when he was eight years old. On Sunday evenings family members would assemble at the Cook household. His mother would sing and Tudor would accompany her.

In 1914, when Tudor was six years old, World War I, the Great War, began. The English did not see the war as a matter of national interest, but rather as a moral issue of right and wrong. With the stereotypical stiff upper lip, the troops went marching off to the strains of *The Rose of Picardy, It's a Long Way to Tipperary,* and *Pack Up Your Troubles in Your Old Kit Bag.*

Mass carnage ensued. At the battle of the Somme alone 60,000 men were lost on the first day, heavier losses than had ever before been sustained by an army. By 1918 one in three of the male workforce, one in two of those between the ages of eighteen and forty-one, were in the armed forces. Over a half million did not return.

The war spawned a heroic group of artists. The poet Rupert Brooke was reputedly so handsome that the author Lytton Strachey, of Bloomsbury fame, swooned when first they met. Brooke's untimely death in the war and his posthumously published poetry made him a national hero. Anti-war sentiment surfaced in Sassoon's *Counterattack* (1918), Robert Graves's *Goodbye to All* (1929), and in the work of Wilfred Owen and Edmund Blunden.

Lord Beaverbrook instituted a policy of sending painters to the front lines to record what they saw, perhaps the first subsidy of the arts by the British government. Percy Wyndham Lewis produced *A Battery Shell* (1918), Paul Nash, *Void* (1917), C. R. W. Nevinson, *Marching Men* (1916), and William Robert, *First Attack at Ypres* (1918). The bleak vision that these artists produced did not exactly commemorate the war in quite the way the government had in mind.

In the dance world, the Diaghilev Ballet was the rage in Paris. Fokine's 1907 ballet *Les Sylphides* revolutionized classical ballet, for it did not tell a story in the way of *Swan Lake* or *Giselle*. Rather, it created an atmosphere and explored the characters without the aid of a plot line. A few years later came Nijinsky's innovative ballets, *L'Après-midi d'un faune* (1912) to the famed score by Claude Debussy and *Le Sacre du printemps* (1913) with Igor Stravinsky's amazing music. Tudor was too much of a child to be aware of all this, however.

Young Antony experienced the war through his visits to air raid shelters. He was later evacuated to Chiswick with its firing range, where he endured the shocks and gun shots that later found expression in *Echoing of Trumpets*. One wonders also how his young mind took in the war and how the experience of those years influenced his later pacifism.

The two Cook boys attended excellent schools with the aid of an uncle who helped pay the tuition fees. At that time, children, especially working class children, routinely finished their schooling at age fourteen, but Tudor won a scholarship to attend the prestigious Dame Alice Owens School for Boys. He entered in September, 1919, soon after the Great War armistice at Versailles, and in 1924 passed the General Schools Examination (GSE).

On 18 December, 1924, just past the age of sixteen, having completed more than two years beyond the legal requirement, he left school. He began working and continued his education in the evenings. Soon thereafter he abandoned his studies because he failed to pass the university entrance examinations.

When Tudor left school, his father helped place him in a position of clerk/office boy in the nearby, renowned Smithfield meat market on Farringdon Street. Since the postwar slump and considerable unemployment had not yet abated, the job was quite a welcome coup. While he worked conscientiously and carried out whatever tasks were assigned him, music remained his real interest.

Every Saturday morning the whole sidewalk of Farringdon Street became second-hand book and music stores.

> I used to walk up and down looking through and buying lots of second-hand sheet music to take home and play. I used to get the star albums which were mostly piano reductions of orchestra scores. That is how I tried to enlarge my knowledge of music.[8]

Tudor continued his piano study for quite a few years, even after he had left home. He studied with several teachers from the London College of Music, including a disciple of Joseph Schillinger.[9] He claimed to have played badly and got only as far as part way through the last movement of Beethoven's *Sonata in C-sharp Minor* (op. 27, no. 2, subtitled "The Moonlight Sonata"). Then he stopped. He could read scores reasonably well. This proved to be an asset to him later in his career; he himself arranged the music for several of his ballets, combining various pieces with musically acceptable regard for key relationships. He made just such a score for his very first ballet, *Cross-Garter'd* (1931).

Tudor's knowledge of music repertory was profound, much of it gleaned as a young man by attending the Promenade concerts at London's Queen's Hall and various chamber music venues. With typical Tudor dry wit he recounted that his first taste for music came through his dentist who played the radio to divert his attention from the agony and then gave him a penny at the end of the session.

## Discovering the Dance and the Stage

In his 1971 lecture series at York University, Tudor spoke of how he discovered dance more or less by accident. As a schoolboy he had to travel to the playing fields for physical education twice weekly.

> To get there was a pleasant ride on a double decker tram and I often sat at the top. Halfway through this trip I passed a triangular-shaped building and level with the top of the tram was a big window. I saw kids doing the strangest things. It was a typical dance studio teaching a little bit of everything. So I joined up.[10]

He attended these first classes at the studio of Suzy Boyle; they were "dreadful." His evenings were mostly spent with amateur dramatic societies.

> Shortly after he left school, Antony Tudor joined a little Amateur Dramatic Society attached to a church in the City Road about seven minutes walk from the Angel crossroads. It was very small and they rehearsed in the church parish hall which lay at the back of the church. It had a platform at one side which could be rigged up into some distant imitation of a stage . . . "You can imagine how lowly this was when I tell you that my first role there was Professor Higgins in *Pygmalion*."[11]

For his second foray he played Malvolio in *Twelfth Night*; he was exactly eighteen years old. This experience surely influenced his choice of the theme for his first ballet, *Cross-Garter'd*. The ballet centered around the comic characters of the play, with the lead role, Malvolio, being danced by Tudor himself.

As time went on, Tudor linked up with better and better dramatic societies; the better the group, the less demanding became his roles. Finally, he joined St. Pancras People's Theatre where his roles were "miserable" and where he first encountered elementary ballet classes.

At St. Pancras one Christmas show required dancers, thus he discovered partnering. He portrayed a devil in his dancing debut, with his partner cast as a bat. At that moment he recognized how much he enjoyed being applauded. Tudor mused that he would have liked to be an actor but his voice was not good enough. "So that ambition went out. I think the really greatest career would have been [as] an orchestral conductor, because he is so powerful."[12]

Very little dance existed in the London of that time. Mostly it took place in the commercial theater—music halls and variety shows, which featured dance more as entertainment than art. What ballet did exist was almost exclusively "Russian." The Diaghilev Ballets Russes debuted in London in 1911 and, except for the war years, played in London fairly regularly through the 1920s. Bronislava Nijinska, George Balanchine, and Léonide Massine[13] provided most of the choreography. Massine also choreographed revues at commercial theaters in London. English ballet was just beginning and no professional company yet existed.

In 1928 (some sources say 1925), Tudor saw the exquisite Anna Pavlova (1881–1931), who illuminated the stage with her grace and lightness and who inspired so many people in the dance world. She enchanted Tudor, even though "she couldn't do pirouettes." He remembered "sitting in the Gods [the amphitheater] of Covent Garden suffering through an interminable performance of *Tristan and Isolde*," to see Pavlova in excerpts from *The Fairy Doll* (*Die Puppenfee*, Hassreiter/Bayer) and *Coppélia* (St. Léon/Delibes). This sold-out performance of *The Fairy Doll* resolved Tudor's destiny. He was captured. Years later he told Richard Philp, former editor-in-chief of *Dance Magazine*, that *The Fairy Doll* was the best ballet he had ever seen and the one that he would most like to see revived.

It was 1926 or 1927 when Tudor saw the Diaghilev company for the first time. By then his impressions had been solidified. Except for the work of Massine, he adored what he had seen, going back again and again, seeing everything he could. According to Tudor, the top soloists, excluding the stars, would not be accepted into any corps de ballet today. He recalled that later, when Tamara Karsavina[14] performed as guest artist with the Ballet Rambert, she had little technique but danced with the elegance of a mature artist. Perhaps memories such as these led Tudor often to opt for dancers with the ability to enter deeply into roles rather than for their technical virtuosity.

## First Steps

Tudor's visits to the Diaghilev Ballet in 1928 during its penultimate season in London included seeing Serge Lifar[15] in Balanchine's magnificent new work *Apollon Musagète* (Stravinsky).[16] The work's great beauty stayed with him until the end of his life. In the flush of the enthusiasm that it engendered, Tudor, in his late teens, sought advice. He had finally decided it was time to get some serious dance training. He telephoned the secretary of the Imperial Society of Teachers of Dancing who steered him to Cyril Beaumont. Beaumont, writer, publisher, and owner of a renowned dance book shop in the Charing

Cross Road in London, advised him to contact Marie Rambert (1888–1982). Rambert was one of the pivotal people in the growth of ballet in England. She had danced with the Diaghilev company and was Nijinsky's assistant for *Le Sacre du printemps*. As a teacher she nurtured many of the most important dancers and choreographers of the period.[17] Wrote Beaumont of the encounter:

> So one day Tudor called and confided something of his ambitions and difficulties. I suggested that he could not do better than study either with Margaret Craske[18] or Marie Rambert, whose addresses I gave him. He first went to Miss Craske but, since his work did not allow him to be free before 4:00 p.m., he could only attend a late afternoon or an evening class, for which there was no provision at the Craske school. He then went to Marie Rambert. [19]

As "someone with the strange desire to aim for a future in that exotic world" Tudor surmised that Beaumont's advice had to be taken seriously:

> [Rambert] was a lady known for her culture, her wide acquaintanceship, and for a wealth of experience that was awe inspiring. It was, therefore, with some trepidation that I went to meet this great Marie Rambert at her studio which was half of a bisected Parish Hall. It was already winter, near the end of 1928, and an appointment had been arranged for the late afternoon. . . I arrived out of the dark and cold, and walked up a narrow passageway to the unimpressive entrance and through it to the sacred ground of the ballet studio. . . There was the small lady in her uniform of black tights with a small wrap-around black silk skirt, and hair tied back into a small knot, exuding energy and command, and alternating between yelling and whistling and laughing. So this was Rambert . . .[20]

# Notes

1. Based on Tudor's description in Marilyn Hunt's interview with him, 11 November, 1986 ( transcript: 45).

2. This quote is from a fragment of an autobiography that Tudor had begun writing. The material was found in the archives of Isabel Brown, which were willed to her by Hugh Laing, Tudor's longtime companion. I would like to extend special thanks to Ms. Brown for all of her help with the research for this book.

3. Antony Tudor, York University lecture #1, Canada, 19 October, 1971.

4. In the 19 October lecture Tudor described the performance as follows: "Water: volumes of waving tulle undulating in light; Fire: on an underlit glass platform; Air: a sprinkling of paper from the flies, a tiresome device one sees in every production of *Nutcracker*." His reaction, he remembered, was ecstatic. He was sixteen years old.

5. Loie Fuller (1862–1928) was a forerunner of modern dance. She was one of the first to abandon pointe shoes and the traditional vocabulary of classical dance. Her main interest was in the effects of fanciful lighting and costuming. At one point she had the idea of embedding radium in her costume for its special glow, but was dissuaded by her close friend Marie Curie, who pointed out the dangers. Fuller also had the questionable distinction of being the first American dancer to have an appeal for copyright of her dances be denied by a judge. He described the function of dance as entertainment for the benefit of gentlemen.

6. Tudor, York University lecture #1.

7. It was the custom during World War I to send the children out of London to protect them.

8. Antony Tudor, York University lecture # 7, 11 November, 1971.

9. Joseph Schillinger (1895–1943) was a theorist who taught a method of composition applicable to music and graphic arts. Among his many famous pupils were George Gershwin and Earle Brown. Schillinger also invented a system of dance notation.

10. Antony Tudor, York University lecture #8, 16 November, 1971.

11. Letter from Vivienne Browning of East Barnet, which appeared in *The Dancing Times* (16 November 1990: 141. The sentence in quotation marks is Tudor's as quoted in the letter.

12. Hunt, Tudor interview.

13. Bronislava Nijinska (1891–1972) was the sister of Vaslav Nijinsky and a talented choreographer. Her *Les Noces* (Stravinsky), *Les Biches* (Poulenc), and *Le Train blue* (Milhaud) were among the dances she made for the Diaghilev Ballet. Léonide Massine (1895–1970), a protege of Diaghilev after the impresario's break with Vaslav Nijinski, was trained at the Bolshoi School. His *Gaîté Parisienne* (Offenbach), *Parade* (Satie), and *Le Tricorne* (de Falla), remain in the current reper-

toire. George Balanchine is one of the most highly respected choreographers of the twentieth century. It was he who founded the New York City Ballet, along with his patron and administrative collaborator Lincoln Kirstein.

14. Tamara Karsavina (1885–1978) was trained in Russia, married the British diplomat Henry Bruce and moved to England. She was a prima ballerina at the Maryinsky Theatre, a charter member of the Diaghilev Ballet, and one of the finest dancers of her day. Her book *The Children of Theatre Street* remains classic reading for any aspiring dancer.

15. Serge Lifar (1905–1986) was a soloist with the Diaghilev Ballet. He went on to become a noted choreographer particularly in Paris where he eventually directed the Paris Opera Ballet.

16. Tudor also spoke of being moved by Balanchine's *Prodigal Son* (Prokofiev), but he must have seen it after beginning to study with Rambert, because it did not premiere until 1929.

17. Chapter 2 deals at length with Rambert's school, company and important contributions. See also her autobiography, *Quicksilver*, published by Macmillan, London, 1972.

18. Margaret Craske (1898–1990) was a renowned teacher of the Cecchetti method of ballet training. She was ballet mistress for Tudor's short-lived London Ballet, his long time associate, and later taught with him at both the Metropolitan Opera and the Juilliard School.

19. Cyril W. Beaumont, "Antony Tudor: Choreographer," *British Ballet*, Peter Noble, ed. (London: Skelton Robinson, 1949): 166.

20. Another fragment from Tudor's autobiographical sketch. The material has been pieced together from several drafts.

Tudor and Eugene Loring in Loring's *The Great American Goof*. Photograph *courtesy of Nancy Zeckendorf*

# 2

# The London Decade: 1929–1939
# Ballet Rambert

## The First Meeting

So this was Rambert, insisting that I must come to a performance of her school in the near future, and then return to talk to her. A few weeks later, and after attending the performance, which bowled me over with admiration, I returned; and this time the tiny lady in her chic, tiny cloche hat asked that I walk her home.[1]

The performance was "The Lilac Fairy Matinee," and among the dances presented was Frederick Ashton's *Leda and the Swan.* Rambert's pupils gave their first public performance as a company on 25 February, 1929 at a small theater in west London, the Lyric Theatre in Hammersmith. The announcement in the *Times* called it the "first production of a company directed by Madame Rambert and Mr. Frederick Ashton."[2] A month later Ninette de Valois, a choreographer and teacher who went on to found the Vic-Wells Ballet, which later became England's Royal Ballet, gave a matinee in the same theater. A group called the Ginner Mawer troupe performed in "revived Greek dances" (students from Ruby Ginner's London school of Greek dance). Other dancers included the following: at the Coliseum, Anton Dolin, renowned classical soloist; at the Queen's Theatre, Angna Enters, an American dancer–mime who toured the world with a one–woman show; and at the Globe, Tokujiro Tsutsui.

No indigenous British ballet company yet existed. The Rambert and de Valois performances were a step beyond school recitals—a large step, but certainly not an established English company nor professional ballet as we know it today. In fact, ballet was synonymous with the Diaghilev Company and the various incarnations of Russian companies which came after. For example, in 1939, both Colonel de Basil's Ballet Russe de Monte Carlo starring Massine and René Blum's Monte Carlo Ballets Russes with Fokine as ballet master performed in London.

Tudor's description of his meeting with Rambert continued:

After we reached her house, she invited me into the famous study, and we had our first conversation. This was rather in the nature of a well-bred inquisition, for Madame had a great curiosity and deep interest in her pupils, particularly this one who came from the "other side of the tracks." She gently reminded me of this when, after I had recited some of the sonnets of Shakespeare,[3] she remarked that I had a not-too-bad but nonetheless impermissible cockney accent. Within a couple of years the cockney intonation was of the past.[4]

Tudor had already taken some classes in "elocution" in his acting days. Taking Rambert's comment seriously, he went to study with "a very expensive" diction teacher in Harley Street. The teacher laid down the editorial page of the London *Times* and told Tudor to read it aloud. He listened painfully then proceeded to correct Tudor's vowels. Shades of Eliza Doolittle!

Elizabeth Sawyer, Tudor's longtime accompanist and good friend, recalls Tudor saying, "Rambert monitored my progress so energetically that she drove me nuts for nearly half a year, but it was Rupert Doone who mainly did the trick." According to Sawyer, Doone, a colorful character on the scene at the Mercury Theatre, was Tudor's chief, though unofficial, speech therapist.

Once rid of the cockney "intonation" Tudor spoke a very elegant if idiosyncratic English. The American television personality Dick Cavett described it as somewhere between Claude Raines and Alfred Hitchcock.

There were probably fewer than a dozen males in the entire United Kingdom who might, in their vanity, dream of having a working future in the insecure and alien world of the ballet. Therefore, the enrollment of an extra male available for double work, with its hoisting and balance supporting, was a prize,[5] and I was not too surprised at being accepted into the school. I had already had a couple of years or so of ballet training of sorts and some amateur theatre experience. But it was surprising that Rambert, having decided that my fast progress was mandatory, arranged that two of her leading dancers, Pearl Argyle and Harold Turner, should alternate in giving me private lessons.

And so in no time at all I was the latest to be recruited as the one who after class must practice with "Mim" [Marie Rambert, familiarly].

To be accorded even a peripheral acquaintance with the artistic circle with which her husband, Ashley Dukes[6] and she had surrounded themselves, was an honor. And useful.

Referring to his later ballets, Tudor explains just how useful:

The backcloth of *Dark Elegies* was from an Irish landscape painting by Nadia Benois, and Hugh Stevenson's painting had provided the impulse for *Jardin aux lilas*. These people had to look after the painting of the scenery themselves, which they did without recompense, for it became an act of love which Rambert was never loath to accept.

Agnes de Mille mentions that, at her introduction to the premises, she came upon Hugh Laing and myself bending over and painting a cloth spread out on the floor. How else would we ever have got our scenery?

Since Tudor had no money to spare, he arranged to pay what he could for the lessons; the remaining balance would be settled at the rate of 15 percent of his earnings when he became professional.

Rambert, herself, was quite impressed with Tudor. She described him as tall and handsome with poetic eyes, someone with intelligence and a deep appreciation of the art of dance. When Tudor first called Rambert he had explained that, because of his work commitment he would have to meet her after 4:00 p.m. She was much impressed.

Thus Antony Tudor, né William Cook, began his fruitful decade–long association with Marie Rambert. He was a diligent pupil, serious and hard working. Agnes de Mille described him as slow, gentle, diffident, humorous, courteous, and much abused. She reported that he watched everything with remembering eyes and drank his tea quietly, wrapped in his ambitious dreams of world renown.

The Rambert faculty taught the Cecchetti method of ballet training leavened with some Russian technique provided by visiting teachers. Tudor progressed rather quickly, although he was at a distinct disadvantage because of his late start. Later, he went to Paris to study with Olga Preobrazhenska. At various times, many of them before his discovery of Rambert, he also briefly studied Spanish dance, tap dance, German modern dance of the Laban school, and ballroom dancing, particularly its overhead lifts. In 1929, Tudor managed to pass the Cecchetti qualifying examination and a year later that of the Imperial Society of Teachers of Dancing.

The same year, while still working as a "clark" at Smithfield Market, he made his professional debut, dancing with the English Opera Company. (He had used his annual two-week vacation from the meat market for the rehearsals.) The production took place at London's Scala Theatre, on 31 December, 1929; the choreography was by Penelope Spencer. The opera has been identified variously as Henry Purcell's *Dido and Aeneas* or *Cupid and Death* by Matthew Locke and Christopher Gibbons. Tudor played the role of a slain lover. Being on stage made him aware that his given name, William Cook, did not exactly spark the imagination. So, he changed it to the more elegant Antony Tudor. That name, with its intimation of royalty, would follow him for the rest of his career. At first he spelled it more traditionally, with an *h* in Anthony.

A wonderful, if clearly apocryphal, story exists about the change from Anthony to Antony. Tudor was sitting, deep in thought, in one of the Cloisters, a branch of the Metropolitan Museum in New York City. An elderly lady sat down beside him. She asked his name. How did he spell his "given" name, she wondered? He spelled it for her; she predicted that he would never get anywhere with that *h*, so he dropped it.[7]

Why did Tudor change his name from William Cook to Antony Tudor? Changing names was common practice in the dance world at that time. The early English ballerinas often assumed Russified names: Hilda Munnings became Lydia Sokolova, Cyvia Rambam first became Miriam Ramberg then Marie Rambert, Alice Marks became Alicia Markova, Margaret Hookham became Margot Fonteyn.

In his enigmatic way, Tudor consistently avoided directly answering any question about the name change. When queried he would reply:

What's in a name? Rambert insisted that no one could take seriously a choreographer named Cook. I didn't think I looked like a Cook, so I gave the problem some thought. The solution didn't take very long. Edris Stannus had transformed herself into Ninette de Valois . . . I decided to be more consistent and remain English (with just that little touch of Welsh).[8]

Throughout his career Tudor adored getting people to change their names. Mildred Herman became Melissa Hayden, Jimmy Hicks trans-

muted to Scott Douglas, and Nora Koreff to Nora Kaye. He gave everyone nicknames. He dubbed Sally Bliss, a Canadian dancer at the Metropolitan Opera, " Maple Leaf Forever." Pina Bausch, a German currently the director of the Wuppertal Ballet and a leading choreographer,
became known as Adolph. Two female dancers from the José Limón
Company who consistently took Tudor's men's classes bore the names
Saul (Sarah Stackhouse) and Tom (Betty Jones.) Perhaps he was only
carrying on the Cockney tradition that referred to Marlene Dirt-track,
Shirley Temper, and Peter Lorry.

Tudor first danced for Rambert in a minor role in Woizikowski's[9]
staging of Fokine's *Le Carnaval* (Schumann) followed by a small part
in Ashton's first successful ballet, *Capriol Suite* (Warlock). The group
performed at Christmas, 1930, at the Lyric Theatre, Hammersmith. In
April, 1931, Tudor also appeared in Fokine's *Les Sylphides* (Chopin)
and in *Façade,* Ashton's hilarious take on the Edith Sitwell/William
Walton work. He may also have danced in Andrée Howard's first ballet, co-choreographed with Susan Salaman, *Our Lady's Juggler,* with
music by Maurice Ravel. Tudor later admitted to rather liking dancing
in the works of other people, although his ambitions as a dancer were
quite modest. He well knew that he had started too late to have a virtuosic technique, so he particularly relished dramatic roles. Tudor never
seemed to regret either the late start nor that he was not a first–rate performer. Rather, he delighted in saying that, had he had ambitions as a
dancer, he would have had to spend too much time on steps and he
hated steps. In a 1935 article reviewing a Rambert season, Fernau Hall
wrote that Tudor's *grands jetés* were "distinctly elephantine." Tudor
concurred, but Rambert disagreed. She thought that he had a very good
figure and quite a jump, but admitted to his not being a distinguished
mover. His partnering, however, was very fine, good enough, for example, for the pas de deux from *Sleeping Beauty.* The stunningly inventive use of lifts in many of his ballets reflected his partnering skills.


## The Ballet Club


In 1930, both England and the United States underwent a period
of economic depression. After the post–World War I prosperity came

Antony Tudor practicing a lift with Helena Dukes, one of the Rambert children. *Photograph courtesy of Ballet Rambert Archive*

the economic fall. The American stock market crashed (1929); in England high unemployment and hard times prevailed.

In the cultural world, excitement and turbulence abounded. In America, Martha Graham gave her first solo recital in 1929 following it with her spare but beautiful *Primitive Mysteries* (music by Louis Horst) in 1931. Doris Humphrey choreographed *The Shakers* (Traditional), and Hanya Holm opened her school in New York. Kurt Jooss's moving anti–war ballet *The Green Table* was premiered in Paris in 1932. In 1933 the newly formed School of American Ballet gave its first concert featuring George Balanchine's *Serenade* (Tchaikovsky). In America, Alexander Calder was exploring mobiles; in England, Henry Moore and Barbara Hepworth experimented with new forms and Paul Nash with surrealism. Colonel de Basil, one of the founders of the Ballet Russe de Monte Carlo, guided the Russian Opera in London beginning in 1925.[10] Arnold Schoenberg's *Chamber Symphony* was premiered in 1935. Architecture took a new turn with the construction of the Empire State Building. When nightclub dancer Sally Rand lifted her fan, she was jailed. The decade of the 1930s saw the National Socialist (Nazi) regime growing in Germany with its lunatic theories of the master race.

In London, 1930, an event occurred that affected the course of English ballet forever. Ashley Dukes acquired premises on Ladbroke Road at Notting Hill Gate adjacent to the Rambert School. By installing lighting equipment, he constructed a small theater. In October, Dukes and Rambert founded the Ballet Club. They planned to give seasons of dance in this new venue named, three years later, the Mercury Theatre. It had a minuscule stage, reputed to be eighteen feet square. The stage was raised four feet and curved outward so that the edge almost touched the front row. Four seasons of three weeks each were projected, with a permanent company being formed the following year. What a bold idea! A company of English dancers, giving regular "seasons," performing choreography by Englishmen in a theater owned and operated by a Briton. Everyone knew that only the Russians could produce ballet magic! Outrageous as the idea seemed, the Dukes's plan did really happen; the Ballet Rambert was formed and became the first resident ballet company in England.

Simultaneously there occurred another, seemingly happy, event. In the midst of high unemployment and economic hard times, Tudor was promoted to a new job as an assessor in his uncle's surveying firm. The Cook household was jubilant. Tudor was devastated. Along with the new employment came new working hours: 9:30 a.m. to 6:00 p.m., making ballet study impossible. He reluctantly accepted the work, but stayed for only a few months.

Fortunately for the history of ballet, with the founding of the Ballet Club, Madame Rambert offered Tudor full-time employment. He accepted a two-year contract as secretary of the club. In addition to dancing, his duties included almost everything: stage-manager, electrician, stagehand, scene painter, teacher of the children's classes, accompanist, letter writer, accounts keeper, and general factotum. For this he earned the munificent sum of two pounds weekly, an amount variously categorized as niggardly or, conversely, not grand, but not insufficient. At the time a laborer earned about one pound a week, if he could find employment at all.

The contract between Rambert and Tudor also canceled what remained of his previous debt. In addition, the agreement provided free tuition and lodging (a bed in a windowless, skylighted room which was used as the male dressing room during performances).

Several of the dancers in the company at the time have memories of Tudor leaving the stage early in order to pull the curtain. Or, quickly slipping out of costume in the pauses to climb ladders, change gels (colored frames placed in front of lights to give the desired color), and even call light cues from onstage. In the archives of the Rambert Dance Company[11] there is a score of Claude Debussy's *L'Après-midi d'un faune* with penciled cues in Tudor's hand. Obviously he played for the rehearsals of the ballet as it was staged for the company by Woizikovsky. On the front cover of the score is a note from Rambert admonishing Tudor to rewrite the cues in ink.

His obligations as accompanist were not minimal:

> The studio was [tiny] with an anthracite stove at one end and a piano between the stove and a door to the back yard. You could sit at the piano and get a chill in your back. There was a day when I was playing for class. Suddenly I couldn't move my head. They had to pick me up under the arms, get me into a cab, and take me down to Mrs. Wilson who started pummeling me and finally got me to move again. I was frozen stiff.[12]

While the volume of these tasks must have been onerous, they provided an extraordinary apprenticeship for the soon-to-emerge choreographer. Throughout his career Tudor was known for his profound knowledge of lighting and production values.

Thus, in 1930, Tudor abandoned the security of full-time, respectable and stable employment for the vagaries of the dance world. He quit his job at the meat market and signed on with the Ballet Club. With customary irony Tudor described his decision to stay in the dance world as a very practical one. He wanted to be in the theater, but could not be a good actor because of his vocal deficiencies. He wanted to travel around the world and ballet dancers did that. Since he knew he'd started too late to be anything but an adequate dancer, the only other job open was that of choreographer. While this is how he characterized his decision, Tudor, like most creative artists, was consumed with a passion to choreograph. He became a choreographer because he had to. It was not a matter of choice.

The cast of characters in the Ballet Club included such future luminaries as guest artist ballerinas Alicia Markova and Tamara Karsavina, the choreographer Frederick Ashton, dancers Pearl Argyle, William Chappell, Betty Cuff, Rupert Doone, Diana Gould (who later became Mrs. Yehudi Menuhin), Andrée Howard (also a choreographer), Prudence Hyman, Maude Lloyd, Susette Morfield, Elisabeth Schooling, Robert Stuart, Antony Tudor, and Harold Turner. Dancers Charlotte Bidmead, Sally Gilmour, Walter Gore (whose talent as a choreographer we know only by legend), Leo Kersley, Thérèse Langfield, Hugh Laing, and Frank Staff joined a bit later. Peggy van Praagh, future director of the Australian Ballet, Celia Franca, who went on to run the National Ballet of Canada, and Mary Skeaping, who later led the Royal Swedish Ballet, also danced in the company. Kyra Nijinsky, daughter of Vaslav, also performed for a short time.

The Ballet Club "season" consisted of a series of Sunday performances, later extended to include Thursdays. Originally scheduled to open in January, 1931, the first season actually began on 16 February. (The postponement allowed the company to give a Christmas series at the Lyric Theatre.) It cost ten shillings to become a member of the Club, with a top ticket price of an additional seven shillings. Only members of the Ballet Club could buy tickets. That year the Club gave two seasons in its own theater and, later, performed in Hammersmith, Manchester, and for the Camargo Society.[13] Soon the Club's membership jumped from 700 to 1,700.

"The aim of the Ballet Club is to preserve the art of ballet in England by forming a permanent company of dancers with a theatre of its own . . . " announced the first brochure. An addendum jubilantly blazed "All first-night seats sold." The Ballet Club audience included the literati of London—all the rather posh friends of Ashley Dukes as well as the important writers, actors, musicians, painters, and sculptors of the period. Royalty such as Anthony Asquith, Lord Berners, Lady Bonham Carter, Lady Oxford, Lady Cunard, Lady Astor, and her son attended in abundance. So did playwrights: W. H. Auden, Christopher Isherwood, T. S. Eliot, and J. B. Priestly. The author Virginia Woolf, the composer Arthur Bliss, the sculptor Jacob Epstein, the producer Charles B. Cochran, the economist Maynard Keynes and his wife, Diaghilev dancer Lydia Lopokova, the Polish and French ambassadors, the designer Nadia Benois and her son Peter Ustinov were also among the spectators. Princess Galitzine sent the dancers cakes from Rumplemeyer's. This very distinguished audience packed the Mercury, partially because Ballet Club performances alternated with plays produced by Ashley Dukes and written by the leading playwrights of the times. The elegant public, decked out in evening dress, mingled in a room which housed an extraordinary collection of prints. They tasted the fine wine selections of connoisseur Dukes (the Print Room and Wine Bar were later additions, not extant on opening night). At one period there was even dancing for the audience members after the performance. Remarkably, without any subsidy, the hard earnings of two theater people generated and sustained this cultured and stylish milieu. Ashley Dukes's writings had built the theater; Rambert's school earnings kept the Ballet Club functioning. Neither received any director's fees for their work. The dancers were modestly paid and any profits were divided among them. Markova, as ballerina, got ten shillings sixpence. Rambert tried to reduce this to seven shillings sixpence, but Markova pointed out that her shoes for each appearance cost her six shillings sixpence and her taxi home (performances ended after the last bus had left Notting Hill), four shillings. How could she draw less than her expenses?

## Beginning to Choreograph

An event that helped shape Tudor's future occurred the same year. The dancer Maude Lloyd (1908–) returned from an eighteen-month stay in her native South Africa to join the Ballet Club for its first season. Lloyd, still a refined, beautiful woman at over ninety, remembers

Maude Lloyd. *Photograph courtesy of Maude Lloyd*

the first person she met: a tall young man standing alone in the studio. "You must be Maude from Capetown. I'm Antony," he said.

Right from that initial greeting she became his trusted and peren- nial companion. They even stood next to one another at Mim's barre. Lloyd went on to become Tudor's leading ballerina in most of his dances in those early London years. Although she vehemently denies being his muse, history challenges her judgment.

> We were doing a season in Manchester with Karsavina, who was with us as a guest. We had an early call on the stage, to do class, I think. And Antony and I happened to arrive first.

> "Would you like to try out a movement for me?" I can even re- member what it was: *rond de jambe en dehors*, moving one's body in a circle at the same time. I tried it. It was rather uncomfortable, I thought. It must have been about the first step he ever set. He didn't say any more. He's not one to talk about what he wants.[14]

Before becoming secretary, Tudor had never mentioned his real ambition: to make ballets, not to dance in them. But when he negotiated that first two-year contract with the Ballet Club, he insisted it include an agreement for him to create ballets. When the company returned to London after appearing in Manchester, Tudor approached Rambert with an idea.

In his York University lecture of 16 November, 1971 Tudor re- lates that he was trapped with the problem of "what the hell to do for my first ballet." His autobiographical notes go on to say:

> My first effort was *Cross-Garter'd.* I tried to play it safe. I put con- siderable effort and study into achieving enough success with this first piece to prove that I had some choreographic talent, and to guarantee my being offered a second opportunity.

> The choice of making a ballet out of the comedy characters of the *Twelfth Night* of Shakespeare was governed largely by the fact that I was well acquainted with the play. The central character in the ballet was Malvolio, a role I had acted in an amateur performance of the play a few years earlier. And I felt secure that I would be able to work happily with the performers available at Marie Ram- bert's Ballet Club. I had trust in them.

> The score always poses a problem but in this case my indefatigable
> haunting of second-hand music stores solved it. At one of these . . .
> I chanced upon some miniature volumes of famous Italian compos-
> ers. . . . Among these was a volume devoted to Frescobaldi and be-
> cause of the extraordinary discovery that he was a contemporary of
> Shakespeare, the stars indicated that this must be the basis, the
> skeleton on which my project should be constructed.

Tudor decided he needed to visit Florence to soak up the atmosphere for the new work. Having found a congenial small hotel he began
to plot the piece. "It was there, with Mr. Frescobaldi's score [of selected organ pieces] beside me, aiding and abetting, that I made my
start on being a choreographer." After spending his summer vacation
working in Florence, he returned to London. He had written down, in
longhand, about a third of the piece. Next he needed to decide on a designer. Rambert had the solution—the theatrical designs of Burnacini.[15]

> This had all the aspects of a miracle for he also was of the period of
> Shakespeare and Frescobaldi . . . I soon discovered that all my la-
> bors in Florence, the written down movements, were stillborn and
> useless. So, very early on I discovered that choreography is an art
> of movements of various human bodies, and that its true life comes
> from working with those bodies in the studio.[16]

When his ideas were all in order Tudor went to Rambert. She
asked to see a solo. He composed a stately dance for Malvolio, the
character he himself expected to dance. Mostly, he walked up and
down with one arm held stiffly out. Rambert asked why. He replied that
he would be carrying his staff of office, which he did. This totally
changed the look of the walk, foreshadowing his later non-traditional
use of the arms and gesture to explicate the drama in his ballets. Rambert then wanted to see a *pas de deux*. He choreographed one for himself and Maude Lloyd, as Olivia. In the dance she constantly struggled
to free herself from his unwanted attentions. Again, this earliest of
works laid out Tudor's territory. His *pas de deux* are never merely
decorative; they serve to further the dramatic action of the ballet.

The piece was premiered on 12 November, 1931, the opening
night of the Ballet Club's second season. Although the ballet was not a
complete success, critics did not dismiss it. Rather, they expressed the
thought that this novice choreographer should, indeed, be encouraged.
Léonide Massine, who at the time was the darling of the London dance
scene, saw the ballet and was most favorably impressed.

Elisabeth Schooling commented about working on *Cross-Gar-ter'd.*

> [Tudor] was apt to get too tied up with himself. It was an awful ef-fort to get anything out. He didn't seem to have a facility for movement as did some other choreographers. We spent a lot of time while he was hemming and hawing to himself.[17]

Tudor himself recognized that some of the steps he had envi-sioned in Florence turned out to be beyond the anatomical possibilities of the dancers. Although in the future he spent a good deal of time thinking about and planning his ballets before entering the studio, he never again worked out *enchaînements* without dancers in front of him.

## Meeting Hugh Laing

> It was in this period [1931] that Hugh Laing [Tudor's lover, life–long companion, friend, and often the leading male dancer in his ballets] entered my life. He had been studying art under Ian Macnab at the Grosvenor School of Modern Art in Warwick Square and met Macnab's wife, Helen Wingrave. Helen brought Hugh to Rambert's studio to visit, without appreciating Rambert's unrelenting energies in discovering talent. With Hugh's hardly knowing what was happening, she had him taking off his shoes and was admiring the shape and flexibility of his feet. . . . Rambert asked if he could do deep *plié*. To her shock he stood up and *pliéd* so deeply that his bottom hit the ground. He was also extraordinar-ily handsome, and had had a background of outdoor activities in Barbados [where he was born Hugh Skinner of British parents in 1911. He died one year after Tudor, in 1988]. Swimming, diving, tennis and climbing trees gave his body marvelous musculature, proportions, and flexibility. Rambert insisted that he start class the very next week, and, males being in short supply in the ballet world, . . . in no time at all he was being sought out as a performer in much of the repertory.

> At about that time a lady from the Abbey Theatre was making a ballet called *Unbowed* in which she used Hugh Laing as a slave boy whom I had to carry offstage over my shoulder when he had been mortally wounded. It stays in my memory largely because the music by Arthur Bliss was contemporary enough to need counting. I seem to remember that on my entrance I had to count "one, two,

three, four, five, six, seven, eight, nine, ten, eleven; one and er, two and er, three and er, four and er; one, two, three, four, five, six, seven; one and er, two and er, three and er," and back to eleven again. It was perhaps then that I became antagonistic to any counting when choreographing or performing.

Tudor became infatuated with Laing and the two soon began a liaison which grew into a life-long relationship. As soon as they could amass the funds, they moved together to a small flat, 45 Holland Park Mews, in the lovely, green Holland Park area of London adjacent to Notting Hill Gate.

Tudor remarked that Rambert and Laing "got on marvelously together in that neither could bear the other. She said he was possessed of the devil and he knew she was the devil."

Laing's temper was legendary:

> Hugh had a marvelous temper. Absolutely fabulous. He could play scenes to the hilt and know he was playing them. Once, in a temper, he slammed the door to a little balcony that overlooked Ladbroke Road so hard he shattered all the glass. Ashley Dukes was coming from the subway [the underground]. He said "My God, he's killed Mim" and ran all the way back to the theatre. [18]

On more than one occasion voices were raised and chairs were thrown. One story, unprovable and perhaps apocryphal, has Laing dragging Rambert across a room by her hair. Laing threatened to throw himself out of the window so often that one window was designated and always referred to as "the chosen one." Rambert would have palpitations and throw herself on the divan; only Maude Lloyd worried and got her water. Everyone else said she would get over it—and she did.

*Tumultuous* best describes the relationship between Tudor and Laing. Laing's temper tantrums were not restricted to Rambert, and Tudor's way with sarcasm and denigrating personal remarks did not spare Hugh. The two were known to humiliate one another both in public and in private. Hugh simply did not filter what he said—whatever came into his mind in any given moment found a voice. Tudor used as a weapon his uncanny ability to understand a person on his deepest level and thus to poke at his greatest vulnerability. Hugh had weak spots; Tudor found them and probed them in the most hurtful ways he could conjure. Hugh ranted and raved; Tudor replied with rapier-sharp barbs. Their behavior toward one another was like fire and ice. At one point in 1936 Tudor confided to de Mille that he felt he must leave Laing because of the many screaming tantrums. Her advice to him was to do it; otherwise, it would weaken and torture him for the rest of his life. Taking her advice, he went on a walking trip in Finland that summer. When he came back, the two men agreed that there were to be no more screaming tantrums and for a while, there were none.

To characterize the relationship between Tudor and Laing solely as stormy, however, would be to skew the truth. Between them there was warmth, enormous mutual respect, loyalty, symbiosis, and a love that survived many tests and endured until their deaths. For most of their years they lived together. Even during Laing's period of wedlock with Diana Adams, they remained close friends. When the marriage failed, Laing and Tudor were together again. In later life, when Tudor moved into a Zen retreat, they no longer shared quarters, but they ate most dinners together, and visited back and forth frequently. They cooked for one another and nursed one another through illness. Tudor often took care of Laing financially; Laing looked after Tudor's professional interests. And, Tudor consulted Laing in all his professional decisions and, more often than not, followed his advice.

It was evident, early on, that the two were deeply enamored of one another. While it was a complex relationship, the two clearly supported one another. Hugh constantly attacked Rambert for not sufficiently appreciating Tudor. He also goaded Tudor to keep him working, protected him when he could, held him to a high standard, and never let him descend to self-indulgent despair. For his part, Tudor devoted endless hours to helping Hugh learn his craft, shaped him as an artist, choreographed extraordinary roles for him that focused on his best points, shared whatever financial resources he had with him, depended on him for his good memory, and respected his sensitivity and his understanding.

The duo of Maude Lloyd and Tudor became a trio with Laing, and later a quartet with Maude's roommate Tiny (Muriel) Monkhouse.

> We spent so much time together, going to the theatre and the cinema and having meals together, laughing and giggling. . . . We had lunch together almost every day at a little restaurant called Sallie's. . . . On Sundays we went walking in the park or we went off to the flea mar-

ket in Petticoat Lane very early in the morning to see if we could find
prints of dancers. He [Tudor] was very interested in dance history.[19]

[Hugh and Antony] needed each in other lots of ways. Hugh pushed
Tudor a great deal. But also, if it hadn't been for Tudor taking on
Hugh and teaching him—he spent an awful lot of time giving him
technical classes outside the usual curricular time—Hugh would
never have become a dancer. Tudor taught him how to stand, how to
work, how to become a dancer. Hugh was already eighteen [He was
actually twenty] when he came. He had extraordinary good looks and
a wonderful presence. He was an artist but he never really acquired a
strong technique.[20]

Laing supported and inspired Tudor throughout their many years
together first as lovers and then as close friends. Tudor credits Laing
with being a complete individualist. In Tudor's opinion no one ever
equaled Laing in any of the roles he created for him.

He was an enormous help because sometimes there wasn't time to
rehearse him. He knew what I wanted so inside out, he could read my
mind. . . . He's a very good critic, too. If he saw me or Agnes or anyone doing something terrible, he would make no bones about it—he
would tell us so. In no uncertain terms, meaning loudly. [21]

Laing encouraged Tudor, chastised him when he felt that Tudor was
turning out mediocrity in rehearsals ("Oh, Antony, really!"), defended
him, pushed him ("Get on with it!"), designed costumes and scenery for
him, touted him, advised him, cooked for him, cared for him, but also
caused him unending consternation.

## Emerging Genius

With his first ballet behind him, Tudor shortly began work on a
second and third. *Mr. Roll's Quadrille* premiered in February, 1932
(either 4 or 11 February; the extant program is undated) and was repeated a few times  thereafter. The dance, a brief divertissement for
Prudence Hyman, Maude Lloyd, and Tudor presented a caricature

Cavorting on the beach. Top: Hugh Laing and Antony Tudor. Bottom: Nigel Gosling, Tudor, and Laing lift Maude Lloyd. *Photograph courtesy of Maude Lloyd*

of the kind of jolly classical ballet that Tudor disliked. Displeased, Rambert only tolerated the dance because it could be mounted without expense by recycling existing costumes and using old English traditional music that

> Dukes happened to have. For the same program Tudor choreographed a very brief solo for Diana Gould entitled *Constanza's Lament* to music by Domenico Scarlatti. It was a charming fillip consisting largely of suspended pointe work and continuous *bourrées* with parallel arms gently lowering from one side, then rising to the other. The floor pattern clearly demonstrates the fact that the stage was minuscule; the dancer travels on the diagonal as often backward as forward. A bit more than a month later, on March 20, followed Tudor's first real success, a ballet based on Aristophanes' *Lysistrata*.

The initial idea came from Ashley Dukes. Dukes first offered it to Ashton, who was not interested. Tudor wanted the ballet to refer to modern times, so he created a wicked tongue-in-cheek comedy.

*Lysistrata* had a literary basis: the fifth-century B.C. play by Aristophanes about a group of Athenian wives who refused to carry on with their wifely duties. They abandon the marital bed to force their husbands to give up warring. The ballet opens with a scene of the wives engaged in domestic tasks. Lysistrata (Diana Gould, later Maude Lloyd) incites them to strike. When the husbands return from battle they are greeted not with loving kisses but with kicks and vituperation. The wives' resolve obliges the husbands to look after their own households, a task which the gentlemen find baffling. The men soon capitulate, making peace with their enemies in Sparta.

Working with Tudor for the first time as the original Myrrhina, Alicia Markova said:

> He brought me down to earth. I was always doing the classics, with the little wings on the back or the wreaths of flowers . . . [Tudor said his work was "entirely different. You're married and you have a husband and a baby."] There was a marvelous *pas de deux* with Walter Gore, who was my husband in it. And the baby–the baby was part of the family. Every time he [Gore] wanted to dance with me . . . I put the baby on the floor and it cried. That was my way of getting back at him. That was typically Tudor.[22]

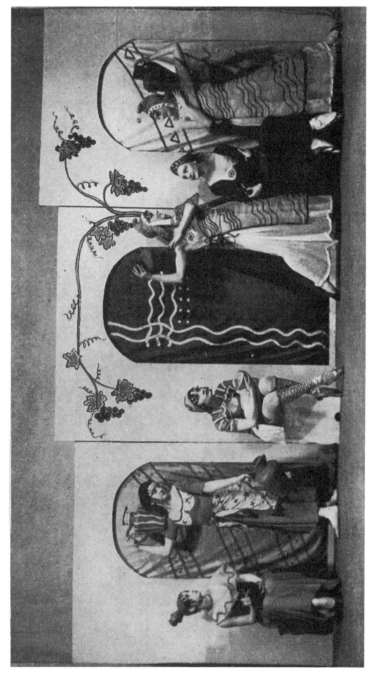

*Lysistrata. Photograph courtesy of Victoria and Albert Museum*

36

Tudor's quotidian characters greatly departed from those in the choreography of his contemporaries such as Massine and Ashton. Hugh Laing vividly recalled this earthiness in his description of Gore's dance with the baby:

> It was utterly charming and delightful. It was full of humor but it was full of humanity at the same time. . . . He'd put the baby down and walk away, and then it cried. So Walter Gore would pick it up again. He didn't know how to cope with it. The wife watches from a distance and laughs at him. . . . This could happen to anybody. You don't have to be a prince or a princess, or have a dragon at your back door. . . . At the same time Walter did pirouettes and arabesques and jumps. It's all classical work, but [Tudor] integrated the human. You were a person, a man with a baby.[23]

Maude Lloyd described the ballet as both funny and touching. She talked about one gentle husband with a virago of a wife whose dance mostly consisted of kicking him around. This was probably Diana Gould as Lysistrata. She was the angry one, with fists, doing *pas de chats* onto pointe. Leo Kersley described the scene in more detail: "Lysistrata came out of the door and Antony cringed. She kicked him and he did two somersaults. He landed from the second somersault with his legs over the edge of the stage, near the piano, a formidable feat of skill and timing."[24]

Lloyd also remembered how Andrée Howard (1910–1968), portraying a gossip, wore a funny little peaked hat emphasizing her long nose. She kept peeking around doors observing the couples squabbling, searching for the baby, and having a great time.

Early in the ballet there is an ingenious dance for the three wives. Sitting on benches attending to their household tasks with their hands, they perform a whole dance with only their feet. Later, when the men have to take over the ladies' work, they repeat the seated foot dance.

Tudor had a row with Rambert when he wanted to have a sheet spread on the stage to represent a double bed. Rambert wouldn't hear of it, disapproving of the realism—such things must only be suggested. Besides, real sheets get dirty. "Diana [*Lysistrata*] was to kick Antony out of bed. On the stage! Rambert hit the ceiling, saying, "I will not have a double bed on my stage." [25]

Tudor chose music by Prokofiev: several piano pieces and excerpts from the second and fourth piano sonatas. Conflicting stories about Prokofiev's reaction when he viewed the dance at the Ballet Club abound. Some reports said he disliked the ballet; others credited him with liking the ballet itself but feeling it inappropriate to use his music for a comedic work. Reportedly, Rambert agreed with him.

William Chappell designed the very successful sets and costumes. He based the black and tan hand painted costumes on Greek dress of that period. The baby was a very simple but effective prop, just a little piece of calico and a skirt. Carey, the carpenter who lived in Rambert's basement, built most of the sets for Ballet Club productions. For *Lysistrata*, out of thin plywood, he cut three arches, one for each couple.

The ballet showed Tudor rapidly developing an original and powerful voice as a choreographer who could draw complex characters sharply and clearly. So successful was *Lysistrata* that it remained in the repertoire for eight years, until 1940.

As early as 1932, in the same month as *Lysistrata*, came Tudor's first work in a medium outside of the concert stage. He invented the dances for a film called *In a Monastery Garden,* which was shot at Twickenham studios with the Rambert dancers. So many films were being made at that studio that the dancers had both day and night shifts; the Rambert dancers finished at 3:00 a.m. Gina Malo, an actress who played a ballet dancer, starred in the piece. Tudor arranged the ballet for her so ingeniously that it required little dance technique. Tudor may have made two other dances because he needed the money: *A Chinese Temple Dance* and *A Toy Cart* starring Madeline Carroll; however, no trace of them remains. As his final work in 1932 he choreographed a version of *Adam and Eve* for the Camargo Society. It premiered on 4 December at the Adelphi Theatre in the West End, near Trafalger Square.

The Camargo Society, founded in 1930, aimed to fill the gap left by the death of Diaghilev. Established by Philip Richardson, editor of the *Dancing Times*, and Arnold Haskell, a dance writer, critic, and later director of the Royal Ballet School, it had as its ultimate goal the establishment of a national ballet. In the event, the society served as a presenter. Both the Marie Rambert Dancers and Ninette de Valois's emerging Vic-Wells Company were commissioned to perform, thus demonstrating to the British public that the seeds of an English ballet company were already in place with native talent in abundance. The initial performances comprised the "Ballet of Nuns" from *Robert le diable* (Taglioni/Meyerbeer); Variations and Coda from *Fêtes Polonaises* by Nicolai Legat, the famous Russian teacher and choreographer who trained Nijinsky; *Pomona* (Lambert) by Ashton; and a *Pas de deux* by de Valois.

For the Camargo Society's second season, which was underwritten by Maynard Keynes with support from Anton Dolin, it commissioned Tudor to create a ballet. Using a score by Constant Lambert originally written for Diaghilev for a ballet by Nijinsky, Tudor created *Adam and Eve.*

> In those days I had nightmares about my ballets. I was at that time tarnished by the idea that you had to have a new angle. Seeing no reason why Adam [Anton Dolin] and Eve [Prudence Hyman] should have all the fun, I ended the ballet with the serpent [Tudor's role] and the archangel [Natasha Gregorova] teaming up for sex.[26]

The ballet shocked some of the audience who thought it lewd. Critics characterized it variously as wickedly irresistible, a merry ballet which aroused the audience to smiles and applause, a childish charade, a delightful *jeu d'esprit,* and a clever excursion into the grotesque. Several of the reviews mention Tudor's outstanding performance as the serpent.

A program note describes the ballet as follows:

> The scenario follows approximately the biblical story, with the important difference that, in accordance with the well-known precedent set by Mozart in the finale of *Don Giovanni,* there has been added a final reconciliation scene of all the characters in the ballet.

> Scene 1: Sinfonia—Siciliana—Sonatina
> Intermezzo Pastoral
> Scene 2: Burlesca—Musette—Tocatta
> Intermezzo Pastorale
> Scene 3: Rondino—Sarabande—Finale

In the final scene, the Serpent, with flaming sword, forces the archangel to taste the forbidden fruit, and the ballet ends in a happy double marriage.

*Adam and Eve* introduced Peggy van Praagh [27] to Tudor's special group of dancers. She played in the corps as one of the dickey birds or fowl of the air. In an interview in 1978 she described working with Tudor:

My first impression of the Rambert was that it was a hothouse of creativity. It was the time of the birth of British ballet. At the end of the first week I was earning two shillings, six pence. Of course we only danced on Sunday nights and not all year round. Tudor was still searching for what he wanted and he worked very much with particular dancers. He got to know you as a person before he chose you. . . . He tried to get into your mind, to know what you were thinking. He was very exciting to work with. . . . He had an extraordinary sense of humour—a rather wicked wit. We became kind of a Tudor group. He used to try to groom us, too. He would suggest that perhaps we were wearing the wrong colour. He sent me off to Elizabeth Arden to learn how to make up. Tudor was a kind of Svengali character. He liked to completely control the people that he was working with—their lives entirely not just the rehearsal hours. Some people didn't like it but I found it very stimulating. His ballets were considered way out.[28]

During the two-week Camargo Society season Tudor saw Olga Spessivtzeva for the first time, in *Giselle*. Her stunning performance completely moved him. Overwhelmed, he presented her with a wreath of orchids that cost every last penny he had. Tudor remembered thinking of her as "a sleazy, very crazy nymphomaniac until I saw her dance. Dancing, she was the embodiment of spiritual transcendence." [29] (Many years later, when he saw Gelsey Kirkland's *Giselle,* he said he could finally forget Spessivtzeva.)

## Tudor the Dancer

What of Tudor as a dancer? All during his early choreographic life, he danced both the roles he designed for himself and those made for him by other choreographers: Fokine, Ashton, even Massine, a choreographer whose work he did not admire.

In certain roles he was absolutely wonderful . . . as a King in Fokine's *Bluebeard* he was brilliant. In comedy, he was magnificent. As the father in Massine's *Aleko,* wonderful—an icon-like figure, and unbelievable, wonderful.

He was a great performer. He was not a classical dancer . . . his legs didn't look like classical legs. And he always said his head was too small. . . . With Maude [Lloyd] in *Elegies,* superb. How they did the *pas de deux*! And nobody has ever done *Jardin* . . . [like him

except] Henning Kronstat. [But performing] was not important. He
enjoyed performing, but he had other fish to fry. [30]

He would never make an Albrecht (the quintessential prince in
*Giselle*), and his classical line left much to be desired. His movement
projected a certain unyeilding stiffness. Yet, he had a flair for comedy.
He was stylistically adaptable, musically sensitive, strong, and concen-
trated. A remarkable actor, he made every gesture count. Only with
difficulty could one find a more superb partner. Celia Franca (1921–),
one of the early Rambert dancers and prime mover in the founding of
the National Ballet of Canada, remarked that she always felt safe when
partnered by him. In later years, critics and audience alike responded to
the *pas de deux* in *Dark Elegies* with wonder. Some of the lifts in *Jardin aux lilas* demand will power and split-second timing. They tell the
story, however, without focusing on the acrobatics of the lifts. In spite
of his technical lacunae, he presented a commanding figure. Extremely
canny in choreographing roles for himself, he highlighted his strengths
and hid his weaknesses.

In 1932, short of male dancers, Ninette de Valois (1898–2001)
"borrowed" men from Marie Rambert for her recently formed Vic-
Wells Ballet, Tudor among them. For a little more than a year and a
half Tudor danced in de Valois's Vic-Wells company, the forerunner of
the Royal Ballet. Like the Marie Rambert Dancers, Vic-Wells was a
germinal company. Although de Valois's promise that he could choreograph lured him there, that opportunity never materialized. He did
choreograph one opera ballet for the company, Gounod's *Faust,* which
premiered on 28 September, 1933.

With both Frederick Ashton and de Valois herself making ballets,
neither time nor space were allotted for Tudor. Perhaps here lies the
genesis of the legendary animosity between de Valois and Tudor. Perhaps that animosity resulted in his ballets not being staged in his native
country. England saw no Tudor work between 1939, when he left for
the United States, and 1967, when he finally agreed to create a new
dance for the young Anthony Dowell. Unquestionably, he did not ever
forgive de Valois for reneging on her promise. As late as 1981, in an
interview with Dale Harris, speaking about de Valois, he comments:
"At that time I didn't know you can't trust anybody in the world of
ballet. Everyone in it is untrustworthy. Like me." [31]

## 1933

Tudor's creative impulses did not lie dormant while waiting for de Valois to live up to her word. On 1 January, 1933, his next work premiered. *Pavane pour une infante défunte [Pavane for a Dead Infanta],* set to the score of the same name by Maurice Ravel, carried little import; however, it did represent the initial collaboration between Tudor and designer Hugh Stevenson (1910–1946). Stevenson, a painter, had appeared at the Rambert school about the same time as Laing, also wanting to study ballet. He had little aptitude for the dance, however. Instead, he collaborated as designer with several of the Ballet Club's choreographers, chief among them Antony Tudor.

Six months after *Pavane,* on 7 May, came a new milestone work, *Atalanta of the East.* The dance, while based on the Greek legend of Atalanta, took place in an Eastern setting. The program describes it as a ballet in two scenes:

> Scene 1: Vikram prays to the Goddess to help him in his quest of the fleet-footed Sita and receives from her the golden apples.
> Scene 2: Sita, secure of victory, accepts the challenge of Vikram, but is vanquished by the ruse of the golden apples which Vikram drops in the race.

Tudor transposed the setting to Asia because, with *Lysistrata* and *L'Après-midi d'un faune* both in the repertoire, the company did not need yet another Greek ballet.

He got some of the ideas from a book on Javanese dance. Maude Lloyd remembers the performance of a Javanese dancer named Robin Mastrojana as also being an influence. Fernau Hall, an English dance writer, critic, longtime Tudor acquaintance and fan, insists that Tudor said he was influenced by the magnificent Indian dancer Uday Shankar, who had performed in London several times in the early to mid thirties. Tudor later denied this.[32] Pearl Argyle played the lead, Sita. The music, an arrangement of Javanese airs by Szanto and Seelig, was a weak link. Rambert commented:

> There was much beauty in that ballet: the opening in the garden of Hesperides with three goddesses swaying in an exquisite group and yet somehow suggesting the immobility of statues; the entrance of Laing begging for the apple to help him outdo Atalanta in the race; and the race itself. But the rest was very dull, and the music was a

poor arrangement of vaguely Eastern tunes which only underlined
the weak passages.[33]

The dance was more a *succès d'estime* than a smash hit. Hugh
Laing characterized it as a resounding flop. Elisabeth Schooling called
it a disaster and wondered at the very idea of running miles and miles
on the minuscule Mercury Theatre stage. She also spoke of watching
while Pearl Argyle ran behind the one-foot space of the backcloth while
it "bonked." Generally the dance garnered the respect of the critics
rather than their accolades; they cited it for its experimental qualities,
beautiful arm movements, satisfying groupings, and ingenious portrayal
of the contest—the race. For Tudor, it represented a first essay into the
Eastern ethos, which became one of the leit motifs of his later output.

The extraordinary series of roles that Tudor created for Laing began with this ballet. Laing described the experience:

> In *Atalanta* he did Oriental. And he'd never taken any oriental
> dancing, as far as I know. We had to bend our hands back and eve-
> rything was in *plié*. It was hell on your legs. Oh, how they hurt. . . .
> It wasn't a successful ballet. It was beautiful to look at, but it
> wasn't successful.[34]

From this very first role Laing went on (along with a few other
such famed dancers of the period as Igor Youskevitch [1912–1994],
Anton Dolin [1904–1983], and Lew Christensen [1909–1984]) to become one of the most sought-after dramatic dancers of his time. He
performed in works by Fokine/Offenbach (*Bluebeard*), Massine/
Tchaikovsky (*Aleko*), de Mille/Gluck (*Tally Ho*), Robbins/Bernstein
(*Age of Anxiety*), and even Balanchine/Prokofiev (*Prodigal Son*). John
Martin, the dean of American dance critics, spoke of his "high-tension
temperament which suffused the simplest gesture with eloquence."[35]
Dame Alicia Markova commented that Hugh "had the theatre grafted
onto his classical training. He was a wonderful stage presence. Hugh
was wonderful with design and make up. With real make up—you treat
it like painting . . ."[36] She also speaks of the dancers making their own
tutus, sitting for hours gathering the tarlatans. Ashton and Laing would
sometimes join in.

Celia Franca, who first danced a Tudor role in *The Planet* in 1934,
tells of just how "naughty" Laing was:

In the Mercury Theatre itself, you just went through a door and you
were [backstage] in the big studio which was running parallel to the
auditorium itself. At the end of the studio was a huge stove to heat
the building. Around the stove were these railings. Right in the
middle of the performance when they were expecting the dignitar-
ies to come "backstage," Hugh climbed up on the railings. All he
had on was a little towel around his waist. He did a step like a *pas
de bourrée* around the railings and lifted the towel, saying "yoo-
hoo." That was Hugh. Hugh was naughty. We loved it." [37]

<h1 style="text-align:center">1934</h1>

On 20 February, 1934, the first of several versions of *Paramour*
to the music of William Boyce  premiered.

We were invited to participate in a production of *Dr. Faustus* by
the Oxford University Dramatic Society and I made a short ballet
which entered the Rambert Repertory as *Allegory.* The music was
by William Boyce. I was Alexander the Great; Laing was the Persian Prince whose domains and possessions, symbolized by his
crown, were envied by Thais, the paramour of Alexander. She demanded that he kill the Persian and give her the "loot." In this
piece I gave Hugh a movement in center stage that to all purposes
was impossible. But he did it. [He had to] raise a leg in the air beside him, parallel to the ground, and then descend on the other leg
through deep plié until he was kneeling with the other leg still extended. [38]

Revised for presentation at the Ballet Club on 22 March, the ballet, of which no record remains, became a *pas de trois* for Walter Gore,
Diana Gould, and Hugh Laing. Later, in 1937, Tudor rechoreographed
it as a *pas de deux* for himself and Maude Lloyd. The *pas de deux* version was presented, first in January, 1937 in a review called *Paleface,*
then broadcast on BBC television on 2 February, under the title *Paramour.* William Chappell designed the costumes.

Maude Lloyd remembered that in her version she *bourréed* backwards toward Tudor as the sleeping Alexander. She had to put her hand
back and shake him, but she reached to the wrong part of his anatomy.
She gave it a good shake, and he never stopped teasing her about it
thereafter.

On 28 May Tudor showed his new ballet, *The Legend of Dick Whittington,* at the Sadler's Wells Theatre as an interlude in *The Rock,* a pageant play by T. S. Eliot. Tudor based the ballet on a legend familiar to all English children. The story tells of a poor boy mistreated by a maid in the house where he works. He runs away, but hears church bells eerily tolling "Turn Back Again Dick Whittington, Lord Mayor of London." The bells encourage him to return to his master's home where his master's daughter befriended him. Whittington owned a cat. He sent it off on a ship where the cat killed all of the rats aboard. Richly rewarding, the cat's windfall changes the fate of its owner, Whittington, who eventually fulfills the prophecy of the bells. He becomes Lord Mayor of London, marries his once-master's daughter, and becomes an enlightened patron of the poor. Everyone lives happily ever after. Reputedly based on an actual fourteenth- or fifteenth-century character, the fantasy of the story connected with a very real and terrifying phenomenon. Rats carried the black plague. Nothing remains of Tudor's ballet except some tales of its wit.

Tudor's first mature work followed on 28 October. *The Planets* had music by Gustav Holst, costumes and scenery by Hugh Stevenson. Originally in three scenes, "Venus," "Neptune," and "Mars," the dance had orchestral music provided live, in reduction, by piano for four hands. For the ballet's later restaging for Tudor's London Ballet he added a fourth scene, "Mercury."

Each section presents a dancer as a planet, with other dancers portraying mortals born under the planet's influence. The strikingly original piece is an important landmark. Each section uses a different movement vocabulary, most often employing atraditional, idiosyncratic arm movement set against more academic use of the feet. This device became characteristic of much of the Tudor oeuvre. Each section of the dance has a special atmospheric quality as well: a lyrical *pas de deux* for the lovers under "Venus," with the planets in gently revolving patterns; the percussive and slashing arms of "Mars" representing war, destruction, and self-destruction; the mystical aura of the "Neptune" scene.

The dance exhibits Tudor's finely honed musicality and departs from usual balletic four-square meter. The "Neptune" section is in 5/4, an unheard-of time signature for dance in 1934. The "Venus" section rides over the music, only coming together in resting points with the musical cadences. The layers and layers of compositional skill include not only fascinating and poetic individual roles, but also planet-like, in-

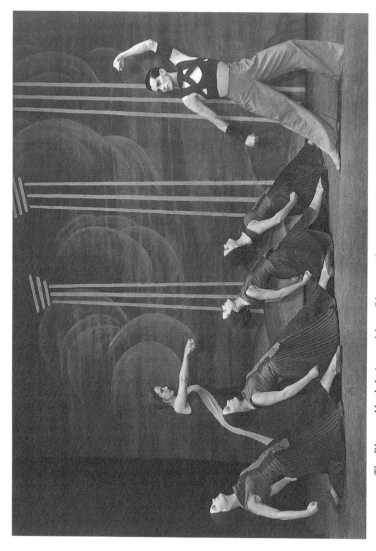

*The Planets.* Hugh Laing as Mars. *Photograph courtesy of Ballet Rambert Archives*

terstellar stage patterns. The work also represented the first collaboration with Hugh Stevenson on a full-length ballet. Stevenson, one of Tudor's favorite designers, worked with him a great deal over the years, most notably on *Jardin aux lilas*. At the time he was choreographing *The Planets*, Tudor had started to read about horoscopes and study the signs of the zodiac. The ballet's casting considered the zodiac sign of each of the dancers. Other influences included the Ballet Mécanique and German Expressionist techniques.

Mary Wigman and *Ausdruckstanz* emerged in the late 1920s. Exploration of non-classical, "expressive" dance foreshadowed Modern Dance as we know it today. Harald Kreutzberg, a contemporary of Wigman, first used the Holst music for a dance. A product of the industrial revolution and World War I, the Ballet Mécanique genre featured an ensemble performing machine-like movement. George Antheil's score, *Ballet mécanique* for pianos, percussion, and airplane propeller, probably best exemplifies the genre musically.

Few of us have had the opportunity to see *The Planets*. I did, however, have the good fortune of spending a week with the late Elisabeth Schooling, one of the original cast, whose memory was legendary. She demonstrated much material from the ballet, which we then checked for authenticity with early Tudor dancers Sally Gilmour and Maude Lloyd. The creative imagination behind *The Planets* idiosyncratic movement vocabulary, its musical sensitivity, and its sheer inventiveness is breathtaking in the context of 1934. There were very few in the ballet world, perhaps only Fokine, de Mille, and Balanchine, choreographing with such originality at that time or for many years thereafter. The sections each differ substantially from one another in vocabulary and structure; each treats the music differently. Moreover, each section has an aura, a perfume all its own.

In the original, Kyra Nijinsky, daughter of Vaslav, played the role of Neptune. Tudor described her as a wonderful character, with limited dance technique but charismatic stage presence. Built like her very famous father, with rather substantial thighs, she was "a bit crazy." Her friend, a Mrs. Freeman, involved her in numerology, also a Tudor fascination. Freeman tried to engineer a marriage between Tudor and Kyra so that Kyra could obtain British citizenship. (Kyra eventually married the musician Igor Markevitch and moved to the United States.)

Rambert said that Tudor tried out some of his ideas for the "Neptune" section with her children on the beach and that the breaking of the waves on the shore gave him the image for some of the basic movements. Maude Lloyd described *The Planets* as follows:

> I adored *The Planets* . . . I was the planet Venus, with Pearl Argyle and Billy Chappell as the two Lovers under my influence. There were four girls who were Venus' retinue. I think it was one of his most lovely ballets. . . . I remember doing *arabesques* with strange arm movements. [Note, once again, the Tudoresque device of traditional footwork with non-classical, gestural arms.]
>
> The ballet started with me *bourréeing* around on the spot with one arm moving up and down, very slowly, over my head, my head very much to the side, and my body undulating as it turned. What I did was very *adagio*—big, slow movements. Mars was written on Laing, who was dynamic in it, with a very exciting corps de ballet. Antony made the last one, Neptune, on Kyra Nijinsky with Antony himself as a satellite Planet . . . It was very difficult, because Holst's music for Neptune has no discernible beat. It just goes on and on. [39]

Lloyd was also impressed with the beautiful way Tudor lit the dance and its three backdrops: red for "Mars;" green underwater coloring for "Neptune," and moon colored for "Venus." Later, when Tudor staged the ballet for his own company, the London Ballet, he added a male solo, "Mercury." Celia Franca remembers dancing Neptune:

> All that mysticism. Tudor's movements were not like any ballet steps you knew—oh, no . . .The last scene of *The Planets* was so clever. He had all of the planets coming back, all revolving as planets do. He was so subtle about it. What a genius! What a gift! [40]

Elisabeth Schooling adds:

> *Planets* had a lovely quality about it. One had to watch very carefully not to make a sound [with the toe shoes]. The music was so quiet, particularly in Venus. I remember literally holding my breath. The feeling of being above the earth, in fact. . . .The illusion of what you wanted to express had to be much as one liked. . . . I didn't like [Mars] one bit. Too central European.[41]

A presentation of *Castor and Pollux* by Rameau, choreographed by Tudor for the Oxford University Opera Club, rounded off this productive year. While it used professional singers and dancers Maude Lloyd and Tudor, the rest of the "corps" were all members of OWLS, the Oxford music society. Tudor arranged one dance for six OWLS who functioned mainly to hold Lloyd up high. The man who later became the Duke of Wellington, according to Lloyd "a beautiful young boy whom everyone fell in love with, but who couldn't do anything," played a Greek Statue. The production was a great success.

Thérèse Langfield, a Tudor dancer who joined the Ballet Rambert in 1934, said of him:

> I was one of his special friends and that was marvelous. . . . I used to explode and make him laugh . . . Amongst my generation, not amongst the older people, you were either a pro Fred or a pro Antony. (I count Schooling as an older person, and Maude too.) He was lovely. Everybody had a crush on Antony. We were all 16–17 years old and ready to fall in love. And there's Antony . . .
>
> [Tudor] was very nice to me. I got married very young and I had my daughter . . . I either took her around with me or I had to get someone to look after her because I never had a nanny. Antony took that in his stride without making any difficulties about it at all . . . He used to let me bring her to rehearsals. I had a crush on him for years."[42]

Tudor's knowledge of music was profound. Customarily he worked with the score at home and came back to the rehearsal with various ideas. He didn't always know how to turn them into movement, however, although, in his head, he knew what he wanted. Never pleased with himself, he harbored terrible anxiety and nervousness.

As he aged he became less and less excited at the idea of doing a new ballet. Not particularly ambitious, he sought neither greater fame nor riches. If he had an idea, he wanted to do it. If not, no matter what the enticement, he wouldn't.

## The Descent of Hebe

Early in 1935 Tudor produced his third major ballet, *The Descent of Hebe,* with music by Ernest Bloch *(Concerto Grosso)* and costumes and settings by Nadia Benois. The work consisted of four sections. In the first, "Prelude," Hebe spilled nectar while serving the gods. She

*The Planets.* Pearl Argyle and William Chappell. *Photograph courtesy of Ballet Rambert Archives*

hoped it would go unnoticed, but Mercury brought a message expelling her to earth. In the second, "Dirge," Night was to bear Hebe away, but Hebe refused to go. Night conjured up a vision of Hercules convincing Hebe she would meet him on earth. The "Pastoral" section showed Hebe, newly arrived on earth, dancing with children when Hercules found and wooed her. A "Fugue" closed the piece in a music and dance apotheosis.

Typically, the ballet came about because sets and costumes already existed. Nadia Benois had designed them for a play, *Jupiter Translated,* by W. J. Turner. Rambert described the ballet as altogether ravishing. The costumes were black and white: Hebe in black and Hercules in white. The striking scenery depicted the black horses of Night's chariot leaping across the backdrop. The way the dancers' movements synchronized with the lines of pink clouds gave a wonderful, if dearly bought, illusion of flight. Some of the performers remembered the ballet:

Maude Lloyd:

> *Hebe* had three layers of clouds and we had to dance between them. It was the most harrowing ballet to perform. Antony had a clear idea of how it should be on a larger stage.[43]

Celia Franca:

> It was a wonderful work. How we ever managed on that tiny stage, I don't know. We had to do these complicated steps, in the middle between two rows of clouds in about two feet . . . What really stayed in me was the musicality of the choreography. It was exactly right for the music.[44]

Elisabeth Schooling:

> The clouds went up and down. Sometimes we were lucky and they went up at the right moment. It was good on a big stage, but it was dicey on a small one. . . . The clouds were made with three–ply wood with gauze around it; nobody would make them that way today. They had to be pulled manually at the Mercury Theatre, so they went up awkwardly. It was supposed to be in a blackout. When it worked it was quite good.

We took *Hebe* to France where it was quite successful. One of the
dancers spoke French slightly so he had to be the stage manager. At
the moment when we should have had the scene of earth coming
down, with the sheep safely grazing and Hebe saying hello to them,
down came a huge building with steps and pillars and God knows
what else. I remember hearing from the wings, *"Felicitations, mes
amis, mais où sont mes moutons?* [45]

*Hebe* was downstage left and Hercules upstage right when she finally succumbed to his charms. She had to run to him, take his
hand and simultaneously get her knee in the crook of his arm. He
was half standing and, at the same time the whole thing turned. It
sounds easy enough, but if you missed that knee getting into that
little bit of space in his arm, it was terrible. It had to look like you
were reclining on his shoulder, airborne. But no, he wouldn't have
that. It would have been safer, but he had to have it the difficult
way.

I used to enjoy the end, the fugue, which was lovely. If I made that
lift successfully, the fugue would be a delight—gorgeous. There
was a little solo. If I danced with real joy, and excitement, and ex-
hilaration there was always a round of applause. If not, it was a
pretty silent audience. [46]

The last movement, the fugue, was a brilliant technical feat of choreography, bringing all of the dancers together in fugal counter-
point analogous to, but not copying, the musical fugue.

Schooling also commented that when Tudor was choreographing,
he disregarded the dancers. She believed he would have preferred to be
alone to have a dialog with only his muse. He didn't particularly want
to see anybody do anything; he preferred the dancers invisible.

Franca also told a story about Hugh in *Hebe.* As practically no
wing space existed at the Mercury, one had to "put the brakes on immediately" on exiting. At a dress rehearsal Laing leapt offstage only to
trip on the milkmaid's stool from *Façade,* which Rambert had carelessly left there. He picked up the stool, went back onstage and threw it at
her.

*The Descent of Hebe.* Antony Tudor as Hercules. *Photograph courtesy of Ballet Rambert Archives*

## Working at the Opera

The remainder of 1935 Tudor devoted mostly to opera, both as performer and choreographer. In late August and early September he danced in the following productions with the Al Fresco Ballet at the open-air theater in Regents Park: *During the Ball* (Richard Strauss, choreography by Nina Theilad); *Allegory* (William Boyce, choreography by Tudor); *Danse Macabre* (Camille Saint–Saëns, choreography by Michael Martin-Harvey); and *The Flower Princess* (Claude Debussy, choreography by Letty Littlewood). During the summer he worked as choreographer primarily for Thomas Beecham's opera season at Covent Garden. Tudor and Beecham became friends. At one rehearsal of *Carmen* Beecham found Tudor trying to both choreograph and play the piano, so Beecham jumped in, accompanying the rehearsal himself.

Those who are convinced that Tudor could only work slowly might be enlightened to see what he produced for the stage that summer. In addition to dancing in the multiple performances of the works mentioned above, he choreographed four operas: a production of Rossini's *La Cenerentola* (1 May) featuring Markova; *Schwanda the Bagpiper* (3 June) by Weinberger, based on Chekhov; Bizet's *Carmen* (4 June); and *Koanga* (23 September), on a voodoo theme performed in blackface to music by Delius. One wonders how much *Koanga* influenced his later ballet about voodoo, *The Divine Horseman,* made for the Australian Ballet in 1969.

Apparently *Schwanda* caused something of a scandal. Its German impresario had in mind a galloping, earthy polka. Tudor produced a very intricate, somewhat avant-garde experimental frolic for thirty or forty dancers. "Antony did some very interesting and delicate things. It was all on the spot using shoulders and feet. It was Antony's idea to be absolutely against the music." When the impresario saw the final "general rehearsal," the dress rehearsal traditionally open to an invited, prestigious public, he was furious. "No, no, no. We cannot have this. This is horrible! We want a polka." [47] He commanded that the dance be completely reworked by the next day's official opening; they had a great row. Changing the piece was an impossibility, of course. The opera went on as Tudor planned, much to the chagrin of the management. The reviewer R. H. in the *Daily Mail* (exact date unknown) seemed to side with Tudor in a rather oblique way: "The clever fugue, with choreography by Mr. Antony Tudor, was productive of expressive dancing."

Tudor also had an idea for a ballet to music by Sibelius. He traveled to Finland and called on the maestro, unannounced. When he returned, having read Finnish legends, he decided to make a huge ballet based on the Finnish epic poem, *Kalavala*. The Sibelius music he chose would require an orchestra of at least eighty players; a two-piano reduction, Rambert's customary musical forces, did not seem practical for the piece. Rambert did not use recordings or tape for performances. The work, to be titled *En Saga,* would make use of rune casting. Scheduled for a premiere in October, 1935, the dance actually went into rehearsal. Lloyd (the virgin mother) was to eat a blackberry and give birth to a baby, Leo Kersley (the Christ Child). Others in the cast included Markova and Peggy van Praagh. Thérèse Langfield and two other dancers were cast as birds with Mona Inglesby (Vredenburg) the lead in the bird section. The corps would dance with the music in 3/4 meter against Mona's solo work in 6/8. Tudor's plan for the ballet looked like this:

*Pohjola's Daughter*

| | | |
|---|---|---|
| Prologue: | Narration of *Kalavala* | Corps de Ballet |
| Creation: | Luontar | Maude Lloyd |
| | The Teal | Mona Vredenburg |
| | Change of scene to Earth | |
| | Birth of Vainamoinen | Hugh Laing and Ensemble |
| | Interlude | |

*Symphony no.3*

| | | |
|---|---|---|
| 1st mvt: | Peasants dance | Van Praagh and Ensemble |
| | Vainamoinen and Joukahainen | |
| | | 2 men (Staff and ?) |
| | Vainamoinen and Aino | Pearl Argyle *Pas de Deux* |
| 2nd mvt: | Water Spirits | Aino's solo, *Pas de Quatre* |
| | Vainamoinen | Male solo |
| | Aino (as a fish) and Vainamoinen | |
| | | Mime scene |
| | Three Golden Cockoos | *Pas de Trois* |
| | Pohjola's Daughter and | *Pas de Deux* |
| | Vainamoinen | |
| 3rd mvt. | Change of scene to Louhi's castle | |
| | Sorcerer's dance | Ensemble |
| | Ilmarinen and Pohjola's daughter | |
| | | Mime and *Pas de Deux* |

         The nuptials and betrothal Ensemble
                         Interlude
En Saga:  Wedding scene              Kyra Nijinsky, A. T. Ensemble
          Arrival at husband's home
                              *Pas de trois*
          Escape and scene in the country
                              *Pas de Deux*
          Brother's house         Scene, solo
          Back to betrothal scene in castle
                              Ensemble
                         Interlude
*Symphony no. 4*
1st mvt:  Marjatta the virgin        Maude Lloyd Solo
          Marjatta and son          *Pas de Deux*
4th mvt:  Crowning of the son, worship
                              Ensemble
          Farewell of Vainamoinen   Solos and ensemble

Finally, Tudor had to give up on the idea for lack of resources; surely the Mercury could never accommodate an orchestra of that size. Apparently Tudor still contemplated doing the ballet as late as 1941. All the while he had another ballet percolating in his mind.

## Jardin aux lilas

*Jardin aux lilas* (*Lilac Garden*) is perhaps the best known and most loved of Tudor's ballets (along with *Dark Elegies* and *Pillar of Fire*). A short story by Aino Kallas (variously identified as Finnish or Estonian) about the *droit de seigneur,* the feudal custom in which the lord of the manor had the right to bed a peasant wife-to-be, inspired the ballet. The choreography departs significantly from that story, however. The main plan for the ballet had its genesis in a suggestion from the designer Hugh Stevenson with the detailed plot purportedly developed by the choreographer and the designer together.

Caroline, the heroine, betrothes The Man She Must Marry in a marriage of convenience. He belongs to the *nouveaux riches* and needs a good name to ensure his legitimacy; she comes from a good family of failing means in need of financial help. The ballet takes place at the final party before the wedding. Caroline's former, probably childhood, first love (The Lover) and, uninvited, the former mistress (An Episode

in His Past) of The Man She Must Marry appear at the party. Through
fleeting, surreptitious meetings, each summarily interrupted by the
partying couples, Caroline and The Lover attempt unsuccessfully to say
their final farewells. For her part, the mistress tries desperately to convince the Man that she sees no reason for their intimacy to end. Neither
couple succeeds in accomplishing its goal, and the ballet ends with
Caroline obediently taking the commanding arm of The Man She Must
Marry and leaving the party.

Tudor began working with music of Gabriel Fauré; eventually he
abandoned it, choosing instead the Ernest Chausson *Poème* for violin
and orchestra. Similar to several other of his ballets, *Jardin aux lilas* is
set in the Edwardian period, the period of his mother's youth, which
held such an attraction for him. Tudor wrote:

> In this ballet I started with the inestimable advantage of working
> within the closely knit family of the Rambert group. I used Maude
> Lloyd, Hugh Laing, Pearl Argyle, and myself as principals but also
> had Elisabeth Schooling to lead the corps. Everyone of them had
> worked perfectly with me several times before and understood my
> approach. Rambert herself did not, and after a few incidents in
> which she, on the sidelines, was trying to influence my dancers to
> show more emotion, which I considered "hamming it up," I had to
> forbid her presence at any of my rehearsals . . . If she as much as
> poked her nose into the door everything came to a halt.

> This ballet concerns itself with the concealing of emotions from
> outward display. Indeed, whenever anyone interrupts others during
> the ballet, then those interrupted retire into their well-brought-
> upness and to behave as their training had required. The ballet goes
> a regular course until the moment of sleepwalking, of divination;
> the immediately succeeding *pas de quatre* should be regarded nos-
> talgically, from a far away point of view, about how wonderful it
> was then, all those many years ago. This is punctured by the future
> husband's bringing on of Caroline's cape and the realisation that
> now all this is of the past and the future is now the present.

> Although the short story by Aino Kallas on the *Droit de Seigneur*
> had been discarded as being too melodramatic, the four principals
> in *Jardin* are *dramatis personae* and only Caroline's friends retain
> the innocent teenage romanticism of youth. The scenery is romantic
> with its moonlight, blue lighting, and its presentation of a deserted
> part of a manor house's garden that is overgrown with lilacs in full
> bloom. At the very opening performance at the Mercury, the audi-

ence felt they could truly sense the heavy perfume of lilacs drifting from the stage into the auditorium. [Rumor has it that at one performance Laing and Tudor sprayed the stage with lilac perfume to provide the right atmosphere.]

The period of the ballet, in the early part of this twentieth century, must be fully understood by whoever is directing the production. It must be remembered that Caroline's family and friends had been brought up in an atmosphere of good manners, good deportment and everything else that was taught them at the expensive finishing schools of the time. It is certain that Caroline was of a generation when virginity was a prerequisite in any marriage. Any contemporary question as to whether Caroline had had an illicit sexual bout with the leading young man of the ballet must not even be posited. They grew up as children together and probably had always harbored the thought and desire that they would eventually be married to one another. Unfortunately Caroline's parents, having no longer the wealth that had once been theirs, have arranged a marriage for their daughter, with her acquiescence, to a very rich man, who is recognised and welcomed into the very best society, for money "talks." He is the self-made businessman and is accustomed to getting what he wants and getting it his way. [The character called] An Episode in His Past should be looked upon as perhaps a stage star, who is recognised in all the best Cafe Society, but is a stranger at this party. She arrives, uninvited, to speak with her rich friend and protector. She loves him and does not wish this longtime relationship to end. She sees no cause for that since his marriage into Caroline's family is to enlarge his circle of acquaintances into that of the very good old families.

The ballet was, and is, a landmark achievement. For the first time in classical ballet, the sequences of movement and the use of gesture (as differentiated from pantomime) expressed all of the action, the emotional climate, and the interplay of the characters. The dramatis personae were clearly and simply drawn. The viewer understands their motivation and their character with not a word needed. The drama unfolds through the sequence of dance events, through the passionate yet contained fleeting encounters always interrupted by the partying group, and through the use of the formal structure of the ballet. The structure evolves from the content. The skill with which Tudor takes us from "real time" at the party into the minds of the characters astounds. So does the incredible moment of stasis which separates the two. Tudor show the influence upon him of the writings of Proust and Freud, and of the Freudian idea of stream of consciousness. Fernau Hall suggests the philosopher Bergson as another influence.[48]

When I questioned Tudor about Bergson, he said that he knew the Bergson family better than the Bergson oeuvre. Bergson's cousin was the father of Goran Gentele's second wife, Marit. Gentele directed the Royal Swedish Opera house during part of Tudor's tenure there. He was under contract to become the intendant of the Metropolitan Opera when the opera moved to its new home in Lincoln Center, but tragically died in an automobile accident before the plan materialized.

As a confirmed film buff, an avid moviegoer, Tudor appropriated filmic techniques as compositional devices. He was totally innovative in his adaptation of these cinematic ways of working to the ballet, the very first choreographer to do so. He adopted and adapted to the stage realities of the ballet, flashbacks and interpolations that reflect the mind-set of his characters. He also coopted the zooming in from large groups to soloists, a fascination with and highlighting of detail, and other similar cinematic devices. It is one among many of the unique contributions that Tudor made to the craft of the working choreographer.

In *Jardin aux lilas,* Tudor's use of traditional footwork overlaid by everyday upper body gesture is the dance equivalent of *"le mot juste."* With every movement being exactly the right one, he has achieved that perfect amalgam of form and content of which every creative artist dreams.

If we listen to Tudor's words about the ballet, we begin to understand how each cast member physically expressed his or her role and how the content influenced the form.

> Caroline always holds herself correctly, shoulders down. When she opens her hand at the beginning, she shows tension as she slides down and grasps [her elbow], but anyone beside her would not know. The Episode in His Past is obviously very fulsome. She sweeps in as though she has a big fan, with huge swinging gestures from the upper arms. I very seldom use wrists—I hate wrists. I take most of my gestures from the upper arms or from the thighs.

> The lover is so open. He has no quirks of any kind, whereas my part [The Man She Must Marry] has nothing but quirks. If he looks at Caroline, it is because she belongs to him. If he gives an arm, it's demanding she take it. . . . The [corps] girl in white I always thought of as being the closest friend. They grew up together and

she was the confidante . . . When I came to the *chassé* entrance I had to go slowly because of its very intricate footwork, which has to look as though it is not intricate. It takes a lot of work to get that feeling . . . With the Chausson that main [musical] theme keeps coming back. Each time it came back I wanted to present it in a different choreographic form, so it wouldn't ape itself. . . . We came to the final statement and it was so *largo*. I said "What on earth are we going to do now?" . . . If you don't know what to do, why do anything? It came out of desperation.

Tudor refers here to perhaps the most famous moment in the ballet in which a complete freeze on stage stopped the action. Caroline, seemingly in a swoon, precipitated a motionless moment (freeze frame) for the rest of the cast. She then began a very simple walking sequence, as if sleepwalking, which led the ballet into a dreamlike, nostalgic final *pas de quatre*.

The change in music from the Fauré to the Chausson seemed to release Tudor, to give him the movement. Apparently the rehearsals first included just Hugh and Maude, later joined by Peggy van Praagh[49] and eventually Elisabeth Schooling. Laing remembered that,

Tudor was finding a new way . . . and we were terribly happy with how things were going. . . . And Mim [Marie Rambert] was not at all happy. She used to come and sit in front of the mirror in the studio at Ballet Club and she would cross her legs and purse her lips and then she'd say, "humph" and walk out. Well, this wasn't very good for Tudor because it [the ballet] was a new approach for him. It was undermining. So Maude and I went to Elisabeth Hewitt, the secretary of the Ballet Club . . . and we said "What can we do about it?" Eventually the three of us got an idea. . . . Every time Mim came in, Maude would suddenly say, "I want to put on my [pointe] shoes," and I'd light a cigarette, and balance on top of the iron rail around the anthracite stove. Mim got very frustrated, but it worked.[50]

Agnes de Mille relates that Tudor was paid seven pounds for the ballet and that Mim kept talking against it. Hugh got Rambert by the throat, called her a wicked woman, and promised that if she didn't stop her propaganda against Antony's ballet he was going to close his hands.

Rambert even tried to call off the first performance of *Jardin aux lilas* .

On Thursday night, at the dress rehearsal Mim started up in one of her moods. She wasn't going to have that "feelthy" ballet on her stage. Tudor asked that they go and get Ashley. He suggested that if it was announced that Mim said he was no good, all his jobs would be jeopardized. It would damage his reputation; therefore, the dance had to be performed in public at least once. Ashley said he was right; they would do it for one performance only. Mim wished to announce this; Tudor insisted it be done after the ballet. After the sixteenth curtain call she hadn't got backstage. [51]

The audience at the Mercury Theatre, on the night of 26th January, 1936, when the ballet was first performed, had no doubt that it had seen a masterpiece. And it was a masterpiece well nigh perfectly interpreted. [52]

Maude Lloyd remembered often going back to the studio at night so Tudor could try some things out.

He would give us a beautiful passage, absolutely lyrical, lovely to dance. You'd think, "Well that's one passage done." Then the next morning during class, he would lean over and tap my shoulder and say, "I don't like what I set last night. . . ." It wasn't good enough for Tudor and out it went. [53]

Celia Franca thinks of her performances in *Jardin aux lilas* as a wonderful experience, the favorite role of her performing career. Although she was only fifteen, Tudor chose her to replace Peggy van Praagh on tour as the Episode in His Past. Learning the role from Tudor himself was a fantastic experience, because he created such an unforgettable atmospheric picture. "Imagine that you have just arrived at the top of the Crush Bar staircase at Covent Garden. Everybody's eyes are on you. And you sweep in." [54] Franca remembered that Tudor could be very sarcastic but that he could also be very kind.

The ensuing years have seen any number of stagings of *Jardin aux lilas,* but Tudor denied the ballet to just as many companies as he permitted. For example, for years he refused to allow Alicia Alonso [55] to stage it with her Cubans, although she requested that he do so many times. Eventually he did capitulate. Tudor's reason for refusing many companies that asked for the dance was as follows:

> This is the ballet most often requested, sometimes even by fledg-
> ling groups with little training either as stage performers or in com-
> pany discipline. The companies see it as requiring a small cast,
> having no obvious scenery problems, and fulfilling the need for a
> romantic piece. This is a mistaken perception. The requirements of
> the ballet are not the province of the talented beginner, and even
> leaders in the world of ballet have failed to achieve its move away
> from egocentricity.
>
> With this ballet the cohesion of the movements with the mu-
> sic is precise even to the turn of a head or a hand as will be clear
> from the Labanotation score. As to the music, whenever the main
> theme returns it must be in *L'istesso tempo* [the tempo in which it
> originally appeared, with the duration of a beat being the same even
> when the meter changes], including the entrance of the orchestra
> after the original exposition by the solo violin. . . . The portrayals
> [of the characters] cannot be handled with ease by some young
> dancer whose sole education seems to have been confined to the
> ballet studio.

As the years passed, faced with requests for permission to mount
the ballet, Tudor became increasingly specific, almost picky, about the
costuming and décor. He complained that the cape Caroline put on at
the end was the wrong color in the Ballet Theatre production. He
maintained that it had faded, and so it should not be copied. Designs
that he provided had to be reproduced exactly. I believe he used the
excuse of a very expensive production to discourage companies that he
did not think would do the work well. He hid behind the expense to
refuse permission. He told me that he was never happy with a set for
the ballet unless it cost at least ten thousand (1950s) dollars.

New casts, even Gelsey Kirkland, often ask Maude to explain the
events of the ballet. "And I say, if you listen to the music, and if you do
the movement exactly, you can't go wrong." [56]

Sallie Wilson, who performed many Tudor roles at American
Ballet Theatre and who often restages his work, complained that she
had trouble getting people to keep the *arabesques* low or mid-height.
Particular arabesques have a particular meaning in the Tudor oeuvre.
They must not read as just an acrobatic pose or trick. When I, myself,
staged *Jardin aux lilas* for the Milwaukee Ballet, I found it most difficult to get the cast to run in a simple, unadorned fashion—an unstyl-
ized, non-decorative run serving only to arrive at a given destination.

After *Jardin aux lilas,* Tudor began to get a bit restless. When the
Ballet Rambert completed its very successful season in Birmingham,

Tudor thought the company should expand and take on more touring, but Rambert and Dukes were worried about finances. Given their restricted resources, they felt the risks too great without outside backing. Their worries resulted in very restricted company touring, thwarting Tudor's ambitions.

## Music Theater

Dance in a theater setting occupied the remainder of 1936. First, on 19 February, came choreography for a new three-act J. B. Priestley play *Johnson over Jordan,* with music by Benjamin Britten and a cast headed by Ralph Richardson and Edna Best. On 23 March, *The Happy Hypocrite* by Clemence Dane, based on a Max Beerbohm story, with music by Richard Addinsell, choreography by Antony Tudor and starring Vivien Leigh, opened in Garrick, Southport. It then moved to His Majesty's Theatre for sixty-eight performances. At the Drury Lane Theatre in September, a musical theater piece called *Careless Rapture* played, with most of its choreography by Joan Davis except for one ballet by Tudor.

The crowning piece (literally) of the 1936 London musical season was a satiric revue about the Duke of Windsor and Wally Simpson. It had an all-star cast including Cyril Richard, Hermione Baddeley, and Viola Tree. Tudor contributed a coronation ballet. The revue opened on 26 November; however, when the Duke abdicated, the ballet "bombed." The revue closed on 12 December. As Maude Lloyd recounted,

> It was called the Coronation. It was going to be [presented] when Edward was crowned King. Antony arranged the ballet for Hugh and me. We did only about six performances, although it was scheduled to run for a year. At the third performance, the curtain closed just before we started, and Edward announced that he was abdicating. The entire chorus was crying. I came down with flu the next night and by the time I recovered, it was all over. [57]

## 1937: Another Busy and Productive Year

Tudor continued working in theater dance throughout 1937. On 6 January he choreographed Johann Strauss's *Die Fledermaus* for Covent Garden. Sir Thomas Beecham conducted; Prudence Hyman, borrowed from the Ballet Rambert, danced the lead.

On 9 January at the Drury Lane Theatre the musical *The Crest of the Wave* appeared. Popular composer Ivor Novello contributed the music and Tudor did some of the choreography.

Meanwhile, a very new medium developed: television. It was very experimental, very daring, with few in the viewing public. Long before the advent of kinescopes or videotape, every program was broadcast live. Preservation was not yet of concern. The programming on BBC tended to be of literary, topical, or cultural content. Only a handful of intrepid people viewed the new invention; very few owned television sets. No mass market, mass appeal sit-coms, soaps, or other commercial manifestations had yet polluted the medium.

The very day after the *Fledermaus* premiere Tudor made his appearance as choreographer for this fledgling form of entertainment. During 1937 he choreographed no fewer than nineteen works for television. The list is breathtaking:

*Paleface* (7 January, starring Cyril Richard and Hermione Baddeley with Tudor and Maude Lloyd dancing a whole series of pieces)

*Paramour* (2 February, choreographed earlier as a *pas de trois,* but rechoreographed, and danced here as a *pas de deux* by Lloyd and Harold Turner)

*Hooey* (2 February)

*Siesta* (2 February, with music by William Walton and décor and costumes by Peter Bax)

A repeat of the formerly choreographed *Constanza's Lament* (4 February)

The ground-breaking *Fugue for Four Cameras* (2 March)

*After Supper* (2 March, a revue)

*Fête d'Hébé* (2 March, a *pas de quatre* for Lloyd, Tudor, Hermione Moir, and Charles Stewart)

*Wienerblut* (2 April)

*The Story of the Vienna Waltz* (2 April, with Lloyd, Tudor, Elisabeth Schooling, and John Andrewes)

*Dorset Garden* (13 April, a restoration revue)

*Suite of Airs* (16 May, period dances to the music of Henry Purcell—it is possible this was rehearsed but never actually aired)

*Boulter's Lock, 1908–1914* (29 June, a revue in this very stylish London setting)

*Cabaret* (5 July)

A staging of Francis Picabia's *Relâche* (8 July; Greer Garson appeared in the cast)

*En Diligence* (14 July, three dances, *En Diligence* with music by Francis Poulenc, *Romeo and Juliet pas de deux,* music by Constant Lambert, and *The Boy David,* music by William Walton)

*Portsmouth Point* (6 September, danced by Peggy van Praagh, Naomi Holmes, Bridgette Kelly, Charlotte Landor [Bidmead], Frank Staff, Elisabeth Schooling, Mark Baring, John Thorpe, and Harry Webster)

*High Yellow* (14 September)

*Full Moon* (25 October)

*To and Fro* (26 November, a revue with Cyril Richard and Hermione Baddeley with Hugh Laing and Maude Lloyd dancing) [58]

Stephen Thomas and Dallas Bower, two avant-garde television directors, particularly liked Tudor's work and the fact that he used "modern" music. The producer Barry Starr, who customarily mounted opera, was also a fan. Tudor and Maude Lloyd were paid ten pounds for every show and in that way earned their keep. Thomas would ask Tudor if he had a piece of music he would like to do. Said Maude Lloyd:

> Sometimes Tudor did marvelous things if he was interested in the music or the idea. If he wasn"t, he was impossible. We'd go to rehearse and he'd say "I haven't an idea. Dreadful music, no idea. Come on, think of something. I'd say, "Well, what about something like this?" and he'd say, "Yes, that's terrible," but we went and did it. . . . He used to laugh at what I thought was sexy.

Lloyd coolly remarked "Of course, at that time television was so small in England that you could really be as highbrow as you like; nobody was watching!" [59]

The *Fugue for Four Cameras* was particularly innovative. A new entrance by Maude Lloyd, picked up by a new camera, represented the entrance of each voice of the excerpt from J. S. Bach's *Art of the Fugue.*

Tudor remembered that he

> did a fugue for four cameras. I had to devise a dance that would fit
> the four-part fugue musically. But instead of another dancer joining
> the movement with the second voice, another camera joined the
> movement and then you saw the dancer in the center of the film
> open up and become a second dancer and then a third voice would
> come in and pick up where she started. We spent a lot of time on
> this, or the cameraman spent a lot of time on this. It was rather ex-
> citing.[60]

The work was about eight minutes long and took place in a very
restricted space. Lloyd remembers it as being ten feet by eight feet. The
choreography, complex and "footsy," had to stay more or less on the
spot. As the *Fugue* drew to a close, the figures dissolved one by one
until the last chord, leaving the original solitary figure.

A month later they repeated the broadcast of the *Fugue*. Luckily
Lloyd had made some notes on the music. She was dancing in Edinburgh that month and took an overnight train, in full stage makeup. She
then rushed to the "Alley Palley" (the Alexandra Palace from where the
television shows were broadcast) in London, to perform.

## Another Tudor Masterpiece, *Dark Elegies*

During the time that he choreographed all of this "dance on order," another work stirred in Tudor's mind, a rather bold undertaking.
Tudor had heard Gustav Mahler's *Das Lied von der Erde* at a concert
and fell in love with it. He was unable to locate a reduction instrumen-
tally suitable for the small forces available at the Mercury Theatre;
however, he did find a piano reduction of another Mahler work, *Kindertotenlieder*. His idea of making a ballet on the theme of grieving for
the loss of children did not win great popularity in 1937. The emphasis
in ballet was still on fairies, sylphs, and glorious processions. Léonide
Massine, who choreographed huge spectacle ballets in the Diaghilev
tradition—grandiose, colorful and fanciful was the darling of London.
The public flocked to see the very Massine ballets that Tudor so intensely disliked. Tudor refused to see them to avoid becoming "in-
fected." The Massine ballets, so full of grandiosity and virtuosic displays, represented the antithesis of Tudor's balletic ideals. But even in
the case of choreographers he admired, such as Kurt Jooss, Tudor

avoided seeing too much in those early days, as he feared being unduly influenced. He wanted to go his own way. Only much, much later had he sufficient confidence in his choreographic path to see a great deal of dance.

Tudor undertook this grieving theme, producing one of the most eloquent, moving ballets of all time. *Dark Elegies* is abstract in that it had no scenario, nor any specific reference to children except in the music itself. It explored the different aspects of grieving with its six soloists (five sections, the second one being a *pas de deux*.) Much of the movement stemmed from the classical canon, using *arabesques,* turns in *attitude, posés à la seconde,* and the like. But the dance also encompassed a vocabulary more referential to modern dance than to ballet: suspensions, falls, skips, and knee work. Although a paradigm of structural clarity and thematic movement development, these devices never impinged on the dance's emotional impact.

The soloist in the first song, a woman, explores her sadness in leaps, small forward and backward rocking steps, and undulating gestures for the arms. The corps remains seated ritualistically in a semicircle around her, moving minimally in abstracted pain. The second song, the *pas de deux,* is one of the most poignant in all of dance literature. With tenderness the man tries to console the woman, to little avail. The amazingly inventive lifts do not seem acrobatic but rather tell this story of attempted consolation. A male soloist and six, then eight corps members dance the third song. The corps performs adaptations of folk dance-like material: chains, circle dances, and crossing steps. The man expresses his grief in sharp, kicking sequences. The dignity of male grief is poignantly explored by alternating outbursts of frustration with consoling movements of group solidarity. The fourth song posits denial and introspection. This quietest of the solos shows a woman who grieves more internally than externally. One senses she cries only when alone. The last song, the fifth, shows a male soloist who begins his grieving by railing against fate. As he jumps and spins, the anger of the solo builds to an almost unendurable pitch. In a remarkable moment, a skip ends with the man turning on the floor on his shoulder. The very intensity of his anger leads to a cathartic moment of frenzy for the entire community.

Slowly the atmosphere transforms itself into one of acceptance and resignation. The ballet ends with a slow, dirge-like walk offstage by the entire cast. By the sense of community the group creates, it has managed to deal in the only way possible with such a catastrophe. The participants accept their fate, and move on.

Rambert tried to persuade Tudor not to undertake the work because of its plot, but of course he was immovable.

> I started to choreograph with the third dance. They do a step which is basic to the work. It came from a tap dance step I learned at Max Rivers studio. . . . I don't think I ever explained what a movement meant in *Dark Elegies*. I think the movement should explain the whole dance. The movement together with the music complete a whole.[61]

Maude Lloyd remembered working on the *pas de deux* in the small, downstairs studio at the Mercury one morning. It had no mirror and each time Tudor lifted her, she would touch the ceiling. She said it was "written" faster than any other choreography he ever did; he never went back over it. He nearly finished it in a single session. Of course, they had no idea what it looked like. They showed it to the designer Nadia Benois and to Rambert. Benois insisted that Lloyd wear just what she was rehearsing in, except for the addition of a skirt. Thus, the ballet remained clothed in practice costumes, with the women wearing head scarves.

The scenery consisted of two backdrops, the first a northern landscape—austere, cold, and frightening. The second backdrop projected more hope and appeared at the moment of acceptance of the fate.

> There is a lot of resignation in what Antony did. You accepted it, with outbreaks of pain. They try to get on with their ordinary life, but every now and again their emotion breaks through, and then they pull themselves back each time. They were people who had to go on living, fishing . . . There are quiet moments broken with big outbreaks of despair, agony of loss . . . You must feel it is really happening to you, and yet you have to be disciplined. You have to get the movement right. . . . The movements . . . were part of your life, although some of them were sometimes odd. They weren't always natural but somehow they became natural. It's a rather frenetic moment after Hugh's song [the fifth song]. Then the music dies down and we all go in together. It is a marvelous moment. Such a sense of community. We close the circle, and we are all holding each other for comfort. It's the last scream, really, before resignation.

*Elegies* is not a gloomy ballet. It's tremendously sad but it's not gloomy because all of the time they are accepting what's happening to them. [62]

Tudor choreographed the fourth song for Agnes de Mille, off pointe. The way she danced the solo greatly pleased him. Rambert was not at all pleased, but Tudor fought her hostility and de Mille performed the role.

Celia Franca, a corps member in the original cast, also has strong memories of working on *Dark Elegies*.

In the first song he said, "sit very simply, with your hands laid in you lap. No nail polish." He explained that they were simple, peasant people. They were there looking out over the sea, into space. And, when his eyes did it, our eyes did it. He was very hypnotic. When he was choreographing the third song, he worked out some of the corps de ballet steps on me. I remember him asking if anybody knew any Irish dancing. I put my hand up and said "I do." . . . In the second half [of the third song] that's where that heel and toe tap dance came from.[63]

The most famous story about *Dark Elegies* took place on opening night. Tudor recounted:

On the morning of the performance I hadn't started on the last dance at all. I'd done a little section of it for [Hugh] the day before and some more early that morning. Hugh had learned his part only that a.m., so it went out of his mind right after the beginning. [While he was performing] he got desperate and would run to someone and say "What do I do next?" He became demented. Toward the end he suddenly remembered that he had to get to this whipping [step]. He picked up then. He threw himself on the floor with such abandon he practically broke his back. [After the performance] he just left the theater and went walking along the Embankment in total depression thinking he had ruined my ballet. He got the most marvelous reviews the next day.[64]

Elisabeth Schooling added that whenever Hugh turned his back to the audience he would mouth "Help me, Antony, help me." Antony was sitting there in the circle of dancers and his "eyes were coming out on stalks." He couldn't move. He couldn't get up and help.

De Mille remembers the cast coming onstage in kimonos before the curtain opened. While the audience, tickets in hand, waited half an hour, Tudor simply told the cast, "You go here and you go there, then bend over backwards and all walk offstage." Numbed, de Mille did what the girl beside her did, thinking, "God help us."

Of Tudor's working procedure Noel Goodwin wrote:

> Because Tudor's genius was in exploring the inward states of mind through dance rather than just the outward emotions, it is understandable that he should not want his community ritual of shared sorrow to become too specific. He kept the dancers from understanding the verbal content of the Ruckert poems for fear they might try to "interpret" the details.[65]

All of the dancers realized, even during the rehearsals, that the work was extraordinary. Even Rambert relented, saying she wanted to take Tudor in her arms and protect him out of fear that something would happen to him before he finished this masterpiece. She admitted that she'd never seen a more beautiful ballet.

Cecil Bates, who danced *Dark Elegies* with the Ballet Rambert much later, reported a phenomenon unique to Tudor works. When the company was performing *Dark Elegies,* all banter and backstage chat would stop. Everyone was quiet. The whole company would come down to the wings to watch.

## Leaving Rambert—Dance Theatre

At the invitation of Rambert, Agnes de Mille originally had come to England in 1929 to perform her solo program at the Mercury.

When she gave her series of solo recitals, Tudor stage-managed. They got on famously, becoming great friends. She recounted how, when she first met Tudor, she did not realize that he was a deeply committed homosexual. She thought of him only as a "bonny, charming" young man. She asked him to lunch; he asked if he might bring Hugh along. At the lunch, Hugh became angry because Antony did not pay him sufficient attention, and he insisted on sitting at another table.

De Mille and Tudor went to see the de Basil ballet together. They were nearly thrown out by the fans because they made derogatory remarks about the great Massine.

She tells a story about how, in 1939, after the break with Rambert, Hugh and Antony moved to British Grove. Since all were short of funds, they proposed that she move in with them.

> They had this very nice house with a yard and a little garden. There was a big studio upstairs with skylights and things. They asked me to come and live with them; that's how close we were. I didn't, for a lot of reasons. It wouldn't have occurred to me to live with two bachelor boys unless I was in love with one of them, which I wasn't. But they did class every morning and I would go out there and take it.[66]

After the performance of *Dark Elegies,* Rambert's negative comments about her dancing so enraged de Mille that she left.

Rambert's appreciation of *Dark Elegies* notwithstanding, Tudor found Mim's meddling and the spatial restrictions of the Mercury Theatre increasingly unacceptable. Somewhat earlier a potential backer had offered to take over the Ballet Club and move it to a bigger space, but Rambert turned the offer down. Maude Lloyd remembered:

> After we'd had a couple of seasons in the West End which had been a big success, Hugh and Antony had an offer from somebody with quite a lot of money, to run the company, to enlarge it, to have a proper orchestra. Rambert wouldn't hear of it. She was frightened. . . . Antony and Hugh were very upset about it.

Before it was given to de Valois, the Sadler's Wells Theatre had also offered Rambert a residency. Rambert was quite happy as long as she was in control, but she was not about to allow anyone to share that control—not even if it would permit of more grandiose productions and less penny pinching. One cannot help but wonder how different the history of English Ballet and the ballet in America would have been, had she accepted the Sadler's Wells' offer.

At the same time as de Mille left, Tudor's disgruntlement with Rambert and his ideas and growing confidence as a choreographer demanded that he, too, move on. Although Tudor abandoned Rambert, he never severed all connection with the company or its founder. Rambert retained his ballets in her repertoire and he returned to rehearse them from time to time. Nor did he forget what she had done for him, writing her glowing tributes on various company anniversaries.

So, in 1938, Tudor and de Mille joined forces. With Laing and Hugh Stevenson they decided to form a company which would have a unique repertoire: suites of de Mille's brand of national dances and works choreographed by Tudor. For the cooperative effort everyone pitched in. Hugh Laing had inherited a small sum from his father, which he threw into the pot, along with some funds contributed by Hugh Stevenson. Agnes de Mille contributed her costumes and fifty pounds, which she had borrowed. They purchased the décor and costumes for three of Tudor's ballets: *The Descent of Hebe, Jardin aux lilas,* and *Dark Elegies.* When not dancing, they were making new costumes; Hugh's mother, visiting London, did the cooking.

The company premiere took place at the Oxford University Playhouse, where they gave a one-week season, 14–19 June. The principals, de Mille, Tudor, Laing, Peggy van Praagh, and Margaret Braithwaite, and the corps dancers were mostly from the Rambert, so no Thursday or Sunday performances could take place. Somehow the fact that it was exam week at Oxford had been overlooked. The exams decimated the expected audience and the company played to only a handful of people at each performance. Rambert came to opening night, among the very few London ballet fans who made the trip. e.e. cummings and his wife were at Oxford and they attended.

Tudor choreographed one new work for the opening program, *Gallant Assembly,* to the music of the *Cello Concerto in D* by Guiseppe Tartini, (1692–1770). The dance was a mid-eighteenth- century romp, full of airs and graces, laden with Tudor's brand of satirical wit,[67] and rather lewd.

> A young couple came to dance for the entertainment of the aristocrats. They were simplicity and beauty itself. The aristocrats, in the funny but rather nasty part of the ballet, were always holding bosoms or bottoms. When the young couple appeared, the aristocrats sort of shrunk into their shells. The young girl wore a simple dress while the rest of the corps sported tremendous finery. I loved it. All of the rather lewd things in it, he did with such a twinkle in his eye." [68]

A. V. Coton described the dance as follows:

> In a mock pastoral episode, the salacious scamperings of a group of "aristocrats in love" are interrupted by the gentle *pas de deux* of a pair of "hired performers." . . . Fascinated by the simplicity and

youth of the young couple, the aristocrats attempt forthwith to se-
duce them both, receiving for all their pains only dignified rebuffs.
. . . A female spectator succinctly summed up the initial performance. "*Gallant Assembly* ought to be called just Dirty Party." [69]

De Mille, who called Hugh Stevenson's décor and costumes for
the piece superb, labeled the seduction scene for Tudor and herself as:

> the most obscene bit of nonsense in the literature of ballet and one
> of the funniest. . . . The company was excellent and danced beauti-
> fully. The repertoire consisted of the absolute best of our
> work—two of Tudor's masterpieces [actually there were three:
> *Dark Elegies, Descent of Hebe,* and *Jardin aux lilas*]. And in the
> cradle of British Culture all we could pull in was between two and
> three pounds a night. But Tudor didn't seem to mind. He delivered
> a gallant and graceful farewell address from stage on closing night
> never mentioning the sparse attendance, and we went out to a party
> which we gave ourselves. The week's kitty was divided equally
> among all members of the company—three pounds a piece. [70]

## 1938: Dance for Television; The End of Dance Theatre

With such a disappointingly small audience at Oxford, Dance
Theatre, of course, lost all of its original investment. Thus, the beginning of 1938 saw Tudor scrambling to earn money in order to live and
to salvage the company. There were few job offers. He made a pittance
teaching classes in his studio at British Grove. He gave a series of lectures at Morley College and at Toynbee Hall. Toynbee Hall became a
very fortuitous venue for the future, for it was the very place where the
next incarnation of a Tudor company, the London Ballet, came into
existence.

At Morley College, the series of six lectures explored such topics
as: "The Development of Classical Ballet," "Period Dancing and the
Influence of Costume," "Ballet, the Synthesis of the Arts," "Ballet
Composition," "Ballet in Rehearsal, Audience in Performance," "The
Completion of a Ballet," "The Use, Misuse, and Abuse of Music,"
"Choreographer and Dancer," and "Ballet, Finite and Infinite." Demon-
strations by Celia Franca and Peggy van Praagh illustrated some of
these lectures:

> It was a very interesting lecture, because he made us both do the
> entrance of the Episode from His Past from *Lilac Garden,* and "The
> Sugar Plum Fairy" from *Nutcracker.* He showed how two different
> artists could do the same choreography, but in slightly different
> phrasing or tempos, and both were right. . . . He was explaining to
> the audience about interpretation. Not everyone had the intellect to
> reach out to the audience in that way.[71]

Television represented a major source of income, and there followed in quick succession a series of works for that medium. In January the second act of *Tristan and Isolde* aired as a masque with mime.
Tudor arranged it for a cast most of whom had had no formal mime
training. Producer Dallas Bower called the hour-long production, which
Tudor rehearsed for a month, his most ambitious undertaking.[72]

On 5 April the BBC presented Tudor's *Wien,* a Viennese entertainment; 24 April, Handel's *Acis and Galatea* with Tudor creating the
ballet. In May, O'Neill's *The Emperor Jones* aired with Tudor arranging dances and appearing in the role of the Auctioneer. Also in May, a
production of de Falla's *Master Peter's Puppet Show* featured Tudor's
mime and his portrayal of the Scholar. Laing appeared as the Page. The
production incorporated a monkey, a recurring player in some of Tudor's later work. And finally, in December, came the presentation of a
one-act opera, *Cinderella,* with music by Spike Hughes.

Elisabeth Schooling told an amusing tale of how they whiled
away the boring hours of waiting during film and TV shoots, and just
how innocent she was in those days:

> We worked in films quite a bit. We were all in *As You Like It.* An-
> tony was not doing the choreography but he was one of us, one of
> the yokels. During the hours of waiting, as there always were with
> films, we played Scrabble[73] [word games and crossword puzzles
> were constant favorites of Tudor and Laing]. We got to P E N I.
> Tudor said, " Finish it, Schooling," and Laing said "Put the S on."
> I was so innocent. I said, "Is that a word?" At 20 years old I had
> never heard the word. Obviously, they were just rolling around the
> floor laughing. Hugh said, "What do you call it, or do you just
> point?" They didn't let me forget that for a long time.[74]

The reincarnation of Dance Theatre or a similarly constituted company
took place later in 1938 when de Mille was hired by a small theater, the
Westminster, near Buckingham Palace. The short presentation of
Gogol's *Marriage* needed a curtain raiser. Agnes asked Tudor to cho-

reograph a new work to augment her own presentations. So, in a sense, she commissioned *Judgment of Paris,* since she split her fee for the evening three ways: a third to Tudor; a third to the dancers who included Laing, Thérèse Langfield, and Charlotte Bidmead; and her own portion of the fee. For the engagement which began on 15 June, 1938 and ran for 21 performances through 7 February, in addition to *Judgment of Paris,* Tudor created *Hunting Scene* and *Joie de vivre.* The three Tudor works along with selections by de Mille were collectively titled "Seven Intimate Dances."

Tudor choreographed *Hunting Scene,* music by John Christian Bach, danced by Tudor, Langfield, and Bidmead, to allow for a de Mille costume change. She described it as "damn good" and she regretted that Tudor neither remembered nor ever revived it. About *Joie de vivre* little is known except that Tudor made the ballet for two women, Thérése Langfield and Charlotte Bidmead. According to an article in the June, 1987 edition of *Dance and Dancers* entitled "The Man Who Changed Ballet" (p. 16), they repeated it in the London Ballet season. Described by Langfield as "a lively and light-hearted beach scene to music by Offenbach, Strauss the Younger, and Weston, it required the dancers to wear old-style bathing costumes under their dresses. While one of them held up a big towel as a screen, the other slipped out of her dress, rolled down the long legs of the bathing costume, and emerged ready for a dip in the waves." [75]

*Judgment of Paris,* choreographed to excerpts from Kurt Weill's *Der Dreigroschenoper* (*Threepenny Opera*), is one of Tudor's gems, the product of his acrid wit, perfectly accompanied by its Kurt Weill score. Laing had suggested the story of its three pathetic prostitutes and their drunken patron. A rather inebriated man about town enters a bar peopled by three "ladies" of questionable repute. Old, tired, and dispirited B girls, rather fat and sleazy, their entrance with half-articulated steps and mock tap dancing is sheer hilarity. The gentleman comes in and sits himself at a table. Each of the women in turn displays her questionable charms. Juno, the youngest of the three, coyly waggles her body as seductively as she can manage, using a black fan as a prop. Venus "dances" with three hoops. In the crowning moment of her performance she manages to step through the hoops, quite a feat given her proportions. Minerva, the final seductress, dances with a very tired feather boa. She tries to do the splits, but cannot make it. The gentleman leers on at the performances, drinking more and more and more. He finally collapses in a heap on the table whereupon the three "graces" stripp him of his worldly goods. The work, infused with the usual Tudor sardonic wit, actually presents a sorry, rather tragic story.

Hugh had seen some early drawings on the kitchen wall of their good friend the painter Vera Cunningham, which gave him the idea for the ballet. He also did the décor and costumes although, because he was not a member of the union, they had to be attributed to someone else. When Marilyn Hunt asked Tudor if he were laughing at the whores, he replied, typically:

> Not at all. They're my central characters. Without them my little piece doesn't exist. I take them very seriously. I know the background of each of the three characters, who is the popular one, who the one whose mother is starving. I know them very well. Agnes is the one with the hoop. . . . She's got it made . . . and she always gets it. She makes the money. The first one is a newcomer. She's trying her damnedest and only succeeds because she has youth on her side.[76]

De Mille added:

> [In the hoop dance] every gesture is a satire of some other kind of bad dancing. I knew what I was satirizing so I became Duncan or Florence Fleming Noyes or whatever. . . . Antony's performance was never recorded, never seen because he was just sitting there in the front. But he was superb. Drunker and drunker. The eyes glazed. And lust, just nearly surfacing, the clouding over until he finally collapses. He was marvelous.[77]

It shocked some of the reviewers a bit but was a hit from the start. The nearly anonymous, very astonished critic F. T. of *the Daily Telegraph* commented, " that a theme so degraded and so sinister should be sponsored by a philanthropic and educative institution with the Archbishop of Canterbury as chairman!" [78]

The work has endured for decades and still is an audience favorite when well performed. Its cast must be drawn from the most experienced dancers; sylph-like, youthful, beautiful ballerinas are very wrong in the ballet.

When Tudor brought the work to New York, he cast Lucia Chase along with Maria Karnilova and Agnes de Mille. Later Chase did the de Mille role.

## 1938–1939: The Jesus of British Grove

Once Tudor had left Rambert and the Mercury Theatre, the Holland Park flat was inadequate. He found it too small and located too close to Rambert. He had to have a place to rehearse his ballets as well as a place to live. So, he and Hugh found a charming small house in British Grove, out past Hammersmith in the Chiswick section of London. It had a garden where they often stored flats from Dance Theatre and later the London Ballet. They lived on the ground floor; upstairs was the studio. Along with rehearsing, Tudor gave classes there to a very loyal band of dancers, acolytes some would say. Their dedication and loyalty earned Tudor the title of "The Jesus of British Grove." Leo Kersley, a Tudor dancer at the Rambert school, explained:

> [When] I went . . . for my first class . . . Tudor spent ten minutes chatting with me in the dressing room—a typical Tudor gesture, for not only did it put me at my ease and make me feel at home; he in his turn had learned quite a lot about me before we began to work together. . . . This quick and unfailing interest in people was not, however, the only reason which drew dancers to Tudor. He aroused in us a devotion to his ideals and achievements which caused certain jealous rivals to dub him "The Jesus of British Grove." [79]

While life continued financially precarious, it seems to have been less stormy temperamentally. In addition to de Mille and Lloyd, "the boys" (Antony and Hugh) were quite friendly with Thérèse Langfield and Charlotte Bidmead. Langfield has many fond memories of that period. She speaks of the group all going to the cinema together quite often, seeing the so-called sophisticated films of the 1930s, particularly those of Claudette Colbert. She also remembers that the boys left little paper notes: "Lotte [Charlotte Bidmead] and Thérèse have been invited to tea by Antony and Hugh. Please reply." So they replied and went to tea.

Thérèse Langfield also remembered that

> The boys had two little dogs: Gita and Tobias. Tobias was normal, not troubled by his former life. Gita was very nervous. If you turned around suddenly he would snap at you.

> My great friend Lotte was going up the steps. . . . He jumped up and bit her hard on the bum. . . . I'm afraid neither Antony nor

Hugh were at all sympathetic. Antony said, "Well, that shows what a lovely waggle you have. I didn't bite Thérèse's bum."

Lotte and I used to spend the night in the upstairs bedroom sometimes when we were rehearsing. There was a bathroom up there and a little kitchen. It must have been a flat at one time. . . . They never trained the little dogs. They used to be left alone there—you opened the door and the smell!! Downstairs was the big room that the boys really lived in. They used to do a lot of cooking, then leave the saucepans on the table. You can't imagine what a hell hole it was.[80]

Peggy van Praagh also had fond memories of the period:

Tudor had his group of friends, and we would go to his flat in Chiswick with its big studio, and we'd rehearse in the evenings. When we got too tired we'd go off to The Doves pub and have sausages, onions and beer, and then go back and do a bit more rehearsing. It was all very informal and great fun, and we'd work very late. . . . He went a great deal to various theaters and we used to go with him—up into the gallery, climbing all the stairs at Covent Garden—and we'd also see a lot of the Kurt Jooss Company. . .

We also went to see Mary Wigman, and I remember how keen Tudor was to watch all the national dance troupes. . . . Tudor tried out everything, exploring the body's movement. In those days he never had a large corps de ballet and he would do very different things for each dancer, not only because of our different physiques, but also because of our different temperaments. That is why he liked us to go to his studio and the pub, so that he got to know us better. . . . We were the instruments through and with which he created the roles and communicated his ideas to the audience.[81]

Tudor had a destructive streak in his personlity. Examples of his sarcasm and cruelty abound in the tales of every dancer who ever worked with him and, more to the point, those who chose not to. Ethan Brown speaks of Tudor's "candid, perverted, vulgar language." Kathleen Moore says he called her a stupid bitch. Alicia Alonso challenged him to make her cry. Almost every day some dancer would run out of his class in tears. I remember in one class his singling out a generously endowed young lady and speaking of the rhythm of her *relevés* as "down, up, bounce, bounce, bounce." In another such incident an unfortunate student came to class with a strategically placed hole in the back of his tights. Tudor made him face the barre and demonstrate a *tendu en arrière* (leg pointing backward) while the rest of the class stood behind him and stared. Nothing would do until someone identified what was wrong with the picture.

Although Tudor could be devastatingly sarcastic, he attracted a totally devoted, loyal group. Over and over again one hears that, while he picked on this one and destroyed that one, while exceedingly remote and rarely showing emotion, he was "very kind and generous to me."

While the dancers claimed to be unaware of making history, his inner circle knew that Tudor was an extraordinary talent doing extraordinary things. Honored to be a part of it, they worked willingly in whatever way he found necessary.

## The London Ballet at Toynbee Hall

All the while that he struggled financially, Tudor was hatching a plan to have a ballet company of his own. Convinced that the only way to present his ballets as he wished people to see them, he believed in his achievements, his talent, and his ability to run a company. The group he planned would have no stars, nor starring roles.

After many months of planning, replanning, interviewing, rehearsing, and conferring, the London Ballet formally came into existence in November, 1938.

The cruel side of Tudor surfaced in his treatment of de Mille when he founded the London Ballet. Although they had been such good friends and close artistic collaborators, he did not ask her to have any part in the new endeavor. When she inquired about it, he bluntly told her that her services weren't welcome, that he wanted a company of young people and she was just too old. Only thirty years old at the time, de Mille considered the comment simply vicious. She believed that Tudor might easily have cited many cogent, acceptable reasons for their collaboration being undesirable, chief among them that their styles were incompatible. As Mim put it, they canceled out one another.

Toynbee Hall developed into the first University Settlement House in England. Located in London's East End and known as "The Working Man's University," it provided self-improvement courses at modest fees in all sorts of subjects. Samuel Barnett, vicar of St. Jude's Whitechapel and a canon of Westminster Abbey, founded it in 1884. He believed that if young Oxford graduates took up residence in the East End, they could conduct educational courses for the local population, learn about the area and its problems, and seek solutions to the horrible poverty and hateful environment that prevailed in late Victorian England.

In 1938 the institution had just rebuilt a 400-seat theater [82] with excellent sight lines, which Tudor could just about afford. In order to attend the theater, one had to purchase a membership at two shillings sixpence annually, thus allowing one to buy tickets priced from sixpence to five shillings. Tudor had already given public lectures and ballet classes there. Toynbee Hall became the headquarters of Tudor's fledgling company, but it provided only the bare walls. All house personnel, such as box office, stage crew, electrician, front of house staff, clerical and secretarial help, lighting personnel, scene painters, and the like were recruited from willing amateur volunteers. The company did not even have its own telephone. The eminent critic A. V. Coton was in charge of box office and publicity; Tiny Monkhouse was the business manager. Margaret Craske [83] taught company classes. Dancers and musicians hand-addressed thousands of circulars. With no financial backing, all expenses for theater rental, production, music, dancers fees, etc. had to be paid for out of Tudor's carefully husbanded, meager savings. An orchestra could not even be considered; musical accompaniment was provided by two pianists: Dorothy Moggridge and music director Hans Gellhorn. On opening night, awaiting the delayed curtain, the eagerly expectant audience heard the sounds of backstage hammering—there had not been time for a dress rehearsal and the scenery was still being mounted.

London's ballet public had experienced a rich year in 1938. In addition to Ninette de Valois's home grown Vic-Wells company, two major Russian groups had performed: Massine's Ballet Russe de Monte Carlo and Colonel de Basil's company, temporarily called the Educational Ballet. Such stars as Irina Baronova, Alexandra Danilova, Margot Fonteyn, Robert Helpmann, David Lichine, Serge Lifar, Alicia Markova, Tatiania Riabouchinska, Tamara Toumanova, and Harold Turner had all performed.

Still, the London ballet world was agog with the news of the new company. Four days before the opening over 90 percent of all seats had been booked for the first two performances, 5 and 12 December. On the standing room only opening night the hall was packed with dancers, press both theatrical and musical, gossip columnists, and ardent balletgoers. Familiar faces included those of Ninette de Valois, Cyril

Beaumont, Margot Fonteyn, Robert Helpmann, and Frederick Ashton. In a bold departure from tradition, ballet had come to the East End.

The East End, hardly high-culture London, was a working-class neighborhood, much like the one in which Tudor had grown up. To him it represented more than just the lure of a new theater and a place where his company could take up a residency. Philosophically Tudor never embraced the elite nature of the ballet, particularly the Russian ballet. Bringing dance to ordinary people was one of his pleasures and goals.

The 31 December issue of *Weekly Illustrated* proclaimed the philosophy of the company:

> To prove once and for all that the ballet is not the pastime of the "intelligentsia," a new professional ballet, known as the London Ballet, is presenting regular performances in the new theatre of Toynbee Hall, the Universities [sic] Settlement in the East End of London. Under the direction of Mr. Antony Tudor, who has lectured on the ballet at Morley College and in Hampstead Garden Suburb in London, the company is intent on living up to its motto "ballet for all." . . . "I knew there were people in the East End making weekly pilgrimages to ballet in the West End," said Mr. Tudor "and I was determined they should have their own company."

For opening night Tudor created *Gala Performance* to round out the program. The other works performed included *Jardin aux lilas, Judgment of Paris,* and *Gallant Assembly.* The evening was enormously successful, with many of the audience staying on long after the curtain came down, discussing the performance, dazed by its professionalism. Much critical acclaim ensued, and many of the succeeding performances sold out.

## The New Works

Tudor had created *Gala Performance* for the very practical reason that his generally darkish repertoire needed a light touch. The ballet revealed itself, in two scenes, with music by Sergei Prokofiev (*Piano Concerto no. 3*, first movement, and the *Classical Symphony*). The first scene supposedly took place backstage. The corps hurried and scurried about, warming up and getting ready for the performance in the face of the usual last minute crises. They actually had their backs to the audi-

ence to simulate the backstage perspective. Three ballerinas entered
one by one. Each in her turn spoofed the national characteristics of her
native land and its style of ballet. The Russian ballerina entered first,
bent over in a parody of poor carriage. She crossed the stage looking
for someone to gobble up in her sure knowledge that she knew the only
way to dance. Snappish and demanding, she sent one of the corps
members off crying. She practiced only her bows, throwing ice cold
kisses to her imagined public. The French ballerina entered next, all
champagne and bubbles, wildly tossing her kisses. Last came the Italian
ballerina, imperious to the point of being ramrod stiff. Every step constituted a magnificent effort which she did not doubt would be greatly
appreciated.

The second scene viewed the "performance" from the opposite
angle, frontally. Each ballerina entered again and performed her solo,
which the corps mimicked in a less exaggerated, but nevertheless
slightly out of control fashion. The Russian ballerina showed a series of
"tricks," which she executed by force of will rather than by technical
prowess. One knew she gritted her teeth before every *pirouette*. The
Italian ballerina milked the audience, taking an interminable time for
each of her over-articulated walking steps to center stage. Every cava-
lier had to kiss her hand, which she barely lifted for him and certainly
did not acknowledge. Such attention was, of course, her due. Every
gesture told a long story. As Tudor showed us, even her *pas marchés*
(walking steps) were a work of art. The French ballerina's upper torso,
as if made of liquid, moved constantly, rarely achieving a centered balance. It did not matter, however, since she never stayed still for a moment. When the three returned to the stage together, sheer bedlam
reigned.

Part of the fun lay in the fact that the corps performed the movement nearly correctly. The dancers lost their balance just a little bit
because they had to deliberately incorporate all the small, subtle technical flaws that one usually works to combat. The faults were choreographed into the sequences. The soloists' attitude toward the whole
affair revealed itself quite transparently: The French one didn't really
care who was best; the Russian one hoped she was best; and the Italian
one knew she was best.

The audience loved this ballet gone wrong. For opening night Tudor did not tell the cast that the dance was funny. They played it absolutely straight, without a hint of caricature. When the dancers came
offstage they said, in amazement, "the audience laughed." Maude

Lloyd spoke of the Italian ballerina being so grand and so conceited that she barely moves at all. And, she warns against performances that vulgarize the piece by making it too broad. (She also remembers that in the spirit of the democratic company, they all took the same salary, five shillings a performance. Five shillings equalled about $1.00 at the time. A laborer earned about ten shillings a day.)

The costumes, by Stevenson, looked lavish in spite of the lack of money. Piggy, the woman who made them,[84] often stayed up all night stitching and wondering where she would find the money to buy the next bit of material.

Tudor described some of his thoughts while choreographing the piece:

[For the Russian ballerina] I saw the towers of the Kremlin and the Russian eagle emblazoned. It was the famous barbary of the Russian I was going for. Wildly extreme arms. Man eating. For the Italian I had a picture of the Forum and Italian monuments—grandeur. Everything immemorial. She's made of stone. Nothing can ever push her over. The French is all frou-frou and petticoats. She never stops curling her hair. She's a mess. . . . The next [second] performance the cast tried to be funny. It was a funeral service it was so dreadful. When people think they are funny, they are not." [85]

Later, when Tudor revived the piece, he called the dance "a lousy piece of work . . . [which] became a big success in spite of my attempts to kill it."

Joining the repertoire after the first night were *Dark Elegies, Descent of Hebe, The Planets,* and another new work, *Soirée musicale.* From 12 December through 26 April, 1939, the company continued to give Monday evening performances on alternate weeks, for twenty-one weeks in all. Two ballets announced for the season were not mounted. Both *Opera Ball,* planned to have music by Heuberger and décor by Stevenson, and *Pavane for Three Cavaliers,* with music by Gardano, had to be abandoned for lack of funds. Instead, beginning on 6 March, the enlarged repertoire added a few works by other choreographers: a *divertissement* which included *Shepherd's Wooing,* a *pas de deux* by George Balanchine for Peggy van Praagh and Hugh Laing; a variation for Maude Lloyd to Tchaikovsky music; and a *pas de deux* from *Italian Suite,* music by Cottrau, arranged by Anton Dolin and danced by

Massey and Bidmead. Later, Tudor's *Joie de vivre* was substituted for the *Italian Suite pas de deux.*

Tudor's *Soirée musicale* also joined the repertoire. Rather an anomaly in the Tudor canon, *Soirée musicale* comprises a light set of variations in various "national styles" danced to the Benjamin Britten arrangement of Gioacchino Rossini's musical *divertissement.* Although this Tudor work received its official premiere with the London Ballet, it was actually created as a demonstration piece for the Cecchetti Society for an annual meeting on 26 November, 1938. The work fits more comfortably into what Tudor referred to as his "dance arrangements" as distinguished from his choreographic works, that is, his dances using unembellished classical vocabulary rather than inventive movement. Its five sections consist of a "March," for six couples with three additional ladies looking on; the "Canzonetta," a *pas de deux* in the style of *Les Sylphides;* the "Tirolese," a foot-slapping Alpine peasant *pas de deux*; a trio of women dancing a rose-in-teeth Spanish "Bolero;" a "Tarantella" *pas de deux,* and a grand finale. In 1959 the Robert Joffrey Ballet revived the dance, and it has since been performed many times by smaller companies.

In sum, the season of the London Ballet was a huge success. The theater filled for all of the performances, critical evaluation remained positive in the main and the audience reacted exceedingly enthusiastically and often quite vocally. Tudor had accomplished what few have ever done in England. He had "presented a complete, unique world of real people seen through the eyes of one person: a vision as valid and individual as that of a great painter or writer or playwright who presents to the public a world which is clearly recognisable, but uniquely his." [86]

It was and remains the only example of an extended "one-man show" (excluding the small offerings in the *divertissement*) in the history of British ballet.

## More Opera, Television, and Theater

The initial season of the London Ballet at Toynbee Hall might have continued had not Maestro Beecham invited the company to dance at the Royal Opera House. Tudor accepted. By performing in opera at Covent Garden the company was able to earn some sorely needed money, dancing in *The Bartered Bride* on 1 May, *La Traviata* on 22 May and *Aïda* on 24 May with Margot Fonteyn as the soloist.[87] For *The Bartered Bride* Tudor choreographed a country dance ensemble, a ballet, and a circus show. The *Times* printed a photograph of the *Traviata* ballet and mentioned that "the ballet and the circus show with its acrobats and tricksters were thoroughly effective." The unnamed critic of the *Sunday Times* of 28 May nearly liked Tudor's work for *The Bartered Bride*, calling the ballets "competent enough, [but it] lacked a dash of inspiration." In his rave review of *Aïda* of 3 June, 1939, W. J. Turner remarked that "it is a great pleasure to see a well-conceived and well-executed ballet."

Tudor did not forswear income-producing television during this busy and productive period. After the 24 January Tudor and Dallas Bower production of *Tristan and Isolde,* on 3 February the BBC broadcast both *Gala Performance* and *Soirée Musical.* On 5 February Tudor directed a production of *The Tempest* using music of Jean Sibelius and featuring members of the London Ballet. April 7 saw his arrangement of the ballets for *The Pilgrim's Progress,* to sixteenth- and seventeenth-century music arranged by Lionel Salter with Langfield, Schooling, and Bidmead having acting as well as dancing roles.

Nor did Tudor's activity in the theater languish. In February he did the choreography for a second production of *Johnson over Jordan.* His first assignment for the producer Charles B. Cochran had consisted of the choreography of two scenes for the 3 April supper-time revue *Nightlights*: "The Argyll Rooms" and "The Fountain." He also worked on Cochran's revue *Lights Up*, repeating "The Argyll Rooms" under a new title, "A Fragonard Picture," and adding a new scene, "An Old Dance Hall." The production did not actually go before the public until February, 1940.

During the summer Tudor occupied himself with plans for the future of the London Ballet. Harold Rubin, an impresario interested in ballet, had approached Tudor. Rubin wanted Tudor to bring the company to his newly acquired Arts Theatre for the upcoming winter season, 1939–1940. After endless conferences and a thorough analysis of every penny spent in the preceding season, plans for a new season emerged. The plans, however, were not to be realized in the way conceived.

Although the London Ballet performed again in the fall, and were, indeed, presented at the Arts Theatre, no longer did Tudor personally lead it. By then he had left for the United States to fulfill a ten–week commitment to Ballet Theatre (later renamed American Ballet Theatre). In an unforeseen development, these ten weeks extended into years as a choreographer and resident in America.

# Notes

1. Antony Tudor, "Rambert Remembered," *Ballet Review* 11, No. 1 (Spring 1983): 62. In his original autobiographical notes, Tudor refers to that evening's performance as "a glimpse of heaven."

2. Selma Jeanne Cohen, *Dance Perspectives* 17 (1963): 7.

3. Originally Tudor stated that the Shakespearean Sonnets were recited "in a beautiful English delivery." Because the sentence structure in the autobiographical notes is unconventional, it is unclear in the original whether the sonnets were actually recited by Tudor or by Rambert herself. In his York lectures Tudor states unequivocally that it was Rambert who recited Shakespeare; she was well-known for doing such recitations.

4. Elizabeth Sawyer, "That Englishman Abroad," *Dance Chronicle* 20, No. 3 (1997): 229. Sawyer quotes a letter from Tudor in which he states, "The Cooks didn't qualify, cockney being a reasonably precise term indicating locale and vernacular speech. . . . I used proper English, but spoke it out of tune." The quote following the excerpt appears on page 230 of the *Dance Chronicle* article. Sawyer's article also contains an interesting and detailed description of the evolution of Tudor's way of speaking.

5. Originally: "hoisting and manipulating the young coryphees, was a gift from heaven, especially if the body seemed of good shape, athletically disposed and of a convenient size."

6. Ashley Dukes (1885–1959) was an eminent playwright, bon vivant, art collector, and sometime producer.

7. While the story sounds like authentic Tudor, the timing does not conform to reality. He was already Antony in the early to mid 1930s, but he didn't come to New York until 1939. In his York lectures, Tudor attributes the suggestion to a Mrs. Freeman, an aficionado of numerology and a friend of Kyra Nijinsky. Freeman suggested that he would never find a good future with the *h* in the name.

8. Sawyer, "That Englishman Abroad," 233–4. From a letter dated 7 September, 1963. While Tudor says Rambert associated the name change with his aspiring to be a choreographer, she did not yet know of this goal when he made his dancing debut under the name of Tudor.

9.   Leon Woizikovsky (1899–1975) was trained in Poland and joined Diaghilev's Ballets Russes in 1916 as a leading character dancer. He performed in the premieres of most of the famous ballets associated with Diaghilev. His long career included teaching and restaging of ballets up until 1974, the year before his death.

10.  Colonel de Basil (1888–1951), originally Vassili Grigorievich Voskrensensky, as assistant to Prince Zeretelli in 1925, was in charge of the London and Paris seasons of the Russian Opera. In 1932 along with René Blum, de Basil founded the Ballets Russes de Monte Carlo, and later was sole director of the Original Ballet Russe (1939–48).

11.  The author would like to express special thanks to Rambert archivist Jane Pritchard, whose assistance in many phases of the research for this book was invaluable.

12.  Marilyn Hunt, interview with Antony Tudor, 11 November, 1986, at the Juilliard School under the auspices of the Oral History Project of the New York Public Library, Dance Collection.

13.  See page 59 for more information about the Camargo Society.

14.  Marilyn Hunt, "A Conversation with Maude Lloyd," *Ballet Review*, (Fall, 1983): 6. Lloyd repeated the tale of this incident in an interview conducted by the author in London, 13 November, 1997.

15.  Lodovico Ottaviano Burnacini (1636–1707) was an architect and scenographer. He designed the Imperial Palace for the Emperor Leopold I in Vienna, and the Teatro di Corte. He is best known for his scenic and costume designs for opera.

16.  This and all otherwise unidentified extended Tudor quotes are taken from his autobiographical writings.

17.  Muriel Topaz, interview with Elisabeth Schooling, Exeter, 15 November, 1997.

18.  Marilyn Hunt, interview with Tudor for the Oral History Project of the New York Public Library, Dance Collection, 1985.

19.  This material was assembled from interviews in London with Maude Lloyd, one conducted by Judith Bennahum on 7 April, 1988 and the others conducted by the author on 2, 10, and 13 February, 1997.

20.  Topaz, Schooling interview.

21.  Marilyn Hunt, "Antony Tudor: Master Provocateur," *Dance Magazine*, (May, 1987): 39–40.

22.  Judith Chazin-Bennahum, interview with Alicia Markova, 11 April, 1988.

Chapter 2

23. Marilyn Hunt, interview with Hugh Laing for the Oral History Project of the New York Public Library Dance Collection, 9 May, 1986.

24. Muriel Topaz, interview with Leo Kersley (1920–), London, 17 February, 1998. Kersley was a dancer with Rambert. He joined the company a few years after Tudor, and was cast in several Tudor ballets. He has written several articles about that early Rambert period.

25. Topaz, Schooling interview.

26. Antony Tudor, York University Lecture #2, 21 October, 1971.

27. Peggy van Praagh (1910–1990) became one of Tudor's favorite Rambert dancers, performing leading roles in many of the early ballets. Toward the end of her life when she became the artistic director of the Australian ballet, she invited Tudor to Australia to choreograph a new work and to restage his *Pillar of Fire*, in 1969.

28. Margaret Dale, interview with Peggy van Praagh, 8 October, 1978. A transcript resides in the archives of the New York Public Library Dance Collection.

29. Antony Tudor, York University Lecture #2.

30. Hunt, Laing interview. Henning Kronstat was a dancer with the Royal Danish Ballet.

31. Dale Harris, interview with Antony Tudor for an article for *Horizons* magazine, May, 1981.

32. In several of our conversations, Tudor expressed his dissatisfaction with the fact that Hall was writing a biography of him. While it would not be out of character for Tudor to contradict himself, several of the dancers I interviewed for this book expressed the thought that Hall had "got it all wrong" in his writing about Tudor. In an interview on 22 May, 1981, Tudor told me that he was not particularly influenced by Uday Shankar. While he did see Shankar, he also saw a visiting Japanese troupe, some Balinese dancers from Java, and other performers from the Orient. He said he was already interested in Eastern material, but not through the work of one person more than another.

33. Marie Rambert, *Quicksilver* (London: Macmillan Publishers, 1972): 151.

34. Hunt, Laing interview (transcription: 97).

35. John Martin (1870–1953), as quoted in Fernau Hall's obituary of Hugh Laing.

36. Dame Alicia Markova, *Markova Remembers* (London: Hamlish, Hamilton, 1986): 15.

37. Muriel Topaz, interview with Celia Franca, Ottawa, Canada, 16 June, 1998.

38. This description appears in Tudor's autobiographical writing about *Jardin aux lilas*.

39. Hunt, Lloyd interview (transcription: 13).

40. Topaz, Franca interview.

41. Topaz, Schooling interview.

42. Muriel Topaz, interview with Thérèse Langfield Horner, Seaford, 20 February, 1998.

43. David Vaughan, video interview with Maude Lloyd, 21 November, 1989.

44. Topaz, Franca interview.

45. "Congratulations, my friends, but where are my sheep?"

46. Topaz, Schooling interview.

47. Topaz, Schooling interview.

48. Fernau Hall, *An Anatomy of Ballet* (London: Andrew Melrose, 1953): 205.

49. Van Praagh was standing in for Pearl Argyle, who could not make the rehearsals. It was not until one week before the premiere that Tudor finally decided to keep van Praagh in the role. In the aforementioned interview with Margaret Dale, van Praagh tells us: "Tudor asked us all to read a lot of Edwardian literature, to steep ourselves in the period. You couldn't learn how they moved from reading but you could learn how they thought and the sort of people they were. . . . One didn't realize at the time that you were making history. It was only later that I realized how important the period was."

50. Hunt, Laing interview.

51. Topaz, Kersley interview.

52. Mary Clarke, *Dancers of Mercury* (London: Adam and Charles Black, 1962): 105.

53. Hunt, Lloyd interview, 10.

54. Topaz, Franca interview.

55. Alicia Alonso (1921–), prima ballerina for many years with various companies including Ballet Theatre, went back to her native Cuba after the Castro-led revolution. She founded an excellent ballet company there. At the current writing, she has finally retired from performing, but until recently she performed in spite of her blindness, often partnered by her grandson.

56. Chazin-Bennahum, Lloyd interview.

57. Chazin-Bennahum, Lloyd interview.

58. I am indebted to Judith Chazin-Bennahum for all of her help, and access to her interview with Janet Rowson Davis. For an in-depth discussion of Tudor's television ballets see Janet Rowson Davis,. "Ballet on British Television, 1933–1939," in the English publication *Dance Chronicle* 5, no. 3 (1982–83).

59. Hunt, Lloyd interview.

60. Antony Tudor as quoted in *Dance Perspectives,* 14.

61. Marilyn Hunt, Tudor interview.

62. Judith Chazin-Bennahum, interview with Maude Lloyd, 4 April, 1988.

63. Topaz, Franca interview. Note that while Tudor attributes the step to his tap dance study, and Franca to her Irish dancing, others attribute it to classical Japanese dance such as Noh.

64. Hunt, Tudor interview.

65. Noel Goodwin, *Dance and Dancers* 462 (August, 1988): 22.

66. Judith Chazin-Bennahum, interview with Agnes de Mille (1905–93), New York, 18 July, 1989. Richard Philp, formerly editor-in-chief of *Dance Magazine*, remembers de Mille herself telling him that they actually did all live together. He also remembers her saying that the situation among the three of them was so complicated that she was in psychiatric treatment for two years as a result.

67. Fernau Hall, *Anatomy of Ballet*: 209. Hall suggests that Tudor "seemed to be applying Bergsonian ideas about the nature of comedy" as described in Bergson's book *Le Rire*.

68. Topaz, Langfield interview.

69. A. V. Coton, "An English Career," *Dance Chronicle* (Winter, 1941–42). As quoted by Kathrine Sorley Walker in *Dance Now* 8, No. 4 (Winter 1999–2000): 37. Note the journal *Dance Chronicle* referred to here was a publication privately produced and circulated in England during World War II. Its main contributor was A. V. Coton.

70. Agnes de Mille, *Dance to the Piper* (New York: Little, Brown, 1952): 221.

71. Topaz, Franca interview. The author remembers having an extended conversation with Tudor on this very topic. He agreed that his enlightened point of view on interpretation was not shared by many choreographers. They usually demanded imitation, getting into the heart and breath of a previous interpreter of a role, rather than allowing the new performer to express the character in his or her own way.

72. Judith Chazin-Bennahum, *The Ballets of Antony Tudor* (New York: Oxford University Press, 1994): 297. Much of the material about the television ballets is based on information in this book.

73. The game was probably either Lexico, invented in 1931, or Criss-Crosswords, invented in 1938, both forerunners of Scrabble, which did not appear until 1948.

74. Topaz, Schooling interview.

75. Kathrine Sorley Walker, "Antony Tudor II," *Dance Now* 8, No. 4 (Winter 1999–2000): 42.

76. Hunt, Tudor interview.

77. Chazin-Bennahum, de Mille interview.

78. F. T., *Daily Telegraph*, 24 January, 1939.

79. Leo Kersley, "Antony Tudor," *Choreographers of Today* series, 13.

80. Topaz, Langfield interview.

81. Peggy van Praagh, "Working with Antony Tudor," *Ballet Today* (June, 1960):13–15.

82. The exact number of seats has been variously mentioned as: 400 (A. V. Coton, *An English Career*); 350 (Janet Sinclair, *The Changes of Time*); and 450 (Judith Chazin-Bennahum, *The Ballets of Antony Tudor*).

83. Margaret Craske was one of the leading ballet teachers in England. She had studied with Enrico Cecchetti, danced briefly with the Diaghilev company then opened a school. She emigrated to the United States in 1946 to become ballet mistress at American Ballet Theatre and then to teach with Tudor at the Metropolitan Opera Ballet School and the Juilliard School.

84. Sorley Walker, "Antony Tudor II" (p. 64), quotes the name of the costumer as Kiki.

85. Hunt, Tudor interview.

86. Janet Sinclair, "The Changes of Time," *Dance and Dancers* (January, 1989): 18.

87. Tudor may have also choreographed dances for Tosca for a 19 May, 1939 production.

# 3

# The First Ten Years at Ballet Theatre

In spite of the growing tension over Germany's aggression against her neighbors, in spite or perhaps because of the growing isolationist sentiment in the United States and the conviction that no war would ever come to its shores, a certain optimism about the arts in America prevailed. Citizens who had lived through World War I were less than anxious to repeat the experience. The ranks of American-based artists began to be swelled by émigrés who no longer felt safe or wanted in Germany. Nor did they wish to subject their art to the constraints of officially approved creativity as popularized in Russia. Arnold Schoenberg, Hans Hoffman, Max Ernst, Fernand Léger, Walter Gropius, and later, when France fell to the Nazis, Piet Mondrian and Marc Chagall, to name but a few, all found their way to the United States. Painters and writers both native and foreign-born hastened to exercise their freedom to make art as they saw fit. Social protest abounded in the very air that they breathed and surely affected their work. The WPA (Works Progress Administration) treated artists as it did all other workers, paying them salaries and recognizing their contribution to society.

The Roosevelt administration introduced the WPA as one way to alleviate some of the hardships of the intractable economic depression. Under its provisions, all workers (and artists were considered workers) were paid the same minimal fee to pursue their work. For most dancers, this minimum wage was more than they had previously received for dancing. It enabled them to give up peripheral employment and devote themselves wholly to their art.

While modern dance was starting to flourish, little ballet existed in the United States. The vaudeville circuit waned. Various visiting

Ballets Russes offshoot companies performed as did the Mordkin Ballet. But, with the notable exceptions of the San Francisco Ballet and short-lived enterprises like the pick-up companies subsidized by dancer/choreographer Ruth Page in Chicago, the Littlefield Ballet,[1] and Lincoln Kirstein's early attempts to form a company, no truly homegrown professional classical group existed. Into this void stepped the would-be Diaghilev Richard Pleasant and an "anonymous" backer, Lucia Chase. Chase, heiress to a Connecticut fortune, had trained in classical ballet and wanted nothing more than to become a professional dancer. Taking what remained of the Mordkin Ballet as a starting point, Pleasant and Chase founded Ballet Theatre, which made its debut in 1940.

In July of 1939, Richard Pleasant sent Tudor a letter inviting him to the United States for a ten-week period to stage two of his ballets. Pleasant originally had Frederick Ashton in mind. He had corresponded with Philip J. S. Richardson, editor of London's *The Dancing Times*, to find out about both Ashton's and Tudor's availability. Ashton would not be free until the beginning of the following year; Tudor, while available at the moment, had to be back in England by October 8. Then war was declared and Pleasant wondered how this would affect either choreographer's plans. At the beginning of September he dispatched letters to both men. Ashton's came back to Pleasant marked "no such address, return to sender"; the letter never reached him. In spite of Tudor's deplorable treatment of her when he founded the London Ballet, Agnes de Mille continued to think of him as a genius. She convinced Pleasant that the man he really wanted was Antony Tudor. She explained not only his extraordinary talent, but his probable availability. He might even be persuaded to stay, whereas Ashton's commitment to de Valois and the Sadler's Wells Ballet precluded any extended residency. Tudor, with his prospects in England quite limited, was interested.

Tudor answered the letter on 5 September accepting the invitation, hoping to earn some much–needed funds to help support his London Ballet. He so fully anticipated a return at the end of London Ballet's vacation period that he did not even tell the dancers of his travel plans. The contract with Ballet Theatre, dated 19 September, 1939, and a telegram dated 18 September, state that he would stage three ballets: *Jardin aux lilas, Dark Elegies,* and *Gallant Assembly.* Ballet Theatre would mount two of the three. The company never staged *Gallant Assembly*, but presented *Judgment of Paris* instead. The contract put Tudor's salary at $150 per week for his services as choreographer and an additional $125 per week as a company dancer. In addition, it provided round-trip cabin-class boat fare. Although Tudor had requested it, Laing's boat fare was not a part of the arrangement; however, after they arrived the company promised to engage Laing as a dancer.

Thérèse Langfield told the story of the evening before Tudor left England:

> He just sprung on Peggy and me that he was going to America. We didn't know. It was really rather naughty of him. He said, "we're off tomorrow." This was typical of Antony. And we said, "How can you be off tomorrow? Have you packed? What's going to happen to your studio?" He said, "It's all paid up to date, so there will be no trouble in his [the landlord's] letting it again." "What about all your furniture?" "Oh, I don't care. Take what you want." They didn't have much furniture, but they had nice bits. There was a whole pile of washing on the floor in the corner. Peggy said "Where are the things you're going to pack?" And Antony said, "Well—there." "You can't go with these things. When you go through the customs they'll be looking at you." "I don't mind about customs; I haven't had time to do the laundry." So Peggy and I started washing. It was about 10 o'clock at night. . . . We were boiling kettles. Then, from dripping wet, we were ironing these things, and the steam was coming out. They were off the next day with damp clothes. There was no way to get them dry.[2]

So it was that Tudor did not resume the directorship of his company, the London Ballet. War was declared on 3 September, 1939; Tudor sailed on 12 October. Only because he had had a previous invitation and a signed contract did Britain allow Tudor to cross the ocean. As it happened, their boat, variously identified as the SS *Manhattan* or the SS *Washington*, ended as the very last one to make the crossing before the banning of all civilian traffic.

Dame Alicia Markova came to the United States on the same boat, as did pianist Arthur Rubenstein, singer Paul Robeson, ballerina Alexandra Danilova, danseur Anton Dolin, choreographer Andrée Howard, and Lord Morley, Speaker of the House of Lords. The ship also carried fifty-four pedigreed dogs sent abroad as a precautionary measure against impairment of championship strains.

Markova described the voyage:

> We were six people in a cabin that was meant for one. It was dreadful. Nobody knew exactly where we were for six days and then we put in somewhere. We couldn't understand [what was being said]. It was Arthur Rubenstein who said, "They're not speaking English." Apparently we were in Bordeaux. We'd gone in to pick up this cargo of champagne and cognac. . . . We

zig-zagged another twelve days and then, afterwards, we discovered it wasn't champagne at all, it was [gold] bullion—the French were getting it out [of the country].[3]

The ship landed in America on Columbus Day. The United States customs did not permit Tudor and Laing to enter the country but took them to Ellis Island instead. Their passports read William Cook and Hugh Skinner, but the work permits were issued to Antony Tudor and Hugh Laing. Not until the following day could they contact someone at Ballet Theatre to straighten out the mix-up; Tudor and Laing spent their first night in America as did so many immigrants—on Ellis Island.

Donald Saddler, one of the original Ballet Theatre dancers, remembers the early days:

The audition [for Ballet Theatre] was a week-long series of classes. The choreographers looked at us: [Mikhail] Fokine, Agnes de Mille, Tudor, [Mikhail] Mordkin, [Adolf Bohm, Anton Dolin, José Fernandez, Andrée Howard, Eugene Loring, Bronislava Nijinska, Yurek Shabelevsky, and Alexander Gavrilov]. At the end of the week, all had to agree to the crop chosen from the audition. I was fortunate enough to be among them. We started rehearsals a week later at the Ned Wayburn studio, 59th and Madison.

Most of that first season Madame Toscanini [Cia, daughter-in-law of Arturo] taught us. Both Hugh and Tudor were in the class. Sometimes Tudor taught. It was like another person in the company choreographing something; it was not like a choreographer coming in. We danced in other ballets together.

In the chorus were Nora Kaye, Maria Karnilova, Alicia Alonso. . . . Opening night we did Loring's *Great American Goof* and Tudor had a role in it.

We all felt we were very privileged. . . . Hugh always treated us as if we were family. Tudor was always curious about what we did at night and would try to find out what our personal lives were like—they were pretty dull.

When we started with Tudor, the first thing we rehearsed was *Jardin aux lilas*. We were very excited. We would go into a room and he would sing with [dance] counts. . . . We didn't know who we were playing or why. He'd just say, "this is it" and show us the movement. He never explained . . . only what we called the Tudor group: Mimi Gomberg, David Nillo,

[Annabelle Lyon], John Shindehetty, Muriel Bentley and Maria Karnilova. We knew we all looked great.[4]

Opening night of *Jardin aux lilas*, 15 January, 1940, at the Center Theatre in Rockefeller Center, proved a major success. During that first season Ballet Theatre performed both *Jardin aux lilas* and *Dark Elegies* to critical acclaim, although John Martin had some reservations about the music for the latter. While experiencing little public exposure and a noticeable lack of interviews, Tudor remained nonetheless confident about his reception. De Mille had prepared people for his work. He was right not to worry. Martha Graham, who choreographed *El Penitente* (Horst) that year, saw his work, liked what she saw, and made that fact known. Both John Martin and Walter Terry, the two major dance critics, raved about *Jardin aux lilas*, with Terry referring to Tudor as a great discovery. The public agreed. During that first season Ballet Theatre also added *Judgment of Paris* to its repertoire and the audience welcomed it just as enthusiastically. In addition to choreographing for the company, Tudor performed in his own and other choreographers' ballets from 1940 into the early 1950s. He came out of retirement as a dancer to perform at least twice, once in 1956 and again in 1958.

An offer of summer employment with an option for more work the next winter followed Tudor's first contract. Tudor visited the British Embassy to ask whether he could offer his services to the war effort in his native land, if they needed him to fight. He was told to remain in the United States. He repeated this exercise many times during the war, but the embassy never permitted him to return. Unaware of this, many of his English compatriots interpreted his leaving for the United States as a defection, a betrayal, and he was not really welcomed back to his native shore until 1967. Many even snubbed him when Ballet Theatre first visited London in 1946, after the end of the war. In fact some of his British colleagues, Ninette de Valois notably among them, never forgave him for absenting himself from the motherland during the hostilities. They ignored or did not know that this was not of his own volition, although he certainly had pacifist leanings all of his life.

Still trying to amass sufficient funds to pay off the debts incurred by the London Ballet (they were not actually finally paid off until 1946), Tudor accepted Ballet Theatre's offer of further employment, an offer renewed many, many times thereafter.

One of the myths that surround the relationship between Tudor and Ballet Theatre posits that in later years union restrictions made it difficult for him to work. Ballet Theatre, however, was a union company from the very outset. In fact, one of the earliest contracts between Tudor and the company, the one dated 8 April, 1940, is drawn up on an AGMA (American Guild of Musical Artists, the ballet dancers' union) form. Of course in later years the union did grow stronger and more restrictive about rehearsal time. And, the way the company organized rehearsal time differed vastly in the 1970s from the 1940s, for example. Dancers rehearsed more and more ballets simultaneously, for shorter and shorter periods, as time went on. Thus, while not totally accurate, some truth lies behind the myth.

The company went on tour to Mexico in the early summer of 1940 where great enthusiasm greeted it. After the first New York season there had been a long lay-off period before that summer engagement—typical of the way Ballet Theatre functioned for many years. During the layoff it became the custom for Tudor to teach "his group" daily. The group consisted of about nine dancers: Hugh, Nora Kaye, Maria Karnilova, Annabelle Lyon, Alicia Alonso, Fernando Alonso, David Nillo, Anton Dolin, and Donald Saddler. After class they would go to an automat around the corner and spend fifteen cents each on food. One of the group would then visit the Ballet Theatre offices to inquire after any news about when they might expect re-employment. In the afternoon Dolin would give adagio classes.[5]

Saddler remembered how Tudor would attack one or another of the dancers in those classes. Tudor made fun of dancers, saying insulting or vulgar things. One day he kept after Alicia Alonso. Everything she did was wrong, starting at the barre. Finally, Alonso put her hands on her hips, opened her eyes wide, full of Cuban rage, and told him that he could not make her cry. He never bothered her again; he knew how far he could go with each of the dancers.

Tudor's first new choreography in this country did not rank among his strongest works. He created *Goya Pastoral*, to the piano music of Enrique Granados as orchestrated by Harold Byrns, for a summer performance in New York's Lewisohn Stadium. The company performed it eight times in August. The idea for the dance evolved because there already existed décor and costumes designed by Nicholas de Molas, originally for an unsuccessful ballet *Goyescas* by José Fernandez. Shades of the Ballet Rambert!

The light-hearted Tudor work told the familiar tale of an older, wealthy woman, the Marquesa, a young man, and a pretty, young girl. The plot line unfolded exactly as one would expect from this cast of characters, enlivened by one twist: a simulated hanging of the young man which sent the Marquesa off in a swoon. The two young lovers ended by enjoying the riches the young man had won from the Marquesa in a card game. John Martin, in his *New York Times* review of 2 August, 1940, said that while "the choreography could be more sparkling and pointed and its action could get under way considerably

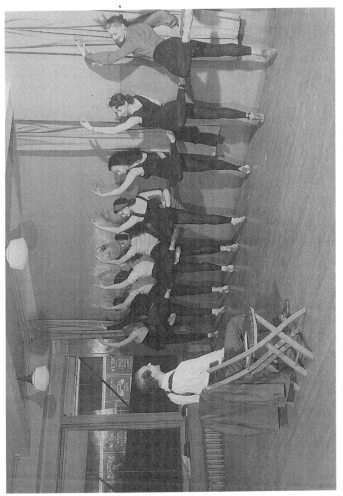

Tudor teaching class. From right to left: Maria Karnilova, Rosella Hightower, Sono Osato, Jean Davidson, Muriel Bentley, three unidentified dancers, one of whom was probably Nora Kaye, Lucia Chase. *Photograph courtesy of Donald Saddler*

sooner than it does," the work was "engaging and expertly done. Every-thing of Mr. Tudor's . . . has been distinguished by his ability to give texture to his compositions."

For Ballet Theatre's second season, Tudor mounted *Gala Performance*, further enhancing his reputation.

In the spring of 1941 Lincoln Kirstein's company, American Ballet Caravan, commissioned Tudor's second new American work for its upcoming summer tour to Latin America. Tudor consented to make only a "little ballet," a minor entry in his oeuvre. He choreographed *Time Table* to the distinguished American composer Aaron Copland's *Music for the Theatre*, a work that had attracted several choreographers before Tudor. Topical for a world at war, the ballet dealt with lovers parting in a suburban railway station after World War I. Kirstein's company first showed the work in New York in May, 1941, to an invited audience before taking it on tour. The later Balanchine/Kirstein New York City Ballet remounted *Time Table* in 1949.

Meanwhile, Tudor had begun a correspondence with his relatives in New Zealand: his brother Bob, Bob's wife Molly, and their three children John, Connaught, and Roberta. Although he professed little family feeling, in actuality he was a devoted and loving son and a fond brother and uncle. He sent Christmas greetings, and birthday cards to his niece and later to his great nephews. In one such later greeting he proposed that his great nephew Chris and his godson Mark Bliss [6] might want to become pen pals. The correspondence with sister–in–law Molly and later his niece Connaught contained warm greetings and thinly disguised expressions of affection.

An exemplary son, he visited his parents in their newly acquired home in Weymouth, Dorset, whenever he returned to England. His parents kept chickens and rabbits there after retiring. A letter from his mother (dated 19 November, no year, but clearly from its contents, during the war) reads:

> My dear son
> Your dear dad passed away peacefully Nov. 14th. Had he got over the operation, I do not think he would have been able to do much on the ground again. It was bladder trouble and it would soon have burst.

The letter goes on to tell of the cremation, the sprinkling of the ashes, and the fact that 200 pounds sterling each had been left to Tudor and brother Bob; however, they could not take the money out of the country at that time. Mrs. Cook refers to a ballet that was supposed to be presented 12 November. Another letter dated 2 December calls the diagnosis stomach cancer as well as bladder trouble. She also mentions

Ballet Theatre tour, 1943. From left to right: Nicholas Orloff, Tudor, Jerome Robbins, Maria Karnilova, and Donald Saddler. *Photograph courtesy of Donald Saddler*

that she had gotten rid of the rabbits, and that she had not yet received the package Tudor sent. Apparently he customarily sent parcels of food not available in Britain during and just after the war. (Thérèse Langfield spoke of receiving such packages from him as well.) In the letter Mrs. Cook thanked him for sending the parcel and told him not to send any more—she had plenty. Later letters spoke about the difficulty of getting letters through, and that packages were even less likely to arrive. She also wrote of the difficulty in communicating with the relatives in New Zealand.

## The Second Muse: Nora Kaye

Just as, in London, Tudor had found in Maude Lloyd at the Rambert a sympathetic and devoted collaborator, so, in the United States, he found Nora Kaye. A new muse, she came into his life at Ballet Theatre. Tudor remembered their first meeting:

> I sat at one end [of the studio] far from the dancers. This girl in a short white tunic, with a bow in her hair, looking like Fanny Brice, kept getting in front of me. Finally . . . she did seven pirouettes. I looked and decided I'd want to work with her. But she thought I didn't see, so she turned her back, walked out of the room, and announced in the dressing room "I'll never work with that Englishman." We started work on the following day.[7]

Once again there developed a trio: Kaye, Laing, and Tudor. After that first season of Ballet Theatre none of them had any money. Tudor and Laing had come over in October and by January the season ended. Most of the time they had earned rather meager rehearsal pay, thus could not put anything aside. They lived at the Windsor Hotel, signed for all their meals and then went to the company asking for an advance. Every night the three of them would play mahjong. They did not go to the bar because they could not afford it, so they brought bottles to the rooms. They formed an inseparable triumvirate.

Tudor decided to mold the completely malleable Kaye. He taught her about what to read, what to wear, how to speak and what to say, how to view life, how to view art. In many interviews she called him her mentor. She felt completely a product of his mind and what he wanted to make of her. They had a Svengali/Trilby-like relationship; he was the most important thing in her life. And he, in turn, that paragon of British reserve, wept openly at the memorial service after her death.

*Jardin aux Lilas.* Nora Kaye and Tudor. *Photograph by Fred Fehl, courtesy of Isabel Brown*

## The First Major American Work: *Pillar of Fire*

At last, in 1941, Tudor signed a contract for a new ballet, to be entitled *I Dedicate*. That ballet became *Pillar of Fire*. The contract stipulated a payment of $400 plus $10 per performance royalty. It also specified that Tudor had the right to choose his own cast and approve the designer. One can only wonder what contretemps had taken place before the signing of the contract that caused these obvious things to be written into the legal document.

During these early days, the relationship between Lucia Chase, as an administrative force in the company, and Tudor was at its most mutually respectful. Lucia, the dancer, was in these early years the sole, but secret, backer of Ballet Theatre. Tudor thought her quite canny. He admired the fact that, contrary to Rambert, Chase left him alone when he was choreographing. He enjoyed her acting ability and loved her performances in the roles he made for her. He also found her fun to work with. And from Chase,

> Tudor does not explain the feeling he wants; he shows emotion by motion, by demonstrating the movement. You have to sense the meaning from him; to find out what he is after, you have to keep doing the movement until you feel it. The movement phrases ride over the music. There are no steps in Tudor ballets, only phrases.[8]

She states that Tudor differed from everyone else, that she admired him greatly, and that he was the one choreographer who sustained her interest in ballet. Eventually their relationship changed, evolving into more one of love/hate,

Tudor began work on his new ballet in the summer of 1941 at Jacob's Pillow (the dance festival in Lee, Massachusetts), the same year that Balnchine choreographed *Concerto Barocco* (J. S. Bach) and de Mille *Three Virgins and a Devil* (Virgil Thomson). Reginald Wright, a friend and patron of Alicia Markova, had leased Jacob's Pillow for her from June to August. Markova, the British ballerina, had first encountered Tudor when she was guest artist with the Ballet Rambert. Anton Dolin (Pat to his friends) directed a summer school at the Pillow. Markova ran the housing and catering, and the two together ran the dance festival, as well as dancing in it. Ballet Theatre was in residence. Hugh and Tudor lived just down the road at Mother Derby's Barn, very primitive accommodations with no electricity, running water, or indoor toilets. Officially the company was on lay-off since Lucia Chase didn't have the money to keep them together and the contract with their new impresario, Sol Hurok, did not begin until September. Technically not working, everyone in the company collected unemployment compensation; they went to New York in a station wagon each week to pick up their checks. Markova remembers that each got $10 of which they gave her $7 to cover the catering. Donald Saddler's memory is of $15; in any case it was not a princely sum. Lucia Chase, choreographer Bronislava Nijinska, ballerina Irina Baronova, and her husband, the new General Manager of Ballet Theatre, German Sevastianov, all came and stayed nearby with families. The mothers of six of the girls in the company, also in residence to keep an eye on their offspring, pitched in to help, and even ran the festival box office for afternoon performances.

Meanwhile, a change in management at Ballet Theatre took place. Richard Pleasant left and Lucia Chase became more visible. Sol Hurok took over the marketing of the company, and German Sevastianov [9] was appointed General Manager. Hurok thought that only Russian ballet mattered, a prevailing attitude at the time. Ironically, Hurok promoted Ballet Theatre, the first company to nurture American talent and put great store in its English repertoire, as presenting "the Best in Russian Ballet." Tudor had to fight for rehearsal time for his new ballet, now called *Pillar of Fire*, just as he so often had to do later, throughout his career.

The Russian companies were in trouble. The de Basil Ballet was folding, so, Sevastianov hired a lot of Russians. In fact, one-quarter of the Ballet Theatre dancers were now Russians and Russian choreography got all of the rehearsal time. Sevastianov had seen some rehearsals of *Pillar* and hated it, as did Hurok. They nicknamed it "Pills of Fire." Desperate, Kaye, Laing, and Tudor enlisted the aid of Hurok's secretary Mae Frohman, Nora's friend, to get Hurok into a rehearsal. Hurok, Sevastianov, and Frohman saw the finished part of the ballet. A conference ensued with the three and Lucia Chase, who had a certain influence. They discussed, Lucia insisted, and Frohman agreed. Hurok remarked that Mae was no help; she liked the ballet. It all ended with Chase triumphant. Hurok announced that henceforth Tudor was to have first call on the dancers. And so he did.

The dance recounts the tale of Hagar, a repressed Victorian whose sexual drive overwhelms her sense of decorum. According to the program notes, "Hagar, whose elder sister is a spinster, foresees the same fate for herself. When the man she loves seems to show a preference for her younger sister, Hagar, in distraction, gives herself to one she does not love. The resulting crisis, however, unites her with the man she loves." The ballet's famous opening scene shows two houses, that of Hagar and her sisters, and the House Across the Way, a house of ill repute. Hagar, sitting on the steps of her home, loosens the high-necked collar of her Victorian dress. The gesture reveals such repression and guilt that, when well done, it carries the message of the whole ballet in that one simple movement. For the majority of the beginning of the ballet, Hagar has little movement, but observes everything that transpires. The corps members represent Lovers in Innocence and Lovers in Experience. In a startling *pas de deux* between Hagar and the man from the House Across the Way, he both literally and figuratively stops her every time she moves to escape from him. He suffocates her with his sexuality and the physical reality of his body, blocking her every dash for freedom and redemption. It is rough, brutal, raw, abusive, and cruelly sexual. Once again the physical details of the movement express the emotional climate and the story. The work progresses to a touching *pas de deux* in which the man she loves accepts her without question. Their consonant *pas de deux* contrasts totally with the dance with the man from the House Across the Way. In this second *pas de deux* Hagar's soon-to-be lover supports, and consoles her, with stunning lifts that never look acrobatic. *Pillar of Fire* ends in a gentle epilogue. Such an appropriately choreographed conclusion makes one soon forget that the ballet probably should have ended with the couple's earlier exit—but more music has to be dealt with.

Tudor worked for nearly a year refining every gesture and having the dancers get to know everything about the characters they portrayed. They internalized their relationships to one another; they knew what kind of wallpaper was in the house, how the elder sister stored her gloves in tissue paper, what kind of rooms they were living in, the shape of the table at which they had tea, the kind of china they used, the food they ate. They explored every nuance.

The actual "steps" ingeniously explicate each character. For example, in the opening, two townswomen enter downstage left. Their walk, mounting to pointe, interrupts itself every few steps by their twisting around to gather up the trains of their skirts with a "proper," socially acceptable, gesture. One knows instantly that such women as these could never be caught thinking of illicit sex, never craving sex of any kind, and certainly never enjoying it. Such a thing just would not be "proper."

Dancer Janet Reed recalls how Tudor prepared the dancers to perform:

> He also did what I seldom see done for a ballet . . . preparation before going on stage. We became the characters while we were still in the dressing rooms. The younger sister is returning from the corner ice cream parlor with three or four boyfriends. She has just had a strawberry soda. It's a hot, sultry afternoon. She wants every man in sight, especially Hagar's.[10]

Tudor struggled for the title. After months of searching, out of the blue (and out of the Bible) came *Pillar of Fire*. Tudor found it apt because, just as Moses guided the Israelites out of their wandering in no-man's land, so Hagar was guided from her role of outcast to civilization by—a man.

Much controversy surrounded Tudor's choice of music, Schoenberg's *Verklarte Nicth (Transfigured Night)*. The score belongs to the composer's early lush romanticism. Although it came before Schoenberg's codification of his twelve-tone system of musical organization, the score did not exactly consist of pretty tunes that the listener walked away whistling.[11] It differed substantially from the kind of music one expected to hear at the ballet—Tchaikovsky's *Swan Lake*, for example.

On opening night, 8 April, 1942, everything was in place: the impressive set by the distinguished American designer Jo Mielziner, the perfect score, *Verklarte Nacht* by Arnold Schoenberg conducted sympathetically by Antal Dorati, and a beautifully coached cast who knew just how special the work was.

Certain he had a good ballet, Tudor arranged a rather wiley trick. He told everyone to get their friends to send flowers—as long as the flowers came, the stage crew would have to keep the curtain going. So, hundreds of bouquets waited backstage in the wings. The event described at the opening of this book took place at this moment: dead silence at first, then tumultuous applause, just after it peaked a staged, delayed entrance of the cast, followed by more applause with the unheard-of thirty-odd curtain calls.

De Mille reacted, not atypically according to other public opinion, by saying that not since the Elizabethans had there been an English work of greater importance.

Nora Kaye described working with Tudor:

> He's the most difficult choreographer I've ever worked with. . . . At that point [when she was cast in *Pillar]* I had already done three ballets for him: a corps role in *Dark Elegies*, the mistress and then Caroline [in *Lilac Garden*, and] the Russian Ballerina in *Gala Performance*. I was a great success in *Gala*. I was very funny; the ballet was very funny. And everybody kept saying to him, "Well, she's all right as a comedienne. That's all she'll ever be. " I think one of the reasons he cast me in *Pillar of Fire* was to show everybody that I had some other kind of scope . . . Anyway, he started *Pillar of Fire* in very small pieces . . . There was one movement which is very sexual. . . . I said "I can't do that . . .What would my mother say? And he said, "You wait and see. You'll do it."

> We went to Jacob's Pillow . . . he started the *pas de deux*. . . . He
> would start a movement and then he would walk around. Then
> he would sit and watch. Then he would do another movement
> and he would walk around and sit and watch. . . . We went on
> tour and we started to work on it more, but it was never a
> straight line. He would always do a piece here and a piece there.
> . . . He would cry "Impossible! I never did that!" . . . Sometimes
> he would walk out. As the rehearsal was scheduled from 2:00 to
> 4:00, I didn't know what to do so I just sat there and cried.
> Sometimes he came back, but more often he didn't.[12]

Tudor coached via images, intuition, and intelligence until dancers internalized the roles. He used natural movement and colloquial
gesture, finding movement that would externalize the inner state of his
characters. Although he knew his own mind and intention, he sometimes had to search for steps to express his vision.

Of those times that Tudor stomped out of rehearsals, Laing remarks:

> I'd yell and scream. I can do a great job of screaming. Tudor
> would say, "What are you doing? I can't work on this now. I'm
> canceling rehearsals. I'll come back in an hour." He'd walk out
> and I'd say to Nora, " Let's have lunch." She'd say, "You're not
> mad?" "I'm not mad. I had to end rehearsal. How else could I do
> it? . . . It was the only way." Because I couldn't say to him in
> front of all the people, " Now this is utter crap." [13]

It was just the kind of behavior Tudor counted upon from Laing.
One wonders what some of the Tudor ballets might have looked like
without Laing's caring and astute critical eye. Tudor highly valued
Laing's contribution and depended on him for it. It was an important
part of their closeness and Tudor almost never disregarded Hugh's
comments.

Laing also remembered how his very famous last walk across the
stage in *Pillar of Fire* evolved. Tudor warned him that he must not
ever behave vulgarly in the role; he had to conduct himself with elegance. He never showed Laing what to do with that last walk, but
merely asked him how he would do it. Hugh demonstrated what he
intended to do and Tudor made him promise not to show the walk
again until the final dress rehearsal or the performance. He knew it
would be done right.

Tudor believed that he had to strip dancers of their superficialities
and their own conception of themselves until he found the core beneath. This process not only took "time, patience, and a little bullying"
but also gave birth to some of the legendary horror stories dancers tell

about working with him. He wanted the dancers to "climb into the skin of the dance" with him—" for a while there are two of you in the same skin. If [the dancer] goes back to herself the performance won't be any good. The dancer needs to completely divorce herself from her own ego." [14]

## 1943: A Productive Year

The success of *Pillar of Fire* brought to Tudor the offer of choreographing *Romeo and Juliet* for the company. Although Sevastianov signed the contract, he was drafted shortly thereafter. The new manager, John Alden Talbot, had a very different attitude toward Tudor. His recognition of Tudor's genius replaced Sevastianov's condescension. Even so, evidence that the path remained strewn with rocks showed in a letter Talbot wrote. He says, "Tudor thinks he is a little [dictator] and gives every indication of behaving like a big one, if he had the power. It is really amazing the nonsense he can think up." [15]

Much of this "nonsense" centered around the treatment of Laing and his billing, a common point of contention in the ballet world. Just as Laing protected Tudor, so Tudor stood up for Laing. And, acting the dictator was completely consistent with statements Tudor himself made over the years. He often said that a company should treat a choreographer like God, following him unquestioningly. Ironically, he clearly enjoyed being challenged and much preferred working with dancers who manifested intelligence, sensitivity, and spirit. Docility was never a virtue for a Tudor dancer. The difficulties of working with him are legendary. Unquestionably, he possessed a cruel wit and a sharp tongue, gleefully embarrassing his dancers. Convinced that, in order to get the performances he wanted, he had to strip away all ego from the dancers, he worked to get beyond the person to the character in the ballet. To do that, nothing was spared. Few rehearsals took place in which someone did not exit crying. In spite of this, or perhaps because of it, dancers felt it a privilege to work with him. A Tudor dancer at that time and even now, after his death, has a certain prestige and cachet in a company.

Kathleen Moore was one of the last chosen Tudor dancers. She has fond memories about working with him both in *The Leaves Are Fading* and in the fourth song of *Dark Elegies*. She described how she found him amazingly musical and remembered that he demonstrated everything (this was shortly before his death). "He would get up and do stuff. It was a whole lot of feeling, and you got the picture very quickly." Moore described a snapshot of him, sitting on the benches outside of ABT's studio 4. "His bearing was like a marble bust. He held himself so beautifully; just sitting there quietly." [16]

Moore went on to say that although people spoke of him as cruel, she thought often it was clearly aimed at getting something he was after. One of the last dancers to rehearse with him just before he died, she told of her most difficult experience:

> *Pillar* was a horrible experience for me. I don't know if he was so cruel in those rehearsals to make the character come alive. To make it be real. To have me be repressed. I can only hope so. I rehearsed it perhaps five hours a day. At every five-minute break I would go into a corner out in the hall and cry hysterically for five minutes and then I would come back. He called me a stupid bitch. Every day he would ask me questions. "What are you doing on these steps? What are you thinking about?" I'd go "uh, uh, uh—I was thinking about" and I would give him something and he would say, "No, that's wrong." He'd tell me what I was supposed to be thinking about. Then the next day I would come in and he'd say, "What are you thinking about on those steps?" I would tell him what he told me the day before and he would say, "No, that's wrong. You're not thinking that. What are you thinking?" I would have to come up with something. . . . He really put the fear of God in me. It was just horrible. Every performance I did of it, I cried. But I think that was just the emotional experience his piece takes you through. . . . It was a joke in the dressing room. "Has she started crying yet (looking at her watch)? Not yet. Ah, there it goes."

Tudor, however, told me he very much liked her dancing and Moore herself speaks of how grateful she was to him for giving her such a big chance—he had plucked her out of the corps. Her experiences in his other ballets, which she love*s,* were quite different.

Cuban ballerina Alicia Alonso, in her letter read at the memorial service for Tudor, explained that:

> He taught me not only that dance movement knows no limits, but he challenged me, as he did other dancers, to dig into memory, to unveil hidden experience and passion, for in no other way could one invoke the tensions and the complex characters he portrayed in dance. No other way could one convey the pain and loss of human relationships . . .

Tudor didn't use a methodology; every case was different, every person an individual.

You've got to get rid of the personal mannerisms to get to the character in the ballet and dancers don't want to let go. Breaking down a person isn't hard. But you cannot break them down unless you are willing to pick up the ashes right away and turn them into the Phoenix. That's the tough thing. You're terribly tempted to lay them flat and walk on them. [17]

## Another Shakespearean Interlude

The Ballet Theatre management came up with the idea of a ballet based on *Romeo and Juliet*. They first approached Fokine with the idea and the Prokofiev score, but he declined. Then they asked Tudor, but he, too, did not want to use the Prokofiev. He found it very beautiful, but too long and repetitive. Nor would he agree to using the Tchaikovsky, which he found to be unsatisfactorily short. He began looking for a score. Being Tudor, he did not wish to make an obvious musical choice. At last conductor Antal Dorati came up with the idea of Frederick Delius.

Tudor's inspiration for Juliet was Peggy Ashcroft. He'd seen her do the role in the 1930s at the New Theatre season when Gielgud and Olivier alternated as Romeo.

The contractual terms included a commission fee of $750 plus a royalty fee of $10 per performance. In return Ballet Theatre obtained a five-year exclusivity with an exception for possible performances by the London Ballet.

The ballet was a beautiful spectacle, a very special version of the story. It emphasized the personal drama of the protagonists, the love story. It opened with a front-of-the-curtain scene for Romeo and Rosaline, progressed to a ball scene with formal dancing highlighting the meeting, a *pas de deux*, several spectacular Capulet/Montague brawls, the balcony scene, and the epilogue in the tomb. Tudor had produced a very stunning choreographed version of the Shakespeare story, the first to be seen in the West.

It is interesting to contrast the ball scene in *The Tragedy of Romeo and Juliet* (April, 1943) with that of Tudor's nearly contemporaneous ballet *Dim Lustre* (October, 1943). *Romeo and Juliet* takes place in a different historical period and the actual steps of the dancers conform to that idea. Whereas expansive waltzes dominate *Dim Lustre*, the steps done in *Romeo and Juliet* move forward and backward on themselves, hardly progressing. The dancers are side by side rather than, as in *Dim Lustre*, in ballroom dance position. In *Romeo and Juliet* they barely touch; the movement projects a pinched, very codified, almost constipated use of space. No one has a glorious time sweeping through the ballet. One can almost feel the plotting and intrigue that might have happened during a dance of that era.

Rather than staged combat or sword play, the fight scenes are all dances. The protagonists suffuse the bedroom *pas de deux* with ethereal, innocent, almost sacred love. They tell us more about vulnerability than about sex. (Compare the *pas de deux* in *Pillar of Fire*.) The ending of the ballet reverberates with passion. It is not a hushed death scene, but a realization of the tragedy, almost an attempt to fight the inevitable.

The company originally proposed Salvador Dali as the designer, but he submitted sketches too outrageous to be considered. For example, for the balcony scene Dali proposed a set of giant false teeth supported on crutches.

Eugene Berman became the final, brilliant choice. His splendiferous designs, inspired by Botticelli, were lush, spectacularly beautiful and in total harmony with the Tudor choreography and the Delius music.

Tudor created the role of Juliet on and for Alicia Markova. It became one of her favorite roles. She felt that the character, who lived her whole life and grew from a child into a woman in the course of the ballet, had a wonderful breathless quality. It was Juliet dancing, not Markova in a ballerina role. To emphasize that, Markova requested a red wig as part of the costume, thus further concealing her own identity.

Work on the ballet began during a five-month residency in Mexico and progressed with intensity throughout the long coast-to-coast tour which followed. Rehearsals even took place in train station waiting rooms to capitalize on travel time interrupted or delayed by wartime exigencies. At the very end Laing and Markova even returned after performances to work through the night.

On the scheduled opening night, 6 April, 1943, Tudor had not yet finished the fifty-minute ballet. Hurok refused to postpone the opening. So Tudor, costumed as Tybalt, went before the audience to announce that the curtain would come down before the unfinished, perhaps four-minute-long, last scene in the friar's quarters. His announcement included the observation that the ballet as choreographed already lasted more than forty minutes. Since most ballets last only twenty to thirty minutes, the audience was not being cheated. He invited the entire audience to come back to see the end of it. They applauded the ballet at its truncated conclusion, loved it, and many did come back when the full ballet was finally presented four days later.

This delay did not exactly please the critics; it disrupted their schedules. Critical response was mixed. Denby found the dance contained innumerable exquisite touches and Martin described it as a play without words rather than a ballet. Some critics didn't approve of Tudor's choice of music while others thought it more than appropriate. Everyone agreed that Berman's costumes and décor qualified as works of art.

After the first or perhaps the second season, Tudor retired from the role of Tybalt and John Taras replaced him. Hugh Laing remembered:

> Tudor wanted to retire; he was working hard. . . . He went out front to see a performance. . . . When he came back I said to him "Tudor, what did you think of the ballet?" And he said . . . "It's a much better ballet than I thought it was. I never had a chance of seeing it before. . . . I was amazed how it held together, how Shakespearean it was, how concise, how it tells the thing with no wasted movements. I was very happy with it."

> "By the way, you haven't said anything about me." He said, "You . . . um . . . you know you looked a much stronger and better dancer than I thought you would appear." . . . I said, "Is that all?" He said, "Isn't that enough?'" I said, "But wasn't I good?" He said, "Oh yes, of course you were good, but you knew that." And he walked out of the room. . . . He left you up in the bloody air. But we put up with those things with each other. And we always fight.[18]

## 1943: The Third Major Premiere

In full creative form, Tudor produced yet another strong ballet in 1943, *Dim Lustre*, choreographed to the Richard Strauss *Burleske*. Perhaps his most Proustian ballet, *Lustre* literally recounts remembrances of things past.[19] A whiff of perfume, a kiss on the shoulder, a dropped handkerchief, evoke, in the characters, memories of bygone love and lovers. The ballet opens on a ball scene, with couples performing elegant traditional partner dances, many of them waltzes. Much of the music used 3/4 meter, unusual in the Tudor canon. The choreography is expansive and space consuming, pure lyricism and flow. When the protagonist gently kisses the shoulder of his partner it causes her to remember with nostalgia a similar incident earlier in her life. On stage, everything stops dead. In a blackout, the scene shifts to her memory of another time, another place. She dances facing another dancer who moves in mirror image. The mirror image dancer signifies a remembered self. The ballet continues in the same fashion, with small occurrences triggering past memories. Each blackout, followed by the mirror image device, transposes the characters to another time frame. The incidents (scenes) carry such titles as "She Wore Perfume," "He Wore a White Tie." In the end the couple leaves—nothing has changed and everything has changed.

The very proper surface demeanor of the protagonists and the Proustian undertones reminded more than one viewer, more than one critic, of *Lilac Garden*. Beneath the protagonists' socially acceptable behavior lay a swirling sea of emotions.

*Dim Lustre* uses split-second lighting cues to introduce a flashback technique certainly borrowed from or influenced by film. During the blackouts the audience has to follow the characters who transform their thinking from reality into a dream-like state of nostalgia. Tudor compared the remembered scenes to blurred photographs. The mirror image technique incorporated another cinematic/choreographic device. The reflected movement of one dancer facing downstage and one upstage, very close to one another, gave the impression of looking in a mirror.

From the archives of American Ballet Theatre came the following written description: "The scene is a ballroom. A ball is in progress. One is made very much aware of a sense of the past. A couple meet and dance together. During the course of their dancing both are reminded of memories of past loves. . . . At the end of the ball the couple part; they will never meet again. Their attraction has only brought back memories of their individual pasts." Tudor described the ballet in the following fashion: "They're basically people. The kind who are haunted by memories. I just bring them on dancing, separate them into another atmosphere, then gradually dissipate their joy with each other and bring them to an easy separation. Most people do separate." [20]

Tudor earned $750 by creating the ballet, while the scenic designer was paid $500. It cost about $1,500 to construct the women's costumes. The general manager, Alden Talbot, projected total production costs at about $6,000. The ratio of payment for work involved seems skewed with the choreographer receiving much less than was commensurate with his contribution to the whole, a practice, alas, that continues to this day.

Contrary to the legends borne out by many true stories of what personal torture Tudor went through when choreographing and how impossible he found it to meet deadlines, he composed *Dim Lustre* in two weeks. From the moment Lucia Chase called him to announce that he could do the new ballet he had proposed to her (so, in honesty, the concept was already in place) to the first stage run-through exactly thirteen days elapsed. The ballet seemed to pour out of him in a most unaccustomed way. Sallie Wilson remarked that, in the ballet *Ronde de printemps* created much later at Jacob's Pillow, the same thing happened, with the same resultant appraisal by the perverse Mr. Tudor. Said he about *Dim Lustre*, "I don't think of it as a major work. Something that pours out from me is not major, and I didn't have time to give it much consideration. If others consider it major, I'll be perfectly happy."

Meanwhile, Tudor enjoyed a rather glamorous social life. In a letter to Laing which begins "Dear Bugs," dated Friday, 26 April, no year, Tudor describes a dinner given by Carl van Vechten and his wife, Fania.

> The nicest engagement of the week by far has been Carl's dinner party, although I was terrified when I arrived and found that the company was to be [the philosopher] Mr. and Mrs. Lin Yutang, [the author] Pearl Buck and her husband, [the publisher] Alfred Knopf and Blanche, Richard Wright [author] of *Native Son*. . . . There and then I decided not to open my mouth for the entire evening. My decision was in vain. A couple of Carl's special cocktails, Dubonnet with whiskey . . . loosened my repressions and my tongue. . . . The first hour [I conversed with] Blanche Knopf . . . who I am taking to see St. Louis Woman next Thursday night. The rest of the evening I was with Pearl Buck, who is a real farmer's wife physically with about eleven children. Carl and Fania insisted upon being told the whole subject of conversation. It was theatre and plays, the respective merits of Oriental and Western theatre, the starving Indians, La Guardia's work on UNRRA,[21] and so on.

Van Vechten was a well-known critic and later photographer and social man about town. He actively fought racial prejudice before that became a fashionable cause célèbre. By bequeathing his archives to a black college, he obliged white researchers to go there to do their work. The van Vechtens, Laing, and Tudor became great friends and there exists a long and interesting correspondence among them, in which Carl often addresses Laing as "Dear Ballerino."[22]

In another letter to Hugh dated only Sunday morning, presumably of the same week, Tudor spoke of going out. He saw an African dance festival at Carnegie Hall (which he found unimpressive except for a selection by the Katherine Dunham group), visited a gallery showing the sculpture of an unnamed Brazilian woman, and then went to the movies, to see *Devotion*. He spoke about a lunch with "a group of long-haired, short-sighted, advanced mathematician types—friends of Einstein," He found it quite exhilarating and the cause for lots of laughter. He referred to a foot operation that Isabel [Brown née Mirrow] had to have, which places the letter in 1945. The final paragraph spoke, as he rarely did, of his affection for Laing.

> I do feel I could start rambling now with great pleasure for a long time, telling how much I have enjoyed being with you these many years, with what pleasure I anticipate its continuance and the things we will do, and make, and enjoy, and get kicks and depressions out of. Love to you, sweet Bugs. . . . My sympathy to your poor old legs, swear at the concrete floor for me, and remember the days on the beach in the offing. Blessings on you, pleasant dreams, a good voice for your practice, and cherishings.

## Another Muse; A Disruption

In 1944, Diana Adams joined Ballet Theatre. Adams had come to New York as a teenager and joined the cast of Agnes de Mille's *Oklahoma* (1943). De Mille, recognizing Adams's qualities, brought her to Ballet Theatre. There, her ravishing beauty and radiant dramatic flair soon brought her solo roles. Adams caught the eye of both Tudor and Laing, and Tudor soon cast her as Caroline in *Jardin aux lilas*; later came roles in *Lady of the Camellias*, *Shadow of the Wind*, *Undertow*, *Romeo and Juliet*, and *Pillar of Fire*.

Diana was another of the Tudor true believers. She said that while sometimes he seemed cruel, there was always a reason for it. When he taught her the role of a Lover in Experience in *Pillar of Fire*, for example, he teased her to help her get over her self-consciousness. Because of her young years and the possibility that the theme would embarrass her, he did not tell her what the birth scene was about in *Undertow*.

> To work with Tudor, you had to be a brilliant dancer. Academically his movements were not strenuous, but they were often uncomfortable. . . . For Medusa in *Undertow*, he wanted a purely classical line, yet the effect had to be hideous. "Too neat" he would say. To me, Tudor's greatest contribution lies in his revelation of intense emotional relationships among the characters on stage. With him, for the first time, ballet became concerned with what happened to people.[23]

Although not ideal for her because, on pointe, she was the taller of the two, Hugh Laing became her steady partner. The partnership developed offstage as well as on.

Meanwhile, the relationship between Tudor and Laing, although always symbiotic, became increasingly stormy. Hugh's temper tantrums and Tudor's sarcasm drove an emotional wedge between them. At that point, just as Nora Kaye and Maude Lloyd before her, Diana Adams became a constant companion of the two men. According to Laing, by 1945 all sexual activity between the two men had ceased. Their arguments became increasingly fiery and more public. Tudor would goad Hugh, with terrible consequences: tantrums and humiliation. In spite of the fact that a strong bond of love tied them together, almost classical in the Greek sense, friends said they were driving each other crazy. Both needed an escape. Diana Adams provided just such an escape for the two men.

Laing's compulsive need to dominate and "take care of" the one he loved at first found a willing victim in the lovely Diana. She was young and a bit lost. Her relationship with Hugh became increasingly romantic. Out of relief or perversity, Tudor encouraged the romance, but, underneath, he suffered. He countenanced it to save face, because he felt he had no other option, and perhaps because of some inherent masochistic streak. At one point, the three of them were practically living together, as very close friends, not as a *ménage à trois*. They ate dinner together every night and spent all of their free time as a threesome. Diana accepted it because, completely dominated by Hugh, she had no choice. Few people really know how the marriage shocked and wounded Tudor. A very private person, he never revealed what he felt. Nobody ever really got close to Tudor. He didn't let anybody totally into his life except his family, not even Hugh, although certainly Hugh came the closest. Inexplicably, Tudor encouraged the Diana/Hugh love affair, all the while raging inside. Although he was searching for some breathing room in his complex relationship with Laing, I suspect the actual outcome took a more serious turn than he anticipated.

In 1947, Diana and Hugh married. Only later did Tudor allow his anger and depression to show, privately of course. Publicly, he continued to declare his delight at the union. Maude Lloyd remembered that in 1946 when the company visited London, Tudor giggled to her that he had left Hugh and Diana alone. He mentioned that the two were madly in love, and that it was lovely to get away. He acted delighted with it.

Hugh and Diana definitely made a loving couple, at least in their first years together. Any lingering doubts that the marriage might be one of convenience is dispelled by their correspondence. One letter from Hugh to Diana reads:

> When I was married to you I was too foolish not just to accept my great blessing, but I had to keep asking you for proof of

your love. I was so frightened of losing you. . . . I spent my time
trying to please you at every turn so that you would have more
reason to love me. . . . The terror of losing you has been great; i t
has been overshadowed by the realization of the great love and
understanding and loyalty that you have shown to me in these
past six years. I think that *now* I can truly say I love you.[24]

The marriage legally dissolved in 1953, although Diana had left
Hugh some time before the actual divorce. Maude Lloyd remembered
Diana saying to her: "The thing is, he wants to possess you, he wants
to mold you, he wants you to do what he knows is best for you, and I
can't stand it." [25] They split up not because Hugh didn't love her, but
because he loved her too much.

        After marriage, Diana remained with the New York City Bal-
let for the remainder of her career. She danced ballerina roles in many
Balanchine ballets and taught at the school. Later, she remarried to one
of American Ballet Theatre's stage managers, Ronald Bates, and had a
daughter. Adams died in 1993. While the friendship between Hugh and
Tudor had never ceased, their roles as lovers never resumed. They remained close companions, sharing living accommodations once again
after the Adams/Laing split. Then, beginning in the early 1960s, they
lived apart for many years. Only at the very end of their lives, during
their winter stays in Laguna Beach, did they actually share quarters
again.

## 1945: *Undertow*

        In 1944–1945, long before the marriage of Hugh and Diana, Bal-
let Theatre embarked on a coast-to-coast tour. The repertoire featured
Tamara Toumanova. It included works of Balanchine, Robbins, and
Massine, as well a substantial group of Tudor's dances: *The Tragedy of
Romeo and Juliet, Pillar of Fire, Dark Elegies, Dim Lustre*, and *Gala
Performance*. In those years several important works were being created
by Tudor's choreographic counterparts. Martha Graham produced *Appalachian Spring* (Copland). Jerome Robbins choreographed his first
ballet, *Fancy Free* (Bernstein), which he soon reworked and expanded
into the Broadway show *On the Town*. Meanwhile Tudor began work
on perhaps his most audacious ballet, *Undertow*. The contract for this
new work, dated 28 June, 1944, had some interesting provisions. The
choreographic fee was again $750 plus $20 per performance royalty, for

Tudor and Laing. *Photograph courtesy of Isabel Brown*

which Ballet Theatre gained a five-year exclusivity. Only if, within the five-year period, they performed the work seventy-five times could they require that it be listed by other companies as "Original production by Ballet Theatre." The specific wording for this is handwritten into the contract by Tudor. The contract also specifies that Tudor must provide a synopsis of the plot for the program, something he never did. The scenic and costume designers only required his approval; they were not his to chose initially. The scheduled rehearsal period began 15 September, 1945, and the ballet was to be ready by 30 October (it actually premiered 10 April). And, most peculiarly, all of the above pertained only if S. Hurok accepted the ballet.

Tudor described the dance in the following manner:

> *Undertow* is a study of a murderer. For this ballet I did a great deal of research. I was intrigued by *Rebel Without a Cause* by Theodore Reich. This was my jumping off point—a young boy murders for no apparent reason. I started to read books on psychiatry—two full shelves up to October of this year [elsewhere he refers to thirty-four books of case histories of psychology]. I slowly evolved the plot. Prologue: Birth. The husband unties the umbilical chord and pulls the woman away. The child is left abandoned of love. The child grows up frightened of women. There are scenes of people in the neighborhood. He is constantly an observer, seeing women in his own distorted eyes: an old school master (based on the *Blue Angel* story); a whore; a man molesting a little girl whom he imagines will grow into a whore. He sees her playing behind the woodshed with little boys and she begins doing things with her skirt. A Salvation Army lady tries to comfort him but then makes a pass at him. Later Medusa, sexually attractive, tempts him and gets him to the point of consummation but he strangles her inadvertently.[26]

The final scene was a solo in which the anti-hero explored his feelings after the murderous act. Describing the Epilogue in a letter to William Schuman, the composer commissioned to write the score, Tudor asked simply for a four-minute essay on fear. Tudor goes on to say Schuman gave him exactly that—marvelously. And, a typical witty Tudorism, "I never expect anything until I get it. And then it isn't what I expected."[27]

Schuman recalled that he interested Tudor both because of his music, with which Tudor was familiar, and because Schuman knew nothing about ballet, just about modern dance.[28] The two men felt at

home in the collaboration; Tudor gave Schuman only a vague outline
of the story line. Mostly it was a question of knowing the emotional
climate and the timing of each section. For example, Tudor described
to Schuman the opening, the birth scene, as a dark, dampish night in
the big city, the kind of night that causes you to look around a corner
before you proceed. The palms of your hands are moist. Schuman was
extremely happy with that kind of instruction. He felt he had the freedom to create the kind of atmosphere the ballet called for without being
restricted by a too literal plot outline. When writing the score for *Undertow* he did not know, for example, that a birth took place onstage at
the opening. Personally as well as artistically the two men had a very
cordial relationship. Schuman remembers Tudor speaking at length
over lunch or dinner about the superiority of red wine over white. Tudor was something of a gourmet, but careful of his health. Schuman
also mentioned that he experienced Tudor as always exhibiting a gentlemanly demeanor, although he did witness the infamous sarcasm and
sadistic wit in Tudor's interactions with others.

Schuman suspected that Tudor was a little stunned and appalled
when he first heard the rather poor piano reduction of the music for
*Undertow*. The composer remembered attending one rehearsal at which
the pianist played something that sounded like humming. He had to
assure Tudor that the orchestral sound would be quite different. When
Tudor heard the full orchestra he agreed it was, indeed, a different matter. The budget allowed for only one general rehearsal with the orchestra after which both men went to Hurok to ask for more strings. Hurok
said he couldn't do it, so Tudor and Schuman chipped in and hired
seven or eight extra string players.

Tudor had similar memories of the working relationship between
the two men. When asked if the music pleased him as he received it, he
replied that it shocked him. He also mentioned not telling Schuman
what transpired onstage, but rather speaking of geographic and atmospheric things, for example something reminiscent of a sunset over the
Brooklyn Bridge.

> [The music] was full of surprises when it arrived because in my
> letters I never told him precisely what I wanted, but mostly just
> gave him an impression of the atmosphere, timing of accents,
> beat of the music. Sometimes, I was quite outraged and shocked
> at what I got [laughing] but I worked it out very nicely. [29]

Tudor was the first choreographer to deal with the psycho-sexual
problems of the male, the tortured view of a boy's passage from a
traumatic childhood, through the cruel temptations of youth, ending in
disaster. The noted critic Edwin Denby characterized the work as based

on the theme of "adolescent neurosis, the terrifying dilemma which presents to him the act of manhood as equivalent to murder."[30]

In typical fashion Tudor achieved the drama by physical means, by embodying the character in the steps. For example, when Tudor taught Diana Adams the role of Cybele, the mother, he gave her only the movement. Only just before the premiere did he let her know that she was supposed to be giving birth. (In real life it was Nora Kaye who was four or five months pregnant at the premiere.)

Sallie Wilson spoke of how incredible it was to watch Tudor teach each character, how he could turn into a fat old man, a voluptuous bride, a little girl picking flowers, a young bride. I had the great good fortune to attend many, many rehearsals of *Undertow* and I, too, was struck by this ability in Tudor. Sitting in his chair, fully dressed in street clothes, he would start to become the character from the base of his spine. One could see it travel up that incredibly expressive back and neck and out of the top of the head. The transformation represented extraordinary acting technique, certainly the best I have ever witnessed. The dancers had to work very hard trying to emulate him. He did not wish them to copy slavishly, but they had before them an outstanding example of how to project a role. Seeing this kind of demonstration made one sympathetic to Tudor's protestations in later years that he couldn't choreograph if he couldn't demonstrate.

Once again Tudor had difficulty in concluding the ballet in the allotted time, and left Laing with sections of choreography unfinished.

> I knew the birth, I knew the *pas de deux* at the end where I kill Nana [Gollnar] and I knew the epilogue. The whole middle section of the ballet was only sketched out for me. I knew a few movements here and there, but he'd say, "I'll come to that later." And the first night I said, "Tudor—" He said, "You know my movements. Do them." I improvised. . . . Only after the first night did I get rehearsals. You see, he used to depend on me a lot. . . . He knew perfectly well I wouldn't go diametrically against his main stream.[31]

In the meantime great upheaval took place at Ballet Theatre. Chase and Hurok were at loggerheads. Hurok continued to insist that he could not sell the company without its presenting "the Greatest in Russian Ballet." He expected artistic control while assuming that Chase would take on total financial responsibility. For years she had been the largest, for all practical purposes the only, backer, picking up each deficit as it came along, much against her better judgment. Talbot sided with Hurok, unwilling or unable to find backing elsewhere. Threats of resignations, letters of support theoretically signed by the company, and a general mess ensued. Hurok wanted no part of *Undertow* and only would agree to its going forward if Chase assumed all the costs of its production. Finally, in 1945, the crisis peaked. Hurok and Ballet Theatre parted company although their contract still had two years to run. It took lawyers' action to annul it. Talbot left, Oliver Smith[32] and Lucia Chase became co-directors, and *Undertow* was performed as planned, albeit in April rather than in October.

Tudor soon became increasingly disenchanted with Lucia. The hate part of their love/hate relationship came into ascendancy. He couldn't abide her penny pinching. Although the money itself did not interest him, having his needs supported did. He thought at times that Lucia acted like a silly woman. He hated some of her casting decisions and he accused her of not keeping her word, particularly in regard to Hugh's contracts. Tudor's attorney sent letters concerning the way the company treated him and Hugh—about billing for Hugh, dressing rooms, first-night casts, and the like. While Tudor was naturally inclined to be rather meek about his complaints against Lucia, Hugh constantly incited him. Although he detested some things about Lucia, he continued to admire her guts and her strength. Tudor applauded her focus on what she wanted, her tenacity, the fact that she financially backed the company she believed in, and her love of dance. Lucia honored and respected Tudor. She thought he was a genius and knew that he *was* Ballet Theatre. He saved her company and she loved him for that. But, she also tried to cheat him; that was Lucia.

## Trying His Hand at Music Theatre

With the company on lay-off for lack of funds, Ballet Theatre had no more work for Tudor for the rest of 1945. So, he took on some assignments for the musical stage. In a letter dated 13 January (no year, but presumably 1945) Carl van Vechten queried Hugh Laing about a rampant rumor—that Tudor planned to "put on the Polynesian dances in the musical version of *Rain* as all the papers have announced." (In this same letter van Vechten tells a story of Nora Kaye's coming off-stage after a magnificent Aurora and asking Tudor how she did. He replied, "You'll be all right in six years, IF YOU WORK.") Tudor did not choreograph *Rain*, but he did accept two other music theater assignments.

In June, 1945, Tudor made his bow on Broadway as the choreographer of *Hollywood Pinafore*, with Viola Essen and John Butler as soloists.[33]

John Martin wrote of the effort:

> When the most distinguished choreographer in the ballet takes
> his first plunge into Broadway "show business" that is an
> event. As a consequence, both the world of balletomania and
> genuine lovers of the dance will be making tracks to the Alvin
> Theatre to see what Antony Tudor has done . . . . The verdict is
> more than likely to be mixed . . . . No matter how extraneous it
> [the ballet] may be, it serves most gratifyingly to bring the
> stage to theatrical life for a few minutes. As a ballet it is no great
> shakes . . . . There are two scenes in it that are very good indeed,
> not only because Mr. Tudor has composed them well but be-
> cause he has Miss Essen to play them, and has built them beau-
> tifully on her gift for comedy.[34]

In his second stab at musical theater, Tudor joined forces with the
noted team, lyricist Alan J. Lerner and composer Frederick Loewe, in a
production entitled *The Day Before Spring*. In the tradition that Agnes
de Mille initiated with *Oklahoma*, the two ballets functioned as inte-
gral parts of the action of the play rather than simply as divertissement.
Hugh Laing and Mary Ellen Moylan danced beautifully in a dream
ballet in the first act and a "view of another life" episode in the second
act. Walter Terry of the *New York Herald Tribune* remarked that although the choreography contained "lovely isolated moments of dance
action, they were spoiled by choreographic clutter." [35]

Tudor's forays into musical theater did not please the Ballet Theatre management, since their relationship with him had, in any case,
frayed. The prevailing attitude that the Russian repertoire was the
mainstay of the company had Tudor feeling slighted. In addition, an
altercation arose concerning Hugh's billing vis-à-vis that of Dolin. Vi-
tuperative exchanges, attorney's letters, threats of leaving and being
terminated flew back and forth. Ballet Theatre even refused to give Tudor a short leave of absence to choreograph *Day Before Spring*  although they did not need him for company rehearsals.

At the audition for *The Day Before Spring* Tudor met another of
his adoring dancers, Isabel (Mirrow) Brown. Isabel and Nora Kaye had
a close relationship, like that of cousins, although Nora was eight years
older. At eighteen Isabel went directly from *Day Before Spring* into
Ballet Theatre. She became a part of "the family clique" of Tudor,
Hugh, Nora, and a little later, Diana Adams. Brown described Tudor's
working procedure:

> He was very, very slow. Maybe a minute a day. But it was fasci-
> nating. He never did anything that didn't have some kind of
> meaning. Even if it was one movement, you understood why he

was doing it, what it meant to him, to the ballet, and to yourself. It was very clear. . . . People who didn't understand him were simply not in his ballets. He gravitated to all the people who had the intelligence and the acting ability to understand what he wanted without him having to discuss it. [36]

Isabel enumerated the characteristics of a Tudor dancer as she saw them: feeling, sensitivity, soul, artistry, lyricism, tautness, and intelligence. She attributed Tudor's custom of always changing things to his perfectionism and genius. When he came into a room, one did not talk or do anything other than what he wanted. She also described the perversity of the relationship between Tudor and Hugh, saying that Tudor would do anything to goad Hugh, asking for the tantrums and humiliation that followed. She reported that as Hugh screamed, Tudor got more and more quiet while Hugh became more and more crazy. Although Tudor really never let anyone into his inner life, Isabel experienced moments of closeness with him. Later in Tudor's life they would buy ice cream together. He'd tell her how angry it made him that he couldn't eat ice cream in front of Hugh because Hugh insisted they follow a macrobiotic diet. Isabel also mentioned that even though, when they were young, both men had passing affairs, there existed always a deep commitment to one another. Each was the true love of the other's life.

She also remembered where they lived after leaving the Hotel Windsor: in an apartment on 57th Street in a brownstone across the street from a famous bar, Tony's. It had two magnificent rooms, but no kitchen. Both Tudor and Laing cooked incredible meals on two burners installed in the bathroom.

## The Return of the Native

Free at last from their obligations to Hurok, company co-directors Lucia Chase and Oliver Smith arranged Ballet Theatre's first outside appearance under their aegis. The two signed a contract with London's Royal Opera House for an eight-and-a-half-week season. The company of fifty sailed for England on 20 June, 1946, aboard the Queen Mary. Fortunately for the future of the company, the engagement was an enormous success.

In 1946, London still labored to recover from its wartime trauma. Signs of the war's devastation remained. People struggled back from the illness and poverty which had resulted from the war. Food was still not plentiful. But, the arts and particularly the art of dance already flourished. The kind of spirit that had led performers to carry on dancing in lunch and tea-time concerts during the blitz now showed itself in the rebirth of the various ballet companies. Ashton, back from the service, choreographed his expansive *Symphonic Variations* (César Franck) and his version of *Cinderella* to the newly composed Prokofiev score. Covent Garden had just reopened; ballet was alive and well in London. For Tudor, returning home at last as a recognized choreographer of genius was momentous. How would his work now be received in his native land?

In the meantime, a smoothing over of the difficulties between Ballet Theatre and Tudor had occurred. The company showed several of his ballets in England, his first choreographic appearance in his native country since he had left in 1939. Those shown included *Undertow, The Tragedy of Rome and Juliet, Pillar of Fire,* and *Dim Lustre.* In the United States, *Undertow* had put off some of the press because of its violent and sexual subject matter. In England, it received considerable acclaim by the, perhaps, more sophisticated and less puritanical critics. *Pillar of Fire* also took London by storm. Tudor's return became a minor triumph. Acclaim notwithstanding, not until 1967 did he actually work again in England.

Administrative high jinks had continued during the rehearsal period previous to the tour. Whether because of Tudor's meddling or by fiat of the board of directors, an artistic committee had been formed to advise Lucia. First organized at the end of the Talbot regime, by the spring of 1946 the committee consisted of Aaron Copland, Henry Clifford, Antony Tudor, Agnes de Mille, Jerome Robbins, Lucia Chase, and Oliver Smith. According to rumor, Tudor had angled for appointment as artistic director because of his difficulties with Lucia. The position was not offered to him; however, he grudgingly accepted the role of artistic administrator, with responsibility for the scheduling of rehearsals and performances among other duties. Some believe his disappointment was extreme. If this is true, Tudor never admitted it. He maintained his stance that, if ever he assumed a company's artistic directorship, his choreographic tastes would not be sufficiently catholic to produce a balanced repertoire. Charles Payne's [37] account of the distribution of rehearsal hours during the time that scheduling was Tudor's responsibility tends to validate Tudor's fears in this regard, as it was less than even-handed.

While in England Tudor had the company purchase for him the rights to a score by Bela Bartok. The ballet did not materialize, however, possibly because of his time-consuming administrative duties.

For the remainder of 1946 and the majority of 1947 the company, Tudor included, toured the United States and made an appearance in Cuba.

*Dark Elegies.* Laing on left, Tudor kneeling. *Photograph courtesy of Jerome Robbins Dance Division, New York Public Library for the Performing Arts*

127

During those two years quite a bit of other choreographic activity was taking place in the United States. Balanchine choreographed *Four Temperaments* (Hindemith) and *Theme and Variations* (Tchaikovsky), while modern dancer Doris Humphrey produced her moving *Day on Earth* (Copland). Martha Graham had a particularly productive year, creating several of her enduring masterpieces: *Cave of the Heart* (Barber), *Errand into the Maze* (Menotti), and *Night Journey* (Schuman).

## 1948: *Shadow of the Wind*

On 13 March, 1948, Tudor signed a contract for a new ballet, *Shadow of the Wind*. According to the contract, the ballet would premiere on 12 April. In retrospect, it seems odd that Tudor should have agreed to such a short gestation period. He may, however, have already started working on the ballet as he was fully employed by Ballet Theatre at the time. In fact, the contract stipulated royalty payments ($25 per performance for the first year, $20 thereafter), but no choreographic fee. The contract also stated that the choreographer should receive appropriate credit, that any choreographic changes needed Tudor's consent, and that subsidiary rights (i.e., film, television, etc.) rested with him.

At last Tudor had the opportunity to choreograph his beloved *Das Lied von der Erde*. This Mahler score had captivated him earlier in his career, when he searched for a score for *Dark Elegies*. At that time he ended up using another Mahler masterpiece, *Kindertotenlieder*. At the Ballet Rambert he had not had the resources to present a ballet with the full orchestral accompaniment *Das Lied von der Erde* required. Now, at last, that opportunity opened for him. He was the first choreographer to undertake the challenge of creating a dance to this extraordinary Mahler piece.

Although much criticized for it, Tudor bypassed the very lush German translations of the text for the Mahler songs, going directly to the spirit of the original Li Po poems. Once again the responsibility for the décor fell to Jo Mielziner. Although Mielziner also received credit for the costumes, they were actually designed by Laing. Not a member of the appropriate union, however, Laing could not claim them.

In *Shadow of the Wind* Tudor returned to his fascination with the Oriental; the movements combined classical dance with a Sino-Japanese influence. Tudor explained that "the ballet symbolizes the impermanence of existence, the Chinese philosophy of accepting the mutations of life and bowing before them. Like the seasons, human experience is cyclical and has no sudden beginning or end." [38]

Many problems arose during the rehearsals and once again Tudor did not finish the work in time for the opening on 14 April, 1948. The dancers had to improvise the ending. Tudor's longtime friend and teacher Margaret Craske insisted that the dance was Tudor's supreme masterpiece. Laing thought that about three-quarters of the ballet was superb; the other quarter, discardable. Isabel Brown said that while a beautiful ballet, it was more fit for a museum than for a theater audience. One could best appreciate it by just sitting and looking as one did with a painting. A very elaborate dance, it seems to have been ahead of its time, as is often the case with Tudor's ballets. It lasted in the repertoire for only six performances.

The dance consists of a series of short sections which bore the titles "Six Idlers of the Bamboo Valley," "The Abandoned Wife," "My Lord Summons Me," "The Lotus Gatherers," "Conversation with Winepot and Bird," and "Poem of the Guitar." Walter Terry, critic of the *New York Herald Tribune,* panned the work; John Martin of the *New York Times* wrote a scathing critique which very much upset Lucia Chase.

Shortly after its premiere Tudor committed, yet again, one of his unforgivable acts. He accused Agnes de Mille, whose new ballet *Fall River Legend* (Morton Gould) received critical accolades, of stealing the idea for it from his *Pillar of Fire.* For several years thereafter, the two barely spoke.

After the 1948 premiere of *Shadow of the Wind,* Ballet Theatre went through one of its now all-too-familiar financial crises. The season at the Metropolitan Opera had a weekly loss of about $12,000. Lucia Chase had invested 30 percent of her income in the company that year and, to make matters worse, the Bureau of Internal Revenue disallowed her claims for a tax deduction for her 1947 contributions. (Only after this did the company establish itself as a non-profit charitable entity.) Chase had no option but to suspend operations, which she did for nearly a year.

Tudor had once again become disenchanted with the company. The poor reception received by *Shadow of the Wind* devastated him and he resented Lucia Chase for taking it out of the repertoire so quickly.

## The Proust Ballet That Never Happened

In May, 1948, Tudor left for one of his extended trips. First came a "dull" sea voyage to Barbados, continuing on to Paris and a gay whirl. Tudor loved Paris and saw lots of dance while there.

He described a party given by Schiaparelli and a surprise birthday bash for Isabelle Kemp attended by many of the French aristocracy. His letters spoke of meeting Nora's boyfriend, going to the ballet, seeing *Cyrano de Bergerac*, going to the movies, swimming, and doing the washing and ironing. In a note from Paris, dated 11 May (no mention of a year), he told of how Rosella Hightower's [39] "Black Swan" had changed the French perception that Americans couldn't dance; that Margot (Fonteyn) made everyone else look silly; that Ninette (de Valois) took sugar and butter back to England, and that all of the women took back nylon stockings. Such activities and gossip filled his days in that loveliest of capital cities. He studied French, but said he could not speak it. He also remarked that he did not go to Geneva because he loved Paris too much.

For years Tudor had wanted to do a ballet based on Marcel Proust's *Swann's Way*. Long before, at the time he danced the role of Tybalt in his *Tragedy of Romeo and Juliet*, Isolde Chapin interviewed him for the January, 1947, issue of *Dance Magazine*. In the interview he speculated that next he would choreograph a ballet based on Proust's *Remembrances of Things Past*. Of course, by 1947, he had already created the very Proustian *Dim Lustre*. Tudor mused to Chapin that he would need a year to do this new ballet. He would start by creating movement sequences for two or three of the minor characters, a way of working that was not at all unusual for him. Tudor speculated that the ballet would last about one and one half hours. He had in mind Gian Carlo Menotti to write the music. He even went so far as to meet and receive permission from the Proust family, but he never actually choreographed the ballet.

The summer of 1948 was mostly spent visiting his mother in Weymouth, and seeing theater and dance in London.

In a letter dated 9 July (no year, but probably 1948) and written to Laing from Weymouth during the visit to his mother, Tudor spoke about rationing. He'd brought along two good joints of beef and veal. (This was post–World War II London, where the shortages of food, petrol [gasoline], and other commodities were still very much a part of everyday living.) He mentioned that while in Paris he had attended a dance given by Madame Mantes Proust for her daughter. He referred to a lunch with Madame Proust, Gian Carlo Menotti, and Samuel Barber. The cast of characters suggests that they discussed the projected but never-realized Proust ballet.

Meanwhile, Tudor's disenchantment with Ballet Theatre simmered. Finally, at the end of 1948, while the company was on lay-off, he resigned his post as artistic administrator. He then accepted an invitation to Stockholm to work with the Swedish Royal Opera Ballet the following year.

In the fall/winter season of 1949 Tudor mostly occupied himself again with social life. That year the Royal Ballet visited the United States for the first time. Balanchine created his *Firebird* (Stravinsky), José Limón created *Moor's Pavane* (Purcell), and the movie *Red Shoes* captivated the country. Tudor's only reference to earning his keep mentioned teaching actors twice weekly; he probably taught elsewhere as well. In a tongue-in-cheek letter to Hugh dated 26 October, 1948, he suggested that it would be wonderful to have Hugh's wife working and keeping them both. He spoke of visiting Menotti for a weekend, listening to Brahms, attending a party for Johnny Kriza after Kriza's first appearance with "Lincoln's Company." Kirstein asked Tudor to revive *Time Table*; Tudor wouldn't answer without advice from Hugh. (Eventually he said no.) He went to a party at the home of Tennessee Williams. Others attending were Balanchine and Maria Tallchief, Paul Bowles, Elia Kazan, and Laurence Olivier. He heard a Menotti opera and liked it, listened to the New York Philharmonic play early Schoenberg. Harald Kreutzberg came to watch class. Tudor reported he was sleeping so little that he forgot to give *tendus* on the second side!

# Notes

1. The Littlefield Ballet Company, later the Philadelphia Ballet Company, was founded in 1934 by Catherine Littlefield and her mother Caroline. It was the first company to employ exclusively American ballet dancers.

2. Muriel Topaz, interview with Thérèse Langfield Horner, Seaford, England, 20 February, 1998.

3. Judith Chazin-Bennahum, interview with Alicia Markova, 11 April, 1988.

4. Muriel Topaz, interview with Donald Saddler, New York, 22 January, 1998.

5. Anton Dolin (1904–1983) was one of the pioneers of British dance and one of its first danseurs nobles. He joined the Diaghilev company in 1921 and created roles in Nijinska's *Le Train blue* and Balanchine's *The Prodigal Son*. In 1935 he founded the Markova-Dolin Company, and in 1939 became a founding member of Ballet Theatre.

6. Mark is the son of Anthony Bliss, who was the intendant of the Metropolitan Opera for several years, and Sally Brayley Bliss, formerly the director of the Joffrey II Company and currently director of Dance St. Louis. Mr. Bliss was instrumental in helping Tudor set up

the legal entity that controls his ballets since his death, and Mrs. Bliss is the Trustee of this entity, the Tudor Trust.

7. Dick Cavett, video interview with Antony Tudor, taped on 19 December, 1979.

8. Lucia Chase, as quoted in the "Proposal Nominating Antony Tudor for National Medal of the Arts," assembled by American Ballet Theatre. The quote appears on page 8.

9. German Sevastianov was born in Moscow and later emigrated to Paris, where he became executive secretary to Colonel de Basil of the De Basil Ballet Russe de Monte Carlo. It was in this capacity that he learned about the operation of a ballet company.

10. Lillie F. Rosen, "Talking with Antony Tudor, a Choreographer for All Seasons," *Attitude* 9 No. 3/4 (Fall, 1993): 6.

11. As founder of the system of musical composition, Arnold Schoenberg was an unlikely choice. His music had little in common with the usual tuneful scores used in much of the ballet up until that time. Other than modern dance choreographer José Limón, no other dancer had yet choreographed to Schoenberg's music.

12. "Nora Kaye Talks about Working with Antony Tudor" (panel discussion, Selma Jeanne Cohen, moderator, Society of Dance History Scholars, Albuquerque, New Mexico, 15–17 February, 1985).

13. Marilyn Hunt, interview with Hugh Laing, 3 May and 17 June, 1986. Oral History Project, New York Public Library for the Performing Arts.

14. Ara Guzelemian, adapted from an interview with Nora Kaye, 13 January, 1974.

15. Charles Payne, *American Ballet Theatre* (New York: Alfred A. Knopf, 1978): 127.

16. Muriel Topaz, interview with Kathleen Moore, New York, 21 April, 1998. The succeeding quote is from the same source.

17. Cavett, Tudor interview.

18. Hunt, Laing interview.

19. It is also the work most obviously influenced by Bergson. In Lincoln Kirstein's *Movement and Metaphor: Four Centuries of Ballet* (New York: Praeger, 1970) he has the entry: "Henri Bergson (1859–1941), particularly Bergson's *Creative Evolution* (1907), stressed the role of duration in experience. With time's passage an observer stores up accumulated experience that becomes a repository for conceptual recall. Incidents or objects take on symbolic metaphorical importance such as Proust's madeleine or Tudor's spray of white lilac."

20. Jennifer Dunning, "Antony Tudor Recreates a Nostalgic Ballet," *New York Times*, probably 12 or 13 May, 1985. The preceding and succeeding Tudor quotes are from the same source.

21. UNRRA, the United Nations Relief and Rehabilitation Administration, was established in November, 1943, in order to work with refugees after the start of World War II. Its work included repatriating, feeding, and initiating programs of resettlement for refugees.

22. Van Vecten's letters have been donated to the New York Public Library by Isabel Brown. Laing's responses reside in the Beineke Library at Yale University. No letters from Tudor to van Vecten are known to exist.

23. Diana Adams as quoted in "Proposal Nominating Antony Tudor for the National Medal of Honor of the Arts," submitted by American Ballet Theatre. The quote appears on page 9.

24. Letter from Laing to Adams dated probably 12 or 13 October, no year. From the collection of Laing's heir, Isabel Brown. The letter was obviously written when the marriage was in trouble.

25. Muriel Topaz, interview with Maude Lloyd, London, 13 February, 1998.

26. Antony Tudor, York University Lecture #10, 23 November, 1971.

27. Hunt, Tudor interview.

28. William Schuman (1910–93) was known for his strong and energetic orchestral music in particular. He was a brilliant administrator as well, heading the Juilliard School and, later, Lincoln Center. He, along with Aaron Copland, was often the driving force for the recognition and appreciation of American music. After *Undertow*, he collaborated with Martha Graham on the music for her *Night Journey* (1947) and *Judith* (1950).

29. Rosen, "Talking with Antony Tudor, a Choreographer for All Seasons," 6.

30. Edwin Denby, *Looking at Dance* (New York: Pellegrini and Cudahy, 1949): 122.

31. Hunt, interview with Laing.

32. Oliver Smith (1918–1994) was a designer for the company and had done the décor for de Mille's *Rodeo* and Robbins's *Fancy Free,* among other ballets.

33. Viola Essen (1926–1989) was a soloist with Ballet Theatre. John Butler (1918–1993), who in addition to being a ballet dancer, had danced with Martha Graham, went on to become an important choreographer, working mostly in Europe.

34. John Martin, "The Dance: A New Role," *New York Times*, 17 June, 1945.

35. Walter Terry, *New York Herald Tribune* undated clipping, probably 17 June, 1945.

36. Muriel Topaz, interview with Isabel Brown, New York, 28 October, 1997. Brown, who danced in *Gala Performance, Romeo and*

*Juliet, Lilac Garden, Undertow,* and *Pillar of Fire*, although not always in the original casts, remained close friends with Hugh and Tudor throughout their lives. She is the heir to all of Laing's papers. She is also the mother of later Tudor dancers Ethan Brown and Leslie Browne.

37. Charles Payne, *American Ballet Theatre*, 152. The text talks about Robbins receiving only fifteen hours and forty-five minutes of rehearsal time for a new ballet (which had to be canceled because it was not ready) while Tudor had fifty-two hours of rehearsal for *Undertow,* which was already in the repertoire. Many years later I saw this situation reversed when there were simultaneous American Ballet Theatre rehearsals for revivals of Robbins's *Les Noces* and Tudor's *Undertow*.

38. George Balanchine and Francis Mason, *The Complete Stories of Great Ballets* (New York: Doubleday, 1977): 571.

39. Rosella Hightower (1920–), one of four ballerinas of American Indian ancestry, danced with Ballet Theatre, and many of the Russian ballet companies of the era. She went on in 1962 to found the Centre de Danse Classique in Cannes.

*At Jacob's Pillow.* From left to right: Ted Shawn, Margaret Craske, and Tudor. *Photograph by Jack Mitchel, courtesy of Isabel Brown*

# 4

# The 1950s

## In Residence at Jacob's Pillow

In July of 1949, Tudor had a residency at Jacob's Pillow, the histori-
cally significant summer school and festival created by Ted Shawn and
actually built by him with his troupe of men dancers. Tudor had taught
at that seminal institution twice before: with Ballet Theatre in 1941,
when Alicia Markova ran the summer program and Tudor began work
on *Pillar of Fire*; and in 1946.

In 1949 Tudor once again taught two daily classes to Pillow students. He also choreographed a small work for Diana Adams and Hugh
Laing called *The Dear Departed* (Maurice Ravel). It premiered at the
Pillow's dance festival in July. Tudor tossed off the dance, one of his
lighter works, quickly. It comprised a short, sometimes witty *pas de
deux*. Laing played an aging Chinese philosopher who pursued a sylph-
like genie, danced by Diana Adams. In the end Adams refused to coop-
erate and go back into her bottle, exiting saucily instead. A short, hard-
to-decipher, filmed excerpt remains the only extant trace of the dance.[1]
It bears witness to the choreographic inventiveness of the piece, the
interesting and original partner work, and the clarity with which gesture
told the story. The Jacob's Pillow Dancers repeated the work in a November tour. Then it disappeared from the repertoire forever.

Such a fate faced many Tudor ballets that did not receive immediate public and/or critical acclaim (and those of many other choreographers, a practice that continues to this day). It is deeply disturbing to
contemplate how many masterpieces we have lost because of this my-

137

opic view of dance. If the history of any art form teaches a lesson, it is that immediate acclaim is not necessarily a reliable measure of the worth of a work—a lesson that the dance world honors only in the breach.

During his 1949 stay, Tudor participated very actively in the Jacob's Pillow Dance Festival. The Festival featured Ballet Theatre as the resident classical company that year and the group performed several Tudor dances. *Jardin aux lilas*, *Gala Performance*, and *Judgment of Paris* all appeared.

Tudor returned twice more to teach at the Pillow: in 1951 and 1953. The year 1951 was particularly productive as, in addition to his teaching, he created two ballets: *Les Mains gauches* (Jacques Ibert) and *Ronde de printemps* (Erik Satie).

In 1951 Shawn delegated the entire ten weeks of ballet production to Tudor, who did the planning, hiring, and producing of the ballet segment of each program during the season. The Pillow paid Tudor a flat fee from which he assumed all the financial arrangements for the imported artists. His own payment for the season and what he did with it illustrates once again his lack of interest in the financial aspect of his professional commitments. At the end of the Festival exactly $125 remained to pay him for all his non-teaching efforts. He immediately contributed this sum to the Jacob's Pillow scholarship fund. For his teaching he was paid $75 weekly.


## Off to Sweden


By September, 1949, after the summer at the Pillow, Hugh and Diana had happily married. Stormy times increased at Ballet Theatre. With the prospect of a long lay-off period as the company tried, once more, to solve its financial and administrative crises, Tudor accepted an offer from the renowned baritone Joel Berglund. Bergland, who directed the Royal Swedish Opera House, invited Tudor for an extended stay with the Opera House's resident company, the Royal Swedish Ballet. [2]

In a letter [3] Tudor apologized to Berglund for delaying his commitment. Lucia Chase had thought a considerable possibility existed for Ballet Theatre to perform in London through September and she wanted Tudor with them. This would have necessitated delaying his starting date in Sweden; however, as late as June nothing definite had emerged with Ballet Theatre. So, his plans now solidified: New York until the end of June, Jacob's Pillow from July through the second week of August, by boat to England, a few days in Paris, overnight in Copenhagen, and then on to Stockholm by train.

His relationship with the Laings at the time seemed cozy and he appeared to accept their marriage. Letters from him to them begin with such phrases as "Dear Love Doves," "Dear Cherubs," "Dear Bugs (his pet name for Laing) and Mrs. Bugs." (One letter ends with him rushing off to play chess.)

He wrote that teaching at Jacob's Pillow was heaven compared with trying to undo thirty years of "bad training" in Stockholm. In another letter he wrote that the girls in Sweden looked like Rin Tin Tin. He complained of having no social life and no glamour. He said that not one of the dancers knew that putting a hand in a certain manner in a certain place (The letter remarked: "this is clean and about work!") could possibly have any importance. He was working on a new ballet with music by Gruenberg, but had no deadline for it. (Originally he had proposed a ballet with a score by the Catalan composer Roberto Gerhard.) He had barely started *Romeo*, and *Jardin* and *Gala* would open shortly. He had also planned to go back to his idea of a ballet on the *Kalavala,* but abandoned it because he felt the dancers were not ready. [4]

Berglund's offer for Tudor to come to Sweden was made partially on the advice of Bengt Hager, a Swede very influential in the artistic life of the country. Hager evaluated Tudor's contribution to Swedish ballet during this initial stay as follows:

> For us here, he was far too fine. He was very much above the company we had at that time. It was a very low period. The school was poor—half of what it should have been.
>
> His most important gift to us at that time was a staging of *Giselle*. Not really an authentic *Giselle*, it was very "interpreted." But it had all the fine points of *Giselle*, all the sensitive things. . . . With great care and with great love Tudor highlighted the things that were Ellen Rasch's [Sweden's leading ballerina at that time] forte. He gave us a really, really wonderful *Giselle* that the audience understood and loved. It gave us a new appreciation of ballet—people took ballet more seriously. Anybody with sensitivity now felt that it was a deeply moving art form. It was especially his *Giselle* that had this effect.
>
> *Lilac Garden* was a little lost here. Then, he did *Gala Performanc.* It is so wonderful, so funny. It was a hilarious performance. The dancers captured it very well and it was a colossal success. [5]

Tudor also mounted *Petrouchka* and *Les Sylphides*. *Romeo and Juliet* did not get staged at this time, nor did the new Tudor ballet which they had hoped for. As Bengt Hager stated, *Giselle* rated as the most important achievement of Tudor's stay. Ellen Rasch alternated in the title role with Gunnel Lindgren. Remarkably, *Giselle* had not been seen in Sweden since its debut in 1845.

Tudor's impact on Stockholm's Opera Ballet is summed up by critic Holger Lundbergh: "That it was a resounding success I am happy to affirm. I have seldom heard such spontaneous applause in the venerable house, nor in years seen a ballet receive such accolades in the Stockholm press. A new dawn had come." [6]

Rasch related:

> This man meant so much to me in my career. At the time I thought he was a mean person; I didn't understand the way he worked. He meant well with his sarcasm. When he was in the mood he seemed to get at your insides. He knew you rather well. He was a marvelous psychologist; he could understand the little things. [7]

Rasch explained that at the time she wanted to be more Russian and was afraid that this Englishman would slow her down, that she would become "a little gray, frumpy." [Having met Ms. Rasch when she was about 80, still ravishingly attractive, I could not take the idea of her ever being frumpy too seriously.] But quite soon, she recounted, she realized how his acute sensitivity and rightness revealed themselves when he told her such things as "if you suffer and cry, nobody else will—certainly not the audience."

When he first gave her the role of Caroline, she found it very difficult. She was convinced Tudor chose her because he didn't like her and wanted her to suffer.

> At five to three on a Saturday, when the people wanted to go home, he insisted that I do this moment of looking at the [imaginary] house [in *Lilac Garden*]. And he did what was customary for him: he opened his newspaper and he said, "I'll tell you when it is right." At quarter past three he finally said, "Well, all right, we'll see how you do this on Monday." I came home and I thought, "I never want to see this man again. I don't want to go back." Of course I came back on Monday, and there he was, sitting on the chair. He asked if I'd had a nice Sunday.

He did the same thing to the woman playing the French ballerina in *Gala Performance*. (Rasch remarked that sometimes she thought that newspaper had a hole in it.) When the poor girl finally broke down and wept, he sent Rasch out of the room to console her, saying that tomorrow she'd be the one crying. "I don't know where it came from, but I said, 'Oh, no. You'll cry before I do.' From that moment on we had a certain rapport." Tudor rather liked people who talked back to him; it took a lot of courage and daring to do so.

Rasch and Tudor soon became friends. Most of the dancers were a little frightened of him. They were reluctant to socialize with him, but he did like being invited. Rasch took him to the theater when Orson Welles, the famous actor and director, was in Stockholm. The two sat next to one another. The curtain got stuck for about a half hour, affording Tudor the opportunity to speak at some length with Welles. He reported very much enjoying the meeting.

A telling incident occurred when Rasch performed *Lilac Garden* for the first time. She was also dancing *Gala Performance* and all the *relevés* gave her a sore heel. Tudor suggested she wear high heels for the rehearsal. One critic present did not bother to come back for the performance; he wrote that it was such a marvelous idea to put Caroline in high heels, so that she stood out from the rest of the women.

Tudor was skeptical about how a ballet company, with the kind of stability and comfort level vouchsafed to the Swedes by their government, could produce first-class work. The dancers' incomes were more than sufficient; most were married and had children. They lived a "normal" life. When they retired they were entitled to an adequate pension. No one expected them to be penurious or to suffer for their art. These circumstances differed substantially from the dancer's world that Tudor knew both at Ballet Theatre and, before that, at the Ballet Rambert. At first, Tudor believed the Swedes could not really become good dancers under these rational circumstances. But soon he came to respect their way of life, to regard Stockholm as a second home and to become good friends with many of the dancers.

In addition to mounting ballets for the company, Tudor taught daily classes. Rasch found them intelligently constructed; Gerd Andersson, another of his ballerina/admirers, thought he made dancing fun. As a teacher, everything he said was new to them and he enthralled them with his extraordinary musicality. He often asked his students to experiment with music. Sometimes he would give *enchaînements* in unheard-of meters like 5 or 9. In another of his favorite devices he would give a combination in 4/4, then ask to see it in 3/4 or 6/8 without the piano, so that his students had physically to understand these different meters.

He nurtured the young talent in the company, giving the dancers opportunities to develop. None of them ever forgot it. He arranged a scholarship to the Sadler's Well Ballet School in London. He encouraged them to venture out, to see things, since during the war they had been isolated from the new trends in art, theater, and dance. In recent interviews with the dancers who had met him at that time, I was struck by the unanimity of opinion about his importance to them. There remains a remarkable bond of affection. Most saw him as a father/lover figure.

Gerd Andersson:

> It was the first experience with a choreographer of that kind, and a teacher. So he meant very much to us at that time and he still does.
>
> He was very sarcastic as everybody knows. I had difficulties in pointing my feet; I didn't have a big instep. And, we had very poor shoes at the time. Once, when he passed me, he said, "Point the foot." I answered, "It's the shoe." He continued on his way, but each time he passed he would say, "Oh, sorry. It's the shoe." He was so funny. But, one felt appreciated, so he could say such things without being offensive.
>
> I might not have continued to dance if it hadn't been for him. I was very uncertain; I wanted to go into theater instead. But, when he came and I saw his ballets and the way he worked, I thought, "This is my life. This is what I want to do and want to fight for." [8]

Viveka Ljung also attributed her career as a dancer to Tudor.

> It was a privilege among my generation to be cast in a Tudor ballet. He was Art and he meant as much to the Swedish dancers as Ingmar Bergman has meant to his actors in Swedish theater and film.
>
> He was a genius and taught us not to do a single step without knowing why. Think and feel before moving. That made it worthwhile for me, for I was more of an artist than a technician. [9]

Mariane Orlando said:

When he first came, I was really too young to understand a lot.
In the beginning I was a little afraid of him; he could be very
sarcastic. But he also had this enormous sense of humor. He
combined the two things so you were never sure when he was
teasing or when he would really hurt. We laughed a lot, but
sometimes we were very tense.

It was just as important to be in the corps of his ballets as to be
a soloist. He could see everyone, even those in the back. You
couldn't escape him. Every movement in the ballet was important. He made you feel that, without you, the soloist would disappear. So we all felt very responsible.

I worked a lot with Mr. Tudor. He gave me the opportunity to
dance great roles. We became very close; I admired and respected him. He was musical and sensitive and had an unusual
ability to teach us how to enter deeply into the character of the
roles. I was lucky to have met and worked with him.

He revolutionized the dancing in Sweden, not only in his own
ballets. What he gave us we could use in everything, in every
ballet.[10]

After he arrived Tudor became upset about the training of the
dancers' feet. He replaced the elderly lady who had taught for many
years. She was not good enough for him. Since she was about to retire
anyway, he eased her out, rather gently, avoiding any scandal. Then he
visited all the different schools in Sweden to see if he could find
somebody to suit him. He found two Latvian dancers, Albert and Nina
Kozlovsky, who had barely escaped on a small boat before the Germans
occupied Riga. The only things they brought with them were a fur coat
and some libretti and music for ballets. They mounted the first *Cor-
saire* in Europe.

When the Kozlovskys finally settled outside of Stockholm they
began a small school. They had only one girl with real talent. Tudor
went to see their classes and saw her. He said that if they could train
this girl, they must be good. So he recruited them for the opera ballet
school where they remained for twenty years.

One rather unpleasant incident took place during this visit. Apparently Tudor made an advance to one of the heterosexual boys in the
company. The boy did not like Tudor and there ensued some conflict
and a confrontation. The young man got very angry and complained to
the board of directors of the Ballet. Somehow it all worked itself out
but it must have embarrassed Tudor, who was never very public about
his homosexuality. He guarded his privacy and, generally speaking, his

associates respected his need for privacy, even though on occasion he did make overtures to young, beautiful boys.

When Tudor left Stockholm, many of the dancers were devastated. Gerd Andersson remembered:

> He went around with his keys in his pocket. We thought he was beautiful. We were all in love—the young girls. He was forty then, and very attractive. When he left we were crying.
>
> We had a party when he was leaving. We were a group of about seven. He gathered us together. As we said good-bye Tudor admonished, "Now, you remember. You are the future Swedish Ballet." It was a great responsibility, but he gave us the confidence to do it. [11]

Lulli Svedlin recalled saying to him, "Oh Mr. Tudor, why must you leave us? You have just made us a company out of your work, and you leave such a hole. How can you do such a thing to us?" He answered, "You will manage. You will manage." [12]

His idyll with the Swedes, however, continued for many years. He visited as a private citizen on holiday at least once, in June, 1952, and perhaps more often. Viveka Ljung remembered Tudor coming to a traditional crayfish party and spending the night as her guest on the archipelago on which she has a house. His postcards to Hugh from Stockholm bear additional witness to that visit.

Tudor returned to Sweden again in 1961 as guest choreographer, staging *Dark Elegies.* He took up residence again in 1962–64, perhaps this time with the title of director, mounting *The Tragedy of Romeo and Juliet, Pillar of Fire,* and *Little Improvisations* (retitled the Swedish equivalent of *It's Raining*). He created *Echoing of Trumpets* for the company in 1963, and, in 1973, received the Carina Ari Gold Medal, a most prestigious award named for the famed ballerina of the Ballet Suédois.[13] Several of his ballets were televised for Swedish television, and later, Viola Aberle and Gerd Andersson convinced Tudor to allow them to make a documentary movie about him. When the Swedish company came to the United States to perform in the early 1970s, Tudor welcomed them and helped in an unofficial capacity.

## Back to the United States; Tudor as Educator

Tudor returned to a new affiliation with the Metropolitan Opera in New York, where he felt he had to produce at least one new ballet each year. Annually, Balanchine did one new ballet and Robbins did one new ballet. Tudor felt he had to do the same. And, he had to be sure that his ballet would be as good as the others, perhaps even a little better. Certainly better than the one he had done the year before. It represented an enormous, if imagined, pressure.

Tudor the choreographer could not easily produce ballets on order. With equanimity, he could wait ten years for an idea to ripen. Only when that idea was strong, and he found both music and a structure for it, did he feel able and willing to choreograph. The notion that he must produce a ballet each year to top the previous year's output would have seemed an impossible task

In March, 1950, Ballet Theatre feted its tenth anniversary. Tudor came back in time to dance in the celebratory season at New York's [Rockefeller] Center Theatre.

In May, 1950, three months after Tudor's return to the United States from his first stay in Stockholm, Ballet Theatre could boast of another new Tudor work. All was not lost when the Louis Gruenberg work had had to be abandoned in Sweden; its reincarnation appeared in New York. During Ballet Theatre's tenth anniversary season, *Nimbus* premiered. It used the Gruenberg *Violin Concerto* as music, with décor by Oliver Smith and costumes by Saul Bolasni. The large cast included Kaye, Adams, and Laing with Jenny Workman, Eric Braun, and Fernand Nault among others in the corps. The ballet told the story of a dreamer whose dream-self conjured up a dream-beau. The action moved from her bedroom to a rooftop and back again. In their reviews both Walter Terry and John Martin classified the work as perhaps not among the best of Tudor. But both thought that, with some revision, it might become a very popular ballet. Unfortunately, this prophecy remained unfulfilled. Martin felt the work signified a new direction. It would, however, be six more years before another Tudor work joined the repertoire of Ballet Theatre. It would not be a new work, but a restaging of *Offenbach in the Underworld.*

In the 1950s the United States experienced a period of conservatism. Being conventional became a priority. The country was taking a breathing space before plunging into the moral turmoil of redbaiting and growing McCarthyism. The Alger Hiss case headlined the news as did Mao's take-over of China. The country soon became embroiled in an undeclared war in Korea. In the mid 1950s Elvis Presley reigned as *the* pop singer of the moment and rock and roll dominated the music of the young. It was the era of the hula hoop, duck-tail haircuts, hot rods, the Edsel, and tail-finned Cadillacs. Everyone watched Sid Caesar on television.

In the world of the arts stirrings of discontent surfaced. Jerome Robbins's *Age of Anxiety*, with a score by Leonard Bernstein, premiered; a year later his ballet *The Cage* (Stravinsky) would appear. In 1953 Anna Sokolow explored her brand of distraught dance expressionism in her *Lyric Suite* (Alban Berg). In 1958 came José Limón's moving war requiem *Missa Brevis* (Zoltán Kodály). Jack Kerouac and Allan Ginsberg along with others of the "beat generation" emerged, while at the movies one could see *All about Eve* and in 1951 *Rashomon*. For lighter entertainment Gene Kelly gave us *An American in Paris* and the June Taylor dancers cavorted on television.

At this time Tudor decided that he could no longer exist on the kind of money he received solely as a choreographer. Reading his contracts one understands why. For example, for staging *Lilac Garden* for the New York City Ballet in 1951, he received $500.00 plus a royalty of $25.00 per performance, fees typical for the time. By comparison, in 1949, under the administration of President Harry S. Truman, the minimum wage was raised to $.75 per hour. A corporate magnate earned as much as $70,000, while a Congressman earned $14,000. The lowliest laborer working for the minimum wage earned in less than three weeks what Tudor was paid for staging one of his masterpieces.

He needed a steady income. Thus began the era of Tudor the educator. It also ended the era of Tudor the dancer. He retired from active performing although he did come out of retirement on a few occasions. Many sources give the date of his retirement from performing as 1950; however, he continued dancing at least through early 1951. He appeared on stage in the beginning of his tenure with the New York City Ballet.

For the 1950 fall season, Ballet Theatre entered into an alliance with the Metropolitan Opera. Tudor accepted the directorship of the Met's ballet school and, a bit later, of the Opera Ballet itself. It proved a very valuable affiliation for a whole generation of dancers, allowing them to study regularly with the master teachers Antony Tudor and Margaret Craske. (See Chapter 5 for the story of Tudor's association with the Metropolitan Opera School and Company.)

In 1951, about a year after his acceptance of the Met's school directorship, came another unique offer. The composer William Schuman, whom Tudor knew from the time of their collaboration on *Undertow*, decided that the Juilliard School of Music (renamed simply the Juilliard School after the Dance and Drama Divisions were added) should develop a professional dance program. Having professional level dance in a conservatory setting was a revolutionary idea at the time. The plan, made in conjunction with director-elect of dance Martha Hill, incorporated both classical ballet and modern dance training for all students, a combination unheard of in that period. Hill assembled a stellar faculty including, among others, Martha Graham, José Limón, Doris Humphrey, and Louis Horst; Tudor agreed to head the Ballet faculty. (For more about Tudor and the Juilliard School see Chapter 6).

## Another Muse

In 1950, on his return from Sweden to Ballet Theatre, Tudor met another dancer, Sallie Wilson. She became important to him both artistically and personally.

> The first time I went to Tudor's class was because I had heard that Lucia was looking for dancers. I was sixteen. During class Tudor went up and down the barre saying "Sallie from Fort Worth." I found out that my teacher had asked Tudor to "put Sallie from Fort Worth in front so Lucia could see her." . . . He placed me way in the back, in the john [loo]. That was my first encounter with Tudor. . . . I got into Ballet Theatre in 1949. Tudor was still in Sweden. . . . I was cast as the old dresser in *Gala* and the fishwife in *Romeo*. During the summer I studied with him. . . . That started the romance of the age. . . . I saw him light up and that's when we started feeding each other. He was wonderful to me. I was just eighteen. [14]

When Wilson first took on the role as the dresser. Hugh was directing the production. He told her only that she had first to walk across the stage carrying a tray, then to re-cross and tap the ballerina's leg. On the third entrance the ballerina slapped her wrist. When first she did it, Hugh screamed at her, as only Hugh could scream: "You have to make a character. You have to know who you are and what you are doing." So she "went home and devised a character who had a hunch back and a limp and wrinkles. We went on tour and I got a review to everyone's shock. I never heard another word about it from Hugh so I knew it was OK." [15]

When Tudor moved on to the Metropolitan Opera, he took Sallie with him. This marked the beginning of their collaboration, one which lasted well past his death. Wilson continues as the person most often

Sallie Wilson in *Gala Performance*. Photograph by Fred Fehl, courtesy of Sallie Wilson

entrusted with the entrusted with the posthumous restaging of the Tudor oeuvre. Once more Tudor had found a muse

Wilson adamantly maintains that the relationship, while having its stormy moments, was one of love and respect. In interviews in December, 1997, and May, 2000, she described their relationship.

Tudor played with people. He toyed with everybody; he manipulated. If he wasn't interested in you he'd say, "That was charming." "Charming" was his biggest insult.

He absolutely drove me crazy sometimes—on purpose with a little smile on his face. I would go out and throw a chair down the hall or something. He would be very happy because I responded correctly. But the next day he would be lovely.

When I was first at the Met studying with Tudor, Hugh got me an apartment in his building. Often I would have dinner with Hugh, and Tudor would be there. We'd eat and then play scrabble or chess. One of these nights, out of the blue, he said, "Sallie, someday you are going to have to fight with me." I was nineteen, worshipful, adoring. I said "What do you mean? I could never fight with you." Then it occurred to me that I was shy and couldn't lose my temper. My emotions were muffled, held in. He was bringing them out. I spent my whole life trying to come out on stage and this was part of my lesson. He encouraged me to talk back to him because it was so hard for me. He liked sass. He didn't like me when I was too docile. He tried to put some spice in.

When I kicked him in rehearsal, he was changing *Dark Elegies*. Carelessly. He knew that would get me. He wasn't angry when I kicked him; he had made his point. I went to the boiling point. He loved to get my goat. So often, when he succeeded, he would be delighted. I would see him turn away and smile.

When I joined the New York City Ballet we had several years during which we didn't speak to each other. It was during a time of some difficulty between Tudor and Craske, so I wasn't taking his class. I found out later that he came and watched me in performances, but he didn't let me know. I didn't know until years later that he was watching over me all that time.

He often brought me back gifts from his travels: a beautiful box of teacups from Japan, a Naguchi lamp that I had until it shredded, a sari scarf from India.

He was cruel sometimes and I thought my world would come to an end. But I found out I survived and he was happy I survived. He made me recognize that I really didn't depend on him. When I realized that, I was free. He mortally wounded me a couple of times, but I didn't end up hating him. I ended up loving him.

## Jacob's Pillow, Continued

In 1951, Tudor taught classes at Jacob's Pillow for part of the summer, until Margaret Craske arrived. Wilson studied with them both. Craske's stint as ballet mistress with Tudor's London Ballet had initiated an extended association between the two teachers. They entirely complemented one another in their teaching. Craske's concentration on a strong, basic technique, allowed Tudor the freedom to explore choreographic devices and musicality. Her teaching permitted him to have the time, in his classes, to expound the fine points of being on the stage. Sallie Wilson describes Tudor's classes as

difficult, both mentally and physically. He was always a devil. They were wonderful, hard classes, full of joy. He would show these impossible movements and make us do them. . . . His classes were imaginative and frustrating; I would cry, then recover and still end the class happily. It was full of all kinds of emotion and problems.

At the Pillow that summer the dancers were like a small resident company, living and working together.

Tudor, assisted by Donald Duncan, an administrator, undertook much of the planning of the ballet presentations at the Pillow dance festival that year. As planned, the Jacob's Pillow season featured performances of "Stars of the New York City Ballet." The "stars" presentations consisted of Adams, Kaye, and Laing in various non-Tudor small works plus excerpts from *Dark Elegies*, the "Pastoral" section of *Lady of the Camellias*, a *pas de deux* performed by Melissa Hayden and Herbert Bliss, and a work with Lillian Moore and Kate Forbes.

During that summer Tudor also produced two new works for Sallie Wilson and his Pillow students-cum-resident company. In a letter to Ted Shawn Tudor complains about being inundated with preparatory work, thus excusing himself for being dilatory in getting program information to the Pillow.[16]

The first of the new works, *Les Mains gauches*, to the music of Jacques Ibert, premiered on 20 July. The piece takes an excursion into the mysterious, the occult, featuring a fortuneteller/oracle and a young couple. A curtain at the back, representing the fortuneteller's booth, allows the characters to appear and disappear as if by magic. A fortuneteller, a figure of fate, confronts a couple in love. The couple visits the booth, disappearing behind the curtain. They put out their hands and the fortuneteller appears and grabs them. A rose appears in the girl's hand and a hangman's noose in the boy's, predicting he will kill her. In the end she becomes afraid of him, and he becomes frightened of her love. An ominous and mysterious atmosphere pervades the ballet throughout; one wonders who these characters are. The choreography presents a stark, geometric picture without a hint of lyricism. The woman sprinkles her movement with many *pas de bourrées,* with the body held rigidly upright and the arms stiffly down at the sides. Knifelike *battements à la second* punctuate the *bourrées.* The *pas de deux* resembles encounters rather than love duets and a certain tension and bite permeate the whole ballet. A particularly fascinating moment takes place when the man marches threateningly from upstage right where the woman is lying, to downstage left dragging the figure of fate on his back. It certainly does not present a traditional, comfortable love story. The cast of the *pas de trois* consisted of Sallie Wilson, Marc Hertsens, and Zebra Nevins. The work later reappeared as the second section of *Concerning Oracles,* a dance choreographed by Tudor for the Metropolitan Opera Ballet.

The second work, *Ronde dup printemps*, premiered on 1 August. Based on the play *La Rondine* by Arnold Schnitzler, the dance tells the story of a round of seductions. Tudor choreographed eight of the play's ten encounters making them into eight overlapping *pas de deux*, eight seductions. The work begins with a prostitute seducing a soldier who, in turn, beds the French maid. The maid then introduces the young son of the house to the glories of lovemaking. He has summoned her and asked her to tie his shoe laces. As she bends to the task, the inevitable happens. Now experienced, the young man goes on to an affair with a wife. Nervous, he keeps looking at his watch, certain the wife won't appear. She does, of course. By that time, however, he has worked himself into a frenzy. When the wife rings the bell, he faints. Fortunately, when he revives and takes her hand, her glove comes off, initiating the disrobing. Later, she erotically ensnares her own bored husband. Next, an actress drags the shy young husband home. Following their contretemps, a diplomat appears who indulges in an after dinner tryst with the actress. In turn, the diplomat ends up with the prostitute. Completely drunk, he doesn't remember what transpires. He seems to say, "My dear, I'm glad nothing happened" to which she seems to reply, "Are you kidding?" Thus, *La Ronde* is completed.

Sallie Wilson remembers that in the episode with the diplomat she had to swing her long string of beads in time with the music. She recalls practicing in the woods for hours. Apparently the sequence was patterned after Beatrice Lilly.

The ingenious scenery consisted of two ice cream parlor chairs and a square board mounted on four legs. In one scene it represented two chairs and a table; in another it became a chaise; in a third scene it was turned so that you only saw the chair backs which resembled twin beds. The dancers, in addition to Wilson, Hertsens, and Nevins, included Francine Bond, Harvey Jung, Jack Monts, and Adelino Palomonos. The work received only six performances. Sallie Wilson remarked that although working on the dance changed their lives, Tudor didn't think of it as serious because it had come easily to him.

> It was clear what he wanted and he just did it. I don't know why he didn't give it the stature that it should have had . . . It would absolutely be a knockout to a New York audience. . . . It was so delicate and full of wonderful things, delicious laughs. . . . He wouldn't let us look at each other's parts. Before my entrance I had to keep my back to the stage. And we all religiously did what he told us. We didn't watch. He wanted each of us to be his or her own character.

> He had such fun doing the ballet. Each episode was delightful. The Pillow was like a vacation for him—a wonderful atmosphere which he very much enjoyed.[17]

Tudor had a unique method of working with individual dancers on their roles. Only late in the process would he allow them to discover how their characters interacted with the others. He encouraged each dancer to explore and internalize the person being portrayed without reference to the other cast members. Thus, when a dancer met the others, it became a true discovery. One didn't have to "act" the process; one actually experienced it. This technique of working resembled that used in theater, but rarely if ever employed by dancers. His work on *La Ronde* seemed to have taken this methodology to the logical conclusion in which the characters were not even allowed to look at the others. While this astute methodology succeeded in getting the kind of performances Tudor sought, it had a tragic outcome for the history of dance. Wilson felt that, had she been permitted to watch the ballet, it would now not be lost.

In 1953 Tudor taught at Jacob's Pillow for the last time. In addition to his two classes each morning, he again took charge of the ballet segment of the ten-week program. This time he invited the National

Ballet of Canada for a residency. The company performed *Lilac Garden*, with Lois Smith, David Adams, James Ronaldson, and company director Celia Franca in the leading roles. Franca told a story about when she arrived at the Pillow and first saw Tudor. He said that he had an engagement so asked if she would teach his classes for him.

> Who is going to say no to Tudor? Not I. I remember teaching this class of slightly undisciplined American dancers and I, coming from a rather strict British upbringing of courtesy and politeness and civility . . . This boy walked right in front of me. I said, "You don't do that, ducky." He said, "My name's not ducky, it's Bucky." Miss Franca was put in her place.[18]

Franca said in the end she did not mind a bit teaching for Tudor. In return he agreed to coach the company in his works; he had not found time to do so before that.

## Working with the New York City Ballet

In the early 1950s a breach developed between Lucia Chase and the Laings. One rumor had it that Hugh would not forgive Lucia because she refused to make Diana a principal dancer.

> They were probably all miffed at Chase, and they were all united. Everyone went in and out of love with Ballet Theatre because of Lucia. She was not an easy lady to work for. Being difficult was the game she played in order to get what she wanted. It was her way of getting things done.[19]

Whatever the reason, the Laings decided to leave Ballet Theatre. By 1951 they had joined the New York City Ballet (NYCB). Nora Kaye soon followed. Tudor, never totally happy in his relationship with Chase and bereft of his usual soloists, decided to defect as well. In 1951 he joined the staff at the NYCB and for a brief period functioned as choreographer for that institution. The collaboration never really achieved a comfortable aesthetic fit.

During his brief tenure at NYCB, Tudor mounted two of his extant works. *Lilac Garden* first appeared on 30 November, 1951, with Kaye, Laing, Tudor, and Tanaquil Le Clercq. The company first presented *Dim Lustre* on May 26, 1954, after Tudor had left the company. Patricia McBride and Edward Villella danced the leads. Tudor also created two new works: *Lady of the Camellias* and *La Gloire*.

The best received of the Tudor repertory was *Lilac Garden*, particularly initially, when danced by Hugh and Nora. Correspondence exists concerning a proposed NYCB revival in 1952. It requests that Tanaquil Le Clercq and Nicholas Magallanes dance the two leads. By that time Kaye and Laing, restive at NYCB and looking elsewhere, could not be counted upon for the season. In fact, Tudor rehearsed Le Clerq and Magallanes in the parts, but, at the first orchestra rehearsal, the company postponed the ballet because they deemed the performance unready.

Regarding *Lilac Garden*, Le Clerq says that she found Nora's role simply too difficult for her, that she wasn't up to it. While to Tudor she professed that she couldn't learn the role, in reality she felt it was just too demanding both physically and emotionally.

Le Clercq spoke about Tudor as an amazing partner. Originally choreographed for Peggy van Praagh, the role of the mistress in *Lilac Garden* was made for a short woman—a woman of totally different body shape from that of Le Clerq. Because of this disparity in height, the lifts became all the more difficult. Tudor, ready for the task, never wavered. "When she [van Praagh] ran across the stage and leapt on him [Tudor], it was very easy. When I ran across the stage it was like spaghetti, but I wouldn't let him change it for me. When I leapt on him I thought he was going to fall down backwards but he was strong. He was like iron." [20]

The first new ballet created for NYCB, *Lady of the Camellias* (1951), has music by Giuseppi Verdi and featured Diana Adams and Hugh Laing. Tudor made a surprise appearance in the role of Armand's (Laing's) father. The ballet, based on the story by Alexander Dumas fils, unfolds in four scenes: *Chez* Prudence; In the Country, Two Months Later; Paris, Several Months Later; Marguerite's Bedroom. It recounts the tale familiar from both the Dumas story and the Verdi opera *La Traviata*, as well as from several other choreographic treatments. Marguerite and Armand are lovers, but Armand's father disapproves of his son's choice, a demimondaine. When the father fails to convince Armand to give her up, he approaches Marguerite, telling her she is ruining his son's prospects. Her deep love of Armand leads her to do as the father wishes. She convinces Armand that she prefers a rich nobleman, *Le Compte de N.*, as her protector and lover. The sacrifice affects her already failing health and, in a poignant ending, as she expires from consumption, Armand discovers her real reason for leaving. Since the ballet, never revived, is now lost, we can only conjecture about its realization. A short filmed sequence from the Pastoral (In the County) section exists, showing a work that hewed closely to the classical canon. While the steps were traditional, the way they were com-

bined is pure Tudor. A sequence of partnered *arabesques* built into a
lift. A series of glissades in a box-like spatial pattern (a sequence Tudor
was fond of and often gave as a classroom exercise) built tension as the
lovers circled one another never losing eye contact. Knowing Tudor,
one would assume that he managed to tell the tale devoid of sentimen-
tality. Contemporaneous writing tells us that the dance reached its ze-
nith in the ending *pas de deux*.

The second new ballet, the 1952 *La Gloire*, did not really suc-
ceed. Tudor himself felt that he had made a mistake in the music he
had chosen. The ballet used three Beethoven overtures: *Egmont, Coriolanus,* and *Leonora no. 3*. From all accounts the music overwhelmed
the dance. Sallie Wilson, on the contrary, thought it a fine ballet which
would perhaps be hailed as great if presented today. Tudor constructed
the ballet so that

> the audience could view the pretended "backstage" area, then
> switch to the pretended "onstage" area then to "backstage"
> again. There were two brocade-like wings on a track. They bi-
> sected the real stage from front to back so that sometimes you
> could see both what was happening supposedly "offstage" and
> the supposed "onstage" performance-in-progress simultane-
> ously. Then the wings would change and you could see Nora
> having a fit "offstage," while the performance was continuing in
> a remote corner. . . . It was exciting, incredibly effective . . . but it
> was called an insignificant little ballet! [21]

*La Gloire* uses the metaphor of theater to explore the theme of an
aging actress (ballerina) constantly distracted and threatened by her
younger counterpart. While "onstage" the diva dances the title roles in
Racine's *Pheadra*, Arnault's *Lucrèce,* and Shakespeare's *Hamlet*, "offstage" the younger ballerina constantly shadows her, practicing the
steps, ready to pounce. The metaphor affords the opportunity to explore
behind-the-scenes backbiting. Tudor had seen *All about Eve* and the
film strongly influenced *La Gloire*.

Neither *Lady of the Camellias* nor *La Gloire* received the kind of
public acclaim for which everyone had hoped. The critics responded in
a lukewarm fashion neither totally negative nor totally positive. Betty
Cage, [22] longtime member of New York City Ballet whose friendship
with Tudor continued for many years, reports that in those days the
company did not pay much attention to the critics. Audience reaction
counted heavily. Dance criticism was in its infancy. In stark contrast to
the important influence of today's critics, the nascent "art" of dance
criticism did not seriously impact repertory choices.

In 1954 Kirstein personally requested Tudor to create another work. He offered Tudor the rare opportunity of starting a work and seeing if the result warranted finishing and presenting. Tudor accepted the offer, wishing such conditions were more the rule than the exception. He confirmed the availability of the Ibert [23] score he planned on using and wrote to Kirstein:

> Although your nice remark about my talents, which I think I share, was wonderful, we choreographers have all had our varied ears pinned back into place by that formidable sale of seats for Nut-cracker [sic]. Congratulations; it is a very good thing to have happen.[24]

Unfortunately, the projected Tudor/Ibert work never materialized. In 1954, Tudor and Kirstein spoke of a revival of *Lilac Garden*, another project which did not come to fruition. That year the company also requested a new ballet, but Tudor was not ready. Twenty years later, in 1974, the company did another revival of *Dim Lustre* with Patricia McBride and Edward Villella in the leads.

While Tudor's 1950s restagings fared better than his new pieces, not enough interest or enthusiasm existed to justify maintaining the works in repertory. Thus there was little for Tudor to do in the company. Eventually he ceased working with them.

According to Betty Cage, in principle, Tudor repertoire would contrast with the Balanchine repertoire and thus they would complement each other. It simply did not work out that way. The company did not find Tudor personally difficult, but the dancers had problems adjusting to his style. Tudor's way of working differed radically from that of Balanchine. Dramatic ballet and Tudor's approach to music baffled them. They liked the man and had no difficulty working with him. It was just that they didn't feel they danced their best or gave him what he looked for.

No severance or rupture ever took place. Tudor's respect for Balanchine long outlived his association with New York City Ballet. The following letter to Betty Cage, written in 1983, attested to this:

> Dear Betty,
>     We only get third or fourth hand rumors or reports, but nonetheless we are dismayed that Mr. B stays in the hospital and seems not interested in leaving it. It is difficult to realise that such a legendary figure, and one who was busy producing new works until quite recently, should be out of circulation. And notwithstanding our understanding of the strange diminishing of the time length of one year, especially when you hit

the seventies, this does all seem to have happened so suddenly, and to us—unexpectedly. People like him are expected to be immortal and even I, who was around and looking at *Prodigal Son* and *Apollo* when they were first exploding on to the ballet world with Diaghilev, can hardly believe that so many years have passed and are presumably taking their toll with him as with all of us. I hope he is coping well with everything and still accepting homage.

> Love to you and him,
> Antony and Hugh[25]

Eventually Laing also left the NYCB and returned to Ballet Theatre. Kaye left in 1954, returning to Ballet Theatre until 1959, then retiring from performing in 1961. Only Diana Adams stayed at the New York City Ballet for many years; she became one of its leading dancers. She remained with the company in 1953 after her divorce from Hugh Laing and was one of George Balanchine's favored ballerinas. Later she remarried, to Ronald Bates a stage manager at NYCB, and had a child. After retiring from dancing, she taught at the School of American Ballet. Adams died in 1993 at the age of 66.

## The Philadelphia Story

Beginning in 1950, as part of his new educational zeal, Tudor had begun commuting weekly to Philadelphia to teach at a private studio. One of his devoted pupils there, Judith Skoogfors, née Gesensway, was fifteen when Ethel Philips, a local teacher, managed to entice Tudor to come. Evidently Philips went to New York and actually handed him a check. Having the check in advance might have convinced him, but, given Tudor's infamous disregard for money, why he actually agreed to go remains a mystery. Skoogfors conjectures that Ethel, a raspy voiced, arthritic, overweight woman with dyed red hair and lots of jewelry, was a genuine character. Tudor was fascinated by characters. Skoogfors remembers the first class:

> There was this rather elegant gentleman. He must have been in his forties. All in beige. He always wore all beige. He very quietly stood up in front of the class and we did nothing but *pliés* for the entire hour and a half. We never got beyond *pointe tendu, demi plié* and *grand plié.* One thing I remember very clearly is that when I left the class, I literally had to grasp the handrail. My calves were so sore I could barely move, but I was

hooked. I was really hooked. There was something about him
that was so compelling. He was very quiet, very gentlemanly. . . .
That first year he taught a class for intermediates (he probably
thought we were beginners). Then he taught a class for teachers
. . . [The second year] he actually taught a children's class, followed by an intermediate class, a pointe and a partnering class.
Later he added some workshops in choreography. They were extraordinary. . . . He would set up a situation: you had to leave a
lover. He had a boy standing at the other end of the room. We
each had to get up and extemporize. . . . I was walking toward
this person and then . . . I started leaving in half circles. I don't
know why I did that. It came from the deepest part of me. . . . He
perked up and looked at this. It seemed to strike a chord. . . . I
was actually using movement to illustrate an emotional situation.[26]

The Philadelphia Orchestra, conducted by Eugene Ormandy, gave
a concert series each year at the huge Convention Hall. In 1953 Ormandy asked Tudor to direct the dances for one of the programs. Ormandy selected the music: Frédéric Chopin's *Les Sylphides*, Claude
Debussy's *Afternoon of a Faune,* and Jacques Offenbach's *Gaîté Parisienne*. [The latter eventually proved to be an unfortunate choice, as
Léonide Massine claimed choreographic rights to the score and threatened legal action.] Rehearsals of Fokine's *Les Sylphides* came first,
starting with the corps de ballet. Tudor spent many hours molding his
motley group of Philadelphia student dancers into a company. In defer-
ence to the disparate footwork skills of the group, he lavished a great
deal of time on the upper body exploring the meaning of each movement. He imported Diana Adams and Michael Lland[27] for the leads,
along with two local dancers, Sylvia Kim and Elaine Wilson. In typical Tudor fashion, near the end of the rehearsal period he insisted that
Kim and Wilson switch roles. For the staging of the Nijinsky *Afternoon
of a Faune* he chose Jon Jones, a black dancer,[28] and Judith Skoogfors
for the leads. For *Offenbach in the Underworld*, his redesign of *Gaîté
Parisienne*, he opted for New Orleans as the locale. His version featured a painter; Degas was known to have visited New Orleans.

Tudor's take on the merry, frivolous café life of the 1870s begins
with a "starving artist" painting a portrait of the innocent young daughter of the café's *patronne*. Various characters enter—a grand duke (His
Imperial Excellency), a diva (The Visiting Operetta Star), a soldier (An

Judith Skoogfors designs for original production of *Offenbach in the Underworld. Illustration courtesy of Judith Skoogfors*

Officer), a courtesan (The Queen of the Carriage Trade), veiled young
ladies hiding their proper identities (Debutantes), and assorted gentlemen and ladies (Les Garçons and Local Ladies). Flirtations and good
times abound as might be expected at such a venue, a less than totally
respectable place where people meet after hours to have a good time.
The ballet features all out dancing from beginning to end. Tudor filled
it with high-energy waltzes, a mazurka, and a can-can, with every
measure packed with "dancey" *enchaînements*. He mined and re-mined
the classical repertoire of steps with wit and charm. If one watches
closely, one can see actual *enchaînements* lifted from various well-
known ballets: a partnered *pirouette* and lift from the *Sleeping Beauty
pas de deux*; a Tudorized send-up of the Rose Adagio; sequences from
every standardized waltz that was ever created. Tudor put them all together in set pieces with amazing phrasing and continuity.

The flirting and carousing lead inevitably to a face slapping challenge that in turn brings on a hilarious *mêlée*. At one point the dancers
end in a pile-up in the middle of the floor. They slowly extricate themselves and a quiet *pas de deux* for the Artist and the Diva follows. The
apotheosis comes in a grand can-can which brilliantly illustrates Tudor's conviction that, if one performs the choreography exactly as it
was made, one becomes the character. The can-can girls (Local Café
Habitués) are tough broads; every movement they make has an earthy,
weighted quality, into the ground, into the hips, often with torso tilted
ever so slightly backward pushing the weight forward and downward.
The contrast between the way they move and the breezy, airy movement of the Diva tells the whole story.

The can-can finishes with everyone falling exhausted to the floor,
at which point the young innocent enters. She cannot quite figure out
what has transpired. Slowly the couples revive, as in a dream, and drift
off, as the café closes. Rather than just ending, Tudor added a post-
script. The Diva enters briefly, gives a note to the Painter and exits.
Curtain.

Michael Lland played the Painter, and Viola Essen, the Diva.
Once again Tudor started out by choreographing for the large groups
and worked his way down to the soloists. In the beginning he didn't
concentrate so much on the steps as he did on the overall movement
patterns.

Skoogfors remembered his talking about a particular movement in
the can-can section of *Offenbach in the Underworld*. It was essentially
a *grand battement* that he wanted to end settling down in the hips with
the pelvis pulled forward. He tried politely to make the dancers just a
little bit obscene. Skoogfors, an art student as well as a dancer, took

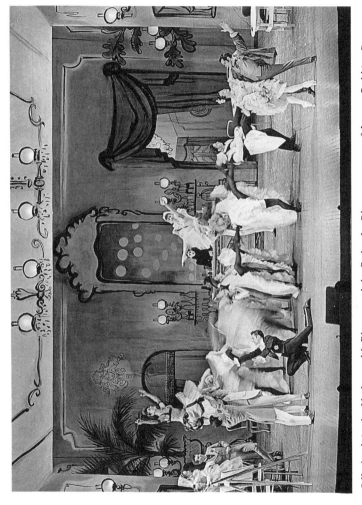

*Offenbach in the Underworld. Photograph by Sedge Le Blanc, courtesy of Jerome Robbins Dance Division, New York Public Library for the Performing Arts*

161

charge of the costumes for both *L'Après-midi d'un faune* and *Offenbach in the Underworld*. Tudor involved himself a good deal in their design. Skoogfors provided him with watercolor renditions that he could take to Japan where he expected to remount the ballet.

Skoogfors relates:

> Then some of us started doing little ballets and he would look at them . . . My father [Louis Gesensway, distinguished composer and violinist with the Philadelphia Orchestra at the time] was involved in a big arts festival at the Academy of Music. Some of the company was working on choreography for it. Tudor helped. He got us out of some sticky parts. When things weren't working he just jumped right in and altered the choreography. . . . Tudor said he would get me a partner from New York. I went up to New York to take class at the Met. Everyone was lined up at the barre when he suddenly said "Paul [Taylor], look like you are going to grab a young girl, rush her into the woods, and ravish her." He made Paul do that, then he turned around and said, "Will that do, Judy?" So, Paul became my partner. It was typical Tudor.

> I've thought a great deal about why he deigned to work with us. First, it was clear that Tudor didn't want to make commitments. He didn't want a company like Balanchine; he didn't want that kind of responsibility. . . . He didn't like people who were aggressive, who wanted to be stars, who pushed themselves forward. . . . I think he loved the idea of a struggling young company. It also could be because he could rehearse with us as long as he wanted to because none of us would leave. We would have stayed till two o'clock in the morning if he asked us to. [29]

The group started as students and coalesced into a nascent company through the performances with the Philadelphia Orchestra. As it grew in confidence, it grew in ambition as well. The dancers found rented space for a studio of their own, named themselves the Philadelphia Ballet, and began teaching and choreographing. Tudor continued to teach in Philadelphia for several more years, but he would not hear of a company being formed under his direction. Once again he refused the responsibility such a commitment would require. He was a free spirit and wished to remain one. Soon he was off to Japan to stage *Offenbach in the Underworld*; eventually he stopped teaching in Philadelphia.

## In England, Briefly

In 1952 the Ballet Rambert had a season at the Lyric Theatre. Cecil Bates, then ballet master of the company proposed an all-Tudor evening as a tribute. The program consisted of *Soirée musical, Dark Elegies, Gala Performance, Judgment of Paris,* and *Jardin aux lilas* (not necessarily in that order).

Tudor went to London for a few weeks to coach the dancers in *Jardin.* Bates reported that Tudor had made some changes for American casts and he was not very happy with the Rambert version, although Bates thought it was quite true to the original. But, "He didn't try to change it too much, because it would have upset the whole balance. He left it as it was." Tudor never actually saw the performance; he had already returned to New York. Apparently the critics found the company too young to fully understand Tudor's work.

Bates also remembers Tudor giving a demonstration of *pas de deux* work to the Cecchetti Society for which Bates and company principal Noreen Insop demonstrated. Said Bates:

> I didn't know he was such a fine teacher. Noreen and I had danced *Nutcracker* and *Swan Lake* together quite a lot. We thought we knew what we were doing, but we were only beginners when he started. He demonstrated the placing of the body for balance doing a lot with fingertip control, placing of the ballerina so she maintained the balance without putting any weight on her partner. The partner was just a source of reference with a very light touch. In fact, you could let go of her and walk away. He placed Noreen's hips and upper back in position. And, suddenly she would be on balance. She didn't need me. That was an eye-opening experience, revolutionary at that time.[30]

## Tudor Visits Japan

Unsurprisingly Tudor, attracted to Asian esthetics and Zen-like ideas even before he discovered Zen itself, accepted the 1954 invitation to work in Japan. The Komaki Ballet company, then a semi-professional group as were all dance companies in Japan at that time, extended the invitation.

He stayed in Tokyo and Osaka from 25 August to 17 September, teaching daily class and staging *Lilac Garden* and *Offenbach in the Underworld*, called *Café Bar du can-can* in Japan. The dancers and the company were very new and untried; he worked very hard to bring

them up to his standard. Although he was very kind to them on this
initial trip, the dancers found him difficult to work with. They did not
understand his thinking; until this visit the company had performed
only standard classical works. He was not mean, as he could and would
be on a later visit. He understood that they were simply not capable of
doing more.

One of the dancers, Yasuki Sasa, later became a Tudor *protégé*.
He described how, at eighteen, he had only studied ballet for two years
and "could do anything but nothing correctly."

> The first day Tudor lined everyone up to choose his cast. He
> picked me out. He said "tch, tch"; My teacher said "Oh no, no,
> no. He cannot do anything." Tudor replied, "This is my ballet.
> I'm going to chose who does it."

When he was picked out, Sasa was very happy, but then he found
out he was to be only a waiter in *Can-Can*. It was not until later that
Tudor cast him as a soloist. Sasa rembers the early classes.

> All he gave me in class was *tendu, passé*. If I tried something
> else, he said, "No, you cannot. Other people can, but not you." I
> was so ashamed. I could turn eight or nine pirouettes, with no
> form, but he said "No, only a single turn." I could not do it. I
> worked on single turns for three months, because I began to re-
> alize what it meant.[31]

The program presented by the Komaki Ballet included *Lilac Garden*, the Offenbach work, and a version of *The Firebird*. It played for
ten consecutive sold-out houses at the 4,000 seat Nichigeki Theatre.
The audience received it triumphantly. Sasa underlined that the Offenbach ballet offered light-hearted entertainment in contrast to Tudor's
darker works.

Tudor returned to Japan in the late 1960s. He also became very
much involved with the training of Japanese dancers, inviting several
of them to study with him at the Metropolitan Opera Ballet School and
at the Juilliard School. Sasa credits Tudor with making him the dancer
and inspired teacher he later became.

## Ballet Theatre Honors Tudor

During the early to mid 1950s, hurt feelings and bruised egos
notwithstanding, Ballet Theatre continued to perform Tudor's ballets.
Most years they presented full evenings of his works. In 1955 he

brought Sallie Wilson back to the company. There she became a principal dancer specializing in the dramatic roles of Tudor and de Mille. In 1956, in honor of the twenty-fifth anniversary of Tudor's association with the company, a gala event took place. On 1 May the company presented a Tudor evening. They performed *Undertow, The Tragedy of Romeo and Juliet,* and *Offenbach in the Underworld* in its New York debut. Tudor came out of retirement to perform with the company that evening. In recognition of his genius, articles were written honoring his contribution to the world of ballet. The evening was a major event.

He resumed working with Ballet Theatre off and on during the next years, although he devoted the majority of his time to his teaching at the Metropolitan Opera and at the Juilliard School. From the early 1950s onward, he did much of his creative work at these educational institutions, where he choreographed dances appropriate for the level of the young professionals and students. At Ballet Theatre he supervised revivals of his older works, trained new casts, and kept his ballets in presentable order. Because of the subtlety and detail of his dances and their rhythmic complexity, errors and misconceptions constantly crept in. Also, the characterizations had to be constantly refreshed. Although he would deny it ("I would never have done that; it's all wrong!"), he also made slight choreographic emendations to better fit the performer with whom he worked.


## Argentina

In 1958, while on a tour in South America with Ballet Theatre, Tudor was invited to Buenos Aires to stage works for the resident ballet company of the Teatro Colon. He mounted *Pillar of Fire (Columna de Fuego)* to enormous acclaim and produced a new work, *La Leyenda de José* subtitled *José y la mujer de Putifar* ("Joseph and Putifar's Woman.") The commission from the Teatro Colon was very specific: the company wanted a ballet based on the Joseph legend using the music of Richard Strauss. The Strauss score was the same music as Fokine had used for a ballet, mounted in 1914 by the Ballets Russes de Diaghilev. Fokine had treated the same subject matter; his ballet had received only a single performance. No scenery or costume credits appeared in the original program for the Tudor piece; perhaps they were recycled from the company stock.

Seven scenes comprised the ballet: House of Putifar's Woman; Patio; Garden; Living Room; Garden; Putifar's Woman's Bedrooms; Patio. A painting by Tintoretto, *Giuseppe e la Moglie de Putifar,* in the Museo del Prado in Madrid, inspired Tudor. The ballet had the look of the early Venetian painters. Tudor adapted the libretto from the tale in the Koran which gives a fuller account than that of the Bible. Since the relationship between Joseph and Putifar's woman lasted too long to be dealt with in a ballet, Tudor chose to cast the work in the form of a classical Greek tragedy. The action took place in the previous twelve hours, starting in the morning and finishing at the end of the day. Carlos Schiafino and Olga Frances danced the leads, backed by a cast of fifty dancers. The work premiered on 19 August, 1958.[32] The ballet, alas, was deemed unsuccessful. It was never revived and is lost.

## Zen Buddhism

All during the 1950s Tudor had also been questioning and seeking to understand his life on a deeper level. Mary Farkas, his colleague at the First Zen Institute of America said that, at that time, one could not easily learn about Zen, not even in Japan.

> [Tudor] was looking for a better spiritual foundation than the Christian ethic or Freud. When he asked what our place was about, I opened my heart to him. . . . The human mind and condition was the object of study; daily life, the field of practice. Living Zen was what we individualistic Americans were concerned with. To take responsibility for our own actions, to communicate with one another heart-to-heart, mind-to-mind, in the world, not out of it. . . . To become realized human beings was our object. . . . Tudor, vowing he never joined anything, became a member.[33]

Tudor started his association with the First Zen Institute of America some time after his 1954 visit to Japan, attending evening meetings. He continued to do this more or less for ten years. Because of his professional obligations he would often arrive late, but would immediately join the meditating group. Farkas spoke of his ability to freeze, absolutely motionless, in meditation. Originally Farkas held these meetings in her own home. Eventually, in the early 1960s, the Institute moved to quarters at 113 East 30th Street. At the time of the move, Tudor accepted to serve as president.

Farkas described Tudor:

> In the 60s and 70s, bolt upright, thin-lipped, bald, robed in black, Tudor could easily pass for the head of a monastery.

When, as timekeeper, he would enter the high-ceilinged room,
in which meditation is practiced at the Institute, and walk bare-
foot down to the window end between the similarly robed figures seated in facsimile of the Buddha posture, he looked every
inch a master. Timing and discipline built in, his movements
commanded respect, even awe.[34]

Actually it took him several years to achieve that correct posture
and to execute a full Lotus, a sitting position with legs bent and en-
twined. The ability to achieve this, in Tudor's words, "legs bent like
pretzels" position, was aided by his practicing of yoga daily for years.

His duties included leading the chanting and formal bows. He
also rang the bells that called the group to morning meditation. After
he moved into the Institute, in 1964, I remember him rather proudly
telling me that he arose by 5:00 each morning because he had been
entrusted with the bell ringing responsibility. As a leader, he could be
very strict and critical. He accepted no slouching or slackening of concentration—an approach not very different from his attitude toward
dance and dancers.

Later, he also gave lectures on Zen to the other residents. On Sat-
urdays and Sundays he did nothing but meditate.

At this time Tudor began deliberately restricting his intake of
food, a practice that many of his admirers viewed with alarm. Sometimes on the weekends he took only a cup of tea for a whole day. This
attitude toward food continued until his death; in the end he followed a
strict macrobiotic regime, imposed on him by Hugh Laing. At a certain
period Hugh had gotten rather heavy and both he and Tudor were drinking quite a lot. In an effort to control his weight and take conscious
steps toward better health, Hugh began experimenting with dietary restrictions. Since Hugh tended toward the fanatic, eventually he adopted
a strict macrobiotic diet with severe restrictions on the total amount of
food eaten. Of course, since he always knew what was best for those he
loved, Hugh insisted that Tudor join him in this new eating regime.
The diet left Tudor painfully thin and rather weakened; it alarmed many
of us who knew him.

The satisfaction of being abstemious both with food and with
possessions was part of Zen for Tudor. In 1964, when he took up residence at the Zen Institute, he divested himself of many of his worldly
goods. For the rest of his life he lived in a simple room, furnished
only with essentials, a mattress on the floor for a bed. He cooked his
own meals in a community kitchen.

Lance Westergard, at the time a devoted student at The Juilliard
School, tells the follwing story. In 1963, just before he moved into the

Zen Institute, Tudor brought into a class many of his possessions:
books, records and the like. He placed everything on the piano and
invited the students to help themselves. He would no longer need these
things, he announced. Lance remembered the frenzied reaction of the
students, all vying to own something that had belonged to their revered
teacher. Lance, himself, could only observe, a bit horrified. Several
days later, Tudor mentioned noticing that Lance had not joined the
fray, and presented him with a gift.[35]

Many of Tudor's friends remarked on the gradual change in Tudor's behavior as he connected more and more with Zen Buddhism. He
became less caustic, mellower. He could more often show his concern
for those around him, less compelled to camouflage it with barbs and
irony. In his own assessment of how Zen affected him he said that it
saved his mind. He felt able to handle everything better.

Tudor's created his next major ballet, *Hail and Farewell*, in 1959
for the Metropolitan Opera Ballet. It is part of the story of his association with the Met.

# Notes

1. The film resides in the collection at the library of the Juilliard
School.

2. Some sources state that Tudor was asked to be director of the
company if not in 1949, then when he returned in 1962–1964; however, Tudor himself "didn't know I was director until I read it in some
book." Yet, in a biography he wrote for the catalog of the Juilliard
School he says that he left Ballet Theatre to be director of ballet at the
Swedish Royal Opera. In the event, the responsibilities he assumed
were well beyond those of a resident choreographer.

3. Letter from Tudor to Berglund dated 11 June, 1949.

4. Letter from Stockholm dated 13 September, 1949, from Tudor
to the Laings, from the collection of Isabel Brown.

5. Muriel Topaz, interview with Bengt Hager, Stockhom, Sweden, 31 October, 1998.

6. Holger Lundbergh, *The American Swedish Monthly* (April,
1950).

7. Muriel Topaz, interview with Ellen Rasch, Stockholm, Sweden, 3 November, 1998. This and all succeeding Rasch quotes are
taken from the interview.

8. Muriel Topaz, interview with Gerd Andersson, Stockholm,
Sweden , 30 October, 1998.

9. Muriel Topaz, interview with Viveka Ljung, Stockholm, Sweden, 29 October, 1998.

10. Judith Chazin-Bennahum, interview with Mariane Orlando, 9 July, 1988. Also a letter to the author dated 6 March, 2001.

11. Topaz, Andersson interview.

12. Judith Chazin-Bennahum, interview with Lulli Svedlin, 28 July, 1988.

13. Carina Ari (1897–1970) studied in Stockholm and later with Fokine in Copenhagen. In addition to dancing with the Ballet Suédois from 1920 to 1925, she choreographed for the Paris Opéra Comique. Ari established a foundation in Sweden to benefit young dancers. The Foundation awarded a gold medal to outstanding choreographers who contributed to dance in Sweden. In addition to Tudor, over the years recipients included Ashton, Jooss, Béjart, Flindt, and Kragh-Jacobsen.

14. Muriel Topaz, interview with Sallie Wilson, 23 December, 1997.

15. Topaz, Wilson interview.

16. The letter, found in the Jacob's Pillow archives, is dated Friday, 21 June (no year),

17. Chazin-Bennahum, Wilson interview. Also, the Topaz interview with Wilson. Wilson rues the fact that she did not watch and learn the ballet. Had she done so, it would not have been lost.

18. Muriel Topaz, interview with Celia Franca, 16 June, 1998. The dancer was probably Buck Heller who went on to become a respected Broadway choreographer.

19. The quote is from a conversation with Nancy Zeckendorf, dancer, patron of dance, longtime board member of American Ballet Theatre, and friend of both Tudor and Chase.

20. Muriel Topaz, interview with Tanaquil Le Clerq, Weston, Connecticut, 13 September, 1999.

21. Judith Chazin-Bennahum, interview with Sallie Wilson, 6 January, 1988.

22. Muriel Topaz, interview with Betty Cage, New York, 5 May, 1999. Cage was long associated with the New York City Ballet.

23. It has been impossible to establish which Ibert score Tudor was considering. In fact, even with works that came to fruition, it was often difficult or impossible to discover exactly which of a composer's works was used. Programs and reviews most often do not mention the actual work, only the name of the composer.

24. Letter from Tudor to Lincoln Kirstein, dated 19 March, 1954.

25. Letter dated Monday, 20 February, no year but obviously in 1983, received by Betty Cage during Balanchine's final illness.

26. Muriel Topaz, interview with Judith Gesensway Skoogfors, Philadelphia, Pennsylvania, 10 June, 1998.

27. Michael Lland (1925–1989) joined Ballet Theatre in 1945, was promoted to soloist in 1956, and became an important ballet master with the company in 1971.

28. Even as recently as 1953 this was an audacious choice. In the 1950s black students had just begun to be admitted to white ballet schools; before that they were largely barred from studying classical dance. Having a biracial leading couple was even more radical.

29. Topaz, Skoogfors interview.

30. Muriel Topaz, interview with Cecil Bates, Adelaide, Australia, 22 September, 1998.

31. Muriel Topaz, interview with Yasuki Sasa, Philadelphia, Pennsylvania, 23 June, 1999.

32. The author wishes to acknowledge the invaluable help of the distinguished Argentine choreographer Mauricio Wainrot in providing access to this information.

33. Mary Farkas, "Antony Tudor: The First Zen Institute," in *Antony Tudor: The American Years, Choreography and Dance,* 1, Part 2, ed. Muriel Topaz (London: Harwood Academic Publishers, 1989): 59–60.

34. Farkas, "Antony Tudor: The First Zen Institute," 61.

35. Muriel Topaz, interview with Lance Westergard, 22 December, 1997, Brooklyn, New York.

# 5

# The Metropolitan Opera

[N.B. The time periods covered in the next two chapters actually occurred simultaneously. The author has chosen to present each of them
as a story in itself, but they must be read as overlapping events in Tudor's life. Some of the material in Chapters 4 and 7 also overlaps Tudor's time at the Metropolitan Opera and the Juilliard School.]

Simultaneous with his return from Sweden to Ballet Theatre in March,
1950, there occurred one of the most significant events in the life of
Tudor the teacher. Ballet Theatre and the Metropolitan Opera reached an
agreement to work together. The new Opera Ballet would function as
sort of a second company to Ballet Theatre and a ballet school would
be established at the Met. Tudor agreed to direct the school, with a
faculty that included Margaret Craske, of course. He also took on the
task of directing the Opera Ballet Company.

At the time, Lucia Chase was thinking of firing Sallie Wilson;
Lucia thought Sallie was too plump. Tudor had seen Sallie's performance as the dresser in *Gala Performance.* He was sufficiently impressed
with her characterization to summon her to his dressing room and
compliment her. When he discovered Chase was about to let Sallie go,
he said: "Don't fire her. Give her to me." Sallie ended up being the
only dancer who did not have to audition for the Opera Ballet Company—all the others went through an audition process. Tudor had taken
her under his wing. It was the beginning of their long and fruitful association.

During his tenure as director Tudor provided the choreography for
the operas. He had not undertaken this kind of task since his early days
at Covent Garden collaborating with Thomas Beecham.

In 1950 he choreographed *Die Fledermaus.* According to Met
dancer, longtime friend, and devoted acolyte Nancy King (Zeckendorf),
it was a uninspired. Suzanne Ames, another Tudor admirer and a dancer

171

at the Met at that time, remarked that the waltz had no spark. Then he choreographed *La Traviata* and later the "Walpurgis Nacht" ballet from *Faust*, which Ames described as brilliant. The *Annals of the Metropolitan Opera*, held in the archives of the Metropolitan Opera, also lists him as choreographer for *Don Giovanni*. (While there are multiple other sources which confirm Tudor's choreography for *Die Fledermaus, La Traviata, Faust* and, in 1960, *Tannhäuser*, only the *Annals* lists *Don Giovanni*.) He also did a tavern dance for *Wozzeck* that director Herbert Graf thought too shocking and ordered it abandoned. Tudor commented "What do you think this opera is about, anyway?"

For Gluck's opera *Alceste* Tudor produced his most successful contribution. He went to Greece to do research for the choreography, taking along his latest protégé, Bruce Marks.[1] Marks starred in the opera ballet production along with Edith Jerell. The dances were a mixture of Greek and sixteenth-century steps. Pina Bausch,[2] another of his Met students, danced in its large cast.[3]

It is interesting to compare two assessments of the ballet he did for *Tannhäuser*. Judith Chazin-Bennahum, one of the Met dancers and author of the only, very valuable, critical analysis of Tudor's work to date, *The Ballets of Antony Tudor*, remembered: "it was so beautiful. It was breathtaking. And, of course, it was in the dark; we were barely lit. [He had] a way of evoking the mood and the atmosphere of the script, the scenario, with bodies that happened to be almost like moving sculpture."[4]

John Martin, distinguished critic for the *New York Times* commented:

> He kept the lights as dim as possible, and in the first half of he ballet he filled the back of the stage with a milling and indecipherable mass of partner-lifting. In the second half, however, he really came to grief. With three forlorn damsels from the corps stranded mid stage, raising a foot tentatively here and tracing a minuscule floor path there, he produced an Olympian longueur, no less.[5]

Suzanne Ames, recalls that one of the most interesting things he did had nothing to do with dance. The 1959 production of *Manon Lescaut* contained a scene during which Lescaut is released from jail and sent to the new world. Each of the girls in the scene, portraying prostitutes, had a name; Tudor decided to do the same thing with the ballet.

Each was given a character and each had to find her own rags from the costume department.

> We spent hours. We were on stage a long time, but we never danced. I chose to be full of myself, young; nobody was going to touch me. One woman was old and shaking. Another was angry and ready to spit and did spit. One was frightened. One was sick. He worked on these characters with us for weeks until we got it right. . . . It was a sensation.[6]

Tudor's role as choreographer for the opera never satisfied him. He complained that there was never enough time, that he could not choreograph the way he wanted and that no one appreciated the seriousness of dance. Always seen as comic relief or frivolous theater, dance had a "bring on the girls" function. The way the opera house was run disenchanted him. He was not really an opera choreographer and he knew it.

A memo from Tudor to Met opera administrators Rudolf Bing and John Gutman expounded on the history of all-ballet evenings of the Royal Ballet in England. It stated that Ninette de Valois began them in 1931. At that point the company already had seven ballets in its repertoire and had danced some of them for the Camargo Society. They gave performances at the Old Vic, not at Covent Garden. The company moved to the large theater only after quite a few additional years of dancing and maturing together. Tudor continued:

> I am invited to produce a ballet at the Metropolitan Opera using its regular corps of dancers. You wish me to utilise some of the costumes already available in the wardrobe, or practice costumes, and to present it without scenery. This is to be done for one performance.

> Any time I have a ballet I wish and am ready to do, I think one of our other ballet companies will be more than willing to present it. I will then be working with a company consisting of a fairly well seasoned *corps de ballet*, several good and experienced soloists and a few stars. I am fairly sure that means will be found to provide me with decor and costumes although it is understood that extravagant ideas cannot be admitted. In addition to my production fee, should the ballet be a considerable success, it may be shown from twenty-five to a hundred and twenty-five times in its first year at a royalty per performance of $25.00.

Question: What are the particular and special possibilities  open
to me at the Metropolitan, as opposed to the established companies, that will counterbalance the seeming disadvantages I
have mentioned?[7]

## Tudor the Teacher

After his first year at the Metropolitan Opera Tudor decided that
he would stay on as head of the school to teach, but would no longer
choreograph the operas. The Opera brought in Zachary Solov as resident choreographer, a happier solution for all. Later on, in 1963, Alicia
Markova took on the task of directing the opera ballet company.

Tudor's greatest contribution to the Met was the school, immeas-
urably enhanced by his impeccable teaching. He gave two classes daily
at the Met: professional classes in the morning three days a week, adagio (partnering) classes, and what he called a production class. Many of
the finest dancers of the time from various companies flocked to the
professional classes. In addition to Nora Kaye and Hugh Laing, one
could see on a random day Lawrence Rhodes, Fernando Bujones,
Patricia Neary, Gelsey Kirkland, or Maria Tallchief among others.

Tudor's teaching profoundly influenced his students—the ones
who had the courage to stick with him. What was it about that teaching
that made him so remarkable?

He inspired dancers to attack the movement and really experience
it. He gave them not just steps, but an approach to dance. He was always probing. Several of the people I interviewed spoke about one of
his devices. He would come up to you and say, "Turn." It didn't matter
which way you turned, but you had to do it with absolutely no preparation. You simply had to find your center and hang on to it. Tudor
never found technical details particularly interesting; he took them for
granted. What the movement said interested him. That is why he and
Margaret Craske made such an excellent and complementary pair of
teachers. He taught what to do and she taught how to do it, the technical details of producing the required movement.

Tudor constructed his classes quite intelligently, except when he
went off on a tangent. What one did at the barre led to what one did in
the center work and prepared one for the traveling combinations. On
occasion these intelligent constructions left out the warming up of
some muscle groups, so some dancers didn't much like his barre. One
did better in his classes if he or she thoroughly warmed up beforehand.
Sometimes Tudor veered off on what he classed as his "bright ideas."

He pursued these tangents because they had some resonance for what he was doing choreographically, or because he had a momentary conviction about the only right way to perform some step.

He gave tremendously complex combinations and he constantly experimented musically. No matter what level you achieved, he pitched the class just a little beyond comfortable. It was always a challenge.

He did not ever want to "see" the dancer do a physical preparation for the next step. He considered preparations an anathema and wanted them as inconspicuous as possible; they interrupted the flow of the movement. Of course he expected the dancer to toss off the virtuosic steps such as quadruple *pirouettes* and multiple *tours en l'air*. He wanted these movements performed effortlessly to be sure, but never done as star turns or the primary concern. What the movement communicated always took precedence. He hated fingers, flourishes, and anything merely decorative.

He loved reversing everything, not only exchanging right for left, but also backward for forward. It forced one to think about the combination. He experimented constantly, giving movement that, on more than one occasion, was anatomically impossible to accomplish. In trying, however, the dancer extended his or her possibilities. He demanded much more than the student thought he or she was capable of, and he got it!

Donald Mahler remembers a time when Tudor asked him to do *glissade, jeté à côte, jeté renversé* in a circle, quite an advanced *enchaînement*. Mahler had studied ballet for exactly two months. "He took me into a studio and put a broom across my shoulders so I would get the feeling of going around the periphery of the circle. He made me do it and I did it—or something like it."[8] I, myself, remember Tudor teaching me how to do *renversé* by putting a waist basket across my back in order to get the appropriate rounded, convex feeling in the upper back.

William Burdick recalls that the classes Tudor gave did not resemble anything else he had ever experienced. They were so full of organic movement.

> The technique was inside you; you had to dance from the motivation that was centered inside the body. . . . He talked about the line and the strength of the back. Whether you had your back to the audience [he would sometimes have the class face the back of the room] or your front to the audience, the back was motivated and carried the whole spirit of the movement.[9]

I remember another of Tudor's favorite devices. He would ask the
dancer to sing while performing a *port de bras*. One could not accomplish this feat unless the throat was open, the back and the lungs extended. For me, this proved much more meaningful than being asked to
open the back and throat. As a student I didn't really know how to do
that. But by singing, I discovered how.

He would often construct an entire *enchaînement* out of a single
step *(glissade, sissonne,* and *temps lié* were among his favorites) by
giving an unbelievable number of permutations. His imagery and
imagination poured into his classes.

Patricia Neary, who became a soloist with the New York City
Ballet, was practicing *pirouettes* in his class one day. Tudor asked if
getting married interested her; did she wish to attract a husband? She
could not figure out what he meant for a while. Finally, she got the
message. At the end of the *pirouette* she tilted her torso slightly backward. She went away from any spectator instead of going forward with
the body weight, presenting herself and appealing to the observer.
Typically, he made her think through the problem by use of a metaphorical message.

Tudor occasionally devoted a class to one student, concentrating
on what that particular student most needed. Often it was somebody he
liked, someone he expected to use in a ballet. Just as often, however,
the least talented student captured his imagination. He would work dili-
gently with him or her, to the amusement and fury of everyone else. His
classes were brilliant, but he was also very perverse.

Tudor's partnering classes were unique—full of fanciful lifts. He
taught such things as where the man's gaze should be on the woman's
shoulder, where to spot when a woman approaches her partner, what to
look for. As he did in his choreography, he arrived at the psychological
through the physical. He taught where and how to place the hands, not
what the man should be feeling when he touched the woman. Of these
classes Donald Mahler recalls:

> Other people teach adagio work: how to lift a girl, how to hold
> her. But he taught partnering: what you two do together. He did a
> lot of *Sleeping Beauty* and *Swan Lake*. But he would teach things
> in them that no one else thought about. He taught a lot more than
> ballet. . . . He taught a way of working and a way of looking and
> thinking about things. . . . For example, when the Swan Queen is
> on the floor, she doesn't have to do so much with the arms be-
> cause the spot light is on her and it picks up the movement. . . . He

was very big on challenging you until you revealed yourself
to other people. It could be very painfu

## Production Class

Tudor's most famous class was the one he called production
class. It resembled "method" acting as taught at the Herbert Berghof
studio in Manhattan. It was akin to the type of training offered at the
Actor's Studio, which produced some of the best-known stars of their
generation, among them Shelley Winters, Ben Gazzara, Eli Wallach,
Geraldine Page, and occasional students Marilyn Monroe and Marlon
Brando. It also brought to mind the Stanislavsky method.

Tudor brought in guests to teach in his production class: Jean
Louis Barrault, the French mime; a teacher of Japanese dance named
Sohomi Tachibana; an unidentified East Indian teacher. He would give
the students problems to solve, a scenario to experience:

> Somebody is coming home after a long time. You hear the door.
> You're standing there. You don't know what the result will be.
> Show what happens, but without raising your arms or moving
> your feet. Do it with the breath alone and the neck.

The neck was very important in Tudor's canon. He would tell you
to take your hair at the back of your head and pull up your neck. One
must not jut out the chin, but should feel the plumb line as if sus-
pended. Tudor himself stood and presented himself this way.

Nancy Zeckendorf found the production classes fascinating. She
said that those who experienced them will never forget them. They
differed from anything that other dance teachers ever taught. She recalls
Tudor asking the students, all professionals, to do a *port de bras* first
in a blue light, then in a gold light, then pink. "What does the back of
your neck feel like? How are you radiating the color from the back of
you neck?" he would ask. One of his favorite devices was to have the
dancers all sit in a circle with their legs crossed. You had to be an umbrella—without moving a muscle. With your eyes closed. You opened
the umbrella, pushed it up and pulled it back down, furled it and then
fastened it. Everyone judged whether you had done it effectively. In
one of the exercises he taught how to laugh and to cry. You had to
keep exhaling so much that you started to laugh. Or you would inhale
so much that you began to cry.[10]

Donald Mahler remembers another problem Tudor gave.

> He wanted the men to act out a young girl in love. Of course,
> nobody could do it. Everybody was mortified. He finally threw
> up his hands and said, "All right, I'll do it." And he did. He be-
> came a young girl in love; it was unbelievable. Miss Craske
> happened to come into the studio during this and stood on the
> balcony watching. Afterwards she said to me: "The trouble with
> you boys is that you are afraid of making fools of yourself." He
> didn't want you to make a fool of yourself, but he wanted you
> to get past that fear.[11]

The effort on his part to get the dancer to get further into a character than he or she thought possible engendered Tudor's cruelty and teasing. He tried to entice the performer beyond "acting" the part. He
wanted the dancer to abandon stopping him or herself, whether con-
sciously or unconsciously, and "become" the part.

Miss Craske and Tudor were the two master teachers at the Metropolitan Opera School. In addition to teaching with Tudor, Margaret
Craske was a very popular teacher elsewhere in New York. She adhered
fairly strictly to the material that the great dancer/teacher Enrico Cecchetti had established. It used set exercises and emphasized the place-
ment of the body in order to achieve a pure line. Not only had she
served as ballet mistress for Tudor's London Ballet and later for Ballet
Theatre, but also for many years she had her own school, backed by a
former pupil, Robert Ossario.

Sometime in the early fifties a rift developed between Tudor and
Craske. Hugh Laing had just returned from a stint in Hollywood performing in the film version of *Brigadoon*. It happened to be a difficult
time for him. Much disgruntled with Lucia Chase, he planned to leave
Ballet Theatre. Apparently Craske habitually invited soloists to the
front of the class. She invited Hugh to the front, but he declined. He
claimed he was out of shape and needed to work at the back of the
class. This exchange repeated itself for several days. Finally Craske
abandoned the effort and ceased to invite him to come forward. True to
form, Hugh was furious and his fury influenced Tudor. Scenes ensued.
At one point Tudor even asked his loyal students, among them Sallie
Wilson, to make a choice, Craske or Tudor. Some did, after much soul
searching, but some, Wilson included, refused. It was a tense time for
everyone. Like history repeating itself, it brought to mind how Tudor
had asked dancers to choose between himself and Marie Rambert early
in his career, when he left the Rambert company to form the London
Ballet. Maude Lloyd had also refused to make the choice.

Tudor and Craske finally agreed to patch up their differences. Craske accepted an invitation to dinner with Tudor providing he promised not to attack her. They went to a restaurant and made small talk. At one point Tudor could no longer suppress his hostility. Miss Craske followed a spiritual leader named Baba. Her belief was central to her life and she had even made a pilgrimage to India during the war years. Tudor looked at her and said, "Baba's done a very bad job on you." She looked right back at him and replied, "Yes, and you're the worst teacher of pointe work in America." In spite of this, a sort of reconciliation between the two followed.

During the warring period, Tudor was teaching class when Craske came down from the dressing room on the balcony at the Met studio. Tudor called out "Miss Crasky, Miss Crasky (what he called her when he was teasing)." "Yes, Tudor." "Do you know that this young man here doesn't know where his backside is?" She looked over and said, "Well, I'm sure you'll show him." Tudor just turned white; his joke had backfired.[12]

Sometime in 1951 Tudor became involved in a film project with Maya Deren, an avant-garde filmmaker. Tudor was to make movement which she would film and then put together into some sort of movie. He decided to work with the students from the Met school. The film turned out to concern a sleepwalker who wandered through the sky and saw the constellations. Deren filmed in negative, so all the dancers wore black body paint. The background was white, like a photographer's paper backdrop. Of course, the dancers perspired and it showed. Donald Mahler remembers the outcome as "just a mess." The work, called *The Very Eye of Night*, consisted of plotless sequences of movement, some of which derived from Tudor's very early ballet *The Planets*.[13]

## Choreographing for the Company

In 1956–1957 Tudor resumed the post of director of the Metropolitan Opera Ballet. He agreed to direct the company once again, for a one-year period. The then company director, Zachary Solov, took a leave of absence as director, but continued on as choreographer. This "one-year" arrangement lasted for seven years, through the 1962–1963 season. From 1961 on, Tudor acted only as artistic director, with Mattlyn Gavers assuming the everyday administrative functions.

Tudor instituted the innovative "ballet evenings," programs devoted solely to ballet works rather than to opera. Not since the 1930s, when the opera dance company was under George Balanchine's direction,[14] had the Met presented such evenings. They turned out to be historic occasions. The first took place in March, 1959. Four ballets constituted the program. John Butler's *In the Beginning* had music by Samuel Barber and a set by Jac Venza, who went on to produce the Dance in America series for WNET television. The ballet featured Bruce Marks as Adam and Lupe Serano as Eve. Alexandra Danilova[15] set a divertissement called *Les Diamants*, with Serrano, Marks, and four women, to the music of Charles de Bériot. Herbert Ross[16] choreographed *The Exchange* to the Poulenc *Organ Concerto*, for Nora Kaye. The Catholic Church picketed the ballet because in it an angel came down and had sex with Nora.

The crowning glory of the evening was a new ballet by Antony Tudor, *Hail and Farewell*, to the music of Richard Strauss's *Festival March, Serenade for Winds,* and *Four Last Songs*. The female soloists were Lupe Serrano, Edith Jerell, Audrey Keane, and Nora Kaye, with William Burdick, and Ron [Sequoio] Murray among the men.

Tudor started with the music and then chose the dancers he wanted for the ballet. He would have the pianist play the music and point out particular moments in the score that fascinated him. William Burdick, one of the dancers spoke of how

> He would talk about who we were—even though it was an abstract work. . . . He wanted us to be young and innocent as if we were dancing for the first time. . . .T he movement was very simple, organic, with long beautiful lines, very flowing like the music. The partnering was gorgeous with the dancers being close to each other, intimately relating to each other, and yet abstract . . . Behind the singer [Eleanor Steber] were a scrim and a platform; we danced up on the platform. . . . It was one of the most exciting things that I have ever done in my life. Unfortunately, that was the end of it. After the initial performances, it was never done again. [17]

According to Elizabeth Sawyer[18] the title comes from an elegiac poem by the Roman poet, Catullus, and had a very special symbolism for Tudor. The work came at a time when he was seriously considering retiring as a choreographer. Conceivably, he planned *Hail and Farewell* as his swan song. The title resonated with many personal associations. It "hailed" his successes; his native land, which he regretted having lost; the loyal dancers who worked with him, most particularly Nora Kaye; the genius of Strauss; and many other things. The "farewell" was directed to Nora who was retiring, to his own ambitions which were more and more in conflict with the Zen principles he was adopting, and, perhaps, to his creative role in dance. In fact, according to Sawyer, the ballet actually contained choreographic snippets of many of Tudor's earlier works heavily edited and camouflaged.

The piece opened with a dance of greeting (hailing) for the corps; the group also danced the second section. There followed four solo episodes: Spring, September, Going to Sleep and In Evening's Glow. This final section was a solo for Nora Kaye. It contained convoluted choreographic reference to Hagar's material in *Pillar of Fire*. Sawyer says that at the end the audience sat hushed for several seconds before starting to applaud.

The work, which received only two performances, had great potential and many beautiful moments. Most critics dismissed the group sections but highly praised the *Four Last Songs*. Tudor's desire to rework the dance was completely frustrated as no company came forward to produce it. (What a pity! We may all have been deprived of yet another Tudor masterwork because he was not given the appropriate opportunity.)

In 1963 Tudor also composed a short ballet specifically for his dancers at the Met. Called *Fandango*, to piano music of Fra Antonio Soler, the ballet used only the familiar classical vocabulary, but with a difference. Presented as a competition, the dance closely mirrored the personalities and idiosyncracies of the five women in the original cast: Edith Jerrell, Suzanne Ames, Ayako Ogawa, Nancy King (Zeckendorf), and Ingrid Blecker (originally Judith Chazin-Bennahum). All of the women had wonderful, distinctive personalities. On the 39th Street roof stage of the old Met, work on the dance started with their first listening to the music. Then Tudor worked with each dancer separately. Original cast member Suzanne Ames commented:

> Edith was sort of stone-faced in her way; Ayako was very outspoken so she spoke out when she danced. Nancy had her own very elegant quiet way of doing things. I thought I could do everything faster. If he said do something once I'd do it twice when once was enough.[19]

Nancy Zeckendorf added:

> It's amazing because each of us was personified in the piece. It was all very intricate but he really played off the personalities of the five people . . . It's a lot of "I can do this better than you,

one upmanship, move over, let me show you how it's done."
And it's very funny. It particularly parodied Suzanne Ames. She
liked to sing, so Tudor put that in for her, and then we all laughed
at her which we sometimes did. She always wanted to work on
pointe, so everything he gave her was on pointe . . . It was the best
piece I ever did in my life. I loved it. It was very hard to pick up
and learn because it was like "knitting."[20]

Ames called the work "a nice, evil ballet" and both she and Zeckendorf described how Tudor set the scene. He spoke of the heat in Madrid in the summer and urged them not to remain cool. He also began
by saying he had no idea what he was going to do, so they should all
try together, playing with the material.

They performed the dance fifteen times in two seasons,[21] mostly
in morning performances for high school audiences, who apparently
had no trouble in understanding the jokes. It was very well received.
*Fandango* was revived at the Juilliard School in 1968, and later, in
1988, at American Ballet Theatre. Being a chamber ballet, it "read"
better in small houses and more intimate settings.

The delightful task of notating the work fell to me, along with my
then student Christine Clark Smith. We did this during rehearsals for
the Juilliard revival. Studying *Fandango* in detail is like taking a course
in choreography. The compositional craft it exhibits is extraordinary. It
contains every kind of formal and rhythmic manipulation of basic material that a choreographer needs to know about as part of his or her
basic equipment. Of course, the formal manipulation is so thoroughly
embedded in the steps themselves or rather in the dance (Tudor hated
"steps") that only through careful and thorough analysis can one recognize the compositional devices.

When Dame Alicia Markova assumed the directorship of the Met
company in 1963, she convinced the intendant Rudolf Bing of the importance of ballet. He permitted her to stage *Les Sylphides* as a curtain
raiser for the opera *Don Pasquale*. Its success led to evenings in 1965
and 1966 devoted solely to ballet.

The third and final of these Metropolitan Opera ballet evenings, in
1966, was another truly historic event. It featured two Tudor works,
one a world premiere and the other a United States premiere. The third
work was the first American performance of August Bournonville's[22]
*La Ventana* coached by one of the world authorities on the Danish
School, Hans Brenaa.

The program opened with the new Tudor piece, *Concerning Oracles*. It is a sprawling work for a large cast in three unrelated scenes.
Each scene concerns itself with a different gift of prophecy. Originally

Tudor planned to tie the scenes together by having a gypsy fortune-teller and two male gypsies appear in each. He ran out of time, however, and did not finish the ballet. Consequently, the men appear only in the first section.

Each section is set in a different historical period. The first, called "Mary Queen of Scots" for some mysterious reason since she never appears in the ballet, is Elizabethan. It featured Edith Jerrell as a young woman confronted by the prophecy of an orb of power, a chaplet of marriage, and a skull of death. For the second section, set in the Romantic era, Tudor reworked his earlier *Les Mains gauches*, originally composed at Jacob's Pillow (See Chapter 4). The cast comprised Ivan Allen and Carolyn Martin with Nira Paz as the fortuneteller. The two sections take place in a sinister, foreboding atmosphere. By all estimations the third section became the run-away hit. Set in the late 1800s, the time of de Maupassant, it depicts a hilarious French provincial wedding picnic, a drunken outdoor affair. The section begins with a reading of Tarot cards, followed by a wedding scene with three brides and one groom. Then it progresses to the main *pas de deux* composed for a very tall woman (Sally Brayley Bliss, five feet seven and one-half inches off pointe) and a very short young man (Lance Westergard, approximately five feet). Lift after lift ends at the last moment with the woman unexpectedly supporting the man. While, starting with contemporary dance of the late twentieth century, such a gender role reversal is not so unusual, at the time it was startling and unheard of, particularly in classical dance. Bawdy and quite daring, the piece exemplifies Tudor's irony and wit.

Sally Brayley Bliss, one of the dancers of the Metropolitan Opera Ballet who was later to become the sole trustee of the Tudor Trust, remembers working on the piece. She recounts how, one Saturday afternoon after they had worked about a week, Tudor said that it was time he started choreographing for the two redheads. She was certain he told her on a Saturday so she would spend the whole weekend puzzling about it. Totally Tudor.

> I was an old maid aunt at this French family picnic. Lance was my dreamy and imaginative nephew. As he approached my part of the table, I stripped off my dowdy dress to reveal a beautiful, sexy, pink peignoir. We started to waltz. As the music built . . . the choreography would develop toward a lift. But at the very last minute, we reve rsed roles and I would lift him. . . . It was absolutely hilarious. Lance and I were very serious about it,

Sally Brayley (Bliss) and Lance Westergard in *Concerning Oracles*. *Photograph courtesy of Sally Brayley Bliss*

which, of course, made the dance even funnier. . . . It stopped the performance.[23]

Bliss thinks Tudor conceived the idea for this section of the ballet in one of his classes at the Juilliard School. He had given a combination to three tall girls. Suddenly he turned to Lance and said, "Do something." Lance, having no idea what to do, wandered around among the girls, running in *plié*. Tudor began laughing out loud.

There is, perhaps, another source for that section. In one of my interviews with Maude Lloyd, Tudor's first ballerina and dear friend, she told of vacationing one summer in Mentoni (or Menton, a small town at the Franco-Italian border). One rainy day she, her husband Nigel Gosling, Tudor, and Hugh Laing wandered into a French family picnic. Tudor became fascinated with the goings on and so, soaking wet, they stayed and watched for a long time. During one of our interviews, Maude told me this tale quite in passing; she had never even seen *Concerning Oracles*.

Bliss spoke of the great difficulty of some of the material. Tudor would demonstrate in his shirt and tie, everything pressed and just right. He would show them what he wanted with his big street shoes on. The dancers would explain to him that it was impossible to do that on pointe. His answer? "Do it!" And they did.

Lance Westergard remembered

He never told me my character's title. And I didn't know it until I saw the big poster outside of the Met. There was a cast list and there it was. The Fool: Lance Westergard, debut. That was the first time I knew my character.[24]

Lance is one of several dancers who feel that Tudor directly influenced their careers:

If it hadn't been for that particular evening I don't think I would have had a career in the concert end of the business or stayed in that side of the work. Because of my height, what I had to offer didn't fit into ballet companies very easily.

Lance went on to dance in the concert field for many years and eventually to be associate director of a company with the dancer/choreographer Kathryn Posin, as well as appearing in Lotte Goslar's Pantomime Circus. He now teaches at Hofstra University.

By consensus the most important and impressive ballet of the evening, *Echoing of Trumpets*, came second on the program. Tudor made this anti-war ballet for his beloved Royal Swedish Ballet in 1963. *Trumpets* marked his return to choreographing major dances after a hiatus of several years. Before its Metropolitan Opera appearance, the dance had never played in the United States. It was clearly an unqualified success—a strong statement and an eloquent and moving ballet. (For more about *Echoing of Trumpets* see Chapter 7.) Walter Terry in his review said:

> Antony Tudor . . . received a standing ovation. . . . The unmistakable hit of the evening was the *Echoing of Trumpets*, for this was the work which had the audience, filling the old house to capacity, hushed and intent during its course and cheering at its conclusion. This represented more than the success of a new ballet. It signaled the return of Tudor, whose choreographic genius seemed to have remained fallow, for the most part, over several years, to a position of distinction once again. [25]

Clive Barnes called the work "massively impressive" and Tudor's most important achievement since the 1945 *Undertow*.[26]

Everybody who was anybody in the dance world was in the opera house that night, among them George Balanchine, Paul Taylor, and Merce Cunningham. To my great good fortune, I was also able to attend. The atmosphere was electric, the audience hushed and respectful. Everyone waited—some for a triumph and others to see Tudor fall flat on his face. Neither actually occurred, although the evening came closer to a triumph. Generous, heartening, and exciting applause made the evening one to remember.

Tudor's contractual arrangements with the Metropolitan Opera are worth examining as they give another insight into his legendary lack of interest in money. His initial contract for directing the school, dated 7 March, 1951, assured him first of all of complete control of the curriculum and standards. He agreed to teach at least fifteen hours weekly for forty weeks. The contract set his remuneration at $100 per week plus 10 percent of any net school income which exceeded $6,000, an arrangement renewed annually for several years. By comparison, the minimum wage at the time reached $.75 per hour and, in 1955, the price of a ticket to a Broadway show was $6.00. As director of the program at the Juilliard School of Music, notorious for underpaying its staff, Martha Hill earned $7,000 annually. Even in 1951, payment of less than $7.00 to teach a one-and-a-half-hour class was niggardly, not to mention virtually no fee being provided for directing the school.

Not until 1956–1957 did Tudor's weekly salary rise to $112.50 and the share of the profits was 12 1/2 percent. For the few years for which figures are available, this percentage resulted in a payment of some $700–800. (Note that in 1956 the minimum wage in the United States rose to $1.00 per hour.) In 1957 Tudor's weekly payment reached $152.50 but for only thirty weeks. A note states the salary was computed on the basis of $11 per hour. Although by contract his fee was to be $135 weekly in 1962–1963, a note appended to the contract amends this to $130 weekly, with Tudor's accord. By the time he left the school, the weekly payment had risen again to $135 and his contractual obligation included teaching only nine hours weekly.

At present, nine contact hours[27] weekly is a normal teaching load at colleges and universities, although dance people all seem to do more than that. In the early seventies a very low salary for a college teacher was about $8,000 annually. For the 1963–1964 season Tudor's salary at Juilliard was $6,500 for the thirty-week academic year. At Juilliard, he taught eight classes (twelve hours) weekly and supervised the ballet department, with some additional compensation for extra classes and rehearsals.

For Tudor's work directing the opera ballet company in 1956 he earned $1,000, raised to $1,500 for 1958–1959, and $2,000 the following year. The fee remained at this level until he left the Metropolitan Opera Ballet, although his duties were much reduced beginning in 1961–1962. In 1960 he earned an additional $1,000 for choreographing *Alceste*. While these fees are not comparable with today's salaries, the dollar having changed its value a great deal, they can hardly be construed as grand.

By the late sixties Tudor had virtually stopped signing contracts. An amusing letter to him from John Guttman, the man then in charge of operational matters at the Metropolitan Opera, begins, "Since for several years now I have not been able to get your autograph on a contract for the Met Opera Ballet School let me try to get a signed agreement with you in this more informal way."[28] The letter stipulated $200 weekly and, for the first time, four-weeks' paid vacation. It also says that he may leave the country if necessary as long as he provides a substitute, who will be paid $20 hourly. Tudor did sign this letter of agreement.

The mid sixties saw the end of Tudor's relationship with the Metropolitan Opera. By 1963 he had ceded the artistic directorship of the company, and in 1966 he relinquished his post as director of the school.

# Notes

1. Marks went on to an international dance career as *primeur danseur* with American Ballet Theatre and, with his ballerina wife Toni Lander, the Royal Danish Ballet. When he retired from performing he directed Ballet West and, later, the Boston Ballet.

2. Bausch is one of the most honored of choreographers, being an exemplary exponent of a new expressionism. Her company, based in Wupperthal, Germany, tours internationally to great acclaim.

3. The material about the Metropolitan Opera was assembled in part from the following interviews all conducted by the author: William Burdick, 23 December, 1997; Nancy Zeckendorf, 22 October, 1997; Donald Mahler, 10 January, 1998; and a collective interview with Burdick, Zeckendorf, and Mahler, 10 January, 1998.

4. Muriel Topaz, interview with Judith Chazin-Bennahum, 31 May, 1991.

5. John Martin, "The Dance: At the Opera," *New York Times*, undated.

6. Muriel Topaz, interview with Suzanne Ames, 5 March, 1998.

7. Unsigned, undated letter found in the Isabel Brown archives.

8. Topaz, Mahler interview.

9. Topaz, Burdick interview.

10. Topaz, Zeckendorf interview.

11. Topaz, Mahler interview.

12. Topaz, Burdick interview

13. This description is based on the Topaz–Mahler interview and a viewing of the film itself. The movie is housed at the New York Public Library Dance Collection.

14. Balanchine was associated with the Metropolitan Opera from 1935–1938.

15. Alexandra Danilova was the very famous ballerina who created many roles for Diaghilev's Ballets Russes. She was Balanchine's companion when they were both in Paris and, after emigrating to America, taught at the School of American Ballet.

16. When he left American Ballet Theatre where he had danced and choreographed, Ross went to Hollywood as a producer and director. Perhaps his most famous film was *The Turning Point*. Ross married Nora Kaye. After Kaye's death Ross remarried, this time to Lee Radziwell, sister of Jacqueline Onassis.

17. Topaz, Burdick interview.

18. Elizabeth Sawyer was Tudor's longtime accompanist and friend. She and Tudor exchanged letters for many years and she is in

the process of writing memoirs about their friendship. A chapter of her proposed book was published by *Dance Chronicle*, Summer, 1997 issue, which was a source for these comments.

19. Topaz, Ames interview.

20. Topaz, Zeckendorf interview. "Knitting" is a colloquial term sometimes used by dancers to describe very intricate footwork.

21. This and most other hard facts about dates and performances of the Metropolitan Opera Ballet were taken from *Annals of the Metropolitan Opera, 1883–1985*, ed. Gerald Fitzgerald (Boston: Metropolitan Opera Guild and G. K. Hall & Co., 1989). *Fandango* was previewed on 1 March, 1963, and received its official premiere on 7 March. Original cast member Edith Jerrell danced in the preview but was replaced by Carole Kroon at the premiere. Ingrid Blecker had replaced the injured Judith Chazin (Bennahum) early in the rehearsal period.

22. August Bournonville, born 1805, was a Danish dancer and choreographer. During his youth he went to Paris where he partnered the reigning ballerina Marie Taglioni. Bournonville's choreography has been carefully preserved by the Danish Royal Ballet and forms the backbone of that company's repertoire to this day.

23. Sally Brayley Bliss, "Antony Tudor: Personal Reminiscences, 1950–66," *Choreography and Dance*, 1, part 2. Muriel Topaz, ed. (London: Harwood Academic Publishers, 1989): 34.

24. Muriel Topaz, interview with Lance Westergard, 22 December, 1997.

25. Walter Terry, "Premiers for Tudor at Met," *New York Herald Tribune*, 28 March, 1966.

26. Clive Barnes, "Metropolitan Opera Ballet Presents 3 New Works," *New York Times*, 28 March, 1966. Mr. Barnes began his career as a dance critic in England and later emigrated to the United States where he was both dance and theater critic for the *New York Times* and later for the *New York Post*.

27. The phrase "contact hours" is academic jargon for the number of hours a teacher is actually in the classroom as opposed to time spent marking papers, holding office hours, or doing preparation, research, student counseling, or committee work.

28. The letter and contracts for previous years were found in the archives of the Metropolitan Opera. The author thanks archivist Pennino for his help.

*Judgment of Paris.* From left to right: Maria Karnilova, Agnes de Mille, and Lucia Chase. *Photograph by Fred Fehl, courtesy of Sallie Wilson*

# 6

# The Juilliard Experiment

> The most important event in the 1951–1952 dance season is already in progress. The new Department of Dance, established by The Juilliard School of Music,[1] has just commenced its first academic year and even at this early date the project has already assumed major significance because of its distinguished faculty and their noteworthy aims.[2]

The school's 1951–1952 bulletin announced that:

> In establishing a Department of Dance, Juilliard School of Music offers for the first time a comprehensive education in this art in conjunction with training in music. The primary aim of the new Department is to train students to become expert dancers, choreographers, teachers, and at the same time develop in them penetrative musical insights. Dance is studied as a major performing art and is considered from more than one particular point of view and technique. In addition to ballet and modern dance, the two major schools of our period, the folk idiom is included and technical studies encompass the important contributions to this art. Repertory works of ballet and modern dance are studied and recreated under the personal direction of the artist–choreographers.

While today there is nothing remarkable about dance being taught in a conservatory or other institution of higher learning, in 1951 it was pioneering. No academic institution prepared dancers for life in the profession; the few colleges which did offer dance prepared the students to teach modern dance. No conservatory offered a program for the profession-bound dancer. In fact, the Juilliard bulletin's very statement labeling the dance as a major art form seemed controversial. Only the extraordinary vision of the then president, William Schuman, and his chosen department head, Martha Hill, brought this idea into focus and

191

allowed it to flower. Not only was the basic idea of such a program revolutionary, but combining training in both ballet and modern dance constituted practically a heresy at the time. Martha Hill assembled an impeccable faculty, among them Antony Tudor, Margaret Craske, Martha Graham, Doris Humphrey, Louis Horst, Agnes de Mille, Ann Hutchinson, and later Hanya Holm and José Limón. Hill also engaged Jerome Robbins as faculty in the original plan, but his other commitments made his participation impossible.

From 1961 on, many dance programs established in higher education based themselves on the so-called Conservatory Model. The curriculum at Juilliard, as conceived by Schuman and Hill and begun in 1951, served as the paradigm for all such programs.

Martha Hill wrote an evocative description of Tudor at the initial press conference:

> Antony Tudor stood out clearly. The press conference was held in a large, anonymous room, probably at the Lotus Club. . . . In the hubbub of meeting and greeting, there was Tudor standing so still and yet so alert, particularly those darting eyes. He stood slightly withdrawn from center stage . . . alone, observing.

> He was so right if he was intuiting undercurrents in the press conference situation other than simple celebration and explanation of the new project to establish a conservatory approach in the teaching of dance. For there were conflicting evaluations in the press articles emerging from this meeting. There was shock at the idea of ballet and modern dance under the same roof. Antony Tudor, Margaret Craske, Martha Graham, Doris Humphrey, Agnes de Mille, Louis Horst joined in the same faculty! Madness, destined for collapse! Added disbelief came from the Russophiles. How could one base training in ballet on the British concept? [3]

## Tudor's Students and Teaching Methods

Fortunately I was among those chosen by stringent audition to attend Juilliard in the first entering class. A motley crew, we found it difficult to understand the criteria for our acceptance. The exceedingly rigorous program made us wonder how much our stamina and toughness counted. A shake-down period ensued during which the faculty as well as the students had to learn how to work together harmoniously. Eventually, if not immediately, they did. In the first three years those students in attendance included Rena Gluck, one of the charter members of the Bat-Dor Company and later director of dance at the Rubin Academy in Jerusalem; Nancy King (Zeckendorf) a dancer at the Metropolitan Opera and on Broadway and for many years a member of the Board of Directors of American Ballet Theatre; Carolyn Brown, longtime soloist with the Merce Cunningham Company and Cunningam's partner for much of that; Richard England, who directed the second companies of American Ballet Theatre and the Joffrey Ballet; Donya Feuer, who worked with the filmmaker Ingmar Berman in Sweden; Pina Bausch, director of the Wupperthal Dance Theatre and the choreographer credited with inventing a new style of theatre–dance; and the famed choreographer Paul Taylor, to mention only those among the thirty or so students who come immediately to mind.[4]

The level of ballet preparedness among those first students left much to be desired. Ballet dancers usually did not attend institutions of higher education; the most talented among them had already joined companies by age sixteen or seventeen. I, myself, had never studied ballet; it was an anathema for most modern dancers of my generation. Imagine taking your first ever ballet classes from Antony Tudor! Not easily ruffled, I could stand up under his barrage of well-deserved criticism, I suppose, but he must have had unbounded patience. He gave of himself in an unprecedented way as long as he felt that students seriously devoted themselves to the work. Only half-hearted or unthinking efforts repeatedly brought out his razor-sharp tongue. He could also be kind, helpful, and supportive to those who brought their minds as well as their bodies to his classes. And, he loved movement audacity and abandon. It took me, personally, several years to begin to understand what dancing full out meant; he encouraged me at every turn.

I remember silly things like the day he told me if I ever wished to get over my fear of pointe shoes, I must wear them even to do the laundry. Or the day he asked me about what image I had when I performed a simple *port de bras* to his liking (a rare event). He knew I had just met the man I was later to marry, so, when I blushed and didn't answer, he said, "Oh, I see." Or how, after he had been difficult with me in class, he would knock on the door of the dressing room and tender a cigarette as a peace offering (We all smoked in the fifties before we knew of its dangers. Tudor was a particularly heavy smoker at that time.) Nancy Zeckendorf has a similar memory of being in Tudor's class, awaiting her turn at the side, nearly hidden from his view. Lost in thought, musing about why Tudor was so important to her, she decided that he fulfilled her need for a father figure. At that very moment, Tudor turned to her and asked her what she was thinking. Tudor had the uncanny ability to divine the innermost workings of the minds of his students.[5] He could watch several things simultaneously; he knew

what occurred in every corner of the class and every area of the stage.
And, he cared about every one of us, although only in the autumn of
his life did he show this overtly.

Questioning played a vital and constant part in the training. Why
are you doing that? What does it mean? Where is the movement going?
What space does it use? Making you think about what you did was one
of his prime teaching devices. When he asked a question, you shook.
You so wanted to have the right answer, not to disappoint him or be
the fool. But so often he phrased the question or comment in either an
enigmatic or a global fashion. One could not answer glibly, and yet
one couldn't really think through the answer under that kind of pressure. I do not believe this was accidental; Tudor wanted you to go
away and think about it.

Bonnie Oda Homsey, among the last generation of students who
studied with Tudor at Juilliard, became a soloist with the Martha
Graham Company. After she moved to California she established (with
Janet Eilber, another former Graham soloist) the American Repertory
Dance Company. Homsey spoke of feelings similar to mine concerning
Tudor's teaching methodology. She recalled one incident among many:

> He had started class with some phenomenally difficult tendu
> exercise. It was an exercise for the brain as well as the arches. I
> was trying to execute it properly when Tudor walked by,
> stopped with his back toward me and said, "When was the last
> time you went to Central Park and just sat and watched people."
> Then he moved on. . . . It took me a while, and I still think about
> it. He was reminding me that one could not become isolated as a
> dancer. What made the whole language of dance so singularly
> expressive was our ability to use what we knew in life and have
> it come out through our bodies. Not only did we have to de-
> velop physical facility via technique, but we had to exercise our
> minds, to begin to understand what we were going to have to
> seek as people in order to bring movement to life.[6]

In a seminar/lecture that he delivered to students in the
1952–1953 season, Tudor quoted Socrates as saying he never had a
student, only friends. Tudor agreed; he believed one couldn't really
teach unless a complete sympathy of understanding existed between
teacher and student.

Tudor taught at Juilliard for twenty years. Most of those years
overlapped with his teaching at the Metropolitan Opera Ballet. While
much of the world thought him a bit lazy, an impression he took pains
to cultivate, his schedule was actually killing. At one point, as a young

notator, I followed him from place to place. The pace was grueling; I found it nearly impossible keep up.
In 1963, his schedule looked like this:

Monday:      Met: 11:00–1:30
             Juilliard: 2:30–5:20
             Met: Production Class TBA (to be
             arranged—originally scheduled for 4:30–5:30)
Tuesday:     Juilliard: 1:00 p.m. on, depending on rehearsal
             schedule
Wednesday:   Met: 11:00–12:45
             Juilliard: 3:30–6:00
Thursday:    Juilliard: 2:30–5:20
Friday:      Met: 11:00–1:30
             Juilliard: 2:30–5:20
             Met: Adagio Class (TBA as above)

In addition, he conducted rehearsals at Ballet Theatre, and made trips abroad. Also in 1963 he created *Echoing of Trumpets* for the Royal Swedish Ballet.

Special arrangements were made between the Met and Juilliard for a few select students to study in both places. Also, many Juilliard alumni went on to study at the Met when they left school. Among those who took classes in both institutions were Nancy Zeckendorf; Lance Westergard; Pina Bausch; Bruce Marks; Paul Taylor; Karen Bell-Kanner who taught for Tudor at the Met for four years and had a fine career in Europe as dancer, choreographer, and teacher; and Yasuki Sasa, a renowned Japanese dancer and teacher. Juilliard alumnae Jennifer Maisley and Ilona Hirschl became members of the Metropolitan Opera Ballet.

Tudor's relationship with Yasuki Sasa shows a little-known side of him. Tudor championed Sasa, one of the dancers that he had met in Japan. He invited Sasa to come to New York to study at both the Met and Juilliard. He became Sasa's mentor to the extent of providing for his classes at no charge and arranging a place for him to live at the Zen Institute. These kindnesses accompanied an autocratic control over what and with whom Sasa studied. Tudor was determined to shape this young dancer. He permitted Sasa to study only with him.[7] He often embarrassed and tongue-lashed the boy in class. Sasa now believes that Tudor deliberately made him nervous and insecure, preparing him for the role of the murderer in an upcoming Ballet Theatre revival of *Undertow*. Later Tudor did, indeed, schedule Sasa to perform the work with the company, but visa problems prevented Sasa from re-entering the United States. The trauma of losing that opportunity because of a visa technicality induced Sasa permanently to stop performing. But he cherishes the memory of Tudor saying on one occasion, "I have developed one dancer in Japan and that is enough."

Other students who trained at Juilliard with Tudor constitute an international who's who of important dancers, choreographers, teachers, and company directors. They include Dennis Nahat, director of the Cleveland/San Jose Ballet; Michael Uthoff, former Joffrey Ballet dancer and at various times director of the Hartford and the Arizona ballet companies; Martha Clarke, illustrious choreographer, opera director, and winner of a MacArthur Foundation "genius grant"; Daniel Lewis, dean of dance at the New World School of the Arts; Carl Wolz, former dean of the Hong Kong Academy of Performing Arts and founding force behind the World Dance Alliance; Jennifer Muller, choreographer and company director; Angeline Wolf, a member of Muller's company; Carla Maxwell, director of the José Limón Company; many, many Limón Company dancers from several generations; Sylvia Waters, Mary Barnett, and Dudley Williams, of the Alvin Ailey American Dance Theater; former Paul Taylor Company soloist Linda Kent; Carolyn Brown, Merce Cunningham's partner for many years; Japanese dancers Bonjin Atsugi, Chieko Kikuchi, and Yasuki Sasa; Israeli dancers Rena Gluck and Rina Schenfeld; Leigh Warren, director of a dance company in Australia; Sirpa Jorassma and Anthony Salatino, former directors of the Syracuse and Fort Worth Ballets; Robert Lupone, who played the original "director" in *Chorus Line*; Buck Heller, a Broadway choreographer; Maria Barrios, who danced with the National Ballet of Canada and went on to found a company in Venezuela; Sue Knapp (Steen) who danced with American Ballet Theatre; Diana Byer, director of the New York Theatre Ballet and founder of a program to provide dance training to homeless children in New York City; Hollywood choreographers Kevin Carlisle and Robert Iscove; former Martha Graham Company dancers Gene McDonald, Peter Sparling, Bonnie Oda (Homsey), Janet Eilber, and Diane Grey; William Louther, one-time director of the Bat-Dor Company; Donya Feue,r who worked closely with Ingmar Berman; Airi Hynninen, who is one of the select few who restage Tudor's dances; and many others. Note that the list includes both classical and modern dancers, as well as those on Broadway and in Hollywood.

What those students had to say about Tudor and his teaching often belies the image of him as an ogre that many dancers held. That image persists particularly among those who either never worked with him, or had a single brush with his wicked tongue and never returned to his classes or rehearsals. Those who stuck with him often had a very different view:

Karen Kanner:

> My whole impression was that I was working with a man of in-
> credible generosity and kindness. He was interested in me as a
> person, not because I was ever going to be a ballerina [Kanner is
> six feet, one inch tall] but because I might develop into a good
> human being. I might make something of my life. He was amaz-
> ingly helpful and amazingly patient . . . He had a great, great in-
> fluence on me which continues to this very day.[8]

Lance Westergard:

> He could come out of his shell that was not always easy to get
> through, and say something meaningful from down deep inside.
> He did this for me all of the time; I think he did it for all of the
> students. Even if he said something horrible to you, he always
> knew how to pick up the pieces before the end of class and make
> you sail out of the room on air. [9]

Bruce Marks (who began as a modern dancer in the company of Martha Graham soloist Pearl Lang):

> Martha Hill, who headed the department, was a Graham person,
> but she made it very clear that everyone had to study ballet. So
> there I was at Juilliard and Tudor walked in and just terrified
> me. I was scared to death. He obviously was tremendously inter-
> ested in me from the first. . . . It was Tudor who really seduced
> me into ballet.[10]

Bonnie Oda (Homsey):

> I was in utter terror of him the first day of class—actually the
> first week. . . . But, there was always something incredibly car-
> ing about him that touched all of us. . . . It was that loving care
> that made me want to do the best I could as a student. To please
> him.[11]

Of course there were the horror stories of how he treated some other students and dancers. Sometimes he would get very frustrated because he could see the potential in someone who held himself back or sabotaged herself. He had no patience for that. He felt that if one had the instrument and the time to work to develop it, one should cut through all of the personal problems and get down to what needed do-

ing. Once the dancer crossed the threshold of the studio, Tudor expected total dedication and hard work. He had neither forbearance nor
sympathy for the person who disappointed him. His rapier wit went
into action.

## The Ballet Arrangement Class

In addition to teaching ballet technique, adagio (partnering), and
ballet repertoire, Tudor also taught a class in ballet composition. Ballet
Arrangement he called this very practical class. He did not start with
theory or improvisation or what a dance should say. He started by asking the students to invent a simple combination. He did not ask for
complexity nor great originality or genius. He wanted just a simple
combination of steps. Then the students would begin to explore permutations of that combination. What would happen if you added a turn? If
you faced a different direction? If you altered the spatial pattern? He
asked the students to take simple movement and embellish it. Then he
would look at the result with them so that they understood how each
new element changed the meaning of the movement. He tried to sensi-
tize the participants to the moment the body knows that the combination works. He insisted the nascent choreographers listen in depth to
music before deciding what score to use for a compositional assignment. He required them to listen so many times that they understood
the underlying structure of the music. They had to ascertain with certainty that the musical structure would serve the dance idea.
        Together the class made a piece called *Pyramids* to Czerny ex-
ercises. Tudor assigned the students to work on something using the
steps from class. One student had to provide a solo, one a duet, one a
trio, etc., up to a *pas de cinq*. Then each showed his or her work. This
interesting process resulted in a dance that was successful and quite
funny. Dennis Nahat, who later became a choreographer, did the opening solo. It presented a major domo-like character. Nahat put the piece
together brilliantly, building on Tudor's academic classroom steps. The
students performed *Pyramids* at Juilliard in 1965 and then toured it to
schools as part of the Lincoln Center Student Program. It was very
well received. One critic, viewing an in–school program for 700 eighth
and ninth graders, wrote: "Even those few skeptics who came to scoff,
may not have actually cheered, but at least they looked. . . . As the
nine exceedingly attractive girl and boy dancers showed not only skill
and beauty, but humor that junior high students readily understood, the
battle of ballet was won."[12]

Lance Westergard remembers that Tudor often gave the class impossible problems to solve:

"I want you to walk on the diagonal, upstage left to downstage right. Show me three changes in level but don't show me how you make the level changes." We would go home and work on the problem for a week then come back and show what we had done. He would never say "good" or "bad," just "uh-hum," or "you weren't successful, were you?" Then he'd show us how he did it in a ballet of his. There was always something you carried away with you. And the way he solved the problem was always so simple.

There was another problem I remember which I think two or three people were successful at. You have 11 dancers and you have 15 counts of music. They all have to come onstage on the first count and be offstage by the last count, but they can't leave the stage at the same time. We would all try solve the problem, then he would show how simply it was done in one of his ballets.

You have 5 dancers. Two are downstage right in a grouping, two are downstage left in a grouping. One is upstage center, but the upstage center one cannot look like a soloist. You had to get the dancers into those groupings. Of course, nobody was successful at that. Then he showed how he did it. It was always a problem he had solved himself. [13]

## Tudor as Mentor (and More)

Tudor was homosexual all of his life. In order to understand his somewhat guarded behavior vis-à-vis his sexual preference, one needs to think back to the context of his youth. Homosexuality was a crime, punishable (and on occasion punished) by a jail sentence. The trial of Oscar Wilde or, much later, the incarceration of the composer Henry Cowell, make us recognize that widespread homophobia existed. Vernacular vocabulary did not include words like "gay" and "coming out." No one seriously considered the idea of legalizing marriage between gays.

Not until 1969 did organized efforts to end the criminalization of homosexuality appear. A police raid on a gay bar in New York City precipitated the Stonewall riot. The riot galvanized several groups to work together and the gay civil rights movement was born.

Tudor had found a lifelong companion in Hugh Laing. In the early years, however, both of them had other affairs as well. They were both extraordinarily attractive men. More than one source establishes the fact that their own sexual relationship, but not their companionship, ended in 1945. Certainly, it did not continue after Laing married Diana Adams. According to their friends, even after Hugh's divorce when their close relationship was reinstated, the sexual part of it did not resume. In fact, in later life the two referred to themselves as "Joan and Darby" an English expression for an old couple together so long that they took one another for granted.

During the fifties and sixties, Tudor's years at Juilliard, he did not have a steady sexual companion. The young men at Juilliard and at the Metropolitan Opera school clearly presented a temptation. In his lonely state some of these youngsters definitely caught his eye. Everyone knew that Tudor was looking for companionship, but everyone not directly involved managed to ignore it. He was, for example, on intimate terms with Bruce Marks at Juilliard and with modern dancer Paul Sanasardo who studied with him at the Met. Surely there were others. Whether or not these intimacies included sex is not publicly known. Tudor remained always a very private man, and those who were close to him highly respected and continue to respect that privacy.

While Tudor certainly pursued his sexual interests, exactly how predatory, or even how successful, he was at seduction is open to question. He had a very proper side. He recognized boundaries and abided by them in all respects. For one thing, he and Laing rarely appeared in public as "a couple." Many years later, when Tudor received the prestigious Kennedy award, he invited Nancy Zeckendorf as his escort, not Laing.

Karen Kanner tells a story illustrative of Tudor's respect for boundaries:

> When I was a student, he invited me to his apartment with another girl, and a boy in whom he was very interested. He cooked a wonderful dinner for us, pork chops with cream. We all talked amiably, but he had his eye on the young man. Towards the end of the evening we were concerned about getting the boy out as he clearly didn't want to stay. Tudor was very understanding. He simply said, "It would have been very nice having some company for the evening." The next day in class everything was normal. . . . It might have been a scene, but it wasn't. Tudor never made any reference to what had happened.[14]

Lance Westergard, another Tudor protégé, spoke about Tudor as a role model for a young homosexual. While Tudor did nothing to deny or hide his sexual preference, neither did he make it an issue. Rather, he conducted his life with dignity. In the 1960s there were few such role models for young men who were struggling with their sexuality.

## Choreography for the Juilliard Students

Tudor took his responsibilities at Juilliard with the utmost seriousness, to the point of restricting nearly all of his creative output during this period to works for the students. While this course proved nothing short of a disaster for the ballet-going public and for the history of dance, it resulted in a miraculous bonanza for the students.

The first of Tudor's choreographic assays at Juilliard was the delightful *Exercise Piece*, a work in three movements to the *String Quartet no.2* by Arriaga. In one part, four girls stood in a circle holding hands, balanced on one pointe with the other leg raised behind in *arabesque*. Even professionals with solid, dependable balance might have difficulty accomplishing this feat. Somehow the students managed it for Tudor. Another section, a multiple *pas de deux*, featured his wonderfully inventive partnering. The dance continued with a hilarious section in which one youngster performed every sequence a few beats behind the rest of the group, which was what she normally did in classes. Tudor based *Exercise Piece* strictly on classroom material. He called it a Dance Arrangement rather than choreography. Ann Hutchinson (Guest), of the dance notation faculty, asked some of the students to record their sections of the work so a student-level Labanotation score survives.

In December, 1953, Juilliard presented a production of *Britannia Triumphans*, a Masque, as part of the "Festival of British Music." The Festival involved the collaboration of the entire school. The Masque, a remounting of a 1637 work, had music by William Lawes. In addition to Tudor, the collaborators on the production included opera director Frederic Cohen, formerly the music director of the Ballet Jooss and composer of the score for *The Green Table*[15]; the noted conductor Frederic Waldman; dadaist Frederick Kiesler, who did the scenic design and lighting; early music specialist Suzanne Bloch leading a lute and recorder ensemble; and Leo Van Witson providing costumes and make–up. Also part of the Festival was an "Evening of Elizabethan Dance and Music," a collaboration between Tudor and Suzanne Bloch. The Festival scored a major success.

*Britannia Triumphans*: The "Cat" Section. From left to right: Charles Wadsworth, Bruce (Kevin) Carlisle, unidentified, Rena Gluck. *Photograph by Frank Donato, courtesy of the Juilliard School Archives*

During rehearsals for these Festival productions, Tudor received word of the grave illness of his mother. Martha Hill remembered:

> On the Saturday that he was to fly to London he started re-
> hearsal early morning and continued all day, until plane time,
> completing each section so that his assistant [Mattlyn Gavers]
> could take over rehearsals. There was no frenzy but a workman-
> like ordering of the whole complex structure. The final form
> emerged firm and clear. [16]

Tudor later staged a rather straight, unmanipulated classical *Pas de trois* to music of Carl Maria von Weber for students Caroline Bristol (Britting), Gail Valentine, and Bruce Marks.

The year 1960 saw the creation of *A Choreographer Comments*, a series of "comments" based on academic ballet steps and on the idiosyncrasies of the student performers. Each section bore a title followed by an explanation. For example: "587 *Arabesques. Arabesque*: A position in which the body is supported on one leg, while the other is extended in back with the arms harmoniously disposed." "224 *Jetés. Jeté*: A spring from one foot to the other." Other "comments" were *"Pas de bourrée,"* a wonderfully funny section danced by Pina (then known as Philippine) Bausch in high heels with a huge egret feather in her cap; *"Quatrième en avant"* an adagio (partnerwork) section; and similar sections, ten in all. The finale consisted of one *pas de chat. "Pas de Chat*: Step of the cat." Although for the rest of the ballet the dancers wore simple tunics, the *pas de chat* girl came out in full cat regalia for her one big moment. The whole was totally engrossing, witty, and charming, a brilliant choreographic feat. Tudor persisted in calling it a "Dance Arrangement" because it used traditional classical dance material. A film of the work exists since Martha Hill insisted that preservation of dance should appropriately be of major concern to a school so influential in the dance world. In spite of the department's extremely limited funds, she managed to convince the Juilliard administration of the vital importance of filming and sometimes notating the works choreographed at the school.

During the 1960–1961 winter season, Eugene Ormandy, conductor of the Philadelphia Orchestra, invited Tudor to present the Juilliard students in excerpts from *The Sleeping Beauty*, accompanied by the full orchestra. The two men had already established a working rapport with *Offenbach in the Underworld*. In the midst of a blizzard the students left for Philadelphia in a cordon of taxis laden with toe shoes and tutus. Performing an hour-long version of a ballet classic proved an especially exciting event for students and faculty alike. Tudor's standards ensured a fine performance, quite an accomplishment for the newly organized dance department.

Assistant conductor William Smith led the Philadelphia Orchestra for the rehearsal, with Ormandy looking on. As they rehearsed, Ormandy was struck not only by the students' musicality, but also their knowledge of music terminology. And, they all knew the score very well. When Smith would suggest beginning at, for example, section A or going back 16 bars or beginning at the *più mosso*, the students knew exactly where to start dancing. Such a phenomenon was not common among dancers of that (or perhaps any) period; it resulted from their intensive training at Juilliard where they studied music daily. Ormandy was so impressed that he took over the conducting of the rehearsal himself.

The musical knowledge of the students stood them in good stead for Tudor's next choreographic project. His 1961 *Dance Studies (Less Orthodox)* used the Elliott Carter "Etude III" from *Eight Etudes and a Fantasy for Woodwind Quartet.* It was less orthodox, indeed. The piece used a trapeze. In order to rehearse the dance properly a trapeze had to be installed in one of the studios. Both Tudor and the students endlessly experimented with all sorts of contortions on it. Some of the results of the experiments in the piece ended up as material used in his later ballet *Shadowplay.* Tudor loved the idea of monkeys and gorillas; obviously one of them would soon make an appearance in one of his ballets. *Dance Studies* ended with a gorilla-suited dancer wandering across the stage, sitting down, and scratching himself.

The extant film shows a student-level performance. It would be interesting to see what a group of more experienced dancers might make of the work which probably could be reconstructed from the film.

Tudor's 1962 ballet production, called "Gradus ad Parnassum," consisted mostly of remountings of works previously done. The dancers repeated *Dance Studies (Less Orthodox)* as well as performing two works previously choreographed for Jacob's Pillow dancers, *Trio Con Brio* and *Little Improvisations.* They also danced a few new studies, frankly labeled with such names as *Ballet 1* "Passamezzi" (meaning the beginner's class).

Five years later the ballet talent in the school had improved considerably and Tudor was no longer siphoning off the best of the ballet dancers to the Metropolitan Opera School. He decided the Juilliard group had reached a level good enough to undertake *Lilac Garden.* Since he had consistently refused to permit small or regional companies to mount the work, his allowing the Juilliard students to undertake it was a great honor. His Caroline was Sue Knapp, a dancer who

*A Choreographer Comments*: Arabesque Section. From left to right: Virginia Klein (?), unidentified (either Jerry King or Benjamin [Buck] Heller), Michal Imber, Chieko Kikuchi, Myron Howard Nadel, and Jennifer Masley (?)

went on to join American Ballet Theatre and to dance the role of the younger sister in *Pillar of Fire* with that company.

The Juilliard dancers brought a notable depth of characterization to *Lilac Garden*. Even though their technical abilities were considerably less than those of professionals, Tudor again had what he so longed for. At Juilliard he had a group of sympathetic, perhaps adoring, performers shaped by him combined with an amount of rehearsal time that would have been economically unviable in a professional company. These factors allowed Tudor the kind of luxurious working environment that he had once had at the Ballet Rambert. He achieved results quite amazing in such a young group of performers. For them and for many of us in the viewing public, the performance provided an unforgettable experience.

On 29 September, 1965, President Lyndon Johnson signed into law the legislation creating a National Endowment for the Arts, the first direct federal aid to the arts in United States history. By 1971 the National Endowment for the Arts (NEA) had made quite a few grants to choreographers of note. Someone at the endowment was truly awake, for Tudor received a letter asking why that most important of choreographers had never applied for funding. The Endowment encouraged Tudor to undertake a project. Although he did not usually seek grant funding, he allowed himself to present a project that he felt meaningful. Many smaller and regional companies had asked for permission to mount his works over the years, but he had always resisted. He felt his ballets unsuitable for production by these groups either because of the limited company production resources or because of the level of technical and dramatic skill the ballets required.

While at Juilliard and at the Met he had created a number of "etudes," "dance arrangements." These he felt were both a learning experience for the young dancers and, while challenging, were appropriate to their level of accomplishment. Why not do the same for those smaller companies hungering to experience a Tudor work?

So Tudor conceived of a plan to create three ballets specifically designed for restaging by small companies. The NEA grant allowed him to hire Juilliard students on whom to create the works. In this way he could use the grant to augment their meager student means, rather than for his own financial advantage. The students would probably willingly have participated in the project for the honor of working with Tudor, but he wished to compensate them. In true Tudor fashion, he kept a strict accounting of the monies dispersed. At the end of the grant period, after producing the ballets as proposed, he returned to the Endowment whatever funds remained, much to their astonishment. It was a very Tudorian gesture.

For the first time since the days of Rambert and the London Ballet he could have the kind of working conditions he liked best: an adoring group of acolytes, trained by him, willing and free to devote to the task whatever time he needed. There was a buzz among the students. Gossip abounded about the grant. Whom would he pick? What would the ballets be like? How many dancers would he use? The students vied for the honor of working with the great man. Tudor sat back and enjoyed every moment of it; he could not be pushed to reveal his plans.

Work started in May, immediately after the school year officially ended. In an amazing spurt of creativity he executed an unparalleled virtuosic choreographic feat. He simultaneously created three ballets, each totally different from the others, and, in one case, totally different from anything he had done before.

I was asked to record the ballets in Labanotation, but in no way could I keep up with the man. It was not possible for me to notate three ballets simultaneously. I did notate one at the time, and attended many of the rehearsals of the others to give me a head start on notating them later. I even discussed the works at some length with Tudor, unearthing whatever thoughts about them that he was willing to disclose.

For the first of the ballets, *Continuo*, he composed a very short, beautiful, lyrical outpouring. To the famous *Canon* of Johann Pachelbel, Tudor created an untroubled paean to young love, a seven–minute work for three couples. It was a miracle of formal construction and intricate partnering, a breath of fresh air in his oeuvre. It presents a gorgeous joyfulness, with no complex psychological overtones. In spite of the difficulties of programming such a short piece, the dance has been restaged all over the world, for small companies and large, for training groups and for professionals. For example, both the students of the *Conservatoire de Paris* and the ballet company of the Paris Opera have performed it. The critics have acclaimed every performance.

The second ballet, *Sunflowers*, presented a more familiar Tudorian tone. The choreography also called for six dancers, but in this case four girls and two boys. The dance had the same sort of ambiguous psychological atmosphere familiar from other of Tudor's works. He spoke of mixed images—Iowa farm country with boundless vistas, and Chekhov. At one point for scenery he suggested a rudimentary fence on stage, *à la* rural Kansas. The opening for the four girls showed them both as *jeunes filles en fleur* (Tudor's words) and confused adolescents. They danced together until the entrance of the boys, when the four friends became competitive and somewhat suspicious. *Sunflowers*, performed to the *String Quartet no.1* of Leos Janácek, reflected the age and personalities of its young dancers, although it can just as well be reinterpreted (not changed, just differently performed) by more mature, perhaps more disturbed personalities. The ballet ended with none of its conflicts resolved. One of the most ingenious secrets of the dance was that the boys' parts required very little technical expertise. They need only good and sensitive partnering skills. Tudor knew that across the United States at least, young male dancers capable of high-level technical displays were a rarity. He never lost sight of his goal of producing works remountable by small or training companies.

The third work, *Cereus*, a substantial, twenty-odd-minute ballet, was perhaps the most ambitious. It constituted a total departure from anything he had ever done before—quite experimental. The story behind its creation took place in the late sixties, a time of turmoil among the youth of many countries. The *Evénements de mai*, the great student unrest in France, took place in May, 1968. In the United States Vietnam War protests wracked the country, the flower children movement flourished as did Haight-Ashbury and the drug culture. I remember a moment at Juilliard, perhaps the least political of any tertiary institution in the world, in which the students of the Dance Division lay down around the fountain in Lincoln Center in protest.

During those years a particular group of students at Juilliard, among them some of the most talented, became something akin to Tudor groupies or an inner circle. In the spirit of the times, they were great party throwers and goers. They often invited Tudor, and finally, he attended one of their parties. He took the subway (underground) out to Brooklyn and sat on a mattress on the floor like everyone else. Perhaps it was the gossip in him. A great gossip, he always wanted to know about the dancers' personal lives and particularly who was sleeping with whom. Or, perhaps he was doing research for a new ballet. In any case, the party became a watershed event not only for the students, but for Tudor himself.

His third ballet of the trio definitely grew out of that very party. The British school marm in him and the man brought up to behave in an always proper fashion, never to show embarrassing emotions, was a bit shocked by the "let it all hang out" culture of the students. Their casual attitude toward sex and sexuality, new to Tudor, perhaps unsettled him a bit. In the event, he choreographed *Cereus*, a work originally for three couples and an extra man. Later he added a fourth couple. The movement vocabulary of the piece departed radically from classical steps. Sexual energy permeated much of the material although in a most abstract and playful fashion. The score, an all-percussion work by Geoffrey Gray, added to the sensuality of the piece. Of course, nothing was explicit.

The piece opened with one of the young men alone on stage performing a pulsating movement. The other three (later four) boys entered, and there ensued an abandoned, macho dance. When the women appeared, the mood changed. The dancers began an episodic adagio with many pauses, and movements which mirrored the *timpani glissandi*. Another part, for one girl and the boys, Tudor referred to as the toothpaste section. He wanted it to flow endlessly like toothpaste been squeezed from a tube. The men hoisted the girl and passed her among them. Her feet barely ever touched the ground. Tudor also referred to it as the giggle section, possibly because it reflected the fast mallet work in the music. In another section, a female solo, he wanted the girl to be cat-like. Bonnie Oda, for whom he created it, said he kept using tiger images to achieve the desired results. The piece ended as it began; the characters were unchanged. The solo boy went skipping off weaving among the couples. Before he left he tapped one on the top of the head. (I wondered if Tudor knew this device sometimes was used by leaders of jazz bands to determine who was high on marijuana.)

The dancers performed the three ballets at a private showing to an invited audience on May 27, 1971. Later, all three dances had official premieres with small professional companies: *Continuo* with the Syracuse Ballet; *Sunflowers* with the Omaha Ballet; and *Cereus* with the (not small) Pennsylvania Ballet. All of the dances have been remounted for other companies many times.

## Tudor Leaves Juilliard

Directly after these performances, in May, 1971, after two decades of teaching, Tudor retired from Juilliard. The reasons for the retirement, like so much about the man, remain ambiguous. Perhaps he simply felt it was time. Perhaps at last he wanted to get back to choreographing. Perhaps he had a new work in mind, for it was not too long after that he created *The Leaves Are Fading* (1975) for American Ballet Theatre. Perhaps he felt his age. Perhaps the move of the Juilliard School to Lincoln Center (which was bruited about for nearly ten years before the actual move took place in 1969) prompted his decision. Perhaps he got wind of the carefully guarded secret that plans were afoot for Juilliard to amalgamate with the Balanchine school. Perhaps the loss to the Balanchine establishment of four of the six studios in the new Juilliard building influenced him.

Shamefully, he was denied a pension by the school in spite of his twenty years of service. In a letter to President Peter Menin dated 3 October, 1970, Tudor asked permission to retire and requested a small pension. The school had finally instituted a pension plan for the faculty by the time of his retirement. Since he retired before reaching sixty-five, however, the institution did not consider him eligible. The lack of pension must certainly have dealt him a financial blow, particularly as he aged and his health, as well as that of Laing, began to fail.

One additional blow is clearly stated in the minutes of the Juilliard Board of Directors meeting of 10 February, 1971:

> Earlier this season Mr. Antony Tudor, major teacher of ballet, requested that he be permitted to retire at the end of the present academic year. . . . Though he is requesting retirement two years before the usual age of 65, the President recommends Board approval for this request, based on accumulated credits.

> As a result of Mr. Tudor's proposed retirement, the President is recommend ing that the degree with a major in ballet be discontinued. . . . This action is also in line with the understanding agreed to by the School of American Ballet.

In essence, Juilliard agreed to emphasize Modern American Dance and the School of American Ballet would concentrate on classical ballet, thereby avoiding similar training in two institutions under the same roof. The initial premise of the founding of the Dance Division, to afford equal training in both classical ballet and modern dance, was thus totally compromised. Not only was the faculty not consulted, but the decision was kept from them until after the arrangement had solidified.

Thus ended a significant era in dance training in the United States. Although the decision to down-play ballet at Juilliard engendered infighting for years, the ballet segment of the program never again achieved the heights it had had under Tudor.

# Notes

1. The Dance Department later became the Dance Division, a more nearly autonomous unit. the Juilliard School of Music officially became the Juilliard School when the institution added a Drama Division under the direction of John Houseman and moved from its old home at 122nd Street and Claremont Avenue to Lincoln Center in 1969.

2. Arthur Todd, "Dance with Music at Juilliard," *Theatre Arts* (October, 1951): 34

The Juilliard Experiment                                    211

3. Martha Hill, "Antony Tudor: The Juilliard Years," *Antony Tudor: The American Years, Choreography and Dance* 1 part 2, ed. Muriel Topaz, 43.

4. A more extensive list of those attending the early semesters also includes Fumi Akimoto, Rachael Armour, Harry Bernstein, Madeline Cantarella, Gloria Fuguet, Phyllis Gershon, Toby Glanternick, Sally Holroyd, Lenore Landau, Sheldon Ossosky, Barbara Rosing, Patricia Sparrow, Charles Wadsworth, John Waller, Ruth Walton, Georgette Weisz, Alec Rubin, and Ellida Kaufman.

5. This ability seems to have extended to those other than students. Richard Philp, former editor-in-chief of *Dance Magazine* told me the following tale: "I was managing editor in 1973 and had insisted on taking my scheduled summer vacation. Our small and overworked staff was already short due to vacations. There was a huge row just before we closed for the day. Two hours later, I was at ABT and, during the first intermission I carefully approached Tudor, whose reputation for irascibility and playing mind-games was widely known. Before I had a chance to speak, he said, 'So you're going to London too!' I was astonished! He got a glittering expression on his face, not at all unkind—something stretched, skull-like, shaved, focused, mischievous—and added, 'I believe there was a great deal of trouble at *Dance Magazine* today.' It had to be some sort of trick, but it was presented and carried out with great skill."

6. Muriel Topaz, interview with Bonnie Oda Homsey, Los Angeles, 4 September, 1998.

7. During the very early Juilliard days some students were permitted to study only with Tudor, both at Juilliard and at the Metropolitan Opera Ballet school. The practice was short lived. After a few years Juilliard students were required to adhere to a prescribed curriculum.

8. Muriel Topaz, interview with Karen Bell-Kanner, London, 12 November, 1997.

9. Muriel Topaz, interview with Lance Westergard, Brooklyn, New York, 22 December, 1997.

10. Francis Mason, interview with Bruce Marks, *Ballet Review* 22 (Winter, 1994): 45.

11. Topaz, Homsey interview.

12. Marion Feman, "Students Dance for Students," *Middletown Times Herald Record*, 1 April , 1965.

13. Topaz, Westergard. interview

14. Topaz, Bell-Kanner interview

15. Tudor was a great admirer of Kurt Jooss. *The Green Table*, choreographed by Jooss in 1932 remains one of the most powerful antl–war ballets ever presented. It had and continues to have an avid

public and is regularly performed by ballet companies the world over. In the United States for many years it was in the repertoire of the Joffrey Ballet.

16. Hill, "Antony Tudor: The Juilliard Years," 51–2.

Tudor choreographing *Dance Studies (Less Orthodox)*. *Photograph by Elizabeth Sawyer, courtesy of Isabel Brown*

# 7

# The Peripatetic Tudor: The 1960s

In the 1960s, particularly the latter part of the decade and especially among young people, great foment pervaded the atmosphere. The "flower children" of the late sixties and early seventies had the slogan "Make love not war." Meanwhile, their elders worried about the drugs many of them were taking. The era celebrated the counterculture, the Hippies, long hair, beards, and mini skirts, "peace, love, and psychedelic drugs," sit-ins and be-ins and the inanities of the Yippies led by Abbie Hoffman and Jerry Rubin. The discovery of the birth control pill presaged the sexual revolution; feminism reached new heights. Rachel Carson wrote her seminal *The Silent Spring* precipitating the environmental movement. The entire moral climate in the United States was changing. Nor did student unrest limit itself to America. Extremism abounded in Germany under the leadership of Danny the Red. In 1968 troops fired on the French students who manned the barricades in the streets of Paris.

The United States finally enacted civil rights legislation but many in the country would not accept the new laws. Students both black and white joined in protesting and passively resisting the ensconced bigotry. Courageous Rosa Parks refused to sit in the back of the bus. The Selma march brought to prominence the heroic black leader Martin Luther King Jr. Medgar Evers was shot in the back; James Meredith integrated Old Miss facing down state militia intervention. Toward the end of the decade passive resistance gave way to the Black Power movement. Race riots riddled the country as did church burnings and school bombings. America, a nation divided, had 200,000 people involved in rioting and looting. Over one million marched to support civil rights. The horrifying assassinations of John F. Kennedy, Martin

Luther King Jr., Robert Kennedy, and Malcolm X all took place in this era.

The United States had become embroiled in its soul-wrenching war adventure in Vietnam, the problems of which the French had earlier abandoned as intractable. Between 1963 and 1968 over two million Americans took to the streets in anti-war demonstrations. The police clubbed and beat peaceful marchers. Four students were shot on the campus of Kent State University, and war protesters fled to Canada to avoid the draft.

The arts reflected the foment. Painters like Jasper Johns and Robert Raushenberg came into ascendance, as did Andy Warhol. The composer Terry Riley wrote his *In C*, precipitating what came to be known as minimalism in music. And in the dance world, Cunningham produced his chilling, in-your-face, *Winterbranch,* and Anna Sokolow her terrifying *Dreams.* In 1960 Robert Dunn began teaching a dance composition class which heralded so-called post-modern dance. Eventually it led to the formation of the Judson Dance Theater. Black dancers were not untouched by what was going on: Alvin Ailey choreographed his masterwork *Revelations* while Arthur Mitchell founded the Dance Theatre of Harlem. Rudolf Nureyev defected from Russia, followed in a few years by Natalia Makarova. In England the Ballet Rambert morphed into a contemporary dance company and Robin Howard with Robert Cohan founded the London Contemporary Dance Theatre.

Tudor, ostensibly an apolitical man, continued his work, not entirely untouched by what transpired around him.

In what activities did he engage during the 1960s? Mostly he continued teaching both at the Metropolitan Opera and at the Juilliard School. In addition to his heavy teaching schedule, his choreographic wellspring did not totally dry up, contrary to conventional wisdom. For his Juilliard students he created *A Choreographer Comments* in 1960 and *Dance Studies (Less Orthodox)* in 1962. At the Metropolitan Opera, he staged *Alceste* and *Tannhäuser* (1960), and choreographed *Fandango* (1963). Later came the history-making evening, the 1966 concert at the Metropolitan Opera for which he remounted *Echoing of Trumpets* (1963) and created *Concerning Oracles* (1966).

While he continued all of this teaching and choreographing, mostly for students, Tudor's artistic life evolved in other directions as well. And, his work reflected all that was happening around him.

## Sweden

In 1963 Tudor returned to Sweden for yet another stay and produced as moving and poignant an anti-war ballet as any that has ever been seen.

Tudor went back to Stockholm first in 1961, as a guest choreographer, to stage *Dark Elegies*. During 1962 through 1964 he kept returning there whenever he could manage it. He staged a lovely program of three ballets: *Pillar of Fire, Les Sylphides,* and *It's Raining,* the name given to *Little Improvisations* for performances by the Royal Swedish Ballet.

During this period, after Mary Skeaping[1] had left the post, various books refer to him as the artistic director of the company. Tudor commented, however, that "they say I've been director of this company. I didn't know I was."[2] According to correspondence with the director of the Royal Opera House, Goran Gentele, Tudor clearly, at the very least, served as artistic advisor. He suggested who might work with the company, which ballets would be appropriate, casting, which companies they might invite to perform in Stockholm, and so on.

In correspondence Tudor complained loudly that nobody informed him about what was going on. Apparently Tudor was not alone in suffering from lack of information. One wonderfully succinct letter, dated 29 October, 1963, from Gentele to Tudor reads:

> Where the hell are you? Are you still alive? I am thinking of the next season: what programs and which choreographers are we going to have? . . . Write, for heaven's sake.
>
> Not very sincerely,

By 1963 the Swedish company's Tudor repertoire included *Jardin aux lilas, Gala Performance,* and *Romeo and Juliet* in addition to *Pillar of Fire* and *Little Improvisations.*

Tudor cast Nisse Winqvist and Berit Sköld as the lead dancers in *The Tragedy of Romeo and Juliet.* Offstage the two were actually about to marry. Winqvist illustrated Tudor's working method with a tale of how, at a stag party given the groom-to-be shortly before the wedding, Tudor kept teasing him.

> They gave me a lot to drink. And I couldn't stop it because they pushed the bottle into my throat. I was very happy. Everyone was very happy. Tudor went on teasing me in the same way as in rehearsals. The more I drank, the more courage I got. I was really angry at him. I thought, "Why did he pick me for the part of

Romeo when he doesn't like the way I do it?" His constant criticism made me desperate. I thought, "Cast another dancer who can do the part as you want it, because I can't." At the party with my drunken courage I couldn't hold back. I took him like this [hands around his neck]. I always called him Mr. Tudor, but I said, "Antony, you are a bloody bastard." That was the only curse word I knew in English. He didn't say a word, just looked at me with a smile. And those eyes! Then he said "That's the anger I want from you in that scene." And then I understood the reason he was treating me like that. I loved the man and we were very good friends from then on. [3]

Sköld remembered Tudor telling her during a rehearsal that she looked as interesting as a pancake. But she, too, was devoted to Tudor. She relates: "It was a stunning experience. We loved him. He was a father to all of us. He was the one who taught us another level in dance." She also told a lovely story about the first performance of Romeo and Juliet. Sköld had been hospitalized with a throat problem for two weeks before the premiere and had returned only for the last two rehearsals.

Before the balcony scene I was standing behind the set. Tudor was sort of shadowing me saying go here, go there, now you change costumes, etc. . . .When I entered that balcony, he stood behind the set, declaiming Shakespeare. It was his way of helping me. Of course I thanked him, but I didn't understand until later, how absolutely marvelous, gorgeous that was.

After *Romeo* came *Echoing of Trumpets*, Tudor's first major new work in a very long time. The company provided him with his favorite kind of opportunity.

I knew I wanted to do one of two pieces: a classical piece to Tchaikovsky and this score of Martinu. . . . I came over in the spring and started work on both. It was not until after I went away on vacation that I realized it would be the Martinu. . . . It was very good working with the company and I enjoyed it fully. They completely adapted themselves to my work. [4]

So, Tudor returned to Sweden in the fall of 1963 and began serious work on his newest project. In his usual manner of professed non-commitment he insisted that he had no idea what he would do nor whether he would actually do it. But he had already studied the music

*Echoing of Trumpets. Photograph courtesy of Sally Brayley Bliss*

and was quite aware that it dealt with the World War II Nazi massacre Lidice in Czechoslovakia. He assembled his chosen cast in a room, played the music for them, then proceeded to choreograph without music. He had already memorized the music; the dancers, of course, had not. Gerd Andersson recalls that he would tell them not to worry about the beat, but to listen for the trumpet, for example. This bewildered the dancers because in 1962 they did not have orchestral tapes, but worked to the sound of the rehearsal pianist or to Tudor's singing. So, of course there was no trumpet to listen to. Somehow they muddled through, but several of the original cast remarked that they never fully understood the coordination of the dance with the music until later, after he had staged it with the Metropolitan Opera Ballet and returned to remount the work for television. Andersson reported:

> The first day . . . we stood there for almost two hours and did nothing. He tried and tried. He was terribly difficult because he was consumed with so much fear and anxiety. He didn't know what to do. He had us scream and do movements. He had us stand up against a wall. It was rather breathtaking, but the hours went by.[5]

Conversely, Berit Sköld and Nisse Winqvist remember with amazement the calm and balance Tudor maintained. It astounded them that he could do so even though it was his first major ballet in a very long time. He did not indulge at all in sarcasm. A very good atmosphere prevailed at rehearsals and the premiere lacked the usual nervous chaos. Of course, by this time, Tudor had become very much involved with Zen.

In casting the ballet, Tudor chose men who did not look or move like traditional ballet dancers. Many of them had gymnastic backgrounds. They had to project a rough, very macho image. At one point Tudor told me that he didn't care if the men could point their feet, but they had to be believable as soldiers.

He worked and reworked the material with the dancers until they believed in what they were doing. Sally Brayley Bliss, the female lead in the Metropolitan Opera Ballet production, remembered spending two or three hours on the part in the "dead man's *pas de deux*" in which she kicked the corpse—two or three hours just on the kick.

The stark and violent ballet opens on a bleak set symbolizing the destruction of war. It consists of ruins of a building and three somber arches supporting a stone bridge. A gibbet and barbed wire top the bridge.The scene begins with a group of forlorn women, the only remaining inhabitants of the village. The lover of one sneaks back into town and there follows a poignant love duet. The soldiers discover the fleeing man lurking in the arches; they brutally murder him and string him up by the heels. More soldiers enter and perform a circle dance reminiscent of Balkan folk material. The choreography conveys their sense of a macho community which subsumes personal identity and denies personal responsibility for cruel and inhuman acts. In one scene a soldier crushes a woman's hand under his boot when she reaches for a crust of bread. A real incident which Tudor had read about reputedly inspired the sequence. In another scene the woman discovers her lover's body, hanging. A chilling duet, both tender and horrifying, for her and the man's inert form, follows. Enraged, she enlists the other women in a plot to kill one of the soldiers. In the midst of a seduction scene she whips off her head scarf and strangles the soldier. A mass rape, explicated by five couples simultaneously performing *pas de deux*, and mass murders are the reprisal price. Another true story heard or read by Tudor inspired this last episode.

The ballet is a deep and heartfelt addition to the dance canon, an addition that still resonates.The program notes announced that the ballet took place in any locale and at any time that civilization left its imprint. The note spoke ironically, of course, because all of the behavior was totally uncivilized. The dance remains as relevant today as when Tudor choreographed it. He spoke of the dance as emblematic of how people continue to dominate and viciously torture one another. The audience reacted strongly:

> After the first performance there was dead silence in the audience. We were petrified. God, was it that bad? . . . But it wasn't. Then [the applause] broke out. I think it went on for seventeen minutes. It is a fantastic ballet—so right. And still relevant in this day, because such things continue to happen all over the world.

> As Tudor said, this could be anywhere in the world where "civilization" has made its entrance. Knowing Tudor one understands the meaning of these words.[6]

Winqvist remembers how exhausted he was after every performance.

> Rape the women; kill the men; hang him up. And we stood there just looking at the corpse. And the crying women. I was wrung out every time. It's a ballet which must keep being performed always. It's about cruelty, and violence, and war. And every time it is given there is a current example. Unfortunately.[7]

Critical reaction included such phrases as: "its epic resonance always shines through. The ballet's images are bleak and grim. . . . It places the sordid and the beautiful side by side" (Anna Kisselgoff);[8] "the subject is big, horrible and topical . . . a triumph of expressive stylisation" (James Monahan);[9] "*Echoing of Trumpets* is one of the few genuinely tragic ballets, concerned with man's inhumanity and the perseverance of the human spirit under oppression" (John Percival);[10] "the action is dense and tense and packed with cruel details . . . it is the obscure and hidden which fascinates him . . . [However] this is a straight forward drama, with the economy and punch of a short story by Maupassant" (Alexander Bland);[11] "the long awaited Tudor masterpiece, ending triumphantly the question of whether this major figure of the 1940s would ever again be a power in the world of ballet." (Clive Barnes).[12]

## Around and About

Free from teaching both at the Metropolitan Opera and at Juilliard in the summers, Tudor once more indulged his very early wish to become a world traveler. In June, 1962, at the invitation of Batsheva de Rothchild, he taught in Tel Aviv and Jerusalem. He advised de Rothchild about the possibility of developing classical ballet in Israel. Apparently he did not encourage the founding of a classical company at that time as he worried that the bodies he saw were not particularly suitable for classical dance. While in Israel he dined with the visiting Martha Graham and de Rothchild, Graham's patron.

He returned to Israel in 1968 for three or four weeks to polish works for the newly formed Bat Dor Company. The company eventually performed three of his ballets: *Fandango* and *Little Improvisations* staged by Naomi Isaacson from Labanotation scores and coached by Tudor, and *Judgment of Paris* which Tudor himself mounted. Ahuva Anbarry, who had studied with him at Juilliard, was one of the three "ladies" in the cast. She remembers Tudor as being quite kind and helpful throughout the rehearsal period, not at all cynical or sarcastic.

In the summer of 1962 he visited Athens, then went on to teach at Kurt Jooss's Folkwang Schule in Essen, Germany. There he staged *Jardin aux lilas*, with his former student, the distinguished expressionist choreographer Pina Bausch, cast as Caroline.

The following summer he staged *Giselle* for the Royal Swedish Ballet and went to London to help rehearse an all-Tudor evening for Ballet Rambert. Starting in 1958 the Rambert company customarily presented full evenings of Tudor's work. They scheduled these evenings both in homage to him and as a reminder to the world that his roots lay at Rambert. After England, he went on to Germany to stage *Jardin aux lilas* with the Berlin Festival Ballet.

Tudor followed all this travel in 1964 with a revival of *Dim Lustre* for the New York City Ballet. Neither the public nor the critics received the revival well. In truth, the production was not a stellar one. The dancers, steeped in the cool abstraction of the Balanchine aesthetic, did not enter deeply into their roles in the customary Tudor fashion. The costumes were dated and hampered the dancers' movement, and the lighting was unsubtle. By that time, audiences had experienced the fantastic lighting effects achieved by modern dance wizard Alwin Nikolais (for example, his *Imago* premiered in 1963) and the capabilities of sophisticated light boards. The on/off technique used by Tudor, with its split-second timing so crucial to the success of the ballet, seemed old-fashioned and abrupt. In 1964 New York City Ballet also wanted to revive *Lilac Garden*, but the project never materialized. Nor did anything ever come of the request from Balanchine and Kirstein for Tudor to choreograph a new work.[13]

In 1965 Tudor returned to Japan, now as a practicing Zen Buddhist. His religious affiliation, however, did not stop him from caustic criticism. Now that the dancers had vastly improved (no fewer than six of them had come to New York to study with him), he thought they could do more than they were doing and said so. He stayed for about a month. In that short period,[14] working five or six hours every day, he mounted five of his works: *Undertow, Dark Elegies, Little Improvisations, Pillar of Fire,* and *Jardin aux lilas.* Once he kept the company rehearsing until nearly 2:00 a.m. Ruriko Tachikawa, who had been the female lead in his ballets on his previous visit, directed the company, the Star Dancers. The stay became very prestigious both for Tudor and for the company. Sponsorship by a large and impressive group ensured a certain status. The Ministry of Foreign Affairs, the Ministry of Education, the British Embassy in conjunction with the British Arts Council, the American Embassy, the American Cultural Center, the Society for International Cultural Relations, and the Yomiuri Press all joined in presenting the ballets. The enthusiastic reception for the evening showed the Japanese public to have a particular affinity for Tudor's work. According to Tomoji Tsutsui, one of the dancers who went to the United States to study

Tudor rehearsing in Japan. *Photograph courtesy of Tomoji Tsutsui*

with Tudor both at Juilliard and the Met, the Japanese audience thought classical ballet very beautiful but a bit boring. Tudor's works, which caught the characters, the passion, and the motivation of each role, looked very new and fresh. Even the harshest critics praised both the dance and the dancers in *Jardin aux lilas*.

A letter written much later bears witness to Tudor's love of Japan. Corresponding with Tsutsui on 10 April, 1984, he spoke of how the staging of *Dark Elegies* pleased him. He always felt the ballet most akin to Japan. He also remembered some of the dancers remarking that *Jardin aux lilas* could be a Japanese ballet about the Meiji (1867–1912) era. He closed the letter by saying, "Please give everyone an embrace for me, especially the 'belle' of Central Park." (When Tsutsui was studying in the United States Tudor would take her for walks in Central Park and once invited her to the theater to see Jean Louis Barrault.)

Tudor visited with a Zen master during this stay in Japan. After many hours of simply sitting near the great man, Tudor realized that nothing else would transpire, so he rose. As he went to leave, the master finally addressed him asking if he could do a dance without movement. Tudor thought "Silly man. He does not understand that dance *is* movement." Speculation has it that the encounter initiated the idea for his later ballet *Shadowplay*.

During this period Tudor never completely severed his relationship with Ballet Theatre. Every few years, when the company had an anniversary, he returned to polish those of his ballets which remained in repertory. Among these were *Jardin aux lilas, Pillar of Fire,* and revivals of *Undertow* and *The Tragedy of Romeo and Juliet.* Although for twenty-five years Lucia Chase begged him to return and create new ballets, he refused. The conditions which had made him leave the company continued to plague it. Nothing had changed about the strain of constant touring, the shortage of rehearsal time, the lack of a home theater in New York, and the absence of company dancers other than Sallie Wilson whom he felt capable of doing justice to his ballets. As the years passed his reputation grew, even though he refused many offers to create new ballets and accepted only a few of the myriad restaging opportunities.

## Home at Last: Choreographing in England

Tudor's appetite for choreographing, however, seemed to be whetted by that famous evening of ballet at the Metropolitan Opera. In 1967 he finally accepted a very special and very fraught offer—the offer that came from *the* company of his native land, the Royal Ballet of London. Circumstances had placed his old colleague and competitor Frederick Ashton, now director of the Royal Ballet, in a difficult position. Kenneth MacMillan, one of company's two resident choreographers, suddenly abandoned his preparations for a full-length ballet. Instead, MacMillan accepted the post of director of the ballet company of the deutsche Oper in West Berlin. To fill the gap, Ashton invited Tudor to create a ballet for the Royal, offering to meet whatever conditions Tudor required.

The invitation was of crucial importance. Ashton's offer provided Tudor, who had never stopped being an Englishman, with the perfect opportunity. The prodigal son could return home—in triumph if at all possible. For once a company would give him sufficient time, his pick of the dancers and a free hand. With trepidation he accepted the offer. In New York, before he left to begin work in London, anxiety and doubt tortured him. He went about looking unhinged, saying, "What shall I do," atypical behavior for Tudor.

His anxiety was not misplaced, for he had great difficulty in getting started. Many rehearsal hours passed before he felt satisfied that he had a beginning good enough to keep. During his six weeks' London residency he lived at the home of his dear friends Maude Lloyd and Nigel Gosling. Lloyd reported that he would come home each day saying he had accomplished nothing, not even one step. One day he told them he would take a bath and just stay in it. To his colleague the British critic Fernau Hall he announced, "You are talking to a man heading for a nervous breakdown."

He didn't know the dancers, didn't know how to talk and joke with them, or how their minds or bodies worked. He only saw them a few hours a day after which they went off to rehearse something else. These represented exactly the conditions that Tudor found the most difficult. Tellingly, Merle Park remembered that the material for the soloists, whom he did get to know, flowed fairly easily; the corps work gave him the most difficulty.

In the new work, *Shadowplay*, the protagonist wanders onto the stage. He sits down under a tree with his back to the audience. Encounters with the Arboreals, chattering monkeys, and the Aerials, squalling birds who swing on an actual trapeze, interrupt his meditation. Then there appears a shadowy figure, the Terrestrial, perhaps a reflection of the boy's own nature or perhaps a father figure. Later the beautiful and seductive Celestial enters with her *porteurs*. After an amorous *pas de deux* and a combative scene with the Celestial, the boy returns to his meditation. At the end he sits surrounded by the mi-

micking monkeys, and, with a typical Tudor twist, scratches his armpit. No matter how lofty his aspirations, he must scratch his itch! The dance deals with an unusual subject for a so-called classical ballet. Its protagonist is The Boy with the Matted Hair; in Indian mythology matted hair represents someone who meditates. The work is clearly influenced by Tudor's Buddhism. Critical descriptions of the work and its meaning differed significantly, revealing its enigmatic, ambiguous, allegorical nature. Concerning the music score John Percival opined it was about "monkeys unsuccessfully trying to make music, setting their vanity and insignificance against the peacefulness of natural things."[15] Percival said Tudor's ballet took off from this idea adding to it the boy's quest for Nirvana. Oleg Kerensky[16] called the ballet a kind of nightmare and allegory showing a boy alone in a jungle in which monkeys and birds become sinister and aggressive semi-human creatures.[17] Richard Buckle called it a ballet of adolescent experience, with the other characters being "invisible angels and demons who hover round the hero's head," and the adventures being those of the mind.[18] Peter Brinson said the ballet told of "a jungle boy's being discovered in a world of animals whose different characteristics mirror the boy's emotions and passage to maturity."[19] Fernau Hall said the story was "inspired by the life of Lord Buddha the Enlightened One." The central figure, One Who Meditates, went "in search of enlightenment and truth, encountering temptations as he [did] so." The monkeys, the Bandar-Log, "symbols of vulgarity and chaos, "were used as "temptations of a Buddha-like figure."[20] Tudor himself described the dance as a philosophical piece about a boy wandering in an exotic forest.[21]

The strong music score for *Shadowplay, Les Bandar-Log* by the Frenchman Charles Koechlin (1867–1950), is the composer's only published work. Tudor found other Koechlin scores in the Fleisher Collection of the public library in Philadelphia. He interpolated one, *La Course du printemps* to flesh out the music for the ballet. The arrangement of the score was done by John Lanchbery.[22] The music is based on Rudyard Kipling's *The Jungle Boy*, and the Kipling tale clearly influenced the choreography as well. For leading dancers, Tudor picked the young and upcoming Anthony Dowell, and the very musical Merle Park. *Shadowplay* was Dowell's first leading role in a ballet and he credited the experience as contributing greatly to his growth as an artist.

For leading dancers, Tudor picked the young and upcoming Anthony Dowell, and the very musical Merle Park. *Shadowplay* was Dowell's first leading role in a ballet and he credited the experience as contributing greatly to his growth as an artist.

One of the recurrent stories about rehearsals concerns part of the scenery, the tree. Tudor, in his usual fashion, asked Dowell what kind of a tree it was and of course Dowell had no idea. At a lunch break Tudor walked to a local fruit market and bought two mangos. Dowell recalled:

> When he started work it was all so vague. He seemed to have a very strong idea of the shape and pattern of the steps, but it was so in the air—it was as if he was grabbing it from the air. You just had to watch carefully and pick it up. Then came the story of the tree, when he asked me a lot of questions—and me being totally blank, for I'd never in my life in a rehearsal been asked to *think* about what I was doing. I just did the steps as well as I could, and that was it. But to be suddenly asked, "What kind of tree is it," made me think " he's mad—what is he on about?" And then the next day came and he said, "Put your hands behind your back," and in this thing went. I asked, "What ever is that?" and he replied, "It's a mango—and that's the kind of tree it is!" [23]

Dowell said he had never seen a mango before, but Tudor insisted he'd seen hundreds of them—up in the tree. From then on Dowell did, indeed, see them in the tree.

Merle Park reported that *Shadowplay* was the hardest ballet she ever danced. In her entrance, her feet never touched the ground. The men lifted her and passed her from one to the other. Then the men threw Park from one of them to the other. "It was quite a distance," remarked Park, rather dryly. At the end of the ballet the men carried her standing with one foot on the shoulder of each of them. They had to parade her around, making sure that they did not open ranks. At the end they did open ranks so that she went into a split and Dowell dove under her to resume his meditations.[24]

She also remembers rehearsing an erotic lift, doing a big body circle nearly down to the floor, then up and leaning back. Eyes dancing, Tudor asked what she was thinking. Although embarrassed, she knew instinctively she couldn't let him get the better of her, so she answered, "It's just like *Sylphides*." From then on they were fast friends.

For both Park and Tudor the strongest memories of working on *Shadowplay* revolved around how much fun they had and how much they laughed. Also, for once, Tudor finished the ballet in time for the scheduled premiere.

Anthony Dowell in *Shadowplay. Photograph by Donald Southern, courtesy of Jerome Robbins Dance Division, New York Public Library for the Performing Arts*

The ballet scored a big success, to everyone's, including Tudor's, delight and amazement. He had been certain no one would understand it. The Paris Opera later restaged *Shadowplay*, but the French dancers with whom Tudor himself did not work, had no understanding of the material. Both Merle Park and Maude Lloyd called the performance a travesty. American Ballet Theatre also restaged the dance with Baryshnikov in the Dowell role.

Typical of his former treatment by the Royal Ballet, the company planned no party or dinner following the premiere. When they discovered this, his hosts, the Goslings, quickly put together an ad hoc celebration with a crowd that included Anthony and Sally Bliss and Rudolf Nureyev among others. From all reports the party was especially lovely.

Tudor's triumphant return to England did not end with *Shadowplay*. The English National Ballet, the touring company associated with the Royal Ballet, also contracted him to create a new work. Tudor went on tour with the company in order to choreograph for them. On tour, of course, he lived with company members, getting to know the dancers well—just the kind of situation in which he did his best work.

Tudor would move out of the hotels that the administration had provided for him, hotels well beyond what the dancers could afford. Then he would move into the hotel where the dancers were billeted. He liked to bring back fish and chips for everybody to eat.

He based the dance he created, *Knight Errant*, on the talents of David Wall, with whom Tudor found an instant rapport. Wall described it as a very easy relationship:

> I was very green, only about twenty-one, so I wasn't conscious of his antics. I had had very little experience, especially with a choreographer of his stature. I think he quite liked that because we were very natural and ordinary together. . . . One simply did the job he wanted as well as one could, obviously with a reasonable amount of accomplishment. Otherwise he would have gone wild . . . I found him always very honest. . . . He wasn't cruel, as so many people warned; he just said what he meant.
>
> He did like to put people into difficult situations in the rehearsal studio. Not so much out of a need to, but to find out how they would react . . . [For example] at the end of the *pas de deux* the Knight Errant stands in a normal second position [feet planted, legs apart] with his hands on his hips. The girl is clasping at his thigh, with her head completely in his crotch. Margaret Barbieri must have been eighteen, with a strict

Catholic upbringing. She was clutching with her head down. He said, "I want you to look up, look up, look up. Now what are you thinking?" It was very embarrassing, but it was very funny.

It was the first time I'd ever seen a choreographer get into one's psyche. By the time the ballet was created it was as if Tudor had slit us from our throats to our navels and exposed our innards to the audience. He achieved this by his incredible ability to observe.[25]

Concerning how Tudor worked in the studio, Wall went on to say:

He was not so interested in the physical shape of the *pas de deux*, but rather the way the dancers moved with each other—how they related. . . . Every look, every touch, every gesture, every *pas* was relevant—never just pretty. . . . It was very meaningful both to the artist, and to the audiences.

Work on the ballet had started immediately after the premiere of *Shadowplay* and continued for five weeks. Beginning with a week in Coventry and two weeks in Glasgow, the dancers worked in old rehearsal rooms, church halls or wherever else they could find. Wall recounts how Tudor constantly changed and remodeled things right up until the very last rehearsal. Tudor was in his element living out of a suitcase without the luxuries that he never did seem to want or need. It was a very happy period for him.

The resultant work, *Knight Errant*, completely differed from *Shadowplay*. On the surface it was frivolous and very sexy; in actuality, a quite serious moral thread ran beneath the bawdy humor. Tudor loosely based the ballet on an incident described in one of the letters in the play *Les Liaisons dangereuses* by Choderlos de Laclos. Although this bedroom farce took place in the eighteenth century, neither its score by Richard Strauss (*Le Bourgeois gentilhomme* and the prelude to *Ariadne auf Naxos*; Strauss was a composer Tudor much admired), nor the décor by Stefanos Lazaridis reflected that period. The ballet deals with the adventures of the *Chevalier d'amour* who, to win a bet, seduces three Ladies of Position (Tudor's very devilish double entendre). The Ladies have different characteristics: one is an innocent, one a vamp, and the third a mother figure. They provided a wonderful opportunity for Tudor to create three distinct but erotic *pas de deux*. The protagonist is chased through doors and windows. To his pre-arranged rendezvous with each woman he sends, instead, her husband. In the final unexpected epilogue, the Chevalier finally gets his due. He is stripped naked, totally humiliated—his tights were designed so that the appliqués came off easily to give the impression of nakedness. The main character is onstage throughout the entire forty-minute ballet and serves the function of a narrator. He often poses near the proscenium arch. He looks out at the audience and communicates choreographically what is happening on stage. Apparently Tudor originally imagined the ballet being presented on a thrust stage, with the Chevalier actually walking out into the audience, but the idea never got realized.

A backcloth and wings dress the stage. A carriage, doorways, beds, and screens all made of L-shaped pieces of wood, 6 feet by 4 feet comprise the set. The dancers combine and turn these wooden pieces to represent the various "furniture" pieces. Lazaridis costumed the dancers in classical frock coats for the men and calf-length, bustled dresses for the ladies. All wear wigs.

In an unfortunate twist of fate, Wall injured himself just before the premiere in Manchester and could not dance. When he recovered enough to re-assume the role, Tudor had already left England. He never got to see Wall in performance.

The work was well received by audiences both provincial and sophisticated. Such respected critical voices as those of John Percival, Alexander Bland, and Richard Buckle spoke positively. Except for one dissenting voice, that of Craig Dodd of *The Dancing Times*, the critics acclaimed Wall's performance as an extraordinary combination of wit, grace, devilment, and casual impudence.

Tragically, the ballet was completely lost. The company kept no record of any sort and Wall does not think *Knight Errant* could ever be reconstructed.

## Visiting Down Under

Following his productive stay in England came a trip to Australia. Peggy van Praagh, one of the dancers from the earliest Rambert days for whom Tudor had created the Episode in His Past character in *Jardin aux lilas*, now directed the recently founded Australian Ballet. The company, only seven years old, had formed from the remnants of the Borovansky Ballet. Van Praagh was devoted to Tudor. "She absolutely adored him. She thought he was God, and she loved his ballets. She importuned him to come for several years. When eventually he agreed to mount *Pillar of Fire* she was thrilled beyond belief." [26]

Somehow she also persuaded Tudor to do a new work for the company, in spite of the fact that he said he did not want to and was not ready. He had never even seen the Australian company and unfamiliarity with the dancers always posed a problem for him. Also, his stay with the company lasted only a month or so—not enough time for his way of working. Uncharacteristically, Tudor capitulated to van Praagh's insistence. He allowed himself, for once, to be convinced to do something against his instincts; it seems to have been a mistake.

When Tudor arrived in Australia in 1969 van Praagh had already prepared the company to worship at his feet. They confronted a tall, domed (Australian for "bald"), extremely handsome, imperious–looking man. While some of the dancers enjoyed getting to know him and working with him, others characterized him as perverse, complex, superior, frightening, cruel, embarrassing, aloof, unapproachable, and worse. His admirers described him as exacting, fascinating, and demanding but not difficult. His detractors felt that what he asked of them was unkind, intimidating, humiliating, and irrelevant.

First he mounted *Pillar of Fire*. Rehearsals for that work went relatively smoothly. Bill Akers, the man then in charge of stage production and lighting, reports, however, that at the final dress rehearsal he kept the whole company

> shaking and on the razor's edge. He dressed them down with passion in his eyes . . . He had them all thinking they were terrible so that they would keep trying, keeping the energy up until the opening night. After the performance he came back and congratulated everyone and said he thought they were wonderful. You could see they all were thinking, "You bastard." He continued "Don't ever relax. Keep it always at that edge or the ballet doesn't work, because by now it is getting slightly old fashioned."

For the role of Hagar he chose Kathleen Geldart in the first cast and Gailene Stock in the second. Their reactions typify the dancers' differing points of view. Geldart did not have one positive memory of the man. She found him cruel and difficult, with sudden unpredictable changes of mood. After she'd performed the role for several weeks she remembered him saying to her that she'd really done it as he wanted that night. "I thought, God, I've been doing it for weeks. What happened to the other performances?"[27] She remembered an incident in rehearsal in which she became confused and missed a musical cue. He yelled at her and she yelled back. "We had this screaming match. I was sure it was all his fault. The next day he asked if I was in a better mood. I said, 'My mood was all right, it was yours.' I was furious."

His second cast choice, Gaileen Stock, became a great fan. Although he ignored her in the rehearsals of *Pillar of Fire*, she felt she learned a great deal from him. When cast posting showed her dancing the lead in a matinee performance, the only member of the second cast given such an opportunity, she panicked. She sailed into van Praagh's office to express her objections. "Impossible," she said. She continued by saying that she didn't know the ballet well enough; she'd never even rehearsed the *pas de deux* with the first cast partner. Tudor grudgingly rehearsed her once, then sent her a huge bouquet of flowers with a sympathy card inside. After that first performance he complimented her, but told her she'd been dreadful after the second. She, herself, thought the second performance had gone well. devastated, Stock asked him how she might improve. He answered that if she didn't know what was wrong she was not an artist. Many tears later she learned that she had actually quite pleased him, but, he did not want her to become secure in the role. "If only he had said so!!"[28]

Akers told a lovely little tale about lighting the ballet. Tudor arrived with a full-color plot for the dance. Akers dutifully followed it, hating it all the while. A complete, very expensive, staff worked three hours to get it just as the plot outlined, with Tudor sitting patiently through it all. "By the end of the evening, about quarter to eleven p.m. I went to Peggy and said, 'Look, I'm terribly sorry but I couldn't possibly let this ballet go on like that. These colors are ridiculous. It should be stark, with sharp shapes and the outline of buildings behind the gauze.'" Van Praagh agreed to talk to Tudor who told her that we could do what we liked with it.

> So we redid all of the cues in about an hour and a quarter. I said, "There now, I hope to goodness that satisfies him!" A voice from the back of the stalls said, "It certainly does, young man." He'd been sitting there hidden all of the time. Thank God I didn't say anything else.[29]

*Pillar of Fire* was a great success with the Australian audiences. It remained in the repertoire for many seasons and has had several revivals.

During Tudor's stay in Australia he made a few new friends. He often went to dine at the home of Dame Margaret Scott. Dame Margaret had danced many of the Tudor ballets with the Rambert company during the 1950s. At the time of Tudor's visit to Australia she ran the school attached to the company. She and van Praagh were fast friends and she often asked Peggy to share family dinner. She invited Tudor along, and he very much enjoyed the relaxed family atmosphere. Outside the studio he was always quite friendly. At dinner the conversation, reportedly a bit cynical, sometimes turned quite gossipy, even bitchy.

He also dined several times with Gaileen Stock and her husband. She invited Tudor without knowing that he customarily turned down such invitations. She found him delightful company and particularly enjoyed his great sense of humor. Once he brought her a bunch of very sad daisies, saying "for the lady of the house with my esteem." Then they both had a good laugh. He repaid her hospitality by inviting Stock and her husband out for a very posh dinner.

Van Praagh asked Ray Powell, her ballet master who had spent many years with England's Royal Ballet, to look after Tudor during his visit. In spite of early misgivings, Powell found that he and Tudor had great rapport. Tudor's wickedness amused Powell. He understood immediately Tudor's goal with his rude rehearsal behavior. Said Powell:

> We used to feed together. When he'd finish work I'd cart him off to friends of mine. We ate and talked. He was good company. Very acerbic, but then we liked that. One day he did something dreadful to me. He invited me to dinner saying that he knew what was done in Australia with avocado pears. He served avocado drowned in tomato sauce [ketchup], saying "Well you like tomato sauce with everything in this country." I could have killed him.[30]

Tudor's combination of devilishness and friendliness shows clearly in an anecdote recounted by Peggy van Praagh's secretary Modesta Gentele. Gentele told Tudor that she had tickets to see the play *Hair*, famous for its nudity. Tudor, with his usual twinkle in the eye, counseled her to be sure to sit in the front row and bring opera glasses.

A young, blond, handsome company member named Rex McNeill attracted Tudor. Tudor absolutely fell in love with McNeill, as had, according to Colin Peasley, "half the world." And Tudor absolutely astounded McNeill:

> I remember very well that first rehearsal. . . . All of a sudden this person walked into the room with a completely shaved, very shiny bald head. I thought he must have shaved and polished it every day. His eyes were incredible—the bluest eyes I'd ever seen. And penetrating. When he spoke to you, it was eyeball to eyeball. The eyes seemed to pierce right through you. It was very disconcerting. He had these long, sinewy fingers and he used to stroke his head. It looked like he was stroking some phallic-type instrument.

At rehearsals I was petrified of the man. He always asked me questions. It was like an exam, but it made the rehearsals fascinating. You had to think about what you were doing. In my solo rehearsals, he even went over various classroom steps for my benefit. Obviously he was very fond of me and he often invited me out to dinner, usually with other friends along. I think he was trying to find out what made me tick, why I was interested in ballet and what I was doing there.

Once he cooked an amazing, beautiful dinner for me. It was a very relaxing night because we didn't talk about ballet. He had a lot of Asian art and we talked about that.[31]

In answer to my question, McNeill reported that he had never had any kind of intimacy with Tudor, only conversation. "Even in rehearsal he never touched me at all. I was only eighteen and he loved to have young people around him. He was interested in their outlook on life and in molding them."

Tellingly, Tudor chose McNeill to play Damballah the snake, a fertility/sex symbol, in his new ballet *The Divine Horseman*. By all accounts the ballet was a miscalculation on Tudor's part. The subject matter, based on a book of the same title by Maya Deren, depicted a voodoo ritual set in the Caribbean. The Australians found the ballet, with its fourth position *pliés* and the pelvic gyrations of the Caribbean culture completely foreign to them and embarrassing. For this young and immature company such movement certainly did not lie within their concept of white glove, proper, English ballet. It contained no tutus, nor Sylphs, nor Swans, nor, for that matter, classical *enchaînements*. Colin Peasley described the ballet in a rather tongue-in-cheek fashion:

All the girls came across the front cloth, looking a little like Aunt Jemima, and then went to full stage where there was a ritual tree, a pole down the middle. It was supposed to be the tree of life where the Gods came down. I played a priest and had a bottle with a snake spirit in it. I drank it and came up with some guttural sounds, calling the Gods while the dancers were rhythmically chanting around me. Eventually they got into a trance. As they did, the Gods descended taking over their bodies and changing their personalities. The snake [Rex McNeill] came down and wriggled around everywhere doing things that I suppose snakes do—things that give ladies nightmares. There was another rather strange little God [Karl Welander] who ran around, Groucho Marx-style, smoking a cigarette and molesting all the ladies. All sorts of other Gods

Heather Macrae and Karl Welander of the Australian Ballet in *The Divine Horseman. Photograph courtesy of the Australian Ballet*

appeared. Lady Gods, too. Eventually everyone recovered from
the trance, got up and wandered home. It was like a white man's
version of a Katherine Dunham revue.[32]

A less colorful but rather more respectful description appeared in
*The Young Ballerina*: [33]

> *The Divine Horseman* . . . deals with the possession of three
> individuals by spirits or "loa" at a religious gathering . . . This
> possession is said to be similar to that of a horse and its rider.
> The "loa," mounting a person, take over conscious power and
> control.

Gailene Stock, whom Tudor chose to be the female lead,
remembered how he prepared her for the role:

> He lined up four boys across the room, shoulder to shoulder,
> but spaced about five feet apart. He said, "You are the Goddess
> of Love; seduce each one in turn. Take your time. When you are
> finished with one move on to the next." So I tried to give
> voluptuous looks to the first one while all the rest stared at me.
> Eventually I moved on to the next and the next. When I finished
> Tudor asked the men if I had "turned them on." They all said
> no. So he said try again. All I could think of was how I wished
> the rehearsal would be over. At the end of the hour he said,
> "Now that we had gotten rid of your inhibitions we can start
> work."[34]

She also remembered that the composing of the dance went very
slowly. At one point, after twenty-one hours of rehearsal, Tudor had
not yet set any of the choreography.

For music, Tudor picked a set of variations on the theme of a
popular song, "Yellow Bird." The German composer Werner Egk had
arranged and orchestrated the score, *Variations on a Caribbean Theme*.
Egk had conducted the Berlin Philharmonic from 1937 to 1941, during
the Nazi regime. There was trouble with the orchestra, quite a few of
whom were Jewish; they objected to playing the work because of Egk's
Nazi connection.

The rather minimal set, designed by Hugh Laing, consisted of a
three-sided corral with posts, arranged around the stage to enclose the
worship area. Authentic voodoo locales as illustrated in the Maya deren
book, also titled *The Divine Horseman*, provided its inspiration. Rex
McNeill spent most of the ballet slithering among the posts, with his
feet never touching the ground.

The costumes were mostly white. The ladies wore ruched and ruffled long skirts and both the men and women wore halters and ban-
dannas. McNeill remembers that at first he had very tight knee-length
pants that had no give in them. At a dress rehearsal, predictably, the
pants split down the back. Tudor made him carry on with the rehearsal,
*derrière* exposed, much to his mortification and chagrin. At the end
Tudor said, "Don't worry, dear, we'll get you another pair of pants."
The second pair was made of stretch fabric.

A funny but poignant story told by Leigh Rowles illustrated the
company's youth and inexperience and its inability to comprehend
Tudor's way of working. He asked Rowles to come very close to him
and be a can of tomato soup (Gaileen Stock remembers it as being leek
soup). When Rowles told me this, I laughed. She continued, "Yes, that
would be my reaction now. Hysterically funny. But at the time I
thought, 'Now, I wonder where the cans of tomato soup comes into
this ballet.' And I was really serious. I felt foolish because I couldn't
come up with what he wanted."[35]

Tudor worked very much by analogy and Freudian-influenced
ideas of free association. He wanted Rowles to think through his
meaning. When you are a seventeen-year-old dancer, however, with a
very limited background, and have been taught only to follow
instructions and trust your teacher, a can of soup is a can of soup.

Ironically, the Australian press was not quite as negative about
the ballet as were the dancers. In her review in an unidentified
publication, Maria Prerauer called the ballet colorful. But, she
continued, in spite of some splendid rhythmic dancing-mime from the
principals, the ballet became curiously tame for such a thrillingly
spooky subject. Another critic, unidentified, said that although the
subject commended itself for a ballet, the company had not yet adapted
itself to the demands of the work. In Sydney, *Mirror* critic Frank
Harris wrote that it was a magnificently conceived ballet, with a robust
line. The *Western Australian* of 18 September said the ballet had
pungency and power. Another unidentified critique called it spell-
binding. This last critic also reported that Tudor was in Australia for
three months, rather than the one month told to me earlier. It seems a
more likely time frame for what he accomplished.

When Tudor finally left Australia, he took a small detour. He
visited his brother's family in New Zealand, the first and only time he
went to see them. A typical Tudorism came out in a press interview
that took place when he first arrived in Australia. He announced that he
would go to New Zealand briefly to see his brother for the first time in
forty years. He had never seen his nieces and nephews. "Not that I
really want to, I just think they ought to see me." These cool

statements contrast starkly with his letters to the family, which show
his true caring and warmth:

To niece Connaught:

> I just don't know what to say. Your father wrote me not so long ago
> and told me what you had done [turned forty years old]. Don't you
> know that it is unforgivable? Just think what it does to the previous
> generation!!! Forty, indeed. Preposterous! And obviously not
> true—Love from dotard almost octogenarian, but still kicking.

In another letter:

> Don't tell your youngsters that [they write well] or they'll get
> swollen heads. They have pretty good reason to feel a bit puffed up
> anyway, with all those athletic events they keep winning. . . . I was
> a champion byke-faller-offer and was always sent into the field at
> cricket where they knew a ball wouldn't come my way. . . And
> even though I came in first in a mile swimming race down the
> Thames, there was a good tide running downstream and they gave
> me a handicap of something like two hours or, translated, some-
> thing like half-a-mile. Or diving, where your father was sort of
> champion class. I only plucked up enough courage to go off the 33'
> board at Highgate ponds once, and that was only because I didn't
> want anyone to see me stealthily skulking back down the ladders.
> And once I did a back dive off about eighteen feet in Barbados.

To great nephew Robert Palmer:

> Here is the apology, dear Great Nephew—So now we wish you
> many happy months, days and minutes until your wonderful fif-
> teenth B'day. And with the "Macho" look of you in the canoe line-
> up you've got it coming.

To great nephew David Palmer:

> I had a note from your Grandma telling me that your father has just
> gone through an unpleasant bit of surgery. . . . It must be very wor-
> rying for you. . . . Give my wishes to Connaught. She is a woman
> who can look troubling times in the face. . . . My condolences that
> Molly [Tudor's sister-in-law] thinks you look a lot like I did in my
> calf days. I hope you'll weather the years better and as a septuage-
> narian look gorgeous with golden locks (not a wig or transplant)
> and a mouth full of live, beautiful teeth (not caps or dentures) and
> skin like a downy peach, not stretched like old lizard skin or dead
> bark. . . . Embraces to all.

And to great nephew Christopher:

> Well, young Christopher—I see that you have already completed your first decade on this earth—I'm sure that you've had a marvelous time with constant new experiences and discoveries—And I assure you that all these marvels are going to continue right on through your next decade. Aren't you lucky! Affectionately, Great Uncle A.

Poignantly, he wrote to Connaught in 1973 that, until her letter arrived he had not received a communication from any of his brother's children except for one brief note from John—"but then you are all very busy people one way or another." In another letter he says, "Like all your family, kids and parents alike, writing is a forgotten chore, and I will continue to say to myself 'No news is good news.' Happy Springtime to all the buds—Tudor."

All through the 1970s and 1980s there was a steady stream of birthday and Christmas wishes as well as news–filled letters to the only family he had.[36]

# Notes

1. Mary Skeaping (1902–1984), a British dancer who performed with Pavolva, knew Tudor since the early Rambert days. She was ballet mistress with the Sadler's Wells Company from 1948 to 1951 and directed the Royal Swedish Ballet from 1953 to 1962.
2. Muriel Topaz, interview with Berit Sköld and Nisse Winqvist, Stockholm, Sweden, 30 September, 1998.
3. This and the following quote are from Topaz, interview with Sköld and Winqvist.
4. From the sound track of a film, *Antony Tudor,* Gerd Andersson and Viola Aberle producers, 1985.
5. Judith Chazin-Bennahum, interview with Viola Aberle and Gerd Andersson, Stockholm, Sweden, 7 July, 1988.
6. Muriel Topaz, interview with Viveka Ljung, Stockholm, Sweden, 29 September, 1998.
7. Topaz, Winqvist interview.
8. Anna Kisselgoff, *New York Times,* 26 May, 1994.
9. James Monahan, *Dancing Times,* June, 1973.
10. John Percival, *The Times,* 20 March, 1980
11. Alexander Bland, *The Observer Review,* 6 May, 1973. Alexander Bland is the *nom de plume* used by Nigel Gosling and

242        Chapter 7

Maude Lloyd who together wrote reviews for *The Observer* for many years.

12. Clive Barnes, *New York Times,* 10 November, 1964.

13. A letter from Betty Cage to Tudor, dated 14 January, 1964 states, "George and Lincoln are still hoping that you will want to do a new ballet for us one of these days. The last time I mentioned it to you, you were not very receptive to the idea. What do you think now?"

14. Another source, a letter from Tomoji Shakuta Tsutsui, who danced in all of the Tudor ballets both in 1954 and in 1965, puts the dates at 28 August to 4 September, 1965. It is impossible that Tudor could have done all of this in such a short period.

15. John Percival, *Times,* 26 January, 1967.

16. Oleg Kerensky was a British critic who wrote for the *Daily Mail* from 1957 to 1971, the *New Statesman* beginning in 1968, and the *International Herald Tribune* beginning in 1971.

17. Article in the achives of the Juilliard School which does not identify the publication or date.

18. Richard Buckle, *The Sunday Times,* 26 January, 1967. In addition to writing criticism, Buckle founded the British magazine *Ballet* which appeared from 1939 to 1952 except for the war years. He authored many books on ballet including a biography of George Balanchine and several works dealing with the Diaghilev period.

19. Peter Brinson, *Times Educational Supplement,* 10 February, 1967. In addition to his critical writings, Brinson lectured at Oxford, Cambridge, and London Universities. He founded the British touring company Ballet for All, and in 1968–1969 he directed the Royal Academy of Ballet. Since 1971 he is the director of the British and Commonwealth Branch of the Gulbenkian Foundation.

20. Fernau Hall, *Antony Tudor: Choreographer of Genius,* undated. Unpublished manuscript: 352–53, Fernau Hall Archive, National Resource Centre for Dance, UK.

21. Antony Tudor, Lecture #10, York University, Ontario, Canada, 23 November, 1971.

22. John Lanchbery is a composer and conductor. He was music director of the Metropolitan Opera Ballet from 1947–1949, principal conductor of the Royal Ballet 1960–1972, and thereafter music director of the Australian Ballet.

23. Hall, *Antony Tudor: Choreographer of Genius*, 240

24. Muriel Topaz, interview with Merle Park, London, 9 February, 1998.

25. Muriel Topaz, interview with David Wall, London, 10 November 1997. Both this and the succeeding quote are from that interview.

26. Muriel Topaz, interview with William Akers, Melbourne, Australia, 17 September, 1998. Both this and the following quote are from that interview.

27. Muriel Topaz, interview with Kathleen Geldart, Melbourne, Australia, 24 September, 1998. Both this and the following quote are from that interview.

28. Muriel Topaz, interview with Gailene Stock, London, 10 July, 1999.

29. Muriel Topaz, interview with Akers.

30. Muriel Topaz, interview with Ray Powell, Melbourne, Australia, 14 September, 1998.

31. Muriel Topaz, interview with Rex McNeill, Melbourne, Australia, 25 September, 1998.

32. Muriel Topaz, interview with Colin Peasley, Melbourne, Australia, 16 September, 1998.

33. Author unknown, *The Young Ballerina,,* December 1969– March 1970, 16.

34. Topaz, interview with Stock.

35. Muriel Topaz, interview with Marilyn Rowe and Leigh Rowles, Melbourne, Australia, 16 September, 1998.

36. All letters provided by Ian and Connaught (Cook) Palmer, during the author's visit to New Zealand in September, 1998.

# 8

# A New Ballet and Failing Health

## The World Traveler Continues

Turmoil in the United States did not cease in the beginning of the 1970s. The war in Vietnam, so virulently opposed that it tore the United States apart with controversy, continued. Two hundred thousand people marched on Washington to protest; 23,000 were arrested. The police gunned down four students at a peaceful demonstration at Kent State College. It shocked the public to learn that at the same time President Nixon mouthed his intention to bring the American troops home, he authorized the bombing of Cambodia. This, however, was only the beginning of the shocks in store. The Watergate debacle, combined with the revealing of the Pentagon Papers and the ensuing cover-up, precipitated the first resignation of a president in the history of the United States. After the humiliation of Vietnam came a further blow. In 1979 Iranians held a group of Americans hostage and the United States proved powerless to do anything about it. In the Middle East came the Yom Kippur War, and in Chile, with the support of the United States, Pinochet ousted Allende in a bloody coup.

As the decade wore on, perhaps as the result of all this turmoil, people became more and more interested in self-gratification and personal freedom. The divorce rate soared. People became increasingly self-absorbed and less willing to work to mend relationships gone astray. By the end of the decade two out of every five marriages ended in divorce. Feminism, sexual liberation, and the reality of an increasing number of single-parent homes began to change the role of women forever. In 1970, 50 percent of women with children between the ages of six and seventeen had employment outside the home. Women constituted as much as 40 percent of the entering classes in many schools of law and medicine. African Americans began to gain political power. Black mayors were elected in Los Angeles, Detroit, Cleveland, Birmingham, and Atlanta.

It was also a time of economic stagnation. Productivity declined, unemployment soared and the welfare roles increased. The country was experiencing an economic recession. By 1975 inflation reached 11 percent with 9 percent of the work force unemployed. Between 1972 and 1977 the standard of living in the United States fell to fifth in the world. And, there emerged a new phenomenon, the working poor.

In the dance world new companies emerged. An inordinate number of them were directed by former Tudor students. Denis Nahat and Ian Horvath founded the Cleveland (later Cleveland/San José) Ballet; Pina Bausch became the director of the Wupperthal Ballet; and Bruce Marks became the director of Ballet West. One of the early choreographer/dancers founding the Pilobolus Company was Martha Clarke. The Broadway musical *Chorus Line* began its life with Robert Lupone in the role of "the director." The Eliot Feld Ballet appeared. (Although Feld was not a Tudor product per se, he came under Tudor's influence during their overlapping years at Ballet Theatre.)

New works choreographed during the seventies included Jerome Robbins's *Goldberg Variations* (J. S. Bach) and *Watermill* (Teiji Ito); Twyla Tharp's *Deuce Coupe* (Beach Boys) for the Joffrey Ballet and her *Push Comes to Shove* (Franz Joseph Haydn and Joseph Lamb) for American Ballet Theatre; *Esplanade* (J. S. Bach) by Paul Taylor; and Philip Glass's *Einstein on the Beach* with choreography by Lucinda Childs.

In the early part of the 1970s, however, Tudor's life continued in a vein not much different from that of the sixties, although traveling did become more of a chore and less of a pleasure. He began to feel his age and a lessening of his powers. He turned down as many offers to restage works as he accepted. Except for the three short ballets he did in his last year at Juilliard, Tudor flatly refused to be seduced into creating a new work. Not until 1975 did he finally capitulate to the pleas of American Ballet Theatre. His agreement to choreograph, at last, resulted in his lovely and passionate paean to life and love, *The Leaves Are Fading*.

Why Tudor did not create new works for major companies between 1969 (*The Divine Horseman*) and 1975 (*The Leaves Are Fading*) remains one of the enigmas that bedevil any student of his life. He, himself, attributed it to the reality that he could no longer adequately demonstrate what he wished. That explanation is problematic given what he accomplished in *The Leaves Are Fading* and the ballets he composed for his students. Certainly until his 1971 retirement from Juilliard his daunting schedule precluded time for the kind of reflection and study he usually undertook before beginning a new work. His general reluctance to suffer through the creative process, particularly at a time when he had found some personal peace through Zen Buddhism may also have influenced him. Obviously he had found neither subject matter nor a musical score which tempted him. And, the fact that between 1945 (*Undertow*) and 1967 (*Shadowplay*) only his *Echoing of Trumpets* received the kind of rapt adulation he had previously garnered (in such works as *Lilac Garden, Pillar of Fire,* and *Dark Elegies*) must have dampened his drive to make new work. Last, he found very discouraging the way that rehearsals had to be conducted: with strict time limits, and working, for a few hours at a time, with dancers he did not really know while they were simultaneously learning roles in other ballets.

Tudor did accept one assignment in 1970, a restaging of *Gala Performance* for the Royal Danish Ballet. The production pleased him in spite of his usual reluctance to remount the ballet. Luckily, a film exists of that production; Sallie Wilson has used it in restaging the work since Tudor's death. The film gives a good picture of Tudor's insistence on subtle rather than broad comedy.

The first of a string of awards to honor Tudor came to him in 1970. St. Andrew's University in Scotland awarded him an honorary doctor of literature degree.

By this time Tudor had thoroughly immersed himself in Zen Buddhism and assumed responsibilities as president of the Zen Institute. He lived at the institute on East 30th Street in New York (Hugh lived in an apartment on the upper West Side). Tudor arose every morning at 6:15 in time to ring the bells, sound the gongs, and lead the chanting. He spent most of his weekend time in meditation. From all reports he was a fairly strict taskmaster. Among other things, he expected perfect posture, and when he took his turn feeding the group, he tended to severely restrict the amount of food offered.

Among his many Zen notes is a document which states:

| | |
|---|---|
| DO NOT | Destroy life |
| "    " | Steal |
| "    " | Commit an unchaste act |
| "    " | Become intoxicated |
| "    " | Slander another by self-praise |
| "    " | Be stirred to anger |
| "    " | Recite the 3 treasures—Buddha, |
| | Dharma, Sanghu |

GUIDING PRINCIPLES
> Simplification of life
> Self independence
> Secret virtue—practicing goodness without a
>    thought of recognition by oneself or others
> Regard and use the world reverentially
> Observe order, order, greatest possible order
> Observe hidden practice—secret activity
> Observe humility, morality, obedience
> Observe responsibility, simplicity, frugality
> Observe earnestness, sincerity (non deceiving)
> In Zen there are no dogmatic tenets
> In Zen nothing goes to waste
> In Zen nothing is expressed under disguise

In May of 1970 Tudor attended Sir Frederick Ashton's Metropolitan Opera Gala Farewell. Then he left for Italy for a short vacation in Positano, a charming beach village on the side of a hill.

In the summer of 1970 he staged *The Tragedy of Romeo and Juliet* for American Ballet Theatre. The English critic Clive Barnes, a newly minted American, roundly excoriated the production. In response Tudor wrote a letter[1] to the dancers of the company:

> I suppose that most of you will already have read or heard reports of Clive Barnes' review in this morning's *[New York] Times* of our Thursday night's *Romeo and Juliet* revival. . . . I suspect that most, if not all, of you will have passed over the most important word of the article . . . *pure* . . . unadulterated, free from defilement, chaste, clear, untainted . . . Pure does not suggest being closed in: it conveys freedom. But freedom . . . is not synonymous with license . . . Please give some thought to this word "pure." . . . Last night one dancer exemplified this purity at Ballet Theatre, and that was Sallie Wilson in *Moor's Pavane*.

The letter goes on to indicate how Tudor is smarting under the critical blows:

> I regret that Mr. Barnes does not approve of my having Romeo, who has inadvertently been the cause of his closest friend's fatal wounding, stay with his beloved Mercutio and wish to comfort [him] through the death throes: that there should be moments of self-recrimination, of shock before the scream of "re-

venge." But obviously my reading of human behavior is not the only one, and it takes all kinds.

In October of that year Tudor flew to England to rehearse *Jardin aux lilas* for a few days. Then he went off to Oslo to look in on *Dark Elegies* and to track down some back royalties which had not yet been forthcoming. Tudor's letters of this period are increasingly scattered with references to money—something very new for him. Hugh had been ill and Tudor worried about medical bills. His financial concerns, however, did not deter him from refusing many offers of work, such as Finland's request to mount *Gala Performance*.

In September and October 1971, Tudor visited Geneva to stage *Jardin aux lilas*. In November, he went to Toronto, both working with the National Ballet of Canada and delivering a fascinating series of lectures at York University. In those lectures he shared some of his musings with his students:

On 21 October:

> Although the motive for seeing dancing is often erotic at a certain level, the art is above eroticism. I consider the performance of Nora Kaye and Hugh Laing in my *Pillar of Fire* as above the area of eroticism. . . . The best performances of my *Pillar of Fire* were always executed in cold blood.

On 28 October, regarding Ted Shawn in Shawn's dervish dance:

> He always told his audiences, after the event, how many turns he did. I counted them and found a great disparity.

And, regarding Martha Graham:

> Martha Graham has almost single-handedly led the modern dance movement to its present apex. She has formulated a method of technique which developed muscles in areas ballet has not explored. . . . The Graham method uses beautiful falls and I like the way Graham dancers use their toes on the floor like fingers. . . . Martha is not a kind lady. She is a marvelous, generous and warm body but ruthless to achieve what is necessary. . . . Graham and I were brought together by William Schuman. . . . Now our relationship is such that she can kick me in the shins in friendship [which she actually did].

Tudor and Martha Graham (hidden on the left of Graham is Louis Horst). *Photograph by Joan Vitale courtesy of Jerome Robbins Dance Division, New York Public Library for the Performing Arts*

On 2 November:

> Jerry [Robbins] asked me to promise him that however success-
> ful he became, I wouldn't be afraid of him. I promised.

On 4 November:

> Dance is human movement to an intended time factor to convey
> an idea. The idea may be movement for its own sake or it may be
> instinctual communication or calculated communication. If in-
> stinctual, the idea probably embraces experiences from one's
> past.

> To my mind the greatest ballet created recently is *Dances at a
> Gathering* [Robbins/Chopin]. It has all the essential qualities
> of real dance. *Moves* by Robbins [in silence] is a masterpiece
> that should be seen by every choreographer.

On 7 November:

> Modern dancers always embrace me because they claim I intro-
> duced modern dance into ballet. That was not my intention but
> in some ways it is true. Both Martha Graham and I saw the future
> as an amalgam of modern dance and ballet. This has already
> happened in many companies like Netherlands Dance Theatre. . .
> a big advance for dance.

In a letter from this period Tudor complains that he's kept too
busy working, ruining his plans for "bumming and playing the para-
site—I hate work but find leisure hours beginning to be a problem—It
was much nicer in the old days when one could stroll gently swinging
a bag." [2]

## Teaching—Again

While the 1970–1971 season was his last at the Juilliard School,
it hardly marked his retirement from teaching. He soon began a long-
term relationship with the University of California, Irvine (UCI). His
colleague from the earliest Ballet Theatre days, Eugene Loring, also
taught there. Each year Tudor spent one academic quarter away from the
bitter New York cold, teaching at UCI and, with Hugh, living in a
motel in Laguna Beach called Vacation Village. According to the archives of the school and the recollection of his colleagues there, his
residencies started in 1972 and lasted through 1978. [3] After 1978, when

he suffered his initial heart attack, Tudor did not go back to teaching although he did continue his annual visits to Vacation Village.

Clayton Garrison, the dean of fine arts at UCI at the time of Tudor's residencies, remembered:

> I was brought into contact with Tudor through Olga Maynard.[4] She thought it would be marvelous if Tudor were brought to the campus. So I gave him a call at some point that spring.[5] He said that it sounded very interesting. We negotiated for [him to teach during] a period of time beginning after the Christmas break and lasting through the spring break—the winter quarter. That appealed to him because it meant he could get out of New York for the cold weather. I thought that it was all arranged, but he telephoned me in November. He said, "Is this Dean Irvine?" In a very cutting voice. Recognizing that voice, I said, "Well, yes, Tudor, this is Dean Irvine." He continued, "Sir. you spoke to me a few months ago about my coming to your school. What kind of a school do you run? You've sent no contract." I had done some background work on Tudor by that time and I knew that he wasn't signing contracts.
>
> He went on and on and on. Finally I said, "Are you finished, Tudor." "Yes," he said, "I'm finished. What do you have to say?" "I'm a man of my word, Tudor. I didn't feel I had to send you a contract. If I tell somebody I'm going to hire them, I'm going to hire them. Now you get on that plane and get right out here." His response was, "Well Deany Irvine, you're just the kind of person I want to work for." [6]

Garrison reports that Tudor was "a splendid teacher, superb. The students would jump high in a normal class but when Tudor walked in they would jump much higher." According to Garrison, Tudor conducted himself in an extraordinarily gracious, kind, and expansive way with the students, contrary to the abundant rumors about how vicious and mean he could be.

One of the members on the dance faculty had worked with him previously. She said he had abused her, made her cry. She thought it outrageous that he was coming to the campus. The whole dance faculty sent Eugene Loring to Garrison's office to demand that he rescind his invitation.

Garrison responded that: "You don't run a school of fine arts democratically. I said no; I'm not going to cancel. He's coming. I'll schedule his classes and he's going to be there." Tudor taught ballet every day for several years, coming on the bus from Laguna Beach. Garrison had offered to drive him, but he would have none of that.

Nora Kaye and Herbert Ross begged Tudor to come and stay at their
guest apartment in Hollywood, but he refused that also, saying he had
to be near the sea.

Hugh always accompanied Tudor to Laguna Beach. They loved
being there. They had separate but connecting rooms. Tudor's accommodation had a bedroom and a kitchen, and Hugh's had just a bedroom. The last two years that Tudor taught they both stayed in Tudor's
room[7] to save money. While there they led a very calm, very quiet life.
The first years they brought along their little dog, Chenpo, who loved
the beach. They had a ritual of walking the dog on the beach four or
five times a day. The two men looked forward to going shopping at the
big supermarket just across the street. They enjoyed preparing meals for
themselves and sometimes invited a few people to join them. They
both read a lot; stacks of books always lay around.

Tudor and Hugh invited Garrison for dinner every few weeks. In
the first years they would begin with martinis, which they all liked.
Garrison described the meals as marvelous. Tudor cooked well and
Hugh was a gourmet cook. At the beginning they all ate copiously.
Starting with the third or fourth year Tudor and Hugh began their macrobiotic diet. They stopped drinking and while Garrison and his wife
were served lovely food, Hugh and Tudor ate rice.

During the dinners, they told endless stories about Ballet Theatre:
the train rides, the seedy hotels, the dusty theaters. They spoke about
how tough it was being a dancer. And the inner motivation they had,
the delight they took in the challenge. As long as they had a place to
sleep and they were eating, nothing bothered them. They did complain,
however, about the collective bargaining that went on with companies
during the seventies. They spoke a great deal about the dampening effect they felt the unions had on the kind of spirit they remembered
from the old days.

Tudor talked about one dancer in particular, Gelsey Kirkland. He
adored her. He felt she was brilliant. She really understood his need to
allow movement and gesture to emerge from inner characterization.
Garrison said that Tudor melted for a moment speaking about her, the
only time Tudor showed any signs of passion—other than passion for
Hugh and for the dog.

Only once did Garrison remember Tudor and Hugh speaking
about their personal lives. Garrison asked about what had ever happened to the marriage between Diana Adams and Hugh Laing. Tudor
gave an impish reply: "You see, he just couldn't resist me any longer."

Garrison, who directed plays at UCI, learned to depend on Tudor's judgment. When he staged something during a Tudor stay, Garrison would bring him to the production. Then they would go back to

Tudor's apartment for a critique. Tudor would always follow up those firm critiques with a lovely note. On the other hand, according to Garrison, not one of the dance teachers ever invited Tudor to see his or her work. They never quite accepted him as one of the group; collegiality did not exist.

During Tudor's tenure at the college he mounted many of his small ballets and "Dance Arrangements." Over the years he staged *A Choreographer Comments, Dance Studies (Less Orthodox), Little Improvisations, Continuo, Sunflowers,* and *Fandango.* Just as at Juilliard and the Met, Tudor had a profound influence on both the students and the program. Many graduates went on to have significant dance careers.

In the last of the years that he taught at UCI, Tudor exhibited a markedly different physical stance. Garrison attributed it more to the macrobiotic diet than to simple aging. There was a noticeable difference in Tudor's carriage, which changed from a sprightly gait to shuffling. His voice lost its incisiveness.

During his time at UCI, a back-and-forth correspondence took place concerning the possibility of Tudor's staging *Dark Elegies* for the Royal Ballet. It was to be performed at the Cathedral at Vezelay to raise funds for decontaminating the stonework. At first Tudor said yes. Then the company said they couldn't do it for practical reasons. Then Sir Fred sent a formal invitation. Then Tudor informally refused. That was in 1973.

In a 1971 letter to Maude Lloyd,[8] Tudor mentions Nureyev for the first time. Lloyd was a close friend of both men, and encouraged the deep respect that existed between them. In the letter written from Toronto, Tudor informed Lloyd of how Rudi (Nureyev) was dancing all around town, performing *Sleeping Beauty* with all of the solos and Limón's "Otello" (*The Moor's Pavane.*) "He certainly does drive himself," writes Tudor. "He knows I love him; his double *cabrioles, passés,* and *pirouettes à la seconde* are marvelous."

Also in 1971, Beryl Grey, director of the London Festival Ballet, began importuning Tudor for a work. In light of the critical reception and the workload he experienced for the recent Ballet Theatre revival, he refused her requests for *Romeo and Juliet.* They finally agreed on *Echoing of Trumpets,* largely because his assistant from Stockholm, Anne-Marie Lagarborg, could do the bulk of the work. The planned staging would take place in February and March 1973, with Tudor coming for final rehearsals in April. In the event "La Lagarborg," as Tudor called her, had to withdraw and Viveka Ljung worked with the Festival Company, with Tudor bearing a greater burden than he had envisioned.

In December, 1972,[9] Tudor wrote from Amsterdam of another unexpected complication. Suffering from a hernia which was to be operated on in March, 1973, he estimated that it would be a minimum of
four months before his next *double renversé* or *entrechat six*." He also
wrote of planning to spend the Christmas/New Year celebration in England with his dear friends the Goslings. Over the years, whenever possible, Tudor would slip away from his European obligations to spend a
few resuscitating days in his beloved London. At home and abroad, he
remained an avid reader of the British newspaper *The Observer*. He
bemoaned the fact that he could not get the paper when he was in
Laguna Beach. He sprinkled his letters to Maude Lloyd with comments
on English politics: how John Harrison was making out with the new
"red" government; how Harold MacMillan was trailing badly in the
polls; how the dock workers wanted £60 for a twenty-hour work week
with five weeks of paid vacation; how England had joined the United
States with bombings in stores, race riots, and transportation strikes. In
spite of his many years in America and his eventual embracing of
American citizenship, Tudor remained an Englishman at his core.

A letter to Peter Brownlee,[10] one of the administrators of London
Festival Ballet, explained Tudor's life-long objection to detailed program notes for his ballets. Tudor had always strongly resisted program
notes. He felt it undesirable to tell the audience in advance what they
were going to see, or to influence their reaction to it. "If the matter of
the work is not made explicit in its own medium, then why bother
with it?" asked Tudor. In the letter, he also made an issue of his given
name being spelled with no *h*, Antony. And, he corrected the biographical information insisting that he did not help found Ballet Theatre nor have his own short-lived companies. Of course, in fact, he did
have two short-lived companies in the 1930s: Dance Theatre (with
Agnes de Mille) and the London Ballet, but he obviously chose to
ignore this. Tudor's sensitivity to his given name being spelled incor-
rectly was further documented in a note scrawled on the back of a bill
for $20 from Dr. Amos Brewster Cobert. The note said, "If he can't get
my name spelled correctly after twenty years, he can wait for his payment."

Tudor's work with the London Festival Ballet was followed by a
trip to Dusseldorf to stage *Gala Performance* for the Deutsche Oper am
Rhein. Then he returned to London, this time for pleasure, not work.

In 1974, *Dance Magazine*, at the time the most widely circulated dance publication in the United States, conferred upon Tudor its
coveted Dance Magazine Award. In the award presentation speech
Agnes de Mille told of her long friendship with Tudor, saying it astonished her that anything could last that long. The other astonishing

256

thing, said de Mille, was: "Why the bloody hell wasn't this award given to you sooner. Didn't they notice?"[11] She cites Tudor's economy ("In *Lilac Garden* there's a man and a woman standing on stage at curtain rise and at the end of eight bars you know that he has power over her, that she doesn't like this at all but that there's nothing she can do about it."); his quality of movement (The movement "has become a form of dialogue, of expression, that is just as explicit and just as communicating as language."); his use of music ("He doesn't play against the music, he plays over and around it and falls from it and comes back. The two are partners."); his costumes (Tudor had "people dressed like his father and mother. And that's extraordinary because . . . you cut the flim flam."); and his ability to see dancers as people ("It amounts to a complete change in our dance medium, in our art. He is a watershed character. He's a landmark."). De Mille finished by stating: "Tudor, in the words of your compatriots, God damn it, sir, you're a ruddy immortal." Tudor replied with his usual wit: "I would like to start by answering one of [de Mille's] earlier questions. This has been bothering me slightly: Why should I be getting an award at this time? I haven't done anything for twenty-five years. And then I knew! They gave me the Award for *not* doing anything."

The honorific recognition of Tudor continued, in 1976, with the Brandeis University Creative Arts Medal, an award rarely conferred on someone from the dance world.

## American Ballet Theatre . . . Again

In 1974, Tudor staged *Shadowplay* for American Ballet Theatre with Baryshnikov in the role of The Boy with the Matted Hair. One can only speculate what influence this role and working with Tudor had on Baryshnikov's eventual decision to become a permanent member of the company and later on, its artistic director.

*Echoing of Trumpets* had been successful in its London Festival Ballet production, which encouraged Beryl Grey to write to Tudor:

> Oh! dear—what can I do about you? Should I come over and serenade you or should I just leave you alone to cheer up? I hope that your last letter to me really wasn't a "No" to doing *Dim Lustre* for us. You surely can't do that to me after our happy cooperation this Spring. I just haven't the heart to tell the Company that you might not come. All the dancers are working hard in the hopes of at least being looked at by you next Spring and I am sure that you could not be quite so cruel as to disappoint not only the dancers but also the Tudor-starved and Tudor-devoted British public. . . . After all, we are

not Ballet Theatre, are we? I do hope you will not penalise us because of your present creative problems with another Company . . . . Dear Antony, please do not disappoint us over *Dim Lustre* for our next Coliseum Season in Spring, 1974. I hope that now all your doubts and anxieties will have fled.[12]

*Dim Lustre* for the London Festival Ballet was one more project that never materialized. In 1974, in a moment of weakness, Tudor agreed to become associate director of American Ballet Theatre. The post carried responsibilities he had avoided for so many years. It precluded his going off to London to stage a ballet.

He described his role at ABT as being willing to associate and willing to direct, nothing more. Of course, even Tudor knew that was only a dodge. "There go all my most sacred declarations of independence, my whole future as a rhapsodic bum and my beginning of waking up in the middle of the night screaming towards heaven 'Where are the choreographers: Where???'"[13] A good director, said Tudor, is a Svengali, a Machiavelli, a Florence Nightingale, an Avenging Angel, a Mama, a Papa, and His Holiness, all at the same time.

Beginning with the 1974–1975 season Tudor assumed the role of associate director at American Ballet Theatre at a salary of $15,000. Additional compensation would be forthcoming for any work on his own ballets involving new casts, or any new choreography. Apparently the possibility of his taking the position had been talked about for quite a time. At this moment he felt Lucia really needed some assistance, something he had never felt before. The time had come for him to help out. In a conversation with Lucia Chase, he protested that he was much too old and not accustomed to taking orders. She assured him that only two people would be in that kind of position. He responded that two were two too many.

As associate director he had responsibilities in the areas he knew best: casting, programming, choosing repertoire and choreographers, working in the studio with the dancers, etc. And, of course, supervising and mounting his own works. That first season the company did *Pillar of Fire, Undertow* (with Fernando Bujones in the lead), and *Jardin aux lilas*. Tudor chose Bujones to do *Undertow* because he felt the role would contribute to Bujones' development as an artist.

No written agreement existed between Tudor and the company. If it all didn't work out, there would be a "friendly liquidation."

American Ballet Theatre celebrated its thirty-fifth anniversary with a gala performance at the City Center (55th Street) Theater on 11 January, 1975. The company performed choreographic excerpts from the classics (*Les Sylphides, Sleeping Beauty*) and from the company's rich original repertoire: Tudor's *Pillar of Fire*, Robbins's *Fancy Free*, de

Mille's *Three Virgins and a Devil*, MacMillan's *Concerto*, Ailey's *The River*. The Russians Mikhail Baryshnikov and Natalia Makarova along with André Eglevsky and Igor Youskevitch danced. Tudor, de Mille, Robbins, Nora Kaye, John Kriza, and Sono Osato all took bows. From the audience many dance luminaries, past and present, also acknowledged applause. Among them were Irina Baronova, Fernando Bujones, Anton Dolin, Hugh Laing, Cynthia Gregory, and Gelsey Kirkland. A very proud Lucia Chase presided over it all. It is not really a mystery that Tudor accepted the associate directorship of Ballet Theatre in spite of his determination never to be so encumbered. It would have been quite difficult for him to have disassociated himself from this group of his colleagues, both new and old.

The job of associate director took its toll on Tudor's health. He became frantically busy and beset by the myriad worries which bedevil every director. In a letter to Maude Lloyd he described his first season:

My loves . . .

This absolutely terrible part time job I took on to be helpful is beyond words of horror. End of enormously successful season, thus, inflated egos, therefore inflated demands . . . Natasha [Ma--
karova] wants Sascha [Alexander Gudonov] for herself, but as he'll be with us at times when she ain't we seem to be needing Kirkland [Gelsey], who, knowing she is *really* . . . necessary, is trying to wring the proverbial blood. Cynthia [Gregory], who has become a marvelous dancer, naturally has to outdo the above situation, and she must have her tall partner and so the big blond Dane [Peter Martins] from New York City Ballet . . . says yes, says no, says yes. We plan programmes . . . then he says no again. Meantime the *Times* is still printing columns about B.T.'s disastrous financial situation. All of this should not concern me but how can you talk programmes or plans without knowing what and who are available?

To my utmost horror . . . I may have to get *Chevalier d'amour* [*Knight Errant*, the work Tudor made for the English National Ballet in 1968] in. But I don't remember anything about it. They [English National Ballet] can't trace the piano score, have no idea of the order in which the pieces were used, and the pianist who played for those rehearsals has not been with them for some time. They never sent me any photographs and I never saw it. I need to know when the Walls [David and Elfreda], Betty Anderson, Mrs. Barbieri Cecchetti, and the girl who took over

Tudor, Lucia Chase, Natalia Makarova, and Eric Bruhn (partially hidden). *Photograph by V. Sladon*

for the tall lady from Australia who got arthritis or something
will be back where I can talk with them.

The letter illustrates the haphazard way the art of the dance is routinely preserved and restaged! No wonder that Tudor planned to have a
notator attached to ABT. He wished all of his ballets to be notated. He
knew that having a notator in the studio was actually an economy. It
would save countless hours of argument: "No, it was this way, no, that
way."
      In his will Tudor stated:

> I request my Trustee, in order to insure the integrity of my bal-
> lets in performance, to require as a condition of any agreement
> entered into or permission given for performance of any of my
> ballets that the performance be based on the best available re-
> cord of the ballet and, specifically, if the ballet has been notated
> by the Dance Notation Bureau or by The Institute of Choreol-
> ogy, that the Bureau or the Institute be consulted and the per-
> formance based upon its notation.

      In the face of the insurmountable difficulties, ABT never restaged
*Knight Errant.* Nor did the Royal Ballet, which had also asked for it.
In fact, no company ever remounted it. The ballet, among many, many
others, is lost for all time.
      Tudor's duties at American Ballet Theatre became increasingly
onerous as his stamina began to dwindle. By the end of the 1974–1975
season, he complained of being completely spent, barely able to get out
of bed for five weeks. The following season, the bedlam at ABT continued. It was business as usual—total chaos.

> Everything's as mad as ever, with Jonas [Kage] and the two
> Kevins [McKenzie, O'Day] and Robert [La Fosse] and one of our
> ballet masters gone, and no [Ted] Kivett or Mrs. [Karina Brock]
> yet, and Baryshnikov in Canada for all of our two weeks of re-
> hearsal, and Cynthia [Gregory] out for the first of those weeks
> with teeth-fixing, and [Dennis] Wayne arriving days late be-
> cause of infected ears in Puerto Rico, it has been bloody murder,
> and yesterday I had six hours in a row, and Friday five, and Gel-
> sey's [Kirkland] still got a bad foot. And isn't it a dumb busi-
> ness!!![14]

      Another description of the chaos shows Tudor's increasing disen-
chantment with the way a company functioned in the seventies. It was
so different from the selfless dedication of the dancers in the Ballet
Rambert days:

Tudor and author Muriel Topaz. *Photograph by M. David Varon*

Dear Maude [Lloyd], Muriel [Monkhouse] and M'Lord Nigel [Gosling] . . . carrissimmi,

You wouldn't believe it. Tomorrow ABT opens at the Met . . . the Alonsos arrived two days ago to get their *Carmen* on next Friday, which also has MY *Romeo and Juliet* which is not quite completed. Then we have our great new *[Sleeping] Beauty* which open*s* *(Deus providierit)* in eight days. In one week we get five sets of the Belle and her Beau and six pairs of Bluebirds. . . . I wish I knew what was really going on in the other three studios but I get in one and am not let out until seven hours later. (No lunch break, but I'm permitted to go wee-wee twice.) Total new casts for *Romeo* and two new trios for *Pillar.* It doesn't seem possible. Marcia [Haydee], [Richard] Cragun, Lynn [Seymour], [Vladimer] Gelvan . . . every time you turn around it's a new someone arriving for a few minutes between their other fortune earning commitments to pick up a couple of steps. Everyone wants to be another Rudolf. It is truly rapacious and ravaging on the rehearsal staff, which is aggravating when you realise that possibly a guest for one performance is paid more that a ballet master putting on the whole ballet. It IS a sad life. I got through without a cardiac stop or a stroke or any hysteria. But now His Most Majestic and Genius of an Eminence [i.e., Tudor] is going to tell them "From now on, never more than four hours a day OR . . . stick it."[15]

In turning down a request from the Ballet Rambert to help celebrate that company's fiftieth anniversary in 1975, Tudor also spoke about his lessening energy. He said that at his "rapidly advancing age" he no longer had the "stamina or the pizzazz" and was "going to have to ration my expenditure of energy if I'm not to join all my auld acquaintances that have already gone on ahead."[16]

Such complaints notwithstanding, in that first year of his associate directorship of ABT came another breakthrough. After a hiatus of many years in his creative output, he produced for ABT one of his most beautiful and remarkable ballets, *The Leaves Are Fading.*

There is no question that at this point in Tudor's life he had begun to be a bit nostalgic. *Leaves Are Fading* is surely related to this softening of his astringency and the wistfulness engendered by the sure knowledge that his days, like those of the autumnal leaves, were slowly slipping away. He gave a clue to this when he complained that people mistakenly called the work "The Leaves Are Falling," dryly stating that he had not fallen yet, only faded.

In the dance, Tudor looks back at the rapture of youth from the viewpoint of calm and understanding that can only come with age. The work is a lyrical outpouring, an homage to love, full of yearning. It explores in depth the joy and pain of relationships in a way that only dance can—on a different level from that of words. Solos, *pas de deux,* and ensemble dances follow one another seamlessly. The dance contains particularly exquisite partnering. The movement, while expansive, ecstatic, rhapsodic, never really deviates from the classical canon. The dance begins and ends with a solo female figure, in a long dress, crossing the stage—looking back over her life. It does not hint at an actual dramatic line or flashback of incidents, but rather concerns a life "reflected in tranquillity."

*The Leaves Are Fading* is one of those rare works in which all of the collaborators outdo themselves and everything comes together. Ming Cho Lee, the set designer, revealed an interesting sidelight about the very lovely painted backdrop:

> I was trained in Chinese Landscape painting. The whole drop is essentially filled with leaves painted with a certain kind of Chinese brush stroke. Chinese painting can be dogmatic. There is a certain way of painting, a certain kind of brush stroke to paint a particular kind of mountain. If you use another kind of brush stroke composition, it becomes a different sort of mountain. If you paint leaves there are certain strokes that represent a particular kind of tree. If you paint little circles, it's another kind of tree. The whole drop was painted essentially with a five stroke pattern. That is why it has kind of an abstraction. I discovered that if you don't know the brush stroke, you can't get it right. Once you know it, it's very simple; you just keep repeating that brush stroke. But if you don't know it, the painting looks dead. When other companies tried to paint a new set, it was not right because they misinterpreted the stroke. They would try to paint a western leaf.[17]

Lee reports that his meetings with Tudor never lasted more than ten or fifteen minutes. These very short conferences were very clear, a no-nonsense approach. At the first meeting Tudor said, "Here is the music and this is what I am going to do. I think at the end she will be pregnant." "Pregnant! Is that Ballet?" Lee thought. Of course, it was not until Tudor's later *Tiller in the Fields* that a pregnant heroine actually appeared.

Lee recalls that difficulties arose with *The Leaves Are Fading* during the technical and dress rehearsal period. While the backdrop was acceptable, the legs were badly executed. ("Legs" are the strips of curtain at the sides of the stage which create the "wings," i.e., the slots through which the dancers enter and exit.) Later ABT realized that to dress the ballet well they needed frame legs. They worried that with frame legs they couldn't tour it. Soft legs never really hang straight; they always wrinkle. ("Frame legs" have some solid material such as wooden slats around them; "soft legs" are made solely of weighted fabric.) Initially Tudor thought they should light the drop from the back, so they painted the initial drop translucently. For some reason the translucent painting did not come out cleanly enough. With the lights behind it, it looked dirty. They tried bringing the lights up and down, but nothing worked and the legs were getting more and more wrinkled. Tudor never got upset. Eventually lighting design Jennifer Tipton and Lee decided to hang the legs at an angle so that the lights didn't hit them at all from the audience's point of view. When Lee saw the ballet in Toronto with the National Ballet of Canada, the production used frame legs and the proper painting stroke. Tipton had reworked the lights. Lee thought the dance really looked "breathtakingly beautiful. Better than my memory of the first season."

*The Leaves are Fading* was one of the few ballets about which Tudor, himself, wrote. His essay concerning its creation gives an excellent insight into his working procedure.[18]

> After watching a performance of *Dances at a Gathering* [Robbins/Chopin], not for the first time, and being overpowered with all of its qualities, I found myself telling Mr. Robbins what a wonderful piece it was, and confessing that I also would like to bring about a ballet like that. And he simply said, "Why don't you?" The challenge rankled, hovered in the background never quite taking hold but equally never letting go. Then the music arrived—I discovered the chamber music of Dvorak. The sense of belonging was immediate, not diminished by my having read that Dvorak's father was also a butcher.

> Then the work of collating a practical score for a ballet got started. After a long time it was completed, with each piece following its predecessor without jarring in the changes of key and with sufficient variety of tempi and rhythmic signatures. It was very rewarding and I looked forward with mixed emotions to working with it, with all the doubts and apprehensions that go with the adventure into a new area.

> As usual I needed to feel my way into it, and with the cooperation of Lucia I was able . . . to get some of the dancers to come and work to see if the piece was willing to give itself to me or not. There was much trouble with the opening and, as usual, the patience of the dancers must have been sorely pressed because for days nothing would happen. Then . . . Glory Hallelujah, the breakthrough and I saw what was going to go on when the cur-

tain went up. So then I felt I could commit myself to the production of the piece. I was so *sympatico* with the music of Mr. Dvorak that I felt I would be able to make many works with him as a mentor. It didn't quite work out that way.

From the first entrance of the *jeunes filles en fleur* with the perfumes and freshness of spring in the air, expanding their lungs and stretching their muscles and their emotional responses, we move through a series of dances until at the last exit we are left with the bittersweet memories engendered by fragrant old rose petals. Every *pas de deux* should have its share of exaltation and exultation, and carry the presentiments of its being "too good to last."

The earliest rehearsals at Washington's Kennedy Center Opera House were rather what one could expect. ... My imagination wandered into Maytime, roundelays, and madrigals. I was up against a brick wall, for everything I tried was wrong, off the track, off key. The gathered dancers endured with utmost sympathy. They could feel in their own bones and muscles that something essential was stopping us. Then came the breakthrough. I discarded the piece of music that was originally intended for the opening of the ballet and used instead the piece which now both begins and ends the dance. There were no further difficulties. The music sang to me and the movement flowed as from an oasis in the desert or as fountains throwing blossoms of reflected sunlight into the air.

For once the results of his labors satisfied Tudor. The rest of the world agreed. Audiences reacted positively and the writings of the critics praised the work. Clive Barnes called it "very beautiful, simple and nakedly unaffected."[19] Allan Kriegsman said it was "brimming with the kind of delicately shaded poetic suggestion for which Tudor is rightly celebrated"[20]; and Anna Kisselgoff agreed that it was "a lovely, complex ballet that makes its points subtly and patiently."[21] The ballet remains, today, one of the most beautiful in the repertoire. In addition to its many triumphs with American Ballet Theatre productions, *The Leaves Are Fading* has been presented all over the world, with particularly moving performances in Japan by the Komaki Company in 1984. The central *pas de deux* became a staple of dance galas, and represented Tudor's works at the very moving memorial service given at the Juilliard Theater shortly after his death.

Between 1975 and 1978 Tudor continued working in much the same vein as before: ABT rehearsals and seasons, spending winters living in California and teaching at UCI. His traveling abroad to set his works became increasingly restricted. In 1976 he did go to Israel to coach a production of *Dark Elegies* with the Bat Dor Company. Letters show that some difficulty about the set arose. The Bat Dor Company wished to have an Israeli designer, but although Tudor met with several painters, nothing came of having the ballet redesigned.

Tudor increasingly reverted to his relaxed attitude about finances. With Ballet Theatre going through hard times as usual, they often didn't actually pay him the sums they committed to. In a 1971 letter, the ABT administrator at the time, Sherwin M. Goldman, had insisted: "Hungry choreographers are not good for our National Image. We shall be honored to pay unto Antony . . . if Antony will just name his price."[22]

In another such letter dated April 27, 1972, Goldwin wrote:

> Of all the artists I have ever encountered, you are clearly the most difficult to remunerate. (Remunerate? Compensate—Impossible. Pay—Offensive. OK—Remunerate.) As best I can determine you have received from us not a sou for staging *Romeo and Juliet*. Granted, you have never signed a contract, so that I am not sure what it is that we were supposed to pay you.

The letter ends with a check enclosed for $2,050.

By this time Tudor had stopped signing contracts. He had changed his opinion. He no longer believed that contracts, at the very least, diminished the possibility of misunderstanding. He now believed they carried little weight and were honored more often than not in the breach. I, myself, tried to have contract negotiations in place between Tudor and the Dance Notation Bureau concerning the licensing of his chamber ballets, to no avail. After a series of unsuccessful attempts, I ended by sending him a copy of the dialog from the wonderful scene in the Marx Brothers movie *A Night at the Opera*. In the scene a contract was destroyed little by little. The dialog read something like: "The party of the first part. . . . We don't like the party of the first part. . . . Rip." I understood from friends that Tudor hung the page of dialog over his mantle where it stayed for a long time.

At one point Tudor even suggested decreasing his ABT salary to help the company regain a financial foothold. For the 1977–1978 season the company offered him a three-year contract at $20,000 per year. He wrote back to Lucia Chase reminding her that he had agreed to work for nothing for a while. He proposed that they pay him pro rata from April through November only, thus reducing his salary from $20,000 to $14,400. His letters to Lucia, Goldwin, and later, general manager Joyce Moffat, all showed how much he valued other matters more highly than money. He exhibited greater interest in the number of rehearsal hours his ballets and the classics he took responsibility for could count on receiving, how many orchestral rehearsals were scheduled, the dress parade and similar concerns. His letters to the company bear witness to his growing dissatisfaction. The restricted amount of time he was allotted for rehearsing the works being produced under his aegis and the conditions under which he had to work on them bothered him. Clearly he cared more about the artistic product than about his compensation.

In 1978, Tudor once more succumbed to the pressure to create a new ballet. Although tired and disheartened, he agreed to go ahead. The resultant work, *Tiller in the Fields*, did not please anyone. The critics universally panned it; the audience reacted negatively. Tudor himself said "I thought it had some beautiful things in it, but it had some very boring sections. I don't think I can make the boring sections less boring."[23] Also, the scenery displeased him—he called it gay Polish Peasant rather than the desired heavily Yugoslav landscape.

It is interesting to contrast Tudor's memories of working on the set for *Tiller* with those of Ming Cho Lee:

> Tudor came with a post card reproduction of a Czech or Bohemian painter. I didn't like the painting; I found it a little gross. It was bad primitivism, a kind of Bohemian Grandma Moses, and I was still in the *Leaves Are Fading* mode. What could I say but yes, yes, very interesting? OK, I'll give it a try.
>
> What I first produced was a continuation of *Leaves Are Fading*, ignoring the post card painter. Tudor said, "But I'm not doing *Leaves Are Fading*; I am doing a very folksy piece." It is still very pastoral, I replied. He said, "Remember, at the end the lady is pregnant. I'm trying to do something that is a little bit more down to earth."
>
> I was vaguely dissatisfied with *Tiller in the Fields*. I felt I didn't go far enough. Tudor said, "It's perfect." I wanted to make some changes, but he insisted it was perfect. I even went to Oliver [Smith] saying I didn't feel I was quite getting there, but he also reassured me it was right.[24]

The ballet begins as a bucolic tale of a young peasant boy gamboling idyllically with other villagers in folk-like patterns resembling eastern European dance. A mysterious gypsy girl enters. She immediately attracts the peasant with her unfamiliar dancing, but, like a dream, she disappears when his friends return. When the friends leave again, the gypsy girl reappears. She seduces the young peasant. After a typically fascinating Tudor *pas de deux*, the two run off. As they do so, the young man offers the gypsy girl his jacket, symbolizing their joining together. At the end of the work the gypsy wanders across the stage once more, this time obviously pregnant. After the peasant's initial shock, the two exit to reap what the Tiller has sown. The gypsy's final waddling stage cross shocked people, both audience and critics.

Tudor had become obsessed, I believe. His antipathy toward the overpolished neatness and heartless precision that had become stylish in the seventies overpowered him. His sole interest was in passion, not uniformity. Thus, the corps work in *Tiller in the Fields* looked sloppy and under-rehearsed (perhaps it was). Consistent with his whole philosophy of dance, he did not want the dancers to look like peas in a pod. Somehow the work took that idea to an unsatisfactory, extreme conclusion. Even the costumes, with their lollipop colors and curlicues, distracted from the clean lines of the movement.

That the showing of pregnancy in a ballet shocked people seems consistent with American prudery. One wonders how a different audience would have received the ballet. That Tudor became the first choreographer to deal with this particular reality in a classical ballet mirrored his output and his personality. He was, after all, the choreographer who explored such subjects as a house of ill repute (*Pillar of Fire*, *Judgment of Paris*), murder (*Undertow*), repressed female sexuality (*Pillar of Fire*), the war between the sexes *(Lysistrata)*, and rape (*Echoing of Trumpets*). The light-hearted approach the ballet took to the issue of unmarried sex doubly troubled American viewers. Americans traditionally have difficulty in admitting to the reality of current sexual practice. We will never have the opportunity for a second judgment of *Tiller in the Fields* as there seems no sign of a company willing to remount and reassess the ballet.

In an interview with Judith Chazin-Bennahum,[25] Fernau Hall conjectured that the ballet had started out as a continuation of themes set out in *The Leaves Are Fading*. Tudor learned midway of Lucia Chase's impending resignation (or being pushed out). The board of ABT soon after (in 1980) appointed Baryshnikov to assume the post of artistic director. Hall maintained that Tudor himself coveted the directorship, and that his deep disappointment altered the course of *Tiller in the Fields*. While a plausible idea, several things militate against its veracity. For one thing, the dates don't really support that theory. Two years elapsed between *Tiller in the Fields* and the Baryshnikov appointment. Other unsupporting factors include Tudor's increasing illness; his disillusionment with the turn that professional dance had taken; his diminished energy; his constant references to the ravages of aging; and his need to escape to sunny California for several months each year. It is

hard to believe that Tudor would have willingly shouldered the burdens
of running a company. Why would he do so at this particular time? It
was a role he had rejected throughout his life.

In fact, in an undated letter to Nora Kaye,[26] he states: "Finally I
got Mme. Moffatt to accept that I am not Ass. Dir. [*sic*] next season
and my picture will not go in the programme as such." He goes on to
give his reason—that he totally rejects mounting the full-length *Bayadere*, budgeted at half a million dollars.

> I consider it scandalous. I don't like dancers either but I liked
> Jiri Kylian—much! And ABT kids, having a take-home package
> of about $150 a week, 36 weeks a year, are very unhappy. Even
> we old one's social security is over $100 a week 52 weeks a
> year. In fact outside of Herbert [Ross, Nora's husband, ex-ABT
> choreographer and newly celebrated Hollywood director], your-
> self and me, I don't know anyone these days who isn't totally
> miserable. So, smile kids.

## The Aftermath

Whatever the reason, *Tiller in the Fields* did not achieve success.
This was, it seems, the final blow. Shortly after, while in California in
1979, on Friday, 12 January, a massive heart attack struck down Tudor. Luckily Hugh Laing was with him and got a doctor immediately.
They took him to the South Coast Medical Center, fifteen minutes
away, where the staff tended to him immediately. On the day of the
attack Tudor had been scheduled to go to Los Angeles to rehearse
ABT. According to his doctor, had he done so, and had the attack occurred while en route, it is doubtful that he would have survived.

By Monday the nurses had Tudor sitting up, albeit still under intensive care. He left the Intensive Care Unit on Tuesday. The prognosis
was good. The doctor assured Laing that with adequate care and sufficient time, Tudor should be able to return to his full schedule. Laing
doubted that would include "jumping around in ballet."

Tudor described the event in detail in a letter to Anthony Bliss,
friend, father of Tudor's godson Mark, husband to dancer Sally Brayley
Bliss, legal advisor, and intendant of the Metropolitan Opera:

> Dear Tony,
>
> After a minute sampling of some of the *plus bas cuisine du
> monde* [worst cooking in the world], I enjoyed the first act of

Luisa Miller—wasn't Sherrill Milnes marvelous? . . . And I could
enjoy it nicely propped up in bed and congratulate myself on how
fate is conspiring with me to attain my ends. It is enabling me to
join the club of so many of my cardiac friends. Aren't you glad that
you have a penultimate son who has a godfather who is always
right. . . . After all one isn't seventy every other day.

So the last of '78 found me being enrolled on my old age
insurance—about $5,000 a year tax free—equal to about $7,000
and I can still earn up to $4,500 a year. Now even they [ABT] had
to admit that it is a better deal than taking home about $9,500 after
taxes, FICAs, etc., and working like a mongrel under tension for it.
Being here I could do a couple of hours or so—five or six a day?—
Which I did once.

P. S. (This is the whole truth and you're the first to get it from the
old horse's mouth.) At just after 6:00 a.m. Hugh would usually
walk Chenpo and me down to the Greyhound and off I'd trip. But
to his surprise last Friday morning I said 'It's early. I'm going to lie
down another half hour' . . . Then I said 'I'm not going to Los
Angeles today and when the people at the desk think the doctor's
office is open give him a call.' Then I went into the bathroom and
threw up. . . . Then the Doctor phoned. So everything functioned
marvelously—I'm in a small hospital with Pacific views and
gorgeous nurses—a most admirable doctor—a definite coronary
and angina and the knowledge that the regime they put you on
makes a better man of you than you have ever been before . . . My
wishes have been granted—no rehearsals—no conferences—no
telephone calls—no visitors [except Hugh]—and now that I've got
what I want I'll not yield to any nagging females.[27]

Tudor spent another two weeks in the hospital and then time in
Laguna Beach slowly recovering. While in the hospital, he so
ingratiated himself that the staff loved him. He was spunky and
generous. Hugh reported that Tudor hadn't decided whether he ever
wanted to leave the hospital. He got so much attention. His doctor
adored him and even kept in touch when they went back to New York.
Eventually Tudor did return to rehearsing his ballets, but some of his
admirers, myself among them, felt that he never fully recovered. His
voice remained weakened, his handwriting shaky, and his attitude
toward what transpired in the dance world continued to be increasingly
disgruntled. [28]

# Notes

1. The letter dated 24 July was found in the archives of American Ballet Theatre.

2. Letter to Maude Lloyd dated 14 November, no year, presumably 1971. Lloyd generously gave her collection of letters to me for reference. They now reside at the New York Public Library for the Performing Arts at Lincoln Center, New York.

3. I question the starting date because I have vivid memories of teaching Tudor how to read the floor plans and other rudiments of the Labanotation scores of *Little Improvisations* and *Fandango* in preparation for his staging the works in California. I believe this would have taken place when we were both on the faculty of Juilliard; however, memory can be faulty. Since he left Juilliard in May, 1971, his time at UCI might have begun before 1972. Conversely, it is entirely possible that these "lessons" took place at the Dance Notation Bureau in 1972 and later.

4. Olga Maynard, a great friend of Tudor, was a writer for *Dance Magazine* among other publications. From their correspondence it seems that Maynard helped Tudor write the required reports for his National Endowment of the Arts Grant.

5. Garrison remembered telephoning him at York University, which would place the call in 1971.

6. Muriel Topaz, interview with Clayton Garrison, 25 March, 2000, New York.

7. In a letter to Maude Lloyd, Tudor states, "For a time it looked like we might not make it [to Laguna Beach]—a 90 percent hike in their rates. With a little rearranging we're going, but risking our beautiful long friendship by deciding that . . . for the second half of the stay we'll move into one room."

8. Letter dated 4 November, 1971.

9. Letter to Beryl Grey dated 10 December, no year. The letter is in the archives of the English National Ballet.

10. Letter dated 14 February, 1973, from the archives of the English National Ballet.

11. All the quotes are taken from *Dance Magazine* (May, 1974): 41 as transcribed and edited by Richard Philp.

12. Letter "On Tour—Carcassonne" from Grey to Tudor, dated 9 July, 1973.

13. Letter to Beryl Grey, dated 28 June, 1974.

14. Letter to Olga Maynard, dated 27 September, 1975, found in the archives of the University of California, Irvine.

15. Letter dated 6 June, no year. The year may be 1976.

16. Letter to John Chesworth, artistic director of the Ballet Rambert, dated 12 May, no year. It is in response to a letter from Chesworth dated 5 May, 1975.

17. Muriel Topaz, interview with Ming Cho Lee, 22 December, 1998.

18. From notes made by Tudor in preparation for the writing of an autobiography. The selection has been edited in minor ways; however, all of the words are Tudor's.

19. Clive Barnes, *New York Times,* 27 July, 1975

20. Alan Kriegsman "Tudor's Fading Leaves," *Washington Post* (Fall, 1975, exact date unknown).

21. Anna Kisselgoff *New York Times,* 9 June, 1977.

22. Letter from Goldwin to Tudor dated 12 March, 1971.

23. Marilyn Hunt, "Antony Tudor: Master Provocateur," *Dance Magazine* (May, 1987): 40.

24. Topaz, Lee interview.

25. Judith Chazin-Bennahum, interview with Fernau Hall, London, 13 March, 1988.

26. The year would have been 1980, when *La Bayadere* premiered. The letter resides in the Nora Kaye Archive at Boston University.

27. Letter to Antony Bliss from Tudor dated only Saturday, West Coast, p.m. The date was probably 22 January, 1979.

28. For example, in a letter to Lloyd dated July 9 (?) [*sic*], he writes: "The company [ABT] is full of bright little technicians but very few that are recognisable as human beings with a bit of the old time glamour, womanliness, manliness, and charisma. What a competent, plastic, cloning civilisation we've come to.

# 9

# The Last Hurrah

## Recovery

For the most part Tudor made an excellent recovery from his heart attack, but he never really regained his full stamina. He no longer traveled except, of course, to visit his beloved Laguna Beach annually. He turned down many requests for his ballets. The few times that he did agree to having them performed around the world, he left the task of restaging to his trusted emissaries, most particularly Sallie Wilson and, in some cases, his notator Airi Hynninen.

In 1980, one year after Tudor's near-fatal heart attack Ballet Theatre's new artistic director Mikhail Baryshnikov surprised him by appointing him choreographer emeritus. Tudor continued work with ABT rehearsing his own ballets and directing revivals. Nevertheless, he complained often and bitterly about the lack of sufficient rehearsal time. He also voiced his unhappiness with the quality of the dancers' devotion and their sensitivity to the nuance so critical to the performance of his ballets.

On 27 November, 1980, the Royal Ballet brought *Dark Elegie*s back to London. While the work had been performed many times in Tudor's native city by the Ballet Rambert, to Tudor's increasing displeasure, the Royals had never done it. The staging, however, came too late in his life for Tudor to make the trip; Airi Hynninen staged the work.

Tudor's failing health, his rapid aging, and his exceeding dis-pleasure with his increasing physical limitations became a leit motif. In a letter to Maude Lloyd in 1982 Tudor expressed his mood: "Everything is more depressed and depressing except for being alive, which is the most extraordinary thing we are gifted with. Thanks to one's parents' deplorable nocturnal activities, God bless 'em."

His macrobiotic regime, strictly imposed by Hugh Laing who was convinced of its benefits, undoubtedly contributed to his decline. The diet eliminated all fried foods, all sugar and all dairy products. Since the regime barely provided the necessary nutrition, Tudor became very thin and frail. In addition, following the diet consumed hours in chopping and cooking endless vegetables. One of his recipes found scrawled on the back of an envelope illustrates its deficiencies:

    1 cup split peas
    1 medium onion diced
    3 quartered carrots
    1/2 cup wakame soaked and finely cut up
    4–5 cups water
Layer the vegetables in a pot:
    1st onion
    2nd wakame
    3rd carrots
    Place washed peas on top
    Bring gently to a boil
    Turn to simmer 1 hour or more

## The Accolades

In 1982 American Ballet Theatre restaged *Pillar of Fire* in celebration of the fortieth anniversary of the work. On the occasion his colleagues had wonderful things to say about Tudor. Martha Graham called him a master, an innovator. She said, "Not only has he brilliance in handling a gesture, he has a way of bringing the intimacy of the human spirit into gestural form. He has a supremely intelligent and introspective approach. I bless Tudor."[1] Agnes de Mille, after recounting tales of her association with Tudor in the early days in London and her role in bringing him to the United States, spoke of her reaction to *Pillar*. "I don't think since the Elizabethans, possibly except for the premiere of *Primitive Mysteries* [Graham/Horst], has there been this feeling in a theater. Tudor has found another way of saying things. This is a permanent work." Lucia Chase, speaking of Tudor the man, told how she felt that he had changed since the early days. He was now in such a fine humor. "Tudor has done wonderful things and has such high standards. Nothing bothers him if he has an idea; otherwise I don't think he cares or is anxious to do anything." Oliver Smith averred that seeing *Pillar of Fire* changed his life, and that he believed Tudor to be the greatest choreographer living. Nora Kaye spoke of her fascination with Tudor's Stanislavskian rehearsal procedures [her father was a Stanislavsky actor]. Maria Karnilova told of how Tudor invited individual dancers to his residence at the Windsor Hotel to work with him. One day she walked out of rehearsal near tears. Tudor said, "I hope you are just going out for coffee," his way of apologizing because he knew he'd gone too far. Speaking of the "old days" Karnilova quoted one of Tudor's *bon mots*: "In those days I had people who happened to be dancers, and now I have dancers who are not always people." And, Cynthia Gregory, then American Ballet Theatre's reigning ballerina, explained how at first she had difficulty learning the role of Hagar, the lead in *Pillar of Fire*. She recounted that this amused Tudor because he enjoyed watching her struggle with the challenge. "He used to make me tongue-tied, but now I enjoy him." Of the evening Tudor wrote to Nora Kaye:

> I am so happy that you were nowhere around here in person last week for *Pillar*'s comeback. You will have heard about it because I'm sure Isabel [Brown] has kept you informed. And her powers of description are better than mine could be because I was struck dumb.

> So the little shindig upstairs was a tiny bit under a pall (not my imagination.). . . . Happily, at the Thursday performance with Lise Houlton back in, we got a performance and beautiful reception again. So I decided not to ossify in permanent horror.

> Also, I'm sure I saw your name on a list of the Dance Notation Bureau, as being a contributor to their Fund for notating the works of Tudor. Can you imagine that they even worked so hard that they got a grant for it from the Government for "Humanities? " [2]

The last paragraph refers to an important project undertaken by the Dance Notation Bureau. The project proposed to document six of Tudor's major works through Labanotation, accompanied by historical and biographical essays, production information and comments on the works by the choreographer himself. As a result of this project Tudor was enticed to write about *Jardin aux lilas* and later *The Leaves Are Fading*. He intended to write about each of his notated ballets. Unfortunately he never finished his contribution to the project. The Dance Notation Bureau proposal centered around documentation of *Dark Elegies, Dim Lustre, Jardin aux lilas* (revised version of the dance score), *Undertow, Shadowplay,* and *Pillar of Fire*. The project itself was of major significance. It broke ground as one of the first, and few, dance-oriented projects ever to be funded in the United States by the National Endowment for the Humanities (rather than the National

Endowment for the Arts). The grant signified recognition by the federal government that dance was an acceptable and appropriate topic for scholarly study. The project came about after a conversation I had with Tudor. I worried that while most of his smaller ballets had been notated at the Juilliard School, his major works remained unrecorded. As part of his lack of interest in money, Tudor was, in principle, always opposed to the whole idea of grants. He saw them as unearned gain. Even though from the start he interested himself in the notation of his works, he had to be convinced to lend his approval to my plan because it involved a grant. His opposition melted, however, when I asked if he wished to be remembered solely by those smaller works. He understood immediately that the documented works would live on.

## Nostalgia

In June of 1982, Tudor's esteemed colleague and mentor, Marie Rambert, died. She was the woman with whom he had both blossomed as a young choreographer and fought with a vengeance for his independence. Five years later, just two months before his own demise, his principal American muse and dear friend Nora Kaye also passed away. Tudor, overwhelmed, even allowed himself to cry openly at the memorial service for Kaye. For a man who guarded his privacy with such tenacity, this most unusual public exhibition of his emotional world signified how that world was changing.

Tudor's waning years brought with them a certain nostalgia. His continuing correspondence with his great friend and early collaborator Maude Lloyd clearly revealed this. In the 1980s and particularly for the last two years of his life, Lloyd and Tudor kept up a fairly frequent and lively correspondence. One letter throws light on how he spent his time. On 1 January, 1986, he wrote to her:

> There can be no better way to start a New Year than rare contacts. Hugh and I celebrated with 1/2 bottle of Champagne Brut and toasted ourselves, our respective parents who started it all, and our best beloved friends, then all of Hugh's pals, the dogs starting with Tobias and going through them till Chenpo. And after all this excitement we got into our beds by our usual 8:30 p.m. Life, as you see, is as quiet as ever, quieter without our little dog to fuss over. We shop, go for walks, chop vegetables and ruminate and are very grateful for the possibilities.

And, on 13 April:

> Once upon a time when I was a lad I collected stamps and knew where the Seychelles were, but now I can't even find them on a map. . . . I hope you didn't have to go there, although with Rudi's [Nureyev] penchant for getting his own way, I suspect you may have done what was ordered. Are you a woman or a mouse? [3] Your letters are endlessly fascinating, especially when you manage to get the red and the black of the tape mixed up. We are kindred spirits in that mechanical gadgets are created by the devil to torment nice quiet well-behaving human beings. . . . And speaking of machines, I do believe that our newer crop of dancers are of the mechanical clan. I have never enjoyed an arabesque that ended with the knee on the top of the head, nor do I like overhead lifts where the girl is in a full backbend and can only see where she's going by peeping out of her crotch. Clever. . . . Everything is getting very busy with Memorial Services[4], Awards, Talks to Graham students [Tudor gave a series of informal talks at the Martha Graham School of Contemporary Dance] and all sorts of dates that one would gladly do without. . . . I am rather pleased with Jane Hermann's coup of getting Rudolf and Misha and their companies on the same stage for a performance.[5] I probably won't see it. I don't like to go out in the evenings and I do like to go to bed betimes. But then I do like to "get up in the morning when the sun begins to shine," and am usually doing my stretching exercises by five o'clock. . . . I haven't seen ABT for a long time, but hear (grapevine) that every one of their new ballets have been flops,[6] but *Elegies* revival had been highly praised. We even enjoyed rehearsing again.

And on 6 November, 1986:

> It is winter and old Will Shakespeare said it all. The old gray goats they ain't what they used to be. We certainly had a lot of good times between us before "Father Time" and "caution." . . . We go Dec. 11th to Laguna Beach and it'll be a joy to be in one room with Hugh. Can you believe?[7] Even the subway trips three or four times a week to visit each other (necessary!) become a wild tribulation. But that must be age creeping up. I'm certainly aiming toward senility, and not doing so badly at it. The adrenaline still works itself into a lather at rehearsals.

Although Tudor rarely articulated his inner emotional life, there is one extant, undated letter to Hugh which reveals these very feelings. It is a simple, direct, and unadorned declaration of love:

These are words that should have been said many times over the years. Since I first set eyes on you I have never failed to love you, and you are the only one that I have ever loved. I hope that we shall have a good period of aging quietly together and will enjoy the pleasures of each other's cares, affections and company. [It is signed simply, Antony.]

By the 1980s Tudor had become an icon of dance in America, in his native England, and in many other places around the world. Recognition, homages, and awards flowed. In 1985 the Royal Academy of Dance in London presented him with the Queen Elizabeth II Coronation Award, received for him in absentia by Maude Lloyd.

## France

In spite of his enormous reputation elsewhere, Tudor and his works were little known in France. In 1985, at the behest of Rudolf Nureyev, then artistic director of the Paris Opera Ballet, this was to be remedied. Although Tudor and Nureyev had never worked together, a great deal of respect existed between them. They had met through their mutual friend, Maude Lloyd, and in correspondence with her often asked after one another. Tudor referred to Nureyev as "that boy." He said of Nureyev, with perhaps a touch of tongue in cheek: "[His is] a great, truly great, career and individual. Started as extraordinary—went thru all the superlatives (the mostest of the mostest) and now I know has arrived at being . . . fabulous."[8] At one point Nureyev even requested that Tudor choreograph a ballet for him. Tudor demurred, just as he had when other "stars" made similar requests (as had Makarova, and Baryshnikov). Nureyev organized a full evening of Tudor ballets in homage to his choreographic genius. The Paris Opera staged and presented the evening for a run of twelve performances. The program comprised *Continuo, Shadowplay, Jardin aux lilas,* and *Dark Elegies.*

According to critics[9] and to Maude Lloyd, the French dancers made a travesty of the performances of *Shadowplay.* They had no idea what the ballet was about and they had little sympathy for such things in a ballet as monkeys. Their exposure to material other than the very classic or, in the case of a specially trained group, the very avant-garde essentially did not exist. They giggled at rehearsals and made a shambles of the performance. They compared Charles Jude, dancing the Boy with the Matted Hair, to Tarzan. At the final performance, the dancers even had the audacity to show their contempt for the ballet by eating bananas on stage.

Nureyev and Tudor. *Photograph courtesy of Maude Lloyd*

*Jardin aux lilas* fared better. The characters were not as foreign to the dancers. Also, the ballet had a very French air, being variously called Proustian and reminiscent of de Maupassant.[10] Some critics wrote that the performance did not convince while others found it captivating. All agreed that both of the female soloists Yannick Stephant/Ghislaine Thesmar as Caroline, Karin Avery/Clotilde Vayer as the Episode in his Past, did a fine job. According to the distinguished British dance critic Clement Crisp the performance of *Dark Elegies* also succeeded. It "caught the proper dignity of tone and of expression. The ballet looked a masterpiece."[11] Everyone agreed that the performances of Wilfrid Piollet and Jean Guizérix were, in the words of Olivier Merlin of the respected French newspaper *Le Monde, "tout en nuances, extrêmement discrète et poétique"*[12] [full of nuance, extremely discreet and poetic].

Both critics and public universally hailed *Continuo*. It was called *"le vrai petit bijou de la soirrée"*[13] [the true little gem of the evening]. . . . *"Neuf minutes pendant lesquelles les danseurs de l'opéra savent montrer une suprématie triomphante dans le monde de la danse, défiant toutes les lois de direction and d'effort."* [Nine minutes during which the opera dancers know how to show their triumphant supremacy in the dance world, defying all laws of directional movement and effort]. The excellent young cast included Sylvie Guillem and Laurent Hilaire.

Tudor, of course, although greatly pleased and much moved by the whole affair, did not attend. Sallie Wilson *(Jardin aux lilas, Dark Elegies)*, Airi Hynninen *(Continuo, Jardin aux lilas)* and Jude Siddall and Christopher Newton *(Shadowplay)* staged the evening. Audience reaction was variously described as "baffled by the extreme originality of the ballets, so different from anything they had seen before"[14] to "French audiences had made up their minds that they liked Tudor very much."[15]

Following the homage, several of the Tudor's works remained in the repertory. *Jardin aux lilas,* and *Dark Elegies* played for several seasons, and the following year the company added *The Leaves Are Fading*.

## The Capezio Award

The honors continued in 1986. In the spring Tudor finally agreed to accept the Capezio Award over the objection of Hugh, who felt that the award was too long overdue.

The Capezio Award provided an opportunity for Tudor's many colleagues to pay homage, which they did quite profusely. Some of the encomiums from those who would follow in his footsteps included:[16]

> Eliot Feld: The difficulty in honoring Mr. Tudor is that he has so honored himself in the making of his ballets, that he has rendered the accolades of our pens paltry and our tongues tinsel. Still, we must attempt to overcome this impediment; and knowing Mr. Tudor as I do, having happily run the gamut of his rehearsals, and having felt the keen edge of the scalpel wit of this, our surgeon laureate, I am confident he will tolerate our effort and relish our fumphering. Antony Tudor has invented ballets that are surely among the most beautiful devised by man or woman. It is not we that confer honor on Antony Tudor. That is beyond our domain. Rather, we join together to acknowledge our appreciation and esteem for a half century of gifts he has shared with us. I believe that the ballets, those elegant and generous inventions of Mr. Tudor's, are nothing less than the building blocks of civilization. It is through his choreographic vision that, as a society and individuals, we inspect our frailties, revel in our accomplishments, and glean our possibilities. . . . Please know, Mr. Tudor, that today's celebration is merely an awkward public expression of a private, deep, and abiding genuflection. Thank you for your ballets.

> Jerome Robbins: What a pleasure to be at this celebration of Mr. Tudor. It was seeing one of his ballets, *Dark Elegies*. . . in 1939, that made me want to join the Ballet Theatre company and to hope to dance in that ballet . . . . There is no way to describe those incredible days of concentrated absorbing work or to detail the wonders of that experience. We were working with one of the most influential people in our twentieth-century dance art. . . . I propose a toast to him in the name of the hundreds upon hundreds of dancers who have worked with him and who have been influenced and educated by him. And I toast him in the name of thousands upon thousands of people who have seen his ballets and have had not only great pleasures but profound insights about our inner lives.

Others who spoke included Dame Alicia Markova, Oliver Smith, and Agnes de Mille. Mikhail Baryshnikov said that he had never been a Tudor dancer because Tudor thought him too expensive. He also said that Tudor thought that Ballet Theatre did his ballets because Lucia Chase insisted upon it. Baryshnikov disagreed: "We do his ballets because we must. Tudor's work is our conscience."

William Schuman, Tudor, and Eliot Feld at the Capezio Awards. *Photograph courtesy of Isabel Brown*

Paul Taylor, with his usual quirky sense of humor, thought it appropriate to relate a well-known tale:

> Martha Graham had premiered a new piece and the rumor was afloat that when Tudor had gone backstage to speak to her, she kicked him in the shins. I don't know if this is true. I didn't see Martha Graham kick Tudor in the shins. Hard. But that was the rumor. Evidently he had said that she was guilty of choreographic compromise.

The eminent William Schuman, composer of the score for *Undertow* read the citation:

> To Antony Tudor, dancer, teacher, master choreographer. His understanding of the profound depths of human emotion has led him to explore the springs of grief, passion, jealousy, and joy in ballets that possess an unparalleled resonance. As teacher and mentor, he has served as a conscience for generations of dancers. His uncompromising standards reflect the artist as a moral force, recognizing that dance can provide both pleasure and insight.

That same year Tudor shared with Martha Graham the first Dance/USA Award and was honored by New York City with its highest cultural accolade, the Handel Medallion. The municipal government first presented the award at a small ceremony at City Hall. The cermony was repeated more publicly on the stage of the Metropolitan Opera House on the same evening, 20 May, 1986. A special event took place that evening in homage to Tudor. American Ballet Theatre presented a program solely devoted to his choreography. The program gave a panoramic view of Tudor's work over the years. It included performances of *The Leaves Are Fading, Dim Lustre, Jardin aux lilas,* and *Dark Elegies*—not an easy evening for either, dancer, or audience but one of amazing depth and quality.

## Kennedy Center Honors

In December, 1986, Tudor received the ultimate award the United States offers, the Kennedy Center Honors. It was a grand affair. The weekend celebration included a reception at the White House for Tudor and his co-honorees Lucille Ball, Ray Charles, Jessica Tandy, Hume Cronyn, and Yehudi Menuhin. It culminated in a production. Agnes de Mille introduced the Tudor segment. It included a *pas de deux* from *The Leaves Are Fading* danced by Leslie Browne and Robert Hill. De

Mikhail Baryshnikov, Mayor Ed Koch, Tudor, and Cultural Affairs Minister Bess Meyerson. *Photograph by Walter E. Owen, courtesy of Jerome Robbins Dance Division, New York Public Library for the Performing Arts*

Mille, in her usual fine form as an orator, spoke of the early years when she first met Tudor and of his work:

> He was young and bonny and hopeful. He didn't know what he wanted to do. He didn't want to be silly. There was an awful lot of that in London and in New York. . . . He always shows the emotional meaning behind the action. Right to the heart, but satisfying the mind. . . . No ballet company can claim to be great without a work of his.[17]

At his invitation longtime friend and supporter Nancy Zeckendorf escorted Tudor to the awards. Among his guests were Isabel Brown, and Sally and Antony Bliss with their son, Tudor's godson Mark (each honoree is allotted only five tickets for his or her box). Margot Fonteyn flew in from Panama for the event. Zeckendorf reported that nothing in her life had ever been as exhilarating and as exciting as that weekend. She did, however, worry about Tudor. He was already quite frail for such an exhausting as well as exciting weekend.

Hugh Laing stayed at home. Debate abounded about why Tudor didn't take Hugh. Consistent with their behavior throughout their life together the two men once again avoided public acknowledgment of their relationship. They never appeared in any public place as a couple. Zeckendorf speculated that Tudor's English upbringing, which frowned upon such "inappropriate" behavior, was a determining factor. According to Isabel Brown Tudor very much wanted Hugh to go to Washington. As much as Isabel begged Hugh, he refused. She speculated on Hugh's complex reasons: He wanted Tudor to have all the accolades; he feared his presence would somehow distract attention; he shunned the obvious conclusion that they were a gay couple; and, he was, in his heart of hearts, jealous of Tudor. In spite of his usual macrobiotic diet, Tudor ate and drank the same food as everyone else during the weekend to no apparent ill effect. Although he had long ago forsworn alcohol, on this occasion he even indulged in martinis.

Tudor, along with the other honorees, watched the extravaganza from a box next to that of then President Ronald Reagan. At the end, there came a very touching moment in which he acknowledged the applause with palms pressed together, fingers up, head lowered, in a Buddhist bow.

Mary Farkas, Tudor's longtime Zen associate and founder of the First Zen Institute where he lived, wrote of this moment: "As he stood taking the ovation of the huge audience, he bowed the Buddhist way, with hands joined, in the beautiful gesture that expresses heartfelt appreciation. With tears in his eyes, with this gesture, he acknowledged this deep source of his inspiration."

Nancy Reagen, Antony Tudor, and an unidentified woman at the Kennedy Center Awards. *Photograph courtesy of Isabel Brown*

Tudor returned from the affair exhilarated but exhausted. Clearly he had enjoyed the occasion. He had even acceded to donning formal attire, something which he had resisted for years. "Even I will have to go through the tortures of a black tie and probably tight shoes. It will play hell with my old man routine" is how he described his feeling about it to Zeckendorf.

Unbeknownst to all, the Kennedy Center Honors were the last opportunity the world had to honor the great man. Tudor returned to rehearsals at American Ballet Theatre, but not for long. The awards took place in December and in the beginning of the following April, he finally succumbed.

## The Final Days

Upon his return from Washington Tudor went into rehearsals of American Ballet Theatre. The company wanted to revive *Pillar of Fire*. Ethan Brown, who performed The Man from the House Opposite, the role originally done by Laing, spoke of the emotionally charged rehearsals. Quite often for his solos Brown had private rehearsals, with only Tudor and Hugh present. Kathleen Moore and at times Sallie Wilson would appear in the studio for work on the *pas de deux*. Brown recounts that sometimes the rehearsals became very tense, sometimes not. Every rehearsal was like a performance. One never knew what Tudor would say. He could be very direct and to the point, or he might be very candid, or use vulgar language. Although both Tudor and Laing had very exigent expectations for Brown, he remembered them being happy with him as long as he tried and gave 100 percent. The company scheduled the initial New York performance for opening night of at the Metropolitan Opera House. Two days before the opening Tudor died. To quote Ethan Brown:

> It was very hard. We were all in a studio. Hugh was there and Sallie, and everyone was crying. I thought "How are we going to perform this?" I had opened the paper on my day off and there it was: "Dance Great Antony Tudor Dead at 79." I just couldn't believe it; I was in shock. I had just worked with him, and the next night was to be opening night at the Met—a very exciting moment. We had to spend the day teching the ballet. [setting the lights and wing entrances]. It was very, very rough. I don't know how we got through that performance.[18]

Mary Farkas described those final hours:

> After rehearsing this ballet [*Leaves Are Fading*] and his first
> masterpiece, *Pillar of Fire*, with Hugh Laing [helping him] . . .
> on Easter Sunday, Tudor was very tired. Hugh Laing . . . was
> spending the night at the Institute. He was awakened by Tudor's
> call for help to get him up from where he had fallen. After being
> helped into bed, Tudor lay there quietly. Hugh asked him if he
> was all right. "Yes,' he replied, 'I'm all right. You can go back to
> sleep.' Hugh went back to his own place and was sitting on the
> edge of his bed when he heard, a few minutes later, a 'Ka-a-a-a.'
> This is the usual spelling for a sound Zen masters make to
> demonstrate Zen. It means they dissolve into the sound. It is
> not a human word, but, like the baby's first cry, the true word of
> nature itself. Perhaps you could say "life force." Some Chris-
> tians would say, "He gave up the ghost." In that moment of the
> death rattle, the heart stops beating. The person is gone.[19]

# Notes

1. Hilary Ostlere, *Ballet News*, April, 1982, 18–19.The succeeding
quotes are from the same source.

2. Letter to Nora Kaye dated 10 May, no year, found in the archive
at Boston University's Department of Special Collections.

3. Lloyd and Nureyev were great friends. After the death of
Lloyd's husband Nigel Gosling in 1982, Nureyev was particularly so-
licitous of her well-being and often invited her to accompany him on
his trips.

4. As early as 1980 Tudor's letters were full of regrets over the
many colleagues he was losing. In one undated letter to Lloyd he mentioned George Skibine, Nana Gollner, Royez Fernandez and Kelley
Brown, and later Eric Bruhn.

5. Jane Hermann was the executive director of American Ballet
Theatre at that time. She arranged a benefit performance at which
American Ballet Theatre with Baryshnikov and the Paris Opera Ballet
with Nureyev both danced.

6. New ballets in the season included *Duets* (Merce Cunning-
ham/John Cage); *Claire de lune* (Peter Anastos/Claude Debussy);
*Carmen* (Roland Petit/Georges Bizet); *Configurations* (Choo San Goh/
Samuel Barber), and *Great Galloping Gottschalk* (Lynn Taylor-
Corbett/Louis Moreau Gottschalk).

7. Since at least the sixties Tudor and Hugh had been living
apart, Tudor in the Zen Institute in the east thirties of New York City,
Hugh in an apartment on the Upper West Side. They dined and spent
evenings together regularly, however, taking turns visiting one another.

There is a certain irony about Tudor's relief in living in the same room with Hugh in Laguna Beach, since, starting with Hugh's marriage to Diana Adams in the fifties, Tudor had seemed to need the independence of living separately from Laing.

8. Letter to Lloyd dated 25 June, 1980.

9. Jann Parry, "A Plague of Monkeys," *Observer,* 10 March, 1985. Also, Fernau Hall, "Tudor Féte in Paris," *Daily Telegraph,* 26 February, 1985.

10. Isabelle Cases, "Tudor: Non, Je Songe," *7 à Paris,* 11 November, 1986. Also Clement Crisp, "Homage to Antony Tudor/ Opéra Comique, Paris," *The Financial Times,* 20 February, 1985.

11. Crisp, "Homage to Antony Tudor."

12. Olivier Merlin, "Un Carnivore en Hibernation," *Le Monde,* 22 *February,* 1985.

13. Brigitte Kehrer, "Paris Fête Antony Tudor," *Tribune de Geneve,* 26 February, 1985.

14 Hall, "Tudor Fête in Paris."

15. Parry, "A Plague of Monkeys."

16. *Ballet Review* (Fall, 1986): 34–37. All quotes are from this source.

17. *New York Times,* 8 December, 1986.

18. Muriel Topaz, interview with Ethan Brown, 22 January 1998.

19. Mary Farkas, *Zen Notes* XXXIV, no. 5 (May, 1987).

Laing, Tudor, unidentified woman, and Michael Ohlbaum, husband of Airi Hynninen. *Photograph courtesy of Isabel Brown*

# 10

# Afterward

## Afterword—In Memoriam

The extraordinary Antony Tudor left this world on 5 April, 1987. The First Zen Institute held a brief but quite beautiful service for him at its headquarters at 113 E. 30th Street, New York. He was cremated according to Zen custom and buried in the Institute's plot at the Woodlawn Cemetery in New York.

For the service the residents of the Institute ushered the small group of invited guests into a strikingly simple room. The hosts were already sitting in lotus position one row facing the other. We, the spectator/participants, lined up behind them. Various gongs and drums occupied one end of the room. After a period of quiet contemplation and some chanting, Mary Farkas said a few words about Tudor. She described him as a model for the Institute's students in the strictness of his own personal practice and quiet determination. She called his sitting, walking, and bowing impeccable. She then called upon the rest of us to speak of him if we were so inclined. First various residents said how they felt about the man. Some impromptu reminiscences from the rest of us followed. It was a moving ceremony of great dignity worthy of the man who had affected so many lives. One of the residents, Clara Maxwell, had been his student at Juilliard. Her salute to him was particularly moving:

> Even if the steps remain only in Labanotation, Tudor's work will stay forever, precisely because when a dancer explores the steps and discovers them for himself or herself there is an irrefutable truth in the body which, almost in spite of oneself, places the dancer into the appropriate feelings. . . . I am at a loss to describe this confirmation of physical truth; I could describe it as *le vol de phoenix* [the flight of the phoenix] or as a form of

transcendence in the German words *aufgehoben, mit flugen die ich mich errungen* (with wings I have built for myself). Tudor's legacy is a presence whose inspiration has nothing to do with aspirations toward immortality but the simple courage to be a human being.[1]

The more official and public memorial to Tudor came later, in June, 1987. Organized mainly by Nancy Zeckendorf, it took place in the Juilliard Theater. As the school had treated him in life, so did it in death. The theater was not actually put at Mrs. Zeckendorf's disposal. Juilliard asked for and received from her the costs involved in opening the theater to the public—some $2,500.

The theater filled to capacity with Tudor's friends, colleagues, and admirers. Most luminaries in the dance world attended, and those who could not sent greetings, in absentia.

Messages came from three of the most celebrated ballerinas of our time. Alicia Alonso called Tudor an awesome figure who taught her that dance movement has no limits. He challenged her to plumb memory, to unveil hidden experience and passion in order to help convey the pain and loss in human relationships. Alicia Markova described him as the great international choreographer with the most British name. She found him a man of inspired visions whose enormous talent allowed him to bring those visions to life. Natalia Makarova's note said that his soul would always be alive in her heart and that she hoped to meet him again in the afterlife, if there was one.

Sallie Wilson, the dancer so closely associated with many of his most important roles, and, along with Hugh Laing, the obvious heir apparent in the staging of his works, described him as compelling, dynamic, beautiful, inspiring, electrifying, all-seeing, perplexing, and magical.

Nancy Zeckendorf expressed what many in attendance felt: that it had been an honor to be part of his life. Words written earlier by the late Nora Kaye referred to Tudor as the most inspiring choreographer of his time, perhaps of any time, and the most important person in her life. Mercedes Ellington, distinguished show choreographer, granddaughter of Duke Ellington, and Juilliard graduate trained under Tudor's watchful eye, also spoke. She recounted how he taught her that one could say as much with the back as the front. Tudor, she said, always spoke his mind and read hers. In later years, when she dined with him in Laguna Beach or bumped into him on the bus, he spoke encouragingly to her about her lineage and her responsibility to it.

Choreographer Jerome Robbins told of a note he received from Tudor on opening night of his first ballet *Fancy Free*. It said, in essence, that the night held great importance for Robbins and for all of them. But, continued the note, "Just don't make it too good." Mikhail Baryshnikov, dancer *extraordinaire* and the then artistic director of American Ballet Theatre, drew laughter with his description of his final encounter with Tudor. Tudor was sitting in the hallway of the ABT studios, resting, totally silent. With both his gaze and his hands in front of him, he sat oblivious to all the rushing and chaos around him. As Russians do, Baryshnikov knelt in front of him and kissed his hand. Tudor didn't change his expression, but said, "I liked that."

Choreographer Agnes de Mille called it a cruel day. She gave a call to arms to the entire dance community to come together to preserve the mind, heart, feeling, and perception of his work—his beautiful eye, his taste, his insistence on quality. "We knew him, we worked with him, we loved him. We've got to see that his works last . . . [because they are] not only works of art but facets of life, itself. Wider. Larger. And we see ourselves. Larger. Bigger. More important. More valuable. The horizons stretch out and out and out. Because he made a statement of absolute truth."

Mary Farkas, describing herself as Tudor's Zen connection, said:

> Tudor's self-imposed discipline was impressive and he was a stickler for form. He could be stern and snappish when he took his turn as leader. He could also be charming and impish. Tudor did not get his Zen style of teaching from Zen. Spontaneity was natural for him. He would stop at nothing to invoke it in his dancers. He had it before he ever heard of Zen.

The critic Clive Barnes speculated that Tudor was difficult to work with because he arrived at every rehearsal with an image of perfection that nothing could ever equal. He also spoke of Tudor's one foot of clay—a disparaging, even bitter self-doubt. Barnes described him as "shy of his talent." Tudor knew in some tiny inner way that he was a genius, But, he was awkward about people taking him for one, and yet, rather hurt if they did not. Francis Mason[2] read a note from Martha Graham:

> Antony Tudor was a man I could call, although I rarely use the word, a truly creative person in his work, in his attitude toward life and in his relationships with people. He had the rare gift of making something live absolutely in terms of feeling. *Dark Elegies* was the first work of his I saw at its New York premiere performance. I knew then that I faced a deeply intuitive person and an astounding creative force for the dance. I've never altered that opinion. It has only grown by the years of seeing his work and finding that he had the capability of true friendship. These are very rare attributes and I am fortunate enough to have

sensed them and to treasure them and to miss them with all my heart. It has been a rare gift to me to meet such a person in my life, a person of such dedication and such essential innocence where his art was concerned.

Last to speak was Hugh Laing, the person closest to Tudor, whose elegant words left few dry eyes:

> I know you loved him. How could you help from doing this? I loved him too. I was luckier than you. I knew him for 55 years and shared everything with him. I am so very grateful. . . . He gave so much more than he ever took. He liked it that way. He asked for little. Just perfection. . . . He was a very simple person—a very complicated simple person.[3]

The service concluded with a lovely, emotional performance of the main *pas de deux* from *Leaves Are Fading* danced by Amanda McKerrow and Robert Hill.

       \*        \*        \*        \*

Thus ended the life of Antony Tudor, one of the most gifted artists of the late twentieth century. His imagination, his intelligence, his elegance, his impeccable taste, and his total inability to compromise his art stand as a paradigm for an artist of any time, any century. Those of us who were fortunate enough to cross his path remain enriched—enriched and ever questioning, for we can never be quite as complacent as we were before.

His personal life remains enigmatic. A man of deep feeling, he found it inappropriate and perhaps in bad taste to reveal his inner emotional life—except, of course, in his choreography. There it blossomed and matured, always expressed through the movement of one of his characters, never through the voice of Antony Tudor the man. He is known to have described himself as a cold-hearted bastard, but one whose characters were never cold.

Although it is too soon to make an unprejudiced assessment of his contribution to the art of our time, it is incontrovertible that it was and remains major. While Tudor the man resists inquiry, Tudor the creative force has left us with a body of work that has changed our perception of dance as an art form and profoundly influenced its course. We still find it moving and relevant. While only time will tell how much of the work will survive, its importance cannot be gainsaid because its influence has already been felt.

He was, indeed, a genius. I salute him.

# Notes

1. Clara Maxwell, *Zen Notes,* XXXIV, no. 5 ( May, 1987).
2. Francis Mason is editor-in-chief of the publication *Ballet Review,* and dance critic for WQXR AM/FM radio. He gives a regular weekly broadcast about the dance. Mason has chaired the board of directors of the Martha Graham Dance Company.
3. All material and quotations are taken from an audio tape recording of the memorial service provided to me by Nancy Zeckendorf.

# 11

# An Envoi

## Afterward

In the wake of Tudor's death, concerts devoted to his memory were presented around the world. Ruriko Tachikawa who had danced in his ballets in Japan, mounted a full evening of his works in Tokyo. In a tribute evening, Donald Bradburn, a colleague at the University of California at Irvine, recapitulated three of the smaller works Tudor had previously staged at the college. Jiri Killian dedicated his dance *Overgrown Path* to Tudor. As part of its fiftieth anniversary celebration in 1990 American Ballet Theatre presented a full evening of Tudor ballets, comprising *Gala Performance, The Leaves Are Fading, Jardin aux lilas,* and *Pillar of Fire.* The company performed the program both in New York and on tour in Chicago, San Francisco, and Washington. On 13 April, 1990, the American public television series "Dance in America," broadcast an hour-long program called "A Tudor Evening with American Ballet Theatre." It featured *Jardin aux lilas* and *Dark Elegies.* Sallie Wilson did the staging. The dances were filmed in Denmark with the music performed by the Danish Radio Orchestra. The program also contained documentary footage of reminiscences by Agnes de Mille, Marie Rambert, and Maude Lloyd. Tudor referred to himself as a "bastard to work with" in his brief cameo appearances. In reviewing the telecast Alan Kriegsman added that this solitary man, a practicing Buddhist, looked "as if he were carved from rock, with the clear-eyed profile of a hawk. . . . But, when he raises a hand to illustrate a point, the subtlety and majesty of the gesture convey the entirely different character of a great artist."[1]

Happily for succeeding generations of dancers and audiences, Tudor had the foresight to provide (or was bullied by me and others into providing) for the continuity of his ballets. About ten years before his death, Tudor approached Anthony Bliss. Bliss, along with his duties as intendant (general director) of the Metropolitan Opera, was a partner in the law firm of Milbank, Tweed, Hadley, and McCloy. Tudor had seen the chaos that ensued after the deaths of Charles Weidman and José Limón.[2] Because of this his friends and colleagues succeeded in convincing Tudor that his works would not die but rather be badly misrepresented. So, Tudor finally decided to write a will. Bliss referred him to Jay Swanson, a young associate, who drew up the will. It had standard provisions: directions for disposal of his remains by cremation, the bequest of all his papers and effects, as well as his residual estate not including the dances to Hugh Laing, a monthly stipend to and payment of medical expenses for Hugh, a small one–time sum to each grandniece and nephew upon Hugh's death. Most important, the will set up the Tudor Trust, to which he left the rights to all of his ballets. The will appointed, as sole trustee and co-executor with Swanson of the estate, Sally Brayley Bliss. Sally, wife of Anthony Bliss, formerly danced with the Metropolitan Opera Ballet and starred in Tudor's *Concerning Oracles*. Apparently, before deciding on Sally Bliss, Tudor had approached Jiri Killian. Tudor had very high regard for Killian. Although the regard was mutual, Killian demurred, feeling he did not have the time to assume that responsibility. Tudor surprised many close associates with his choice of trustee. Laing was mortally offended. Clearly he felt that the responsibility of caring for the ballets should have been left to him. He was angry as only Hugh could be, and he never really forgave Sally Bliss.

Perhaps Tudor was wise in his choice. He well knew Hugh's volatility and how difficult he could be in a dance studio. One proof, if such a thing as proof existed, that Laing would perhaps not have been the wisest choice exhibited itself immediately. Laing, in a fit of pique, destroyed many of Tudor's papers and archives before they could be rescued. Hugh's health presented a second issue. He had been ailing for a long time, and, in actual fact survived Tudor only by a year.

Hugh, along with Sallie Wilson, did supervise an American Ballet Theatre revival of *Gala Performance* just after Tudor's death. Hugh refused to accept any compensation for his work on the ballet. Baryshnikov, artistic director of American Ballet Theatre at the time, wanted to show his appreciation in some way. He knew that Hugh's financial position was precarious. On the advice and with the help of Isabel Brown, ABT sent Hugh a new television set. Isabel knew that Hugh avidly watched and enjoyed television and that his TV set was about to expire. At first Hugh refused the gift, then raged against it, and finally accepted it.

Speculation is that Tudor thought of the disposition of his ballets as an administrative and legal matter. He thought of it as a burden with which he did not wish to encumber Laing. I suspect what he imagined would happen is what actually is happening for the most part. Mrs. Bliss has enlisted the knowledge and services of those closest to Tudor for rehearsing the works while she herself bears the burden of the administrative detail. Also, the fact that she was married to Anthony Bliss, the lawyer to whom Tudor had turned for help, must have been a factor in the choice.

## The Tudor Trust

In setting up the Trust the will stipulated that all remountings of the works be undertaken with the aid of the notation. In accordance with Tudor's life-long belief in the corrupting power of money in individual hands, the financial benefits of the Trust went to three nonprofit organizations: the Dance Notation Bureau, the Dance Division of the Performing Arts Branch of the New York Public Library, and a third entity to be chosen by the trustee. In the event of the trustee's becoming incapacitated, the responsibility of running the Trust would pass to Nancy Zeckendorf. Later, when Swanson left the law, Jonathan Bell of Paul, Weiss, Rifkind, Wharton, and Garrison assumed the legal duties vis-à-vis the trust. The trustee also has the responsibility of appointing an appropriate successor.

Predictably, a certain amount of skepticism about how Sally Bliss would run the Trust surfaced. Many wondered whether the works of Tudor would or could be authentically revived. Bliss has a philosophy which markedly differs from that of Tudor himself. He often denied requests for his ballets, worried about overexposure, in principle preferred to say no rather than yes. He searched for the perfect circumstances, retracted ballets when he was not entirely satisfied with casting and in general made it difficult for a company to have a Tudor ballet in its repertoire. On the contrary, Sally Bliss feels that the world can and should have the opportunity to experience the genius of Tudor whenever possible. The one caveat, of course, is that a company must be capable of doing a creditable job with the material. She bears, not lightly, the burden of seeing that the works are set as faithfully as possible.

I feel that when dancers today work on a Tudor ballet, they are affected in a positive and profound way. That is why all companies who can do Tudor, should. His work gives a whole other dimension to dance."[3] But, every time I see a performance or coach dancers, I hear his voice in the background. There is always something not quite perfect, but because of the enigmatic nature of the work, it never can be perfect. Tudor thought so as well. We must try to do them in the best possible way, so they continue to live into the next century and beyond.

It is also her policy to suggest a more appropriate work if a company requests a ballet that she believes beyond its current resources and capabilities.

Sally Bliss has organized well the business end of the Trust. In accordance with Tudor's wishes, license and royalty fees remain very affordable. Usually the license for a dance lasts for a three-year period. The ballet must be staged by an official representative of the estate, one of a handful of people, all of whom worked personally with Tudor.[4] A representative of the Trust must approve major cast changes. The most active of the official representatives at the time of this writing are his ballerina Sallie Wilson, his notator Airi Hynninen, and Donald Mahler. Mahler studied at the Metropolitan Opera with Tudor and danced his ballets with the National Ballet of Canada. I am proud to say that I, too, as an official representative of the Trust, have staged some of Tudor's ballets, mostly the chamber works that he created when he was on the faculty of the Juilliard School.

Also, in league with Tudor's faith in people rather than in contracts, the license must be reviewed after any change in the artistic direction of a company. There is a schedule of minimum rehearsal hours to be guaranteed for each work, and a stipulation about who is to keep the ballet after the representative of the Trust leaves.[5]

In the years since his death Tudor's dances have been in demand all over the world. Companies that have not petitioned the Trust for a ballet are fewer than those that have. In just two years, from 1998 through March, 2000, twenty-five companies have had Tudor works added to their repertoires. Recent stagings have ranged from Japan (Star Dancers Ballet, New National Theatre Ballet) to England (Royal Ballet) to France (Ballet de Bordeaux) to Canada (Royal Winnepeg Ballet, Les Grands Ballets Canadiens, Alberta Ballet) to Australia (Leigh Warren Dancers). In the United States companies from Arizona to Washington, from American Ballet Theatre to the San Francisco Ballet and groups in eleven other states have performed Tudor. In the same time period there have been twelve stagings of *Lilac Garden,* five of *Leaves Are Fading,* four of *Judgment of Paris,* three of *Offenbach in the Underworld,* and mountings of *Pillar of Fire, Echoing of Trumpets,* and *Gala Performance*. Most notable was the controversial revival of *Dark Elegies* by the José Limón Company, the first time a modern dance company undertook a Tudor work. For this viewer, the Limón Company managed a most moving performance.

This list does not include the many stagings of Tudor's chamber ballets such as *Continuo* and *Little Improvisations*. These works are licensed by the Dance Notation Bureau rather than the Tudor Trust, a continuation of the practice instituted by Tudor himself during his lifetime.

One highlight occurred in 1991 when *Jardin aux lilas* and *The Leaves Are Fading* were mounted in St. Petersburg at the Maryinsky (Kirov) Theatre with the Kirov Ballet. In a letter to Sally Bliss, Airi Hynnenin described the performance: "beautiful dancers and an audience which would not let them go." She wrote of how the mayor, Anatol Sobtshak, personally thanked her (it was she who staged *Leaves Are Fading*). To her surprise, and horror, Jerome Robbins attended the performance. Fortunately he loved what he saw. The company even brought the Tudor works to the United States in 1992, a bold stroke.

One of the missions of the Trust is to see to the preservation of the ballets. To this end, Labanotation of *Echoing of Trumpets, Gala Performance,* and excerpts from *The Planets* have been undertaken. Definitive revisions of the dance scores of *Little Improvisations, Continuo, Offenbach in the Underworld* and *Jardin aux lilas,* reflect Tudor's late choreographic preferences. Bliss set about amassing for the Trust authentic production information and film or video recordings. A substantial collection now exists.[6]

The Trust has also assumed the task of making sure that "accurate" versions of the dances are being performed. Although he vehemently denied it, Tudor made changes and emendations in his choreography from time to time. It is often only with difficulty that one can say that a remounting is authentic. As a rule, the restager may never change the "steps," but at times notation or video tapes of the various versions of a particular passage may offer alternatives from which to choose. In some cases Bliss has established what she considers to be an official version. In others she has left decisions up to the restager, since each of them has had the personal experience of working under Tudor. In no case may the material be changed by the restager. He or she may only choose one version set by Tudor himself over another of his own versions.

The incarnation of the Ballet Rambert under Richard Alston's direction, renamed the Rambert Dance Company, produced the most difficult (and sole, to this date) example of the kind of policing that is the Trust's responsibility. Over the years, as the Rambert company had evolved more and more towards modern dance, Tudor had become increasingly unhappy with its renditions of his ballets. Referring to a performance given as early as 1960, in a letter dated August, 1982, addressed to the Dance Collection of the New York Public Library, he indicated his displeasure:

> Dear Custodians and Defenders of the Faith:
>
> Recently I have received letters from two people asking permission for them to view the so-called *Jardin aux lilas* film made with the Ballet Rambert in 1960. I had to ask you to refuse permission in these cases. The reason is that after recently seeing this for the first time, I was in a state of shocked disbelief that one of my pieces could have gone so far away from my originally choreographed piece of the mid-thirties. Not only was it unrelated to the music, not only were the principal characters not recognizable as Caroline and her partner since the intents of the ballet were missing, but if people very occasionally entered stage at the right place at the right time, they proceeded to perhaps move in totally opposite directions from those of my choreography and make movements without any relation to my ballet. And this happened from the beginning right through the end.

Although it is obvious that Tudor exaggerated, his displeasure is patently clear. In 1982, when the Rambert company toured the United States, he refused permission for them to perform his works, particularly *Dark Elegies*.

This is the background upon which the dispute over the Rambert's production of *Dark Elegies* took place in 1988. The company, as a memorial to Tudor, mounted the ballet. John Chesworth and rehearsal director Sally Garbutt, set the ballet. They based the version on a 1980 revival directed by Sally Gilmour. Gilmour had danced in the ballet one year after Tudor had left Ballet Rambert. Chesworth's experience in the work began in 1952. Neither had actually worked with Tudor himself. Since the legal status of the ballets which Tudor originally did for the Ballet Rambert had always been murky, there never having been any formal agreement or payment of royalties, only by chance did the Tudor Trust hear of the revival. Sally Bliss felt obliged to send someone to be sure the restaging of the dance would represent Tudor's wishes. Sallie Wilson visited the company. What she saw did not satisfy her. She reported that both the steps and the nuances were wrong, but that the dancers were fine. She added that the errors could easily be corrected. Maude Lloyd, of the original cast, corroborated that the production didn't seem "right." To complicate matters, the production production would not use the Benois set. The Trust offered Wilson's services and even agreed to assume the costs of her work with the company.

Richard Alston, then director of the Rambert Dance Company, refused. He was convinced that he had the "original version." He did not wish to perform "the American version." "To comply with this request would be to betray everything that Rambert herself cared for and nurtured in the Tudor works,"[7] said Alston. Leo Kersley, an early Tudor dancer, found the Rambert version accurate. Celia Franca, Kersley's wife in those early days of Rambert, equally insisted that, except for the opening of the fifth song, the "American version" as performed by American Ballet Theatre was true to the original.[8] In the event the Rambert Company went ahead with the announced performances, although it expected and was nearly subject to the legal action the Trust threatened. Alston even appealed to the public for funds to fight the case in court. The two entities finally reached an accommodation out of court. It stipulated that the Rambert company could perform "their version" during no more than five seasons in each twenty-five-year period commencing on 1 January, 1990.

Critical reaction to the performance was not encouraging. Critic Edward Thorpe suggested that while the steps seemed right, he found the performance bland and inexpressive. He also lamented, as did other reviewers, the lack of the Benois backcloths.[9] Judith Cruickshank said it was in no way a worthy tribute to Tudor's memory. She found the dancing stilted and perfunctory, lacking in weight, passion, and understanding. She compared it to a skeleton without muscle, flesh, or spirit.[10] Mary Clarke called it a bleak account of what was once a profoundly moving work.[11] And from Clement Crisp:

> The present ensemble, skilled in dealing with the unemotional choreographic styles of Cunningham and Richard Alston, seems to me lacking in that psychic density, that controlled humanity, which was once essential in making real the grief of a community suffering appalling bereavement. The resultant performance was careful, as blanched as the lighting, unconvincing.[12]

## Looking to the Future

As of 2001, the Tudor Trust continues its exemplary work in arranging for the stagings of his ballets the world over. And, for the most part, the dances continue to receive critical acclaim, audience appreciation, and the sense among the dancers of having had a profound experience.

\*        \*        \*        \*        \*

     The legend of Antony Tudor has been much distorted by time, circumstance, and by his own masking of his life and accomplishments. The myth that he produced only a tiny repertoire is belied by the actual number of works: forty-three ballets plus seven smaller works for students; eleven operas; and thirty-three dances for theater, film, and television. The idea that he ruined lives and was universally hated is simply not borne out by the facts. So many of the dancers who worked with him ended by adoring him. Many believe that he had a profoundly positive effect on their careers. Contrary to the "cold- hearted bastard" image that he chose to project, his acolytes found him kind, helpful, sensitive, and considerate. He was a wonderful mentor to them. Many choreographers felt and expressed their admiration and awe at what he had taught them by example. None of this negates the fact that he could be cutting, embarrassing, vulgar, hyper-critical, and even cruel. These were not, however, his only nor even his major, characteristics. Tudor was an indefatigable worker although it amused him to encourage the idea that he was a lazy lout. He was an amazing intellectual despite his humble beginnings and truncated education. His abilities as an autodidact cannot help but impress as does his enormous originality. His contribution to ballet in America is universally underrated. For all practical purposes, he was Ballet Theatre. His output surely ranks among the major accomplishments of our era.

     We pay homage to all those engaged in the effort of preserving and performing Tudor's important body of work. His contribution to the art of the twentieth century cannot be overstated. He is one of the true geniuses of our time.

# Notes

     1. Alan M. Kriegsman, "Tudor Style, Mastered by ABT," *Washington Post,* 13 April, 1990.
2. Charles Weidman (1901–1975), one of the early pioneers of modern dance, partner of Doris Humphrey, died intestate. There was a mad,

acrimonious scramble among his students and associates for control of his dances. While José Limón (1908–1972), dancer and choreographer *extraordinaire*, did write a will and had established a Foundation, he did not mention his works in the will. Consequently, the rights to the dances went to his family who were neither dance professionals nor knowledgeable about the works themselves. A messy period of limbo ensued before the activation of the Limón Foundation and the assignment by the family of control of the dances to it.

3. Muriel Topaz, "The Tudor Legacy: Masterpieces in Trust," *Dance Magazine* (February, 1996): 96. The quote that follows in the text is from the same source.

4. At this writing those so approved to stage one or more Tudor works are: Sally Brayley Bliss, Celia Franca, Els Grelinger, Ann Hutchinson Guest, Airi Hynnenin, Vivika Ljung, Donald Mahler, David Richardson, Sirpa Tepper, Muriel Topaz, Marilyn Vella Gaat, Lance Westergard, and Sallie Wilson.

5. The Tudor Trust may be contacted at the following address: c/o Sally Brayley Bliss, 4514 Pershing Place, St. Louis, MO 63108.

6. In addition to the collection of the Trust and that of the Performing Arts division of the New York Public Library, a project was undertaken by the Dance Notation Bureau. It documents the exact whereabouts of production information of Tudor ballets around the world, as well as filling in, when possible, missing data. The results of this project are in the files of the Dance Notation Bureau Library, 151 W. 30th Street, New York City, 10001, fax 212-904-1426, email notation@mindspring.com.

7. John Percival, *Dance Magazine* (September, 1988).

8. There were plans, never put into effect, for the Joffrey Company to add *Dark Elegies* to its repertoire in 1986. Celia Franca was to set the dance for the company. In a letter to her, dated 30 September, 1985, Tudor states: "It'll be good to see an earlier version before I started playing around *too* much with the opening 18 bars of the fifth dance."

9. Edward Thorpe, *Financial Times,* 9 June, 1988.

10. Judith Cruickshank, *Times,* 9 June, 1988.

11. Mary Clarke, "Rambert Dance," *Guardian,* 10 June, 1988. Clarke was longtime editor of *The Dancing Times* and author of many books on dance in Britain.

12. Clement Crisp, *Financial Times*, 10 June, 1988.

Tudor. *Photograph by Elizabeth Sawyer, courtesy of University of California at Irvine, Special Collections Archive*

# Appendix A

# Chapters 2–8: The Ballets and Critical Response to Them

## The Rambert Ballets (Chapter 2)

### Cross-Garter'd

Music: Girolomo Frescobaldi, selected organ works.
Set: Pamela Bocquet
Costumes: after Burnacini
Premiere: 12 November, 1931, Mercury Theatre, London
Original Cast: Olivia: Maude Lloyd; Maria: Prudence Hyman; Malvolio: Antony Tudor; Sir Toby: Walter Gore; Sir Andrew: Rollo Gamble
Later casts: Olivia: Diana Gould; Maria: Sally Gilmour; Sir Andrew: Rollo Gamble; Malvolio: John Andrewes; Sir Toby: Frank Staff; Sir Andrew: Antony Tudor

Critical Response:
*Music Lover,* 2 November, 1931: *Cross-Garter'd* . . . was the "trial run" of new choreographist, Antony Tudor, the Club's stage manager. Of course, though it was officially a first attempt, one cannot occupy such a post and remain a novice. Hence it is not surprising that he made a genuine success of it, particularly at the opening.
*Dancing Times,* 31 December, 1931: Antony Tudor, the Secretary of the "Ballet Club," who has also danced in many of the Club's productions made his debut on this occasion as a choreographer. . . . Mr. Tudor has an excellent idea of design in detail, but the ballet regarded as a whole lacked a definite shape. The dances gave the impression of having been most carefully and painstakingly arranged, and if this

really be a first attempt, Mr. Tudor, as a choreographer, should be given encouragement. Incidentally he himself made a striking Malvolio.

*Dance Journal,* December, 1931, by Cyril Beaumont: Mr. Tudor has very wisely tried to work out his ideas in his own way. The result was a workmanlike little ballet which impressed by its obvious sincerity, while the dances and mime really did express the story. The steps were simple, the mime was simple, but it was all done in the lusty spirit of the text. The production would be improved by a little condensation. . . . Lastly, Maria and Olivia's attendants must restrain their impetuosity. At present they lift up their legs in a manner that would never have been permitted in the dance of Shakespeare's day.

### *Mr. Roll's Quadrille* (also called *Mr. Roll's Military Quadrilles)*

Music: Old English music
Costumes: Susan Salaman (re-used from *Carmen* )
Premiere: February, 1932 (probably 4 or 11 February), Mercury Theatre, London
Original Cast: The Leaders: Prudence Hyman, Antony Tudor; Pas de Trois: Maude Lloyd, Elisabeth Schooling, Betty Cuff.

### *Constanza's Lament*

Music: Domenico Scarlatti
Premiere: February, 1932 (probably 4 or 11 February), Mercury Theatre, London
Original Cast: Diana Gould

### *Lysistrata* (After Aristophanes)

Music: Serge Prokofiev (Piano pieces from Op. 2, 3, 12, and 22, and from the second and fourth sonatas), played by Hugh Bradford
Costumes and Décor: William Chappell
Premiere: 20 March, 1932, Mercury Theatre, London
Original Cast: Myrrhina: Alicia Markova; Cinesias: Walter Gore; Lysistrata: Diana Gould; Her Husband: Antony Tudor; Lampito: Andrée Howard; Colnice: Prudence Hyman; Her Husband: William Chappell; Other Athenian Women: Elisabeth Schooling, Betty Cuff; Handmaid to Myrrhina: Susette Morfield

Myrrhina was later played by Pearl Argyle, June Brae, Margot Fonteyn, Maude Lloyd, Prudence Hyman, Elisabeth Schooling, Sally Gilmour; Cineas by Harold Turner; Lysistrata by Maude Lloyd, Pamela Foster, Celia Franca; Her Husband by Hugh Laing, Frank Staff, Rupert Doone, Leo Kersley; Lampito by Elisabeth Schooling, Mona Inglesby, Susette Morfield, Peggy van Praagh, Sally Gilmour

Critical Response:
*Herald Life,* May, 1932, by Dion Byngham: The interpretation of this classic comedy provides a superb opportunity for spirited choreography, which Mr. Tudor has seized with gay genius, and for clarity of line and vividness of colour which Mr. William Chappell has exploited to admiration in the costumes and setting. The theme of the Athenian women who, weary of the wars waged by their husbands, and led by Lysistrata, swear an oath to refuse wifely duties until peace is made, sparkles with inspired common sense. They carry their plan into effect (notwithstanding many temptations) and their men are compelled to sheathe the sword and return. The incidentals of this "strike of wives" are made exquisitely amusing. Besides being piquantly enjoyable in itself as a first-rate work of art, this ballet drives home a vital point.
*Observer,* 3 May, 1936, by H. H.: On Sunday night we were invited to see Miss Margot Fonteyn, the rising star of the Vic-Wells Ballet, make her [Ballet] club debut in a revised version of Mr. Antony Tudor's *Lysistrata.* We have said, and still believe, that her future may be brilliant. The *Lysistrata* seen, of necessity in these intimate surroundings, as a sketch, is ingenious in design and amusingly explicit in action. Mr. Tudor has taken what he wanted from Aristophanes and makes good fun of the plight of the Athenian veterans whose war–weary wives, refusing any longer to treat their husbands as heroes or to make their homes fit for heroes to live in, drop the distaff, abandon the babies, and stiffen passive connubial resistance with violence.

### *Adam and Eve*

Music: Constant Lambert, *Suite Dancée,* written for Serge Diaghilev; later incorporated into the score for *Romeo and Juliet,* choreographed by Vaslav Nijinsky
Costumes and Décor: John Banting
Premieree: 4 December, 1932Adelphi Theatre, London
Original Cast: Adam: Anton Dolin; Eve: Prudence Hyman; The Serpent: Antony Tudor; The Angel: Natasha Gregorova; Seraphim: Ci-

celey Grave and Felicity Andreae; Fowls of the Air: Peggy van Praagh,
Susette Morfield, Christine Rosslyn, Molly Brown


Critical Response:
*Glasgow Herald,* 5 December, 1932: After they [Adam and Eve]
had been introduced to each other by the fowls of the air, with the approval of two seraphim, there entered the serpent. . . .This gentleman
was a cheerful drill-sergeant in a spiked helmet. The episode of the
apple was then enacted. Then the serpent had another idea. He seized
the avenging angel and forced her to share a bite of the apple with him.
All ended happily with a double marriage, conducted by the seraphim.
*Daily Telegraph,* 6 December, 1932, by H. E. W.: Everyone was
delighted with the new *Adam and Eve* Ballet at the Camargo Society's
performance at the Adelphi Theatre. . . .The light touch with which
Mr. Antony Tudor, the choreographer, and Mr. Constant Lambert, to
whom the music is due, handled an old story was infinitely pleasing.
. . .It was the sort of burlesque that only the delicate art of the ballet
could carry through successfully.
*New Statesman and Nation,* 10 December, 1932: Finally, a modern version of the Book of Genesis, *Adam and Eve* . . . the Serpent and
the two Seraphim were particularly good—brought with it a breath of
gaiety and satire.
*Time and Tide,* 10 December, 1932: Antony Tudor's wicked
commentary on the first book of Genesis "improved" on the original in
a final tableau in which the Angel with the flaming sword is induced to
taste of the fruit of the Tree of Knowledge and apparently finds it good.
But the choreographer has failed to realise his comment in the terms of
his medium, and though wit is implicit in grouping and situation, it is
absent from the *pas.*
*Evening Standard,* 12 December, 1932: Mr. Dolin and Miss Prudence Hyman . . . threw themselves into this example of later Di-
aghileffism partly, I think, to keep warm, for their costume of leaves
was the sort of thing that leaves inactivity out of the question on a
December night. The fun was equally scanty.
*Saturday Review:* The one vigorous event was Mr. Lambert's
*Adam and Eve* ballet, brilliantly produced . . . it has . . . a scenario
that is witty and impudent to the point of being indecorous. Its touches
of profanity do not heighten its wit.

**In a Monastery Garden**

Film
Made in March, 1932 at Twickenham studios

## *Pavane for a Dead Infanta*

Music: Maurice Ravel
Costume: Hugh Stevenson
Premiere: 1 January, 1933, Mercury Theatre, London

## *Atalanta of the East*

Music: Authentic Eastern airs arranged by Szanto and Seelig, played by
Charles Lynch
Costumes and Décor: William Chappell
Premiere: 7 May, 1933, Mercury Theatre, London
Original Cast: Atalanta (Sita): Pearl Argyl; Vikram: Hugh Laing; God-
dess: Diana Gould

Critical Response:
  *Morning Post,* 8 May, 1933: A beautiful new ballet—full of ingenuity, grace and creative ideas. . . . Here we have a cold, frankly
conventional, but still fascinating transference of the old Atalanta story
to a fantastic semi-Mongolian realm. . . . The race itself is managed
with extreme cleverness; for the apple is dropped not once but every
time the two pass across the stage, Atalanta losing her lead at each lap.
Otherwise everything is as static as could be. . . . Altogether a most
haunting affair—beautifully conceived.
  *Time and Tide,* 13 May, 1933: Mr. Tudor conveys the race with
Atalanta as a ritual—a rather syrupy ritual of a synthetic orient. But the
dancers are engagingly grave, and they move through the work, a
rhythmic frieze with most articulate hands and immobile faces. The
race is conveyed with swiftness and skill—no mean achievement on so
small a stage.
  *Music Lover,* 13 May, 1933: Transports the Greek legend to some
undetermined country, apparently lying between Burma and Java. . . . I
must congratulate Tudor on the patterns and groupings, which were not
only good compositions in themselves, but evocative. The movements
may have been equally good, but somehow our people cannot quite
capture the Oriental spirit in movement. There is something subtle,
perhaps feline, that evades us . . . the whole thing was a remarkably
good show.
  *Observer,* 14 May, 1933 by H. H.: Pictorially, this ballet is
charming: for Mr. William Chappell, whose ingenious costumes
"dance" well, and blend their black and silver, and yellow and gold
harmoniously, has effected a happy compromise between Far Eastern

modes and Kensingtonian models. Bracelets of bells tinkle prettily, and fluttering hands display their long gilded fingernails in subsidiary passions. Otherwise, the ballet seemed to me uncertain in composition, and to hesitate when the action should have soared. The race itself, when the runners entered and left to complete imaginary laps, and the spectators rotated to follow their flight, recalled other less classic events run on less eclectic stages. This is not to say that the ballet fails. Its pictures and nicely danced detail prevent that.

## *Faust*

Music: Charles Gounod
Premiere: 28 September, 1933, Sadler's Wells Theatre, London
Cast: Freda Bamfold, Antony Tudor, Ailene Phillips, Nadina Newhouse, Elizabeth Miller, and *corps de ballet*

## *Paramour* (Originally called *Allegory*)

Music: William Boyce (Extracts from *Symphonies* nos. *1, 2*, and *6* in an arrangement by Constant Lambert)
Costumes: William Chappell
Premiere: 20 February, 1934, Town Hall, Oxford
Original Cast: Walter Gore, Diana Gould, Hugh Laing

## *The Legend of Dick Whittington*

Choreography and production by Tudor
Music: Martin Shaw
Scenery: Eric Newton
Costumes: Stella Mary Pearce
Premiere: 28 May, 1934, Sadler's Wells Theatre, London
Original Cast: Patricia Shaw Page, Joan Birdwood-Taylor, Reymonde Seton, Gladys Scott, Eileen Harris, Phyllis Bull, Betty Percheron

## *The Planets*

Music: Gustav Holst, arranged for piano and strings by Vally Lasker
Costumes and Décor: Hugh Stevenson
Premiere: 28 October, 1934, Mercury Theatre, London

Original Cast: "Venus": Mortals born under Venus: Pearl Argyle, William Chappell (later casts: Elisabeth Schooling, Deborah Dering, Sally Gilmour, Lisa Serova, Gerd Larsen, Jean Stokes, Antony Tudor, Frank Staff, Leo Kersley, Walter Gore, David Paltenghi, etc.); The Planet: Maude Lloyd (Elisabeth Schooling, Daphne Gow, Anna Lendrum, etc.); with Tamara Svetlova, Nan Hopkins, Joan Lendrum, Margot Hawkins

"Mars": Mortal born under Mars: Hugh Laing (Antony Tudor, Harold Turner, Walter Gore, Leo Kersley, Frank Staff, R. Harrold, etc.); The Planet: Peggy van Praagh or Jeanne Garman (Pamela Foster, Anne Ashley, Charlotte Bidmead, etc.), with Susette Morfield, Helena Cornford, Thérèse Langfield, Isobel Reynolds, Cicely Robinson, Florence Rawson

"Neptune": Mortal born under Neptune (The Mystic): Kyra Nijinsky (Maude Lloyd, June Brae, Peggy van Praagh, Celia Franca, Gerd Larsen, Joan McClelland); The Planet: Antony Tudor (C. Boyd, J. Moore, M. Kerr, D. Martin, David Paltenghi, P. Franklin White, etc.); with Nan Hopkins, Joan Lendrum, Tamara Svetlova, Daphne Gow

Added for the London Ballet on 23 January,1939: "Mercury": Mortal born under Mercury: Peggy van Praagh (Sally Gilmour); The Planet: G. Massey (Frank Staff)

Critical Response:
*Observer,* 4 November, 1934 by H. H.: On Sunday we went to see Mr. Anthony [*sic*] Tudor's attempt to express Gustav Holst's popular suite, *The Planets,* in dancing terms. This is just the kind of experiment for which the Ballet Club exists, and to which its intimate limitations are suited. Though of necessity a sketch, I did not think it altogether successful. The astronomical observations seemed too astrological. Venus, Mars and Neptune were in the ascendant, and Neptune was the planet I preferred. The Holstian rhythms happily inspired the motions of heavenly bodies through interstellar space. Indeed, the choric passages throughout seemed to me the best, though the lovers born under Venus, the Mars-inflamed Fighter, and Neptune's mystic protégé were bravely danced, and the music of the spheres was firmly transmitted.
*Birmingham Gazette,* 9 June, 1936: Nothing was more illustrative of this directness of approach last night than the very dynamic ballet called "The Planets." Scenery, dancing, everything combined to suggest elemental forces giving violent birth to portents and strange things. It was an imaginative tour de force.
Unidentified publication, 15 November, 1947: Most impressive of this week's new presentations by the Ballet Rambert at the Princess Theatre is Antony Tudor's highly imaginative work *The Planets.*

Unidentified publication (*Birmingham Gazette?*), T. C.: *The Planets* has been included each year that the Ballet Rambert has been to Birmingham, and it is evidence of Antony Tudor's sound choreography that *The Planets* not only makes a vivid impression at first sight, but also improves on acquaintance.

*Morning Post:* "The London Ballet." Holst's music is admirably suited to ballet . . . and Tudor's choreography interprets it with ingenuity and intelligence, though there is a certain monotony of effect which might, perhaps, be lessened by more careful production. Still the result was agreeable, not least in the "Mercury" section, which owing to some mischance or other had to be presented without scenery or costumes.

### Castor and Pollux

Music: Jean-Philippe Rameau
Costumes and Scenery: Derek Hill
Premiere: November, 1934, Oxford University opera club, Oxford
Original Cast: Maude Lloyd, Antony Tudor, and members of the Oxford Music Society

### The Descent of Hebe

Music: Ernest Bloch, *Concerto Grosso* played by pianist Charles Lynch and a string quartet
Costumes and Scenery: Nadia Benois
Premiere: listed by various sources as 7 April, 1935 (note: this date must be incorrect as the reviews are 8 and 9 February. Premiere was probably 7 February.), Mercury Theatre, London
Original Cast: Hebe: Pearl Argyle; Mercury: Hugh Laing; Night: Maude Lloyd; Hercules: Antony Tudor (Rollo Gamble); Attendants on Jupiter: Susette Morfield, Ann Gee, Norah Whitworth; Attendants on Night: Tamara Svetlova, Joan Lendrum, Cecily Robinson; Children (later dropped from the production): Bridget Kelly, Bitten Nissen, Cyril Hay, Paul Forbes

Critical Response:
Unattributed publication, Monday 8 February, 1935 by G. W. B.: The chief thing in the programme new to the West End was *The Descent of Hebe,* by Antony Tudor, to music by Ernest Bloch. The cho-

reographer lacked something in invention. The movements were inclined to be repetitive.

*Morning Post,* 9 February, 1935: Indubitably the most successful
was *The Descent of Hebe,* a charming and amusing essay in pseudo-
classicism on which the author, Antony Tudor, and Nadia Benois, the
designer of the scenery and costumes, may heartily be congratulated.

*New Statesman:* There is a certain *naïveté* in this treatment of a
classical theme; Mercury wears a little hat perched forward ("how
sweet!"—from the stalls) which might have come out of Bond Street;
the appearance and miming of Hercules is comically unsubtle. Nevertheless, despite some childishness and an occasionally indeterminate
choreography this ballet has charm and variety. It is certainly worth
seeing again.

*Times,* 9 February, 1935: The invention falters a little in the Pastoral, but the first two movements are fanciful, and the final Fugue
builds up strongly into a massive ensemble for the whole company.

*Birmingham Post,* 13 June, 1936, by T. C. K.: Last night saw its
first public performance and, while some untidiness and mistiming
were apparent especially in the second movement, the ballet as a whole
emerged as a sound piece of work. The Pastoral, covering the wooing
of Hebe by Hercules, was marked by an apt choreography, and the
fugue displayed some enjoyable ensemble dancing.

*New English Weekly,* 23 May, 1935, by R. H.: *The Descent of
Hebe,* Antony Tudor's new ballet is still unfinished. The ballet is, in
fact, planned on such a scale that it will stay unrealised until it reaches
a larger stage . . . [The ballet] thoroughly well justifies what has been
said, here, in prophetic praise of the choreographic talent of Antony
Tudor. Its last movement, a Fugue, works ten dancers into as satisfying a contrapuntal intricacy as I know; and, as a whole, it is a strangely
mature work, in which a lovely formal structure is no longer overlaid
and blurred by overmuch detail . . . for one thing, giving the upper part
of the body more significance than it has had.

*Apology for Dancing,* a book by Rayner Heppenstall (London:
Faber and Faber, 1936): His work on the whole, seems to me, is richer
and more pregnant than any other work being done in the ballet. . . . I
am convinced that it [*The Descent of Hebe*] is the most vigorous piece
of choreography that London has seen since Balanchine's *Cotillion.* It
is Mr. Tudor's distinction to have come to the understanding that what
cannot be translated wholly into movement is valueless in ballet.

*Birmingham Post,* 13 June, 1939: Antony Tudor's *The Descent of Hebe* has become one of the most popular of the original Mercury Ballets . . . There is a crisp hilarity about this frolic on Olympus. Hebe and Hercules desport themselves with such vigour in the classical wooing that the descent paradoxically changes direction and becomes an ascending triumph. Choreographically this piece is soundly constructed in four stories topped by an attic.

### La Cenerentola

Music: Gioacchino Rossini
Premiere: 1 May, 1935, Covent Garden, London
Cast: Alicia Markova and others

### Schwanda the Bagpiper

Music: Weinberger
Premiere: 3 June, 1935, Covent Garden, London

### Carmen

Music: Georges Bizet
Premiere: 4 June, 1935, Covent Garden, London

### Koanga

Music: Delius
Premiere: 23 September, 1935, Covent Garden, London

### Jardin aux lilas

(Originally *Jardin des lilas;* when first performed in the United States the title was anglicized to *Lilac Garden* although Tudor preferred the title in French.)
Music: Ernest Chausson (*Poème* for violin and orchestra)
Premiere: 26 January, 1936; Mercury Theatre, London
American Premiere: January 15, 1940, Center Theatre, New York

Original Cast: Caroline: Maude Lloyd; Her Lover: Hugh Laing; The Man She Must Marry: Antony Tudor; An Episode in His Past: Peggy van Praagh (in the original program she is listed as Margaret van Praagh); Elisabeth Schooling, Frank Staff, Ann Gee, Tatiana Svetlova, Leslie Edwards

After 1939 Tudor increased the number of guests so that there were eight dancers in the corps.

Other Productions: Ballet Theatre, New York City Ballet, National Ballet of Canada, Royal Ballet (England), Royal Danish Ballet, Australian Ballet, Royal Swedish Ballet, Zurich Opera Ballet, Les Grands Ballets Canadiennes, Paris Opera Ballet, Ballet Nacional de Cuba, Kirov Ballet, etc.

A Few Other Casts:
Ballet Theatre: Viola Essen, Karen Conrad, Maria Tallchief; New York City Ballet: Nora Kaye, Tanaquil LeClercq, Diana Adams, Yvonne Mounsey; Royal Ballet: Svetlana Beriosova, Donald MacLeary, Desmond Doyle, Georgina Parkinson; Alicia Markova, Alicia Alonzo, Sallie Wilson, Gelsey Kirkland, Leslie Browne, Celia Franca


Critical Response:
*Daily Telegraph,* 27 January, 1936, by Arnold Haskell: Antony Tudor's choreography is not yet fully developed. Deeply interesting in patches, especially in a fine *pas de quatre,* it is too jerky as a whole, and on such a small stage exits and entrances need handling with far greater tact. . . . An innovation is the playing of the music, Chausson's *Poème (Opus 25),* on an electric gramophone, which gives the dancers the rare privilege of Menuhin as accompanist. In time this should work into a period picture of great charm and distinction.
*Times,* 16 February, 1937: Mr. Tudor has ideas, but he has still some way to go before he acquires the certainty of touch possessed by Miss Howard and Mr. Ashton. His *Jardin aux lilas* falls to the ground between the conflicting claims of choreographic, dramatic, and musical logic, though it has the merit of establishing and possessing a consistent atmosphere of the nineteenth century. He is apt to misinterpret the music.

*Diaries* of Lionel Bradley, 24 October, 1937: *Jardin aux lilas* rouses all my romantic feelings. I continue to admire the apparently fortuitous but effective way in which the characters cross and recross

*New English Weekly,* (not dated) by R .H: Antony Tudor's new ballet has still not got him the acclamation he should have. And yet, why *should* such a talent be popularized! There remain some roughnesses to polish away, but *Jardin aux lilas* is the first true *ballet intime,* the first occasion of pure choreographic lyricism.

*New York Times,* 21 July, 1940, by John Martin: The poignancy that Mr. Tudor succeeds so admirably in achieving derives less from the immediate circumstances in which his characters find themselves than in the basic problem that lies beneath the circumstances, the conflict between the human passions and the conventions of ordinary living. The formality of the garden party, its movements highly stylized and unreal, constitute the dominating background for the torrent of feeling that breaks through only in flashes of reality, inhibited almost before they come into being. . . . With sure and simple strokes his choreography projects haste in leisure, turbulence in ordered calm, mute desperation in constraint. This is a remarkably free dramatic use of the academic dance, in every way modern and in a sense even anti-classic. Obviously this is the true vein of Mr. Tudor's talents. . . . The Ballet Theatre is to be commended for bringing him to this country, and could not do better, now that it has him here, than to give him every possible opportunity to create new works. There are so few creative choreographers in the ballet that the emergence of such a one is somewhat in the nature of a miracle.

*New York Herald Tribune,* 17 November, 1941, by Walter Terry: There is no other ballet which can match in richness of emotion and dramatic power Antony Tudor's *Lilac Garden.* . . . Antony Tudor has taken the traditional steps of ballet and woven them into phrases of movement as articulate as poetry, as eloquent as spoken drama. . . . The tremor of the body, the desperate clutch of a hand, the searching turn of a head reveal the anguish of broken lives, disclose the almost unbearable longing of lovers who are to be torn apart.

*Observer,* 1967, by Alexander Bland: *Lilac Garden* [was] mounted by the choreographer at Covent Garden last Tuesday. Thirty-two years have passed since its original presentation by the Rambert company, and many ballets have derived from it. For this was a seminal work. . . . Tudor's new idea was ballet with a human face. The characters here are no mythical or allegorical figures, but flesh-and-blood men and women, caught at the climax of a tight romantic tangle.

*Financial Times,* 20 February, 1985, by Clement Crisp, "Homage to Antony Tudor/Opéra Comique, Paris": The staging lacked inevitability, and that is the key to Tudor interpretation. Yannick Stéphant as Caroline understood the discretion of utterance which must inform even the most heartbreaking moments for the young woman forced into a marriage of convenience, and told also of the nervous tension in her every move. Much of the surrounding performance had a hectic air, as if incidents were rushed, and it is an essential quality of this masterpiece that, for all the urgency of the farewells between Caroline and her lover, between her future husband and his mistress, emotion and action should have time to reverberate, with ripples of feeling spreading further and further into their consciousness, and ours.

On 11 April, 1947, the BBC broadcast a program of works from the repertoire of the Rambert company, among them *Jardin aux lilas.* The cast was Leila Roussova, Hans Zulig, Michael Bayston, and Joan McClelland, with Angela Ellis, Deborah Dering, Josephine Leigh, David Ellis, and Stanley Newby. Note that Angela and David Ellis are members of Marie Rambert's family.

### Johnson over Jordan

Music: Benjamin Britten
Scenery: Edward Garrick
Costumes: Elisabeth Haffenden
Premiere: 19 February, 1936

### The Happy Hypocrite

Music: Richard Addinsell
Scenery and costumes: Motley
Premiere: 23 March, 1936, His Majesty's Theatre
Original Cast (dancers): Peggy van Praagh, Hugh Laing

***Careless Rapture.***  "The Temple of Nichaow"

Music: Ivor Novello
Premiere: 11 September, 1936, Theatre Royal, London


***To and Fro***

Music: Nat Ayer Jr. (*I'm on My Own*); Sergei Prokofiev *(Symphonie Russe);* Lord Berners (*Let's Take a Chance*)
Scenery: Horatio Taylor (ballets designed by Sophie Fedorovitch)
Costumes: Derek Skeffington
Premiere: 26 November, 1936, Comedy Theatre, London
Cast: Maude Lloyd, Hugh Laing


***Die Fledermaus***

Music Johann Strauss
Premiere: 6 January, 1937, Covent Garden, London
Cast: Prudence Hyman


***Crest of the Wave***

Music: Ivor Novello
Scenery: Alick Johnstone
Costumes: René Hubert
Premiere: 9 January, 1937, Theatre Royal, London
Cast: large cast


A group of dances choreographed for television during 1937 were:

***Paleface,*** a revue in which the dances were *Paramour, Romeo and Juliet pas de deux.*
Premiere: 7 January, 1937, for television
Cast: Hermione Baddeley, Cyril Richard, Antony Tudor, Bobby Tranter's Girls

*Romeo and Juliet (pas de deux)*

Music: Constant Lambert, originally written for the Diaghilev Ballet
Premiere: 7 January, 1937, for television
Cast: Maude Lloyd and Antony Tudor

*Paramour*

Music: William Boyce, *Sonata no. 2; Symphony no.1* and *Symphony No. 6* as arranged by Constant Lambert
Premiere: 7 January, 1937 in the revue *Paleface*; under the title of *Paramour*, February 2, 1937, for television
Cast: Maude Lloyd, Antony Tudor

*Hooey*

Dances consisted of *Paramour, Romeo and Juliet pas de deux,* and *Siesta*

*Siesta*

Music: William Walton
Scenery and Costumes: Peter Bax
Premiere: 2 February, 1937, for television
Cast: Maude Lloyd, Antony Tudor

*Constanza's Lament* (from *The Good Humoured Ladies*)

Music: Domenico Scarlatti
Costumes: recycled from a previous production
Premiere: 4 February, 1937, for television
Cast: Pamela Foster

*Fugue for Four Cameras*

Music: Johann Sebastian Bach

Premiere: 2 March, 1937, for television
Cast: Maude Lloyd

*After Supper,* a revue in which the dance was *Fête* d'Hébé

### Fête d'Hébé

Music: Jean Philippe Rameau (*Minuet no. 2*)
Premiere: 2 March, 1937, for television
Cast: Maude Lloyd, Antony Tudor, Hermione Moir, Charles Stewart

### Wienerblut

Music: Johann Strauss
Premiere: 2 April, 1937, for television
Cast: Maude Lloyd, Antony Tudor, Hermione Moir, Charles Stewart

### The Story of the Vienna Waltz

Music: Johann Strauss
Premiere: 2 April, 1937, for television
Cast: Maude Lloyd, Antony Tudor, Elisabeth Schooling, John Andrewes

### Dorset Garden

A restoration revue
Premiere: 13 April, 1937, for television

### Suite of Airs

Music: Henry Purcell (selections from *The Fairy Queen* )
Premiere: originally for television but never aired
Theater premiere: 16 May, 1937, Mercury Theatre, London
Note: This ballet was probably never aired on television, although it
may have been originally created and rehearsed for that purpose.

Critical Response:
    Uncredited: A series of Jacobean measures ranging from the Déco-
rous and courtly to the lively and unrestrained. The Rambert Company
is very much at home in these short series.


*Boulter's Lock, 1908–1914*

A revue which depicts a microcosm of London life and fashion during
these years.
Premiere: 29 June, 1937, for television
Cast: Maude Lloyd, Antony Tudor


*Cabaret*

A revue
Premiere: 5 July, 1937, for television

*Relâche*  (A ballet originally conceived by Francis Picabia)

Music: Erik Satie
Premiere: 8 July, 1937, for television
Cast: Maude Lloyd, Elisabeth Schooling, Hugh Laing, Charlotte Lan-
dor [Bidmead], Antony Tudor


*En Diligence*

Music: Francis Poulenc *(Waltz no. 10)*
Cast: Antony Tudor
Premieree: 14 July, 1937, for television


*The Boy David*

Music: William Walton

Premiere: 14 July, 1937, for television
Cast: Maude Lloyd
Lloyd and Tudor repeated their *Romeo and Juliet pas de deux* on this program.


***Portsmouth Point*** (a re–creation of Thomas Rowlandson's cartoon)

Music: William Walton
Premiere: 6 September, 1937, for television
Cast: Peggy van Praagh, Naomi Holmes, Bridgette Kelly, Charlotte Landor [Bidmead], Frank Staff, Elisabeth Schooling, Mark Baring, John Thorpe, Harry Webster


***High Yellow***

Music: Spike Hughes
Premiere: 14  September, 1937, for television
Cast: Peggy van Praagh, Charlotte Landor [Bidmead], Elisabeth Schooling, Bridgette Kelly


***Full Moon***

Music: Herbert Murrill
Premiere: 25 October, 1937, for television
Cast: Antony Tudor, Margaret Braithwaite


***La Femme rejoint son fauteuil***

Music: Erik Satie
Premiere: 31 December, 1937, for television
Cast: Margot Fonteyn, Antony Tudor


***Dark Elegies***

Music: Gustav Mahler *(Kindertotenlieder)*

Scenery and Costumes: Nadia Benois
Premiere: 19 February, 1937, Duchess Theatre, London
Cast: First Song: Peggy van Praagh and corps
Second Song: Maude Lloyd, Antony Tudor
Third Song: Walter Gore, with Antony Tudor, John Byron, and corps
Fourth Song: Agnes de Mille
Fifth Song: Hugh Laing and corps
Corps: Daphne Gow, Ann Gee, Patricia Clogstoun, Beryl Kay, Celia
Franks [Franca], John Byron
Singer: Harold Child

American Ballet Theatre Premiere: 24 January, 1940, New York
Cast, 1940: Nina Stroganova, Miriam Golden, Lucia Chase, Hugh
Laing, Dmitri Romanoff, Antony Tudor
1990: Cynthia Anderson, Martine van Hamel, Kevin O'Day, John
Gardner, Kathleen Moore, John Renvall
A Few Other Companies: National Ballet of Canada (1956); Swedish
Royal Ballet (1963); Royal Ballet (1980); Metropolitan Opera Ballet
(1986); Ballet du Rhin (1992); José Limón Company (1999)

Critical Response:
     *Diaries* of Lionel Bradley, 19 February, 1937: Unvarying grief
can hardly be represented by dancing for half an hour on end. . . . The
set is a rugged Swiss scene with rocks and a suggestion of a lake
changing at the end to a peaceful view of the entire lake.
     By 23 October, however, Bradley wrote: "*Dark Elegies* is an as-
tonishing and most successful combination of strictly academic movements and what might be called almost a primitive funeral ritual.
     And, in February, 1939, Bradley says the ballet is . . . as hyp-
notically moving as ever.
     *Sunday Times,* 19 February, 1937 by A. B.: There was some
clever and effective dancing by Miss Maude Lloyd and Mr. Tudor in
their duet, and a highly expressive solo on the part of Miss Agnes de
Mille, but between times there were a good deal of processional
movement of a not-too-purposeful order, and too little call upon the
foot-techniques to hold the eyes' attention though the permutations
were often ingenious.
     *Times,* 20 February, 1937: The ballet fails, because our interest
is centered in the voice of the singer and all these solemn posturings
can add nothing to the emotional effect of the music. To an irreverent

eye the spectacles might appear to be that of a very serious dress–reform colony going through its morning exercises.

*Prejudice for Ballet,* 1938, by A. V. Coton: The combined structure of music and movement expends itself in an outburst of grief and despair, the exposition of the reaction towards some kind of hope, a resurrection of faith and finally, the evocation of the renewed trust in, and love for, those still left to us after the visitation of death.

*New York Times,* 24 January, 1940, by John Martin: For all his taste and creativeness Mr. Tudor was defeated by Mahler from beginning to end. [Elsewhere in the review Martin says of the score "a drearier musical background has certainly never been chosen for a ballet."] It is impossible, nevertheless, to dismiss it lightly, for if it fails, it does so, nobly and with distinction. It has been composed with great sensitiveness and a remarkably fresh and authoritative use of movement and design.

*New York Herald Tribune,* 25 January, 1940, by Walter Terry: Sensitivity, ingenuity of movement and simplicity of pattern, qualities we have come to associate with Tudor works, were again in evidence, and *Dark Elegies* emerged as a work that was frequently telling.

*New York Herald Tribune,* 26 April, 1944, by Edwin Denby: Tudor's *Dark Elegies* . . . is Ballet Theater's [*sic*] *Parsifal.* . . . Miss Kaye and Mr. Laing, the stars who interpret his work so brilliantly, are said to consider it his masterpiece. The reviewer feels respect for these opinions, but he does not share them. . . . The actual dance detail of *Dark Elegies* is willfully spare, but it is also of a remarkable elegance in its arrangement. The timing of the accents, the placing of the dancers, the correspondences of dance phrases to musical ones, the variety of invention—all this is completely interesting. The look of helplessness in the men's arm movements, in the women's toe-steps and in the remarkable lifts has a distinct pathos. The running circles at the climax are very effective. But the fact that this helpless and impoverished tone is continued so long, and continued even during the consolatory last section, leaves me with the feeling that at the end there has been no dramatic progress, that the stage characters have exhibited their suffering and have gone off content with that. It gives the ballet a faintly stuffy, holier-than-thou expression.

*Ballet,* July, 1947 by A. V. Coton: *Dark Elegies* . . . is a work of great choreographic beauty and dignity. Formally, it mingles classical and "free" movements with remarkable effect. . . .The work is never less than dignified, and in modern times has not been surpassed by any other ballet as tragedy of the highest order.

*Modern English Ballet,* by Fernau Hall, (London: Andrew Melrose, Ltd., 1949): *Dark Elegies* went so far beyond existing conceptions of the proper scope of a ballet the critics made very little of it on its first night; the most common remark was that it was "monotonous." To do the critics justice, there was nothing in the current English or "Russian" repertoire to give them any standard by which to measure *Dark Elegies.*

*Quicksilver,* 1972, autobiography by Marie Rambert: *Dark Elegies* was Tudor's masterpiece and has remained the greatest tragic ballet of the English repertoire so far.

Fernau Hall, critic of the *Daily Telegraph,* in an interview with Judith Chazin-Bennehum on 13 March, 1988: *Dark Elegies* changed my life. It made me change my whole image of dance. . . . *Elegies* is all pure dance images. He [Tudor] drew upon his profound knowledge of Kabuki, of Indian dance, of modern dance—German and American—of Balkan dance. . . . He explained that the first song, the person has inward turned movements which expressed the crashing by fate of the death of the children, but also outturned movements which represent opening up, coming through and survival. This person is a stoic. In the pas de deux the woman is very weak and always falling. . . . The choreography was like a sculpture in movement creating images in time and space. The whole of my development as a person and a critic has been built around *Dark Elegies.* And everyone who has ever danced *Dark Elegies* or been involved with it has the same experience.

*New York Times,* 1 July, 1990, by Jennifer Dunning: *Dark Elegies* is a quietly cathartic work about bereavement and resignation, danced by the rough-dressed inhabitants of what appears to be a bleak and windswept fishing village. It is a ballet without many recognizable ballet steps or even much of a ballet body line or impetus—a ballet that looks, often, like a folk ritual. The plainness and simplicity of this 1937 work are astonishing as is the way Tudor expresses everything in the curving or carefully flattened lines of the dancers' torsos.

*Financial Times,* 11 June, 1992, by Clement Crisp: If the text itself differs from the old Ballet Rambert version we knew for many years, it yet remains the most powerful expression of grief that dance has yet given us, and the Ballet du Rhin does not betray it.

**Gallant Assembly**

Music: Giuseppe Tartini, *Cello Concerto in D*
Scenery and Costumes: Hugh Stevenson
Premiere: 14 June, 1937, Playhouse Theatre, Oxford
Cast: Aristocrats in Love: Agnes de Mille, Peggy van Praagh, Victoria
Fenn, Charlotte Bidmead, Antony Tudor, Hugh Stevenson, Margaret
Braithwaite, Hugh Laing

Critical Response:
   *The Isis,* 16 June, 1937, by John Irving: In a rococo setting and
with magnificent baroque costumes by Hugh Stevenson, a divertissement, or comedy of manners, is danced by four ladies, two gentlemen,
and two hired performers. . . .The theme—which presents the central
figure, Agnes de Mille, as a nymphomaniac—gives the opportunity for
an elaboration of a square dance. And into the middle of this, a classical *pas de deux.* . . .This ballet seems to me to have been successful in
getting beyond a mere compromise to a real blending of the two techniques. It is obviously something one must see several times before
one can decide whether it is really a valuable development.
   Lawrence Gowing, "Antony Tudor and The Dance Theatre," Notes
on a New Venture: [*Gallant Assembly*] is the justifying creative
achievement of the group, in every way a welcome addition to current
repertoires. The action, an inconsequential and pleasantly disreputable
Rococo frolic, is related with a most original wealth of invention. By
way of example, Miss de Mille . . . dances the part of an ineffectual
old maid seeking some gallant's regard; she moves at the outset in
short, rapid steps making with her hands movements of rotation most
subtly indicative of her state of mind. They suggest an old maid's fingers busy with needle or spinning wheel. . . . There is nothing nebu-
lous about the work of Antony Tudor; it is distinguished by an integ-
rity which he shares only with the other workers at the Ballet Club.
   *Theatre Diaries,* 20 March, 1939, by Lionel Bradley: a rather te-
dious display of the eroticism of the farmyard.
   *Dance and Dancers,* January, 1989, by Janet Sinclair: Most delightful ballet in the London Ballet's repertoire.

## *Tristan and Isolde*

Music: Richard Wagner
Scenery and Costumes: Peter Bax
Premiere: 24 January, 1938, for television
Cast: Oriel Ross, Basil Bartlett, Mary Alexander, Paul Jones, Hugh Laing, Anthony Hyndman

## *Wien*

Music: Johann Strauss
Premiere: 5 April, 1938, for television
Cast: Antony Tudor, Hugh Laing, Charlotte Landor [Bidmead], Peggy van Praagh, Robert Dorning, Prudence Hyman

## *Acis and Galatea*

Music: Georg Friederich Händel
Premiere: 24 April, 1938, for television
Cast: Maude Lloyd, Hugh Laing, Peggy van Praagh, Sally Gilmour, Antony Tudor, Elisabeth Schooling, Celia Franks (Franca), Charlotte Landor [Bidmead], Thérèse Lang field

## *The Emperor Jones*

Music: unidentified composer, a collage of songs sung by the Chipika singers: "Swingtime in the Rockies," "Deep River," "Mwama We Pfumo Chera"
Premiere: 11 May, 1938, for television
Cast: [given name unknown], Hugh Laing, Guy Massey

## *Master Peter's Puppet Show*

Music: Manuel de Falla
Premiere: 29 May, 1938, for television
Cast: Antony Tudor, Hugh Laing

*Cinderella*

Music: Spike Hughes
Premiere: 13 December, 1938, for television
Cast: Thérèse Langfield, Charlotte Bidmead, Jacqueline Saint, Susan
Reeves, Antony Tudor, Hugh Laing, Guy Massey, Anthony Kelly

Presented as a curtain raiser for Gogol's play *Marriage,* were a group of
works by Tudor and de Mille called "Seven Intimate Dances." Tudor
contributed the following three dances.

*The Hunting Scene*

Music: Johann Christian Bach
Premiere: 15 June, 1938, Westminster Theatre, London
Cast: Agnes de Mille, Antony Tudor, Charlotte Bidmead, Thérèse
Langfield

*Joie de vivre*

Music: Jacques Offenbach, Johann Strauss, Weston
Premiere: 15 June, 1938, Westminster Theatre, London
Cast: Charlotte Bidmead, Thérèse Langfield

*Judgment of Paris*

Music: Kurt Weill (from *The Threepenny Opera*)
Scenery and Costumes: Hugh Laing
Premiere: 15 June, 1938 (This date is disputed by Katherine Sorley
Theatre, London
Cast: Agnes de Mille, Gerd Larson (or perhaps Thérèse Langfield),
Charlotte Bidmead, Antony Tudor, Hugh Laing

Ballet Theatre Premiere: January 23, 1940

Cast: Maria Karnilova, Agnes de Mille, Lucia Chase, Antony Tudor and Hugh Laing

Critical Response:
*Diaries* of Lionel Bradley, 5 December, 1938: Sordid satire with an acrid undercurrent of tragedy.

*Diaries* of Lionel Bradley, 9 January, 1939: There is a bitter tang in its humour, like a salted almond, but the sense of sardonic satire prevents its realism from being merely unpleasant.

*New York Times,* 1940, by John Martin: It is an extremely witty and thoroughly indelicate trifle. Suffice it that the goddesses concerned are enthroned not on Olympus but in a boulevard cafe whither the Paris in question resorts in search of entertainment.They compete for his favor and, with champagne as their ally, eventually relieve him of his purse and valuables.

In another *New York Times* review by Martin: Juno, danced by Maria Karnilova, employed to coy approach, and abetted by a fan, she did her best to sell Paris on her charms. Agnes de Mille was by far the funniest. Starting off with a grim, fallen-arch amble, she pointed out her individual qualities with the aid of two hoops, which she slithered up and down legs, arms, and torso. Such was the Cafe Venus. Lucia Chase, a weary Minerva, looked beaten before she began. A few half-hearted flicks with her feather boa, and she gave up the battle. But the minute Paris passed gently out of the picture, the girls turned on the energy and rifled his pocket at what looked like a professional tempo. Although *Judgment of Paris* is not very subtle satire nor very important dance, there are plenty of laughs in it and that alone makes it a valid addition to the Ballet Theatre's repertory.

*Twentieth Century Ballet,* by A. H. Frank, 1954 as quoted in "Antony Tudor II" by Katherine Sorley Walker in *Dance Now* (Winter 1999–2000): Despite its snatches of Rabelaisian humour, [it] expresses with great poignancy the most sordid of human tragedies. . . . [It] unfolds its simple and sordid theme by an elegant language compounded so skillfully of mime and movement that not one discernible break appears. . . . To me the work can lay just claim to recognition as high art.

*Times,* 22 October, 1980, by John Percival: A little black comedy brilliantly capturing the spirit of Kurt Weill's music.

*Sunday Telegraph,* 26 October, 1980, by Nicholas Dromgoole: At one level this is a cheerful romp; at another, with its three harlots seedily enticing a drunk. . . . Weill's music and Tudor's choreography just manage to outface incalculable bitterness and despair with a fierce grin.


## Soirée musicale

Music: Gioacchino Rossini, arranged by Benjamin Britten
Costumes and Scenery: Hugh Stevenson
Premiere: 26 November, 1938, Palladium Theatre, London
London Ballet Premieree 12 December, 1938, Toynbee Hall, London
Cast: "Canzonetta": Gerd Larsen, Hugh Laing; "Tirolese": Maude Lloyd, Antony Tudor; "Bolero": Peggy van Praagh, Charlotte Bidmead, Thérèse Langfield (Rosa Vernon was the third "Bolero" dancer when the work was performed by the London Ballet); "Tarantella": Monica Boam, Guy Massey

The ballet was first revived in 1959 by the Joffrey Ballet, staged by Peggy van Praagh.

Critical Response (to London Ballet performances):
    *Dancing Times,* June, 1939: A gay trifle in the nature of a divertissement. . . .The five dances of which the ballet consists are varied, the gay "Tirolese," is brimful of spirit, the "Bolero" fascinatingly Spanish in feeling, and the "Tarantella" lightly Italian; Antony Tudor has gained all this atmosphere by suggestion and not by a forcing of authentic national steps.


## Gala Performance

Music: Sergei Prokofiev, *Piano Concerto no. 3,* first movement; *Classical Symphony*
Scenery and Costumes: Hugh Stevenson
Premiere: 5 December, 1938, Toynbee Hall, London
Cast: Russian: Peggy van Praagh; Italian: Maude Lloyd; French: Gerd Larson; and Antony Tudor, Guy Massey, Hugh Laing, Monica Boam, Rosa Vernon, Sylvia Hayden, Charlotte Bidmead, Susan Reeves, Katharine Legris, and Thérèse Langfield as the Dresser (and later the French ballerina).

Cast for Ballet Theatre restaging, February 11, 1941: Russian: Nora Kaye; Italian: Nana Gollner; French: Karen Conrad; Hugh Laing, Edward Caton, Tania Dokoudovska, and Antony Tudor; later casts included: Janet Reed, John Kriza, Fernando Alonso, Kenneth Davis, Stanley Herbert, Robert de Voye, Margaret Banks, Muriel Bentley, Patricia Barker, Shirley Eckl, Barbara Fallis, June Morris, Rozsika Sabo, Dorean Oswald, Cynthia Riseley, Marjorie Tallchief; other casts included Thérèse Langfield, Dmitri Romanoff, Sallie Wilson, etc.

Critical Response:

*Time,* 6 December, 1938: A brief prologue shows the stage of a Parisian theatre immediately before the rise of the curtain. The *corps de ballet* and the rival "stars" practice their steps among inhabitants of the *vie de coulisse* [life in the wings] which is recorded in the canvases of Degas. A second scene shows the performance proper, the rival ballerinas competing for public acclaim. The little comedy of jealousies suggested by the prologue is not, however, very amusingly exploited. . . . Bravura, the quality that the manner and period of the ballet seemed most to call for, was not forthcoming.

*Daily Telegraph* and *Morning Post,* December, 1938 by F. T.: *Gala Performance* . . . proved slight but agreeable, representing a ballet before and during performance.

*Diaries* of Lionel Bradley, 6 December, 1938: The ballet is not of very great importance but it could perhaps be revised into something better.

*Diaries* of Lionel Bradley, 9 January, 1939: [The ballet has been] completely revised and improved in every way.

*New York Times,* 16 February, 1941 by John Martin: Mr. Tudor has strengthened the conviction, never exactly a weak one, that he is nothing less than a genius.

Another *New York Times* review from 1941 by John Martin: Tudor has not been content merely to string together amusing tricks, but has composed a work that has form and identity in the theatre. There will be few, however, who will care to stop laughing long enough to worry about niceties of composition.

*New York Herald Tribune,* 16 February, 1941, by Walter Terry: Antony Tudor is English, but his *Gala Performance* is meat for an American audience. In this land where nothing is safe from the lampoon, it is wise to make fun of yourself before any one else does it for you, and that is exactly what Mr. Tudor has done: he has made hilarious fare of the foibles of ballet. . . . The dripping charm, the coquettish mugging, the scrambled movements and the rampant glamour of *Gala Performance* are so close to the real thing—ballet at its very worst—that you'll find yourself loving all ballet for the simple reason that it can see humor in itself.

### The Tempest

Television broadcast directed by Antony Tudor
Music: Jean Sibelius
Premiere: 5 February, 1939
Cast: members of the London Ballet

### Johnson over Jordan

Music: Benjamin Britten
Scenery: Edward Carrick
Costumes: Elizabeth Haffenden
Premiere: 22 February, 1939,  New Theatre, London

### Nightlights,  a suppertime revue

"The Argyll Rooms 1850–1878"
"A Fragonard Picture"
Music: Elsie April, arranged by Antony Tudor
Costumes: [for Fragonard] Karinska
Premiere: 3 April, 1939, Trocadero, London

Critical Response:
        Unknown source: ["A Fragonard Picture" is] a singularly inept strip–tease in the style of Fragonard.

### The Pilgrim's Progress

Television presentation for which Tudor arranged the dances

Cast: Charlotte Bidmead, Thésèse Langfield, Elisabeth Schooling
Premiere: 7 April, 1939, for television

### The Bartered Bride

Music: Bedarich Smetana
Costumes lent by the Prague Opera
Premiere: 1 May, 1939, Covent Garden, London
Cast: The London Ballet

### La Traviata

Music: Giuseppe Verdi
Premiere: 22 May, 1939, Covent Garden, London
Cast: The London Ballet

### Aïda

Music: Giuseppe Verdi
Premiere: 24 May, 1939, Covent Garden, London
Cast: Margot Fonteyn (or Peggy van Praagh in later performances) and
the London Ballet

### Lights Up, a revue

"A Fragonard Picture"
"An Old Dance Hall"
Music: Elsie April
Premiere: 9 February, 1940, Savoy Theatre, London

## The First Ten Years at Ballet Theatre (Chapter 3)

### Goya Pastoral

Music: Enrique Granados

Scenery and Costumes: Nicholas de Molas
Premiere: 1 August, 1940, Lewisohn Stadium, New York
Cast: Alicia Alonso, Nora Kaye, Jerome Robbins, Donald Saddler, Hugh Laing, Eugene Loring, Antony Tudor, Tillie Losch, Lucia Chase

Critical Response:
*New York Times, 2* August, 1940, by John Martin: To an amusing libretto by Mr. de Molas, Mr. Tudor has created a light-hearted little ballet. Actually, its choreography, which makes no pretense at being authentic Spanish, could be more sparkling and pointed, and its action could get under way considerably sooner than it does, but once the plot starts to move, it is engaging and expertly done. Everything of Mr. Tudor's that has been presented here has been distinguished by his ability to give texture to his compositions, and the present work, though it is assuredly not his masterpiece, is no exception to this rule. The most amusing role is that of an elderly Marchioness beautifully played by Lucia Chase.

"The Short Story Ballet," *Dance,* June, 1942, by George Beiswanger: The Spanish dance is hardly up Tudor's alley as yet; his intensity, though it reaches down to the same roots in the passional life, is not of the same order. Nonetheless, even this dancewright chore was done with care, with evident affection and with an unmistakable quality that flowed—a lyric fluid—through the whole revised work and pulled it together.

## *Time Table*

Music: Aaron Copland, *Music for the Theatre*
Scenery and Costumes: James Stewart Morcom
Premiere: 29 May, 1941, Little Theatre of Hunter College, New York
Cast: Zachary Solov, Gisella Caccialanza, Lew Christensen, Lorna London, Charles Dickson, Beatrice Tompkins, Mary Jane Shea, June Graham, John Kriza, Newcomb Rice, Georgia Hiden, Jack Dumphy

New York City Ballet Cast: Marie–Jeanne, Francisco Moncion, Walter Georgov, Jack Kauflin, Beatrice Tompkins, Georgia Hiden

Since the ballet was shown in New York only once in 1941, as a preview of the upcoming South American tour of Kirstein's company, there are no New York reviews of the original production.

Critical Response (to the NYCB production):
*Herald Tribune,* 14 January, 1948, by Walter Terry: There are moments eloquent in their communication of tenderness and desire,

there are large-scale movements and impulsive gestures which define mood and character in masterful fashion but there is also a good deal of superficial romantic dance and pretty obvious horseplay which, though pleasant enough, are hardly worthy of the distinguished choreographer's known skills . . . If *Time Table* is not a superior work intrinsically, it is, at least, an important addition to this company's repertory . . . Further, it is harmless, mildly diverting, and occasionally moving.

*New York Times,* 14 January, 1948, by John Martin: It is interesting to see the fragments and phrases here that anticipated the great work that was to follow [*Pillar of Fire*]. It is also interesting to see certain premonitions of Jerome Robbins's *Fancy Free* that was not to come along until 1944. *Time Table* is definitely minor Tudor, but it is charming and atmospheric and admirably made.

## *Pillar of Fire*

Music: Arnold Schoenberg, *Verklarte Nacht*
Scenery and Costumes: Jo Mielziner
Premiere: 8 April, 1942, Metropolitan Opera House, New York
Cast: Nora Kaye, Hugh Laing, Annabelle Lyon, Antony Tudor, Lucia Chase, Maria Karnilova, Charles Dickson, Jean Davidson, John Kriza, Virginia Wilcox, Wallace Seibert, Jean Hunt, Barbara Fallis, Sono Osato, Rosella Hightower, Muriel Bentley, Jerome Robbins, Donald Saddler, Frank Hobi, Balina Razoumova, Roszika Sabo

Critical Response:
*Dance,* 1946, Tudor Publishing Company, New York, pp. 87–8: It dealt probably for the first time in ballet's history, with sex as a psychological instead of a purely romantic subject, and may properly be considered as inaugurating a new era for the ballet as a medium for the expression of profound and penetrating insight into human experience . . . Tudor has been extraordinarily successful in bringing out qualities in individual dancers which perhaps they themselves have not been aware of and which the conventional repertoire would be unlikely to discover.

*Dancing Times,* London, by Lillian Moore, pp. 490–91: Perhaps once in a generation a work of art is created which completely realizes the aims towards which many other obscure and incomplete efforts have been directed. One work achieves what many have attempted, and becomes eventually the symbol of a school or of a period. Only time can reveal what ballet will emerge as representative of the present renaissance . . . It can only be said that in *Pillar of Fire* Antony Tudor

appears to have created a masterpiece worthy of this distinction. . . .
*Pillar of Fire* [is] a searching portrayal of human emotion . . . actually
revealing the innermost thoughts and feelings of a young girl possessed
and torn by a tragic obsession. Mr. Tudor transcends his medium, and
succeeds in expressing through the technique of the ballet emotions and
situations which one would have thought it impossible to translate into
dance form . . . All the resources of bodily movement and mime are
used in such a way that the clear firm structure of the work is never
obtrusive, and form seems to be subordinated to meaning. Actually
*Pillar of Fire* achieves the perfect synthesis between form and content.

## *The Tragedy of Romeo and Juliet*

Music: Frederick Delius ("A Walk to Paradise Garden" from *A Village
Romeo and Juliet; Eventyr; Over the Hills and Far Away; Brigg Fair*)
Scenery and Costumes: Eugene Berman
Premiere: 6 April, 1943 (incomplete); 10 April, Metropolitan Opera
House, New York
Cast: Hugh Laing, Alicia Markova (later Nora Kaye), Nicholas Orloff
(Fernando Alonso, Enrique Martinez), Jerome Robbins (Michael
Lland), Antony Tudor (John Taras, Darrell Notara), Lucia Chase (Cath-
erine Horn), Dmitri Romanoff, Sono Osato (Sallie Wilson), Borislav
Ronanine, Miriam Golden (Susan Borree), John Taras (Edward Caton),
Galina Rozoumova (Nansi Clement), Richard Reed (Vernon Lusby),
Hubert Bland, Rex Cooper, Stanley Herbertt, John Kriza, Donald Sad-
dler, Michael Kidd, Robert Lindgren, John Duane, Rosella Hightower,
Nicola Vassilief, June Morris, Hilda Wagner, Jean Hunt, Billie Wynn,
and the Misses Muriel Bentley, Davidson, Virginia Wilcox, Gomberg,
Roszika Sabo, Shirley Eckl, Barbara Fallis, Albia Kavan, Georgia Hi-
den

1971 Cast: Vane Vest, Ivan Nagy or John Prinz, Dennis Nahat or Al-
exander Filipov, Ian Horvath, Frank Smith, Bojan Spassoff, Gaudio
Vacacio, Bruce Marks or Royes Fernandez, Robert Brassel, Richard
Cammack, David Coll, Richard Rein, Paul Nickel, Marcos Paredes or
Rory Foster, Jan Fisher, Rosanna Seravalli, Carla Fracci, Martine van
Hamel or Maria Youskevitch, Bonnie Mathis, Carol Foster or Naomi
Sorkin, Warren Conover, Buddy Balough, Marianna Tcherkassky,
Zhandra Rodriguez, the Misses Amy Blaisdell, Busch, Dishong, Dob-
son, Nanette Glushak, Jorgenson, Wesche, Wolf, Sue Knapp, Bryan,
Highton

Critical Response:

*New York Herald Tribune,* 12 April, 1943, by Edwin Denby (as quoted in *Dance Perspectives* 18, 57): It is made up of innumerable exquisite touches, ranging in style from quattrocento poses to a reference to Judo. It is full of nuances and pacing, like an Eisenstein film. And it does not sweep through the story. It is, so to speak, a meditation on the play. But it is strangely moving. Its strength is that of an intensely and consistently poetic attitude.

*New York Times,* 18 April, 1943, by John Martin (as quoted in *Dance Perspectives* 18, 58): It is a play without words rather than a ballet . . . The balcony scene takes place much as in the play, lacking only the justification of its lyric verse, which the choreographer has not attempted to replace. Its physical action is virtually nil, and its value as dance consequently negative . . . Juliet, at least, is an individual in her own choreographic right. She has visual eloquence and would certainly seem strong enough to be separated entirely from the literary and dramatic line of the play and placed bodily in a choreographic development of the same essential themes.

*Arabesques,* (London: Newelle Wolsey Ltd., 1948) by Alan Story: *Romeo and Juliet* . . . is a ballet in the grand manner in both concept and design; but its failure is threefold: (1) The music . . . is not suitable for dancing because of its unemphatic and irregular rhythms and because of its subjectivity, (2) The choreography is too stylised and (stranger still for Tudor) too impersonal for the nature of the ballet, (3) There is a lack of purpose and design in the choral movements . . . Tudor's ballet is in many ways a beautiful thing; once again he reveals his versatility in approaching each new theme from an entirely different angle. He has created some unforgettable stage pictures; yet it is precisely because they remain so obviously "pictures" that the ballet fails.

*Ballet in America,* (New York: Duell, Sloane and Pearce, Inc.: 1949) by George Amberg: [*Romeo and Juliet*] is a magnificent spectacle and probably the most lavish and exquisite theater piece on the contemporary ballet stage.

## Dim Lustre

Music: Richard Strauss (*Burleske in D Minor for Piano and Orchestra*)
Scenery and Costumes: Motley
Premiere: October 20, 1943, Metropolitan Opera House, New York

Cast: Nora Kaye, Hugh Laing, Muriel Bentley, Michael Kidd, John Kriza, Rosella Hightower, Janet Reed, Antony Tudor, Albia Kaven, Virginia Wilcox

Later cast members: Barbara Fallis, Harold Lang, June Morris, Kenneth Davis, Roszika Sabo, Fenando Alonso, Fern Whitney, John Taras, Margaret Banks, Alpheus Koon, Roy Tobias, Patricia Barker

New York City Ballet revival, 26 May, 1954, Cast: Patricia McBride, Edward Villella

American Ballet Theatre revival, May, 1985: Cast: Johan Renvall/John Meehan, Anna Spelman/Leslie Browne, Clark Tippet, Amanda McKerrow, Bonnie Moore.

Critical Response:
*New York Herald Tribune,* October 21, 1943, by Edwin Denby: Ballet Theater [*sic*] presented at the Metropolitan last night the world Premiere of *Dim Luster* [*sic*], a ballet by Antony Tudor, the brilliantly original choreographer of six other ballets in the company's repertory. *Dim Luster* is weaker than any of the others, both in the inventiveness of the dance detail and in the general over-all dramatic effect. It seems to me that the one real distinction it has is Tudor's name on the program.
*New York Times,* 24 October, 1943, by John Martin: For those . . . who complain that the ballet makes no appeal to the intelligence . . . Antony Tudor has created a little piece called *Dim Lustre* which for sheer brilliance is guaranteed to keep busy as keen an intellect as you happen to be equipped with. He calls it a "psychological episode," but that, like the title itself, finds him with his tongue in his cheek. . . . One wag at the opening performance was heard to nickname it "Strange Interlude in the Lilac Garden." . . . Mr. Tudor has never before been so perky, and though the marks of his personal style are all over this new work, it is altogether different from everything he has done previously. . . . When it is all over, the journey itself has been so engrossing that there is a strong desire to make it again, straightway, in order on the second trip to enjoy the scenery. If there ever was a ballet that will stand a second seeing . . . this is it. . . . Tudor's devices for telling his story are ingenious and remain completely within the realm of choreography. . . . It is very simply done, and is both convincing and imaginative. The choreography itself is rich and full in design and the stage is constantly in motion without losing its formal clarity.
*New York Times,* 15 May, 1985, by Anna Kisselgoff: The dancing by this first cast is so rocky and disjointed that the clarity of the

action is sacrificed to a turbulent and disconcerting blur of movement. This is by no means a criticism of the ballet itself . . . in all, [it is] a fascinating ballet whose dancers need to find an anchor.


## *Undertow*

Music: Commissioned score by William Schuman
Scenery and Costumes: Raymond Breinin
Premiere: 10 April, 1945, Metropolitan Opera House
Cast: Hugh Laing, Diana Adams, John Kriza, Nana Gollner, Alicia Alonso, Janet Reed, Lucia Chase, Shirley Eckl, Patricia Barker, Regis Posers, Stanley Herbertt, Michael Kidd, Fernando Alonso, Kenneth Davis, Roy Tobias, Roszika Sabo, Cynthia Riesly, Dick Beard, Marjorie Tallchief, June Morris, Mildred Ferguson

Critical Response:
"The Ballet," *New York Herald Tribune,* 11 April, 1945, by Edwin Denby: *Undertow* . . . is interesting, distinguished, perfectly executed, but it seemed at its first performance to miss fire as a dramatic work . . . at the end some of the audience professed not to understand what had occurred. . . . If Tudor has failed this time to be as effective a story teller in dance form as he has repeatedly proved himself to be in other works (and a second performance may perhaps change this impression) he has in any event filled his "murder mystery" with brilliant detail. . . . The relations of the characters to one another and to the hero are both subtle and precise; they are expressed in fragmentary dance passages beautifully stitched together.
*New York Herald Tribune,* "Tudor's *Undertow*," 15 April, 1945, by Edwin Denby: *Undertow,* Tudor's new ballet which Ballet Theatre is giving at the Metropolitan, is well worth seeing. Though not so effective theatrically as *Pillar of Fire* or *Romeo* it is a highly interesting, a very special piece and a notable credit to the season. *Undertow* tells a story which appears to happen more in a young man's mind than in objective reality. . . . The theme of *Undertow* is that of an adolescent's neurosis, the terrifying dilemma which presents to him the act of manhood as equivalent to murder.
Unidentified clipping, 25 April, 1945, by R. S.: One of the most baffling, and at the same time one of the most fascinating ballets of modern times had its world Premieree at the Metropolitan Opera House on the evening of April 10, when Antony Tudor's *Undertow,* a study in sexual frustration and murder, was given by the Ballet Theatre. Others of Mr. Tudor's works have been more completely integrated, but

none of them has been so bold, so revolutionary and so psychologically disturbing as this one. A powerful score by William Schuman added to the impact of the work, which was created "after a suggestion by John Van Druten."

*New York Times,* 11 April, 1945, by John Martin: A curious and baffling work it is. Mr. Tudor has never been so difficult, indeed, and it will take half a dozen visits and the closest concentration to be sure exactly what he is driving at.

*Newsweek,* 23 April, 1945: Antony Tudor had promised that his newest ballet, *Undertow,* would be a psychological murder drama. The audience . . . was stunned when it got murder—and childbirth too . . . *Undertow* was tough going. . . . The cast listings didn't help, either. Although the tortured young man (Hugh Laing) was called The Transgressor, the rest of the dancers were all identified with obscure Latin and Greek names. . . . *Undertow* is a fine illustration of what can make ballet an exciting and challenging art form: close collaboration of the best in dance, music, and painting.

### Hollywood Pinafore

Music: Arthur Sullivan; Lyrics: George S. Kaufman
Premiere: 31 May, 1945, Alvin Theatre, New York
Cast: Viola Essen, John Butler, Stanley Herbertt, Barbara Heath, Helene Constantine

Critical Response:
*New York Times,* 17 June, 1945, by John Martin: From the out-of-town Premieree in Baltimore right on through the New York opening, the ballet . . . nightly stopped the show. This is not to be attributed, however, exclusively to any surpassing brilliance as a ballet, but rather to a virtually reflex welcome by the audience of something with movement about it in an otherwise static evening. . . . Mr. Tudor (or his librettist) has remained too faithful to the style and form of the surrounding material.

### The Day Before Spring

Music: Frederick Loewe; Lyrics: Alan J. Lerner
Scenery: Robert Davison
Costumes: Miles White
Premiere: 22 November, 1945, National Theatre, New York
Cast: Hugh Laing, Mary Ellen Moylan

Critical Response:
    *New York Herald Tribune,* by Walter Terry: As the "villain" en-
deavors to lure the lovely heroine from her state of wedded bliss to the
enchantment of elopement with him, his words resolve into the action
of dance. This sort of dream sequence should have given visual support
to his romantic plea, but, like too many dreams, it was cluttered up. . .
There were many moments in the fine dancing . . . that revealed the
great Tudor. . . .These fragments of dance pattern were inventive in
design and dramatic in effect, but they were not sustained, and their
possible effectiveness was spoiled by the ambling activities of the
corps. . . . The ballet in the second act . . . suffered from the same
faults as the first: there were lovely isolated moments of exciting dance
action spoiled by choreographic clutter.

### Shadow of the Wind

Music: Gustav Mahler, *Das Lied von der Erde*
Scenery: Jo Mielziner
Costumes: listed as Mielziner, but designed by Hugh Laing
Premiere: 14 April, 1948, Metropolitan Opera House, New York
Cast: Alicia Alonso, John Kriza, Muriel Bentley, Nana Gollner

Critical Response:
    *New York Herald Tribune,* 18 April, 1948, by Walter Terry: A
new ballet by Antony Tudor is something of an event in the theater of
dance, for Mr. Tudor is one of the great choreographers of our time . . .
[The critic] may, as in the case of *Shadow of the Wind* . . . be disappointed in the results of a Tudor project but he cannot dismiss its va-
lidity of purpose, its eagerness to explore new areas of dance. *Shadow
of the Wind* is a disappointment, a rousing disappointment, for it is
stylistically confused, tentative in its conveying of mood, often superficial in effect and dim in dramatic imagery. Portions of it, of course,
are wonderful Tudor, but the vast expanse . . . is more tenuous than the
image evoked by the title itself and not as poetic . . . [It is] mainly
concerned with vague Orientalisms, some rather sketchy pantomime
and only passing choreographic reference to the themes of the dance and
the dynamic intensities of the music.
    "They Create New Ballets," Unidentified source: In *Shadow of
the Wind* English-born, forty-year-old Antony Tudor has produced the
major work of his distinguished career. . . . Diffident and serious-
minded, Antony Tudor calls his latest work "an exposition of Chinese
philosophy of the eighth century."

# The 1950s (Chapter 4)

## *The Dear Departed*

Music: Maurice Ravel (*String Quartet,* 4th movement)
Premiere: 15 July, 1949, Jacob's Pillow, Lee, Massachusetts
Cast: Diana Adams, Hugh Laing


## *Nimbus*

Music: Louis Gruenberg, *Violin Concerto,* conducted by Max
Goberman; Broadus Erle, Violinist
Scenery: Oliver Smith
Costumes: Saul Bolasni
Premiere: 3 May, 1950, Center Theatre, New York
Cast: Nora Kaye, Diana Adams, Hugh Laing, Virginia Barnes, Jacque-
line Dodge, Dorothy Scott, Jenny Workman, Eric Braun, Jimmy
Hicks, Fernand Nault, Holland Stoudenmire

Critical Response:
    *New York Times,* 4 May, 1950, by John Martin: It would be dif-
ficult to go into any ecstasies about Antony Tudor's new ballet *Nimbus.* . . . As usual, Mr. Tudor has devised some highly original lifts
and has composed for the individuals of his story with phenomenal
awareness of their abilities. He has provided Nora Kaye with some
truly wonderful movement, full of character and comment. . . . Diana
Adams . . . has a long opening sequence which explores her lyric po-
tentialities and the strong, clean technical force that underlies them,
with extraordinary beauty and touches of wit and warmth. . . . And that
is about all there is to it at the moment . . . ultimately [it] may prove
to be a pleasant and popular work, if never a major.
    *Herald Tribune,* 4 May, 1950, by Walter Terry: *Nimbus* is an
atmospheric ballet in which fantasy and amusing dashes of realism are
mixed, and, for the most part, successfully. Mr. Tudor . . . has created
some marvelous moments of dance and pantomime in his newest work.
The initial sequences . . . are rich in fresh and exciting movement. . . .
A large audience greeted the new work warmly and demanded many
curtain calls.

*Lady of the Camellias*

Music: Giuseppe Verdi (from *Nabucco, Sicilian Vespers, Macbeth,* and *I Lombardi,* selected and arranged by Antony Tudor)
Scenery and Costumes: Cecil Beaton
(scenery and costumes recycled from a previous production choreographed by John Taras for Alicia Markova)
Premiere: 28 February, 1951, New York City Center, New York
Cast: Vida Brown, Diana Adams, Brooks Jackson, Hugh Laing, Antony Tudor

Critical Response:
"A New Tudor Ballet," *New York Notes,* undated, by Lillian Moore: Tudor has long been an acknowledged master of the narrative ballet, and his *Lady of the Camellias* confirms this reputation. The lyrical quality of movement so typical of his work is perfectly adapted to the romantic theme. . . . He has simply translated a familiar and well-loved story into balletic terms, and the result is eminently appealing.
*New York Herald Tribune,* 1 March, 1951, by Walter Terry: The newest version of the novel by Alexandre Dumas [*Marguerite and Armand*] is by far the most satisfactory of the three [recent versions], although it must be said that Antony Tudor, the choreographer of *Lady of the Camellias,* has not succeeded in matching the dramatic, operatic or cinematic versions of a poignant and haunting tale. . . . In certain details, then, one may admire Mr. Tudor's choreography while not applauding his ballet as a whole.
"Ballet by Tudor in Premiere Here," *New York Times,* 1 March, 1951: Antony Tudor's ballet *Lady of the Camellias* had the first performance of what should prove to be a lengthy career last night. . . . It is far and away the most substantial creation Mr. Tudor has given us in years, and though there is still work to be done on it, since it was completed in record time by a man who is by nature a slow and careful composer, it is marked by an extraordinary originality and an unusual sensitiveness of texture. . . . What Tudor has produced is in effect a choreographed novel of the late nineteenth century . . . its action unfolds in terms of what might be called abstract dialogue, varying from a hint of the formal miming of the nineteenth-century ballet, through fairly natural gesture, to a heightened expressiveness of inward feeling when the situation touches deeper emotional levels. There could scarcely be a more inspired method of approaching the story.

*Les Mains gauches*

Music: Jacques Ibert
Premiere: 20 July, 1951, Jacob's Pillow, Lee, Massachusetts
Cast: Zebra Nevins, Sallie Wilson, Marc Hertsens


*Ronde de printemps*

Music: Erik Satie
Costumes: Hugh Laing
Premiere: 1 August, 1951, Jacob's Pillow, Lee, Massachusetts
Cast: Francine Bond, Harvey Jung, Marc Hertsens, Jack Monts, Zebra
Nevins, Adelino A. Palomonos, Sallie Wilson


*La Gloire*

Music: Ludwig van Beethoven (Overtures: *Egmont, Coriolanus,* and
*Leonora no. 3*)
Scenery: Gaston Longchamp
Costumes: Robert Fletcher
Premiere: 26 February, 1952, New York City Center, New York
Cast: Nora Kaye, Hugh Laing, Barbara Walczak, Beatrice Tomkins,
Francisco Moncion, Doris Breckenridge, Edith Brozak, Arlouine Case,
Kaye Sargent, Tomi Wortham, Gloria Vauges, Jacques d'Amboise,
Una Kai, Walter Georgov, Stanley Zompakos


For the remainder of 1952 through 1953 and the first half of 1954, and
again in 1956, Tudor was mainly concerned with teaching at the Metropolitan Opera, at the Juilliard School, in Philadelphia, and at Jacob's
Pillow. His creative output was limited to works for the students most
of which he considered "Dance Arrangements" rather than choreography. The six works thus created were:

*Trio Con Brio,* music by Mikhail Glinka, costumes by Marie Nepo
and Adolphine Rott, which Premiereed at Jacob's Pillow on 27 June,
1952. The choreographer is listed as Vispitin because Tudor did not
wish the piece to be thought of as his choreographic work. The cast
was Tatiana Grantzeva, Nicholas Polajenko, and Ralph McWilliams.

*Exercise Piece,* using the *String Quartet no. 2* of Arriaga, Premiered
on 7 May, 1953, at the concert hall of the Juilliard School. The work

was based on classroom steps; among the dancers were Carolyn Brown, later to become a soloist with Merce Cunningham and his partner for many years, and Nancy King (Zeckendorf), later a dancer at the Metropolitan Opera Ballet and on retirement a member of the Board of Directors of American Ballet Theatre. (See Chapter 6.)

***Little Improvisations,*** music by Robert Schumann *(Kinderscenen),* a *pas de deux* choreographed (or rather, according to Tudor, arranged) for Yvonne Chouteau and Gilbert Reed at Jacob's Pillow, Premiereing on 28 August, 1953. The piece has been restaged many, many times all over the world.

***Elizabethan Dances,*** music by Orlando Gibbons, Anthony Holborne, Thomas Morley, William Byrd, John Gamble, and Thomas Tomkins, presented as part of "A Festival of British Music," on 7 December, 1953, at the Juilliard School. (See Chapter 6.)

***Britannia Triumphans,*** music by William Lawes, scenery by Frederick Kiesler, costumes by Leo Van Witsen, Premiereing on 11 December, 1953, at the Juilliard School also as part of "A Festival of British Music." (See Chapter 6.)

***Pas de trois,*** with music by Carl Maria von Weber (Overture to *Euryanthe* ), danced by Caroline Bristol, Gail Valentine, and Bruce Marks and premiered on 26 April, 1956, at the Juilliard School (See Chapter 6.)

### Offenbach in the Underworld

Music: Jacques Offenbach *(Gaîté Parisienne)*
Costumes: Judith Gesensway (Skoogfors)
Premiere: 8 May, 1954, Convention Hall, Philadelphia
Cast: Michael Lland, Viola Essen, Ruth Anne Carr, Paula Mainwaring, Sylvia Kim, Michael Lopuszanski, Maurice Phillips, Elaine Wilson, and Jon Jones, William (Billy) Wilson, Judith Gesensway, Odette Phillips, Laura Campbell, Phyllis Dersh, Barbara Flaxman, Dorothy Greathead, Elizabeth Mozley, Claire Shirli, Robert Daley, Vincent Gonzales, Olin Kearse, Joseph Plomchok, Conchetta De Prospero, Ann Garrick, Sybil Klein

Critical Response:

*Philadelphia Inquirer,* 9 May, 1954, by Samuel L. Singer: The ensemble—and the soloists—shone again in *Offenbach in the Underworld,* with buoyant choreography by the able Tudor. This is a French ballet in spirit and choreography, with the setting listed as New Orleans in the 1870s. It contains all the usual characters of popular ballets set to music by Offenbach and Strauss–cafe habitués, "local ladies," visiting celebrities, and others. The fast-moving ballet commanded rapt attention from start to finish, but the high point was the realistic free-for-all . . . a superbly staged ensemble sequence.

*Philadelphia Bulletin,* 10 May, 1954, by Max de Schaunesee: Two ballets bore the unmistakable stamp of Mr. Tudor's fastidiousness and taste, his apt and personal touches, which are never hard to detect. . . . The present choreography (for *Offenbach in the Underworld*) seems much more spontaneous than the old one (Massine's *Gaité Parisienne*) and Mr.Tudor has given his ballet . . . many charming psychological strokes of the brush. There was verve and gaiety and the stage never seemed needlessly cluttered. A stage free-for-all (a cafe brawl) was the best this writer has ever seen depicted on a stage.

### *La Leyenda de José (José y la mujer de Putifar)*

Music: Richard Strauss
Premiere: 19 August, 1958, Teatro Colón
Cast: Carlos Schiafino, Olga Frances, and fifty corps de ballet dancers

## The Metropolitan Opera (Chapter 5)

### *La Traviata*

Music: Giuseppe Verdi
Premiere: 11 November, 1950, Metropolitan Opera House, New York
Cast: Tilda Morse, Nana Gollner, corps de ballet

## *Faust*

Music: Charles Gounod
Premiere: 12 December, 1950, Metropolitan Opera House, New York
Cast: Nana Gollner and corps de ballet

Critical Response:
  *New York Times,* 13 December, 1950, by Olin Downes: Nor can we say that Mr. Tudor's choreography is any more germane to the theme than Gounod's music. [The ballet music was added ten years after the opera was written.] It is unoriginal and mannered, and contains nothing genuinely symbolic of the meeting of Faust and Helen of Troy and the union of German romanticism and Greek art as symbolized in Goethe's poem.

## *Die Fledermaus*

Music: Johann Strauss
Premiere: 20 December, 1950, Metropolitan Opera House, New York
Cast: Nana Gollner and corps de ballet

## *Hail and Farewell*

Music: Richard Strauss (*Festival March, Serenade for Winds, Four Last Songs.* Texts for the songs are by Hermann Hesse and J. V. Eichendorff)
Costumes: Motley
Premiere: 22 March, 1959, Metropoliton Opera House, New York
Cast: Lupe Serrano, Edith Jerell, Audrey Keane, Nora Kaye, Hlenka Devon, William Burdick, Ron Murray, Vincent Warren, and Suzanne Ames, Meredith Baylis, Ann Stone, José Gutierrez, Harry Jones, Donald Martin, David Milnes, Alek Zybine, Margaret Black, Louellen Sibley, Ann Etgen, Fronda Sobel, Eleanor Steber, Soprano

Critical Response:
  *New York Herald Tribune,* 23 March, 1959, by Walter Terry: Of major interest, of course, was the new ballet—his first large-scale effort in some years—by Antony Tudor, the Met's ballet director. . . . It turned out to be the best Tudor choreography in a good many years. It

is without story but is, at least in the *Four Last Songs,* rich in mood. The opening sections . . . are not particularly impressive. . . . But with the Songs, Mr. Tudor came into his own and gave us four gentle, tender but gloriously styled solos. Here, Mr. Tudor created glowing choreographic images, haunting and exquisitely lyrical.

*Alceste* (some sources spell this as *Alcestis* )

Music: Christoph Willibald Gluck
Premiere: 6 December, 1960, Metropolitan Opera House, New York
Cast: Metropolitan Opera Ballet

Critical Response:
*New York Times,* undated, by John Martin: To Mr. Tudor, not unnaturally, go top honors, for his work in the revival of *Alcestis* was clearly that of a major artist. The fact that he was lustily booed at the opening performance constituted a real scandal, for even if he had fallen flat on his face, one does not boo an outstanding master. To do so heaps dishonor on the booers rather than the booee. But he could scarcely have been farther from falling on his face, for what he created was choreographically of genuine distinction. That Mr. Tudor is not a theatrical choreographer or one with a gift for the extroversions of the operatic medium cannot be news to anybody.
"The Opera Ballet," *New York Herald Tribune,* 7 December, 1960, by Walter Terry: One thing which may be said about Antony Tudor's choreography for the Metropolitan Opera's new production of *Alcestis* is that it has range. It ranges from the charming to the near-ridiculous. Matters get off to an agreeable dance start in the first scene, for here Mr.Tudor has used his chorus not only in frieze-like patterns of considerable loveliness but also given them gestural actions which mirror both the mood of the music and the sense of the scene itself . . . the choreography took a dip in the second scene, act I.
*Dance Observer,* January, 1961, by A. T.: Tudor's contributions to *Alcestis* are among his most inspired in any field in the last decade. . . . The stepping off point in this production is the plastic conception of this work that appears to be derived from Rodin . . . [It is] considerably more Etruscan than Greek in his hands. . . . *Alcestis* is approached as art.

## *Tannhäuser*

Music: Richard Wagner
Premiere: 17 December, 1960, Metropolitan Opera House, New York
Cast: Metropolitan Opera Ballet

Critical Response:
   *New York Times,* undated review, by John Martin: He kept the lights as dim as possible, and in the first half of the ballet he filled the back of the stage with a milling and indecipherable mass of partner-lifting. In the second half, however, he really came to grief. With three forlorn damsels from the corps stranded midstage, raising a foot tentatively here and tracing a minuscule floor path there, he produced an Olympian longueur, no less.

## *Fandango*

Music: Fra Antonio Soler
Costumes: Estaban Francis, recycled from *Vittorio*, a ballet by Zachary Solov
Premiere: 26 March, 1963, Town Hall, New York
Cast: Carole Kroon (substituting for Edith Jerell), Suzanne Ames, Ayako Ogawa, Nancy King [Zeckendorf], and Ingrid Blecker

## *Concerning Oracles*

Music: Jacques Ibert, (*Suite Elisabéthaine, Capriccio, Divertissement*)
Scenery: Peter Harvey
Costumes: Peter Harvey
Premiere: 27 March, 1966, Metropolitan Opera House, New York
Cast: Nira Paz, Donald Mahler, Jan Mickens, Edith Jerell, Carolyn Martin, Ivan Allen, Lance Westergard, Sally Brayley (Bliss), Susana Aschieri, Nicolyn Emanuel, Sylvia Grinvald, Rhodie Jorgenson, Janet Morse, Sharon O'Connell, Robert Davis, Martin Fredman, William Maloney, David Milnes, Franklin Yezer, Josef Gregory, Howard Sayette

Critical Response:
   *New York Times.* 28 March, 1966, by Clive Barnes: *Concerning Oracles* was a moderately serious diversion, both sinister and comic.

Set to three disturbingly different Ibert scores, it concerned itself, twice
gravely and once brightly, with the gifts of prophecy . . . choreography
that was always sweet and sound yet excellent only in parts, imaginative only in moments.
   *New York Herald Tribune,* 28 March, 1966, by Walter Terry:
*Concerning Oracles* was a far less impressive affair. It contained many
of the choreographer's traits of style . . . but they were so tenuous and
unfortunately effortful that most of the ballet was singularly jerky. . . .
*Oracles* hit its stride only in its last scene, a wonderfully funny, almost slapstick, near vaudeville bit in which a tall girl and a diminutive
youth danced together with the girl giving the boy as much muscular
support as he gave her.

## The Juilliard Experiment (Chapter 6)

### *Exercise Piece*

Music: Arriaga, *String Quartet no. 2*
No scenery or costumes
Premiere: 7 May, 1953, Concert Hall, Juilliard School of Music, New
York
Cast: Juilliard students including Carolyn Brown, Nancy King (Zeck-
endorf), among others

***Elizabethan Dances***   (presented as part of "A Festival of British
Music")

Music: Orlando Gibbons, Anthony Holborne, Thomas Morley, Wil-
liam Byrd, John Gamble, and Thomas Tomkins
Premiere: 7 December, 1953, Concert Hall, Juilliard School of Music,
New York
Cast: Lucille Badda, Donya Feuer, Sally Holroyd, Patricia Sparrow,
Jerry Kurland, Vernon Long, Barrie Schenker, Charles Wadsworth

***Britannia Triumphans***   (presented as part of "A Festival of British
Music")

Music: William Lawes

Scenery: Frederick Kiesler
Costumes: Leo Van Witsen
Premiere: 11 December, 1953, Concert Hall, Juilliard School of Music,
New York
Cast: Lucille Badda, Sally Holroyd, Jerry Kurland, Robert Moery,
Charles Wadsworth, Karen Kanner, Gene McDonald, Vernon Long,
Barrie Schenker, Joel Schnee, Rena Gluck, Martha Schuh, [Kevin]
Bruce Carlisle, John Coyle, Yvonne Brenner, Madeline Cantarella,
Hazel Chung, Patricia Sparrow, Elizabeth Stanley, Gail Valentine, Bru-
ria Aviezner, Margaret Bayer, Jan Feder, Crystal Needle, Julie Oser,
Muriel Topaz

## *Pas de trois*

Music: Carl Maria von Weber (Overture to *Euryanthe* )
No scenery or costumes
Premiere: 26 April, 1956, Concert Hall, Juilliard School of Music,
New York
Cast: Caroline Bristol, Gail Valentine, and Bruce Marks

## *A Choreographer Comments*

Music: Franz Schubert *(Octet)*
No scenery or costumes
Premiere: 8  April, 1960, Concert Hall, Juilliard School of Music,
New York
Cast: Philippine (Pina) Bausch, Chieko Kikuchi, Jennifer Masley, Mi-
chael Imber, Jerry King, Virginia Klein, Myron Howard Nadel, Carol
Lipman, Koert Stuyf, Benjamin Heller, Mabel Robinson, William
Louther, Carol Egan, Barbara Hale

## *Dance Studies (Less Orthodox)*

Music: Elliott Carter ("Etude III" from *Eight Etudes and a Fantasy for
Woodwind Quartet)*
No scenery or costumes
Premiere: 8 March, 1962, Concert Hall, Juilliard School of Music,
New York
Cast: Juilliard Dance Ensemble

***Ballet 1*** "Passamezzi"

Music: Antonio Gardano
Premiere: 8 March, 1962, Concert Hall, Juilliard School of Music,
New York
Cast: Juilliard Dance Ensemble


## *Continuo*

Music: Johann Pachelbel (*Canon*)
No scenery or costumes
First Showing: 27 May,1971, Juilliard Theater, New York
Professional  Premiere: 20 February, 1976, Syracuse Ballet
Cast: Sirpa Jorassma (Salatino), Anthony Salatino, Deborah Weaver,
Raymond Clay, Madeline Rhew, Blake Brown


## *Sunflowers*

Music: Leos Janácek (*String Quartet no. 1*, "The Kreutzer Sonata")
No scenery and costumes
First Showing: 27 May, 1971, Juilliard Theater, New York
Professional Premiere: 13 May, 1972, Omaha Ballet
Cast: Madeline Rhew, Airi Hynninen, Pamela Knisel, Deborah
Weaver, Anthony Salatino, Larry Grenier


## *Cereus*

Music: Geoffrey Gray (*L'Inconsequenza, Quartet for Percussion*)
No scenery or costumes
First Showing: 27 May, 1971, Juilliard Theater, New York
Professional Premiere: 16 November, 1972, Pennsylvania Ballet
Cast: Jerome Weiss, Sylvia Yamada, Larry Grenier, Bonnie Oda
(Homsey), Lance Westergard, Angeline Wolf, Marc Stevens

# The 1960s (Chapter 7)

## *Echoing of Trumpets (Ekon av Trumpeter)*

Music: Bohuslav Martinu, *Fantaisies Symphoniques (Symphony no. 6)*
Scenery and Costumes: Birger Bergling
Premiere: 28 September, 1963, Royal Opera House, Stockholm
Cast: Gerd Andersson, Catharina Ericson, Viveka Ljung, Kerstin Lust, Hervor Sjostrand, Kari Sylwan, Annette Wiedersheim-Paul, Mario Mengarelli, Jacques De Lisle, Eki Eriksson, Ulf Gadd, Nils Johansson, Nisse Winqvist, Richard Wold, Svant Lindberg

Critical Response:
*New York Times,* November, 1964, by Clive Barnes: He has given us a profoundly antiromantic ballet about war—a ballet that is real, terrible and yet still beautiful in the scarlet way of tragedy.
*Dance and Dancers,* June, 1973, by Peter Williams: One of the most distinguished twentieth century works the company has ever taken into its repertoire.
*Set to Music,* May, 1980, by Cormac Rigby: The most eloquent of all war ballets.
*Times,* 30 April, 1973: A ballet about a fact so stupendous that the imagination balks at contemplating. Tudor's achievement is to present oppression, resistance and suppression on a human scale that prevents any side-stepping of the issues. . . . Tudor uses the traditional steps of classical ballet with an immediacy and meaning no other living choreographer can match. His actions do speak louder than words.
*Dancing Times,* June, 1973, by James Monahan: A triumph of expressive stylisation . . . blended with realism . . . the sum of it being horror distilled and understated into thoroughly effective theatre. No one but Tudor could have made ferocious arabesques and pirouettes say so much or could have mixed academic artificialities with utterly natural movements to produce a convincing unity.
Unidentified publication, by Noel Goodwin: One of the most harrowing dance-dramas of this or any other year . . . shows the firm style of a master within two minutes of the first dance sequence in character, mood and personality. His ballet reaches out . . . to a reconciliation with grief through a remembrance of what cannot be forgotten, making its appeal to heart and mind alike.

*Shadowplay*

Music: Charles Koechlin, *Les Bandar-Log* and *La Course de Prin-
temps*.
Scenery and Costumes: Michael Annals
Premiere: 25 January, 1967, Royal Opera House, London
Cast: Anthony Dowell, Merle Park, Derek Rencher and Kenneth Ma-
son, Lambert Cox, Keith Martin, Geoffrey Cauley, Peter O'Brien,
Donald Kirkpatrick, Ann Howard, Marilyn Trounson, Frank Freeman,
Ann Jenner, Jennifer Penney, Deirdre O'Conaire, Christine Beckley,
Roslind Eyre, Diana Vere, David Drew, Paul Brown.


Critical Response:
   *Times,* 26 January, 1967, by John Percival: It is a richly sugges-
tive piece, provoking ideas about the human condition . . . it is full of
fine dancing.
   *Sunday Times,* 29 January, 1967, by Richard Buckle: [Tudor]
wrestled with his angel and made a work prickly with poetry.
   *Observer,* 29 January, 1967, by Alexander Bland: In this rich,
original and ambiguous work—like all good things it leaves a nagging
doubt that several layers of interpretation remain hidden . . . a work of
dense atmospheric texture which contains not only some marvelous
moments . . . but also a great variety of carefully disorganised.
   *Times Educational Supplement,* 10 February, 1967, by Peter Brinson: *Shadowplay* continues . . . that penetration into character, the
probing and touching of nerve ends of emotion beneath the surface,
which Tudor pioneered in his first psychological ballets before the war
and which remains still a personal trait in his approach to other people.


*Knight Errant*

Music: Richard Strauss, from *Le Bourgeois gentilhomme* and the over-
ture to *Ariadne auf Naxos*
Scenery and Costumes: Stefanos Lazaridis
Premiere: 25 November, 1968, Opera House, Manchester, England
Cast: Hendrik Davel (later David Wall), Caroline Southam (Jane Lan-
don), Alfreda Thorogood, Margaret Barbieri, Elizabeth Anderton and
Spencer Parker, Michael Ingleton, Peter Fairweather, Victor
Kravchenko, Yvonne Saunders, Vicki Karras, Susan Lawe, Kathleen
Denley, Brigid Skemp, Adrian Grater, David Gordon, Kerrison Cooke,
Terence Hyde, Christopher Carr, Michael Bears, Alan Hooper, Nicholas
Johnson, Brian Bertscher

Critical Response:

*Observer,* 25 May, 1969: Intensely a Tudor work—subtle and calculated, laced with a detached and dandified mockery of human endeavours. It emerged as a rare small treasure . . . a cabinet of curious and elegant delights.

*Times,* 2 February, 1969, by John Percival: Entertaining at first sight, *Knight Errant* grows more impressive on better acquaintance. . . [a] strange, amusing and finally moving conception . . .

*Sunday Times,* 2 February, 1969, by Richard Buckle: Subtlety is the keynote of the ballet: the scandalous situations, the erotic poses are delicately sketched and lovers learn, yearn, perform, are jealous and suffer with a smile. . . . It was a wonderful performance of an extraordinary work.

"Two Faces of Tudor," *Dancing Times,* January, 1969, by Craig Dodd: *Knight Errant* manages to be completely unintelligible for most of the time. . . . Not, of course, that one expects deep psychological motivation in a ballet of this type, but without any at all there is a need for brilliantly controlled construction. And this is precisely what is lacking . . . we are left with what looks like a sketch for a Massine ballet. We are even denied sustained dance sequences of any consequence which emphasised too clearly that Tudor's strength has never been to produce pure dance sequences as, say, Ashton or Balanchine.

### The Divine Horseman

Music: Werner Egk, *Variations on a Caribbean Theme*
Scenery and Costumes: Hugh Laing
Premiere: 8 August, 1969, Her Majesty's Theatre, Sydney, Australia
Cast: Rex McNeill, Gaileen Stock, Karl Welander, Colin Peasley and Alida Chase, Julie da Costa, Jo-Anne Endicott, Ann Fraser, Heather Macrae, Suzanne Neumann, Carolyn Rappel, Leigh Rowles, Lucyna Sevitsky, Janet Vernon, Ronald Bekker, Frances Croese, Gary Heil, Graeme Hudson, Graeme Murphy, Paul Saliba

Critical Response (in Australian periodicals):

"Ballet," by Maria Prerauer: A hectic Caribbean spiritualist meeting . . . is the basis of Antony Tudor's colourful *Divine Horseman,* a world Premiere . . . it became curiously tame for such a thrillingly spooky subject.

Unidentified Publication: Tudor's work is just the type that commends itself as a subject of a ballet, and I am sure the choreography amply illustrates the notion. I feel, however, the company has not yet adapted itself to the work. Despite worthy efforts of Peasley and the three principals, the dancing generally was notably dispirited.

"On Stage," *Mirror,* by Frank Harris: Judged as pure dance, it was magnificently conceived ballet, with a robust line that seemed to stem from a folk dance mood.

*West Australian,* 18 September, 1969, by Peter Hellstrom: The ballet has pungency and power. Control of bodily motions in the wild gyrations and incisiveness in the many quick and difficult leg and foot postures combined with channeled verve brought out the primitive element to its maximum without over simplification.

Unidentified Publication: *The Divine Horseman* held me spellbound . . . The concept and realisation of the work succeeds . . . This was a real "world Premiere," with all components of the company combining to a considerable achievement.

"New Ballet Is a Hit on All Points" by Howard Palmer: *The Divine Horseman* was a waste of time . . . The Caribbean bit about people being possessed in ecstasy is best left to the West Indians and others whose blood pounds naturally that way.

## A New Ballet (Chapter 8)

### *The Leaves Are Fading*

Music: Antonin Dvořák, *String Quintet* opus 77, third movement; *Cypresses, II–VIII* and *XI; Terzetto,* opus 74, Scherzo; and *String Quartet* opus 80, third movement
Scenery: Ming Cho Lee
Costumes: Patricia Zipprodt
Premiere: 17 July, 1975, New York State Theater, New York
Cast: Kim Highton, Marianna Tcherkassky, Amy Blaisdell, Nanette Glushak, Linda Kuchera, Kristine Elliot, Hilda Morales, Elizabeth Ashton, Christine O'Neal, Michael Owen, Raymond Serrano, Charles Ward, Richard Schafer, Clark Tippet, Gelsey Kirkland, Jonas Kage

Critical Response:
*Eddy,* 7 Winter 1975–1976 by Toby Tobias: Eagerly awaited was Tudor's exquisitely elegiac *The Leaves Are Fading.* At first view it appears storyless, but we all know that no Tudor ballet is ever plotless. In the autumn of her life, and into a lovely Ming Cho Lee autumnal setting, walks Kim Highton dreaming of her own Springtime and savoring the recollections of couples wrapped in warm, roseate dreams of young love. Lyric, classic, uncluttered by irrelevance, the ballet looses

a sunny, languid interplay of movement. . . . This is . . . a mellower, more muted Tudor possibly retrieving a few hours of his own vanished youth.

*Village Voice,* 11 August, 1975, by Deborah Jowitt: The heart of the whole work is the extraordinarily beautiful duet for Gelsey Kirkland and Jonas Kage. . . . When it's over you feel as if you've observed the process of love as much as you've watched wonderful dancing. . . . You watch, holding your breath at the dancers' bravery and graciousness. The movement, like love, affords them no preparation.

*New Yorker,* by Arlene Croce as reprinted in *Going to the Dance,* (London: Knopf, 1982): It's just that both in composition and in performance the piece is uneven. Its sensibility is wonderfully fresh and striking from the start with an opening group dance that doesn't quite pattern. This is a Tudoresque statement . . . but the piece doesn't rise to a major statement until the entrance of Gelsey Kirkland.

*New York Times,* 27 July, 1975, by Clive Barnes: The piece is very beautiful. . . . Mr. Tudor has always clung to simplicity as if it were a hair-shirt. It is here his saving grace. There is lovely choreography here, simple and nakedly unaffected.

*Entertainment,* by Alan Kriegsman: *Leaves* is a hauntingly lovely ballet, brimming with the kind of delicately shaded poetic suggestion for which Tudor is rightly celebrated.

*Observer,* by Alexander Bland (exact date unknown, but written about the premiere): Characteristically it was totally uncharacteristic—neither enigmatic nor dramatic but gently charming and lyrical in a wistful English way. To a tuneful Dvorak score young people meet and flirt and part, visions in the memory of an older woman. Deft and fluent, it opens up a fascinating and promising new Tudor vein.

*New York Times,* 9 June, 1977, by Anna Kisselgoff: Gesture with emotional connotations is always incorporated into his choreography and there is always an unmistakable mood to a Tudor ballet. . . . *The Leaves Are Fading* is a lovely, complex ballet that makes its points subtly and patiently. Mr. Tudor constructs his mood through shifts in patterns and through the structure of the ballet itself.

*New York Times* (unattributed, undated, summer 1987): This was the first time since Antony Tudor's death on April 19 that a work by the company's choreographer emeritus and onetime associate director had been performed by the Ballet Theatre. On this occasion, Mr. Tudor's 1975 ballet *The Leaves Are Fading* seemed to communicate an extra poignancy at the Metropolitan Opera House. Perhaps the dancers were paying tribute to the great English-born choreographer who had rehearsed them up to the end. But perhaps one should also recognize that this extra dimension of feeling is inherent in all Tudor ballets—it is their signature.

## *The Tiller in the Fields*

Music: Antonin Dvorák, excerpted from *Symphonies nos. 2* and *6, In Nature's Realm*
Scenery: Ming Cho Lee
Costumes: Dunya Ramicova
Premiere: 13 December, 1978, Kennedy Center, Washington, D. C.
Cast: Patrick Bissell, Gelsey Kirkland and Nancy Collier, Cynthia Gast, Camille Izard, Lucette Katerndahl, Christie Keramidas, Lisa Lockwood, Lisa Rinehart, Kristine Soleri, Brian Adams, John Gardner, Robert La Fosse, Danilo Radojevic

Critical Response:
    *Dance Magazine,* September, 1979, by Richard Philp: Tudor's newest work *Tiller in the Fields* . . . in its mood and comfortable pacing might be viewed as an extension of *Leaves.* . . .Together they are among his richest works as far as the abundance of dance is concerned. The ballet has a punchline which seemed out of step with the idyll which comes before: Kirkland enters wearing Bissell's jacket and dances a solo with a thoughtful autumnal feeling to it, then reveals to Bissell that she is pregnant. Things snap unhinged. He overreacts, his horror carrying across the lights to the last row of the top balcony; she stands there, swollen like a watermelon. Then: he mellows, she melts, and they drift off happily.
    *Dance News,* October, 1975, by George Jackson: Enter Gelsey Kirkland in a horrendous gypsy *outfit*. She's a bundle of nerves aimed at big, boyish Patrick Bissell whom she seduces. . . . Is *Tiller* Tudor's wry reply to the "baby" or "Ballerinadom" dilemma posed in that soap opera, *The Turning Point?*

# Appendix B

# Glossary of Ballet Terms

*adagio*
> In musical terminology, "slow"; used in ballet to denote a male and female dancer working together in a supported sequence of slow movements and lifts.

*arabesque*
> Standing on one foot with the other leg lifted behind.

*attitude*
> Standing on one foot with the other leg bent and lifted either behind or in front.

*battement à la seconde*
> Beating (extending) one leg to the side.

*bourrée*
> See *pas de bourrée.*

*chassé*
> "Chased"; a sliding step in which one foot chases (replaces) the other.

*divertissement*
> A diversion; a short dance within a longer ballet.

*double cabriole*
> A hop, usually performed by men, in which the performer, while in the air, beats one leg on the other two times.

*enchaînement*
> A "chain" of steps linked together to form a phrase.

*entrechat six*
> A jump in which the legs, extended downwards, change their front/back relationship three times. The number six comes from the fact that the legs open a bit (1), close with the foot that was in back now in front (2), repeat (3, 4), repeat (5, 6).

*glissade*
> A traveling, linking step in which one leg slides open front, side, or back; the weight is then transferred to the open leg followed by a quick closing of the opposite leg.

*grand battement*
> A raising of one leg usually as high as possible with minimal displacement of the rest of the body.

*grand jeté*
> A large leap traveling forward with the legs split forward and backward.

*jeté à côté*
> A small leap traveling to the side.

*jeté renversé*
> A leap followed by a turn. During the turn the upper body curves to the side, then remains in that spatial direction throughout the turn causing it to arch backward, then curve to the opposite side.

**knee work**
> Movements performed while on the knees; a term used in modern dance.

*largo*
> A musical, not a ballet, term meaning a slow, expansive tempo.

*pas de bourrée*
> A series of small traveling steps.

*pas de chat*
> Step of the cat; a small leap in which the legs pick up under the body, one after the other.

*pas de deux*
> A couple dance.

*pas de trois*
> A dance for three people.

*pas marché*
> A series of stylized walking steps.

*passé*
> A movement in which one leg is lifted in a bent position until the foot touches the knee of the standing leg.

*piqué*
> A traveling step or slight spring from one foot onto the full or demi pointe of the other.

*pirouette*
> A turn on one foot.

*pirouettes à la seconde*
> Multiple turns on one foot with the other leg lifted to the side.

*plié*
> Bending the knees.

*port de bras*
> Literally "carriage of the arms"; a series of harmonious arm gestures moving from one position to another.

*posé à la seconde*
> The term *posé* is synonomous with *piqué*; *posé à la seconde* travels to the side.

*relevé*
> Rising to half toe or full *pointe*.

*renversé*
> See *jeté renversé*; a simple *renversé* is not preceded by a leap.

*rond de jambes en dehors*
> A circling of one leg from front through side to back.

**second position**
> Standing on both feet with legs apart in a side-to-side relationship.

*sissonne*
> A spring taking off from two feet, landing on one.

**suspension**
> A term used in modern dance, similar to a ballet *tombé*; the body seems suspended in a tenuous balance for a moment before falling.

*temps lié*
> Literally "connected time"; a movement in which one foot brushes open, the weight is transferred to it smoothly or sprung, and the second leg slides to a closed position. This is all done with prescribed appropriate arm movements.

*tendu*
> Literally "stretched"; one leg is extended free of weight in a stretched fashion.

*tombé*
> A falling movement.

# Appendix C

# Chronology

## 1908–1913

**Tudor**: April 1908—Tudor is born

**World**: Social legislation begins in England: Pension plan in 1908, progressive taxation in 1909, unemployment compensation and health insurance in 1911; First Model T Ford produced in United States; Perry reaches the North Pole in 1909, Amunsen, the South Pole in 1911; *Titanic* sinks in 1912

**Dance**: In 1907 Mikhail Fokine choreographs *Les Sylphides* (Frédéric Chopin); First Parisian season of the Diaghilev Ballet (1909); Vaslav Nijinsky choreographs *L'Après-midi d'un faune* (Claude Debussy) in 1912 and *Le Sacre du printemps* (Igor Stravinsky) in 1913; Rudolf Laban teaches at Monte Veritá

**Other Culture**: George Bernard Shaw, H. G. Wells, Rudyard Kipling writing; Amateur theater groups popular; Gilbert and Sullivan; Music Hall; and pantomimes for entertainment; Anton Webern writes *Six Pieces for Orchestra* in 1910; Igor Stravinsky writes *Petroushka* in 1911; Georges Braque exhibits first Cubist paintings; Ashcan School exhibits in New York; in 1910 Amedeo Modigliani exhibits at the Salon des Indépendants; in 1911 Kandinsky and Franz Marc found "Der Blaue Reiter"; Armory Show in New York, 1913

## 1914–1922

**Tudor**: Sees Lois Fuller, the Lorraine Sisters; Evacuated to Chiswick

**World**: World War I begins in 1914; Sinking of *Lusitania* in 1915; Woodrow Wilson reelected and Rasputin assassinated in 1916; Tsar Nicholas II abdicates and Bolsheviks overthrow Russian government, T.E. Lawrence captures Aquaba in 1917; World War I ends with Treaty of Versailles in 1919; Fascist Party founded by Mussolini in 1919; Woman's suffrage amendment passes in 1920

**Dance**: Denishawn Company founded in 1915; Léonide Massine choreographs *Three-Cornered Hat* with music by Manuel de Falla and décor by Pablo Picasso in 1919; Mary Wigman opens her school in Dresden in 1920; Bronislava Nijinska choreographs *Les Noces* (Stravinsky) in 1923; Josephine Baker appears in first black Broadway show, *Shuffle Along* with music by Eubie Blake in 1921

**Other Culture**: Poets are Ezra Pound, Rupert Brooke, Robert Graves; Bloomsbury Group writing as is Ernest Hemingway; Painters: Percy Wyndham Lewis, Paul Nash, C. R. W. Nevinson, William Roberts; James Joyce's *Ulysses* published in France; 1913–1928 Marcel Proust writes *Remembrance of Things Past*. 1916 Dada group is formed; George Grosz, Piet Mondrian, Georges Rouault, and Giorgio de Chirico all produce major works; 1919 Bauhaus is founded by Walter Gropius; Duchamp exhibits the Mona Lisa with beard; *The Cabinet of Dr. Caligary* is produced; Pop tunes: "Keep the Home Fires Burning," "If You Were the Only Girl in the World"; In 1920 Arnold Schoenberg becomes preoccupied with serialism

# 1923–1928

**Tudor**: Leaves school and begins working at Smithfield Market, joins amateur theater groups and begins studying dance with Suzy Boyle; Sees Diaghilev Ballet for first time in 1926 or 1927; in 1928   sees Pavlova and decides to study dance seriously

**World**: Hitler, in prison, writes *Mein Kampf* in 1924; Lindbergh flies across the Atlantic in 1927; Penicillin discovered

**Dance**: Diaghilev Ballet performs in London throughout 1920s; Colonel de Basil in charge of Russian Opera in London beginning in 1925; Mary Wigman developing *Ausdruckstanz* in Germany in late 1920s, makes her London debut in 1928; Martha Graham gives first New York concert (1926); In 1928 students of Marie Rambert give first public recital; de Valois's students also perform; Appearing in London: Ginnar Mawer's Greek revival troupe, Anton Dolin in solo program, mime Angna Enters; First Humphrey-Weidman concert in New York; Balanchine choreographs *Apollon Musagète* (*Apollo*) (Igor Stravinsky); Humphrey choreographs *Water Study* (in silence); Helen Tamiris choreographs *Negro Spirituals*; Bill "Bojangles" Robinson stars in *Blackbirds of 1928;* Enrico Cecchetti dies; First publication of Laban's dance notation (1928)

**Other Culture**: In 1921 Edgard Varèse composes *Amériquse* and Arnold Schoenberg writes *Pierrot Lunaire*; Bertold Brecht and Kurt Weill collaborate on *Threepenny Opera;* Robert Frost's first book of poetry published; George Gershwin composes *Rhapsody in Blue*; Stuart Davis paints *Lucky Strike* anticipating Pop Art; André Breton, Juan Miró, René Magritte, André Masson all produce major works as does Max Ernst; Claude Monet completes *Water Lilies*; Babe Ruth sets home run record; Charles Lindberg crosses the Atlantic in a solo flight

## 1929–1930

**Tudor**: Begins studying with Marie Rambert; Passes Cecchetti and Imperial Society of Teachers of Dancing exams; Professional debut with English Opera Company; changes name from Cook to Tudor; Dances in works by Ashton, Fokine; Leaves Smithfield Market to become secretary of Ballet Club

**World**: Stock exchange crashes in United States; England in a period of economic depression and high unemployment; Beginning of the rise of Nazism

**Dance**: Ashley Dukes acquires Notting Hill studio; Ballet Club is founded; Ashton choreographs *Capriol Suite* (Warlock); Andrée Howard and Susan Salaman choreograph *Our Lady's Juggler* (Respighi); Dorothy Alexander forms concert group that becomes Atlanta Ballet; José Limón joins Humphrey/Weidman group; Mary Wigman tours United States; Léonide Massine choreographs *Le Sacre du printemps* starring Martha Graham, for the Roxy Theatre; Diaghilev dies

**Other Culture**: Working artists: Alexander Calder, Henry Moore, Barbara Hepworth, Ben Nicholson; Salvador Dali exhibits in Paris for first time; Popular songs of the 1930s: "The Very Thought of You,"

"Thanks for the Memories"; The era of big bands: Tommy and Jimmie Dorsey, Guy Lombardo; Movie: *All Quiet on the Western Front*

# 1931

**Tudor**: Choreographs first ballet, *Cross-Garter'd* (Girolamo Frescobaldi) which premieres on 12 November; Meets Laing and they become lovers; Works with Maude Lloyd

**World**: Japan invades Manchuria

**Dance**: First performance of Ballet Club, 16 February; Ninette de Valois founds Vic-Wells Ballet; Ashton choreographs *Façade* (text by Edith Sitwell, music by Walton); Graham company performs *Primitive Mysteries* (Louis Horst); Humphrey choreographs *The Shakers* (Traditional); Final Denishawn concert; Hanya Holm founds school in New York based on Wigman's teaching; Pavlova dies

**Other Culture**: Henry Cowell, introduces use of "tone clusters"; Empire State Building is erected; Era of Swing

# 1932

**Tudor**: Choreographs *Mr. Rolls Quadrille* (Traditional), *Constanza's Lament* (Domenico Scarlatti); *Lysistrata* (Sergei Prokofiev), first really successful ballet, premieres 20 March; Choreographs first film, *In a Monastery Garden*; *Adam and Eve* (Constant Lambert) premieres 4 December; Dances with Vic-Wells Company

**Dance**: Camargo Society is formed for which Ballet Rambert and de Valois's Vic-Wells Company are commissioned to perform; "Ballet of the Nuns" from the opera *Robert le diable* (Giacomo Meyerbeer) given along with works by Nicolai Legat, Frederick Ashton, and Ninette de Valois; Olga Spessivtzeva dances *Giselle*; Kurt Jooss' *The Green Table* (Frederic Cohen) wins Paris Competition; Ballet Russe de Monte Carlo formed; Martha Graham gives dance concert at Bennington College, Vermont and in New York where police are called out to handle the traffic

**Other Culture**: Käthe Kollwitz memorial to her dead son unveiled in Belgium; Founding of Abstraction in painting; David Alfaro Sigueiros, advocating public art, begins frescos for Plaza Art Center in Los Angeles

## 1933

**Tudor**:  Does choreography for Gounod's *Faust* for Vic-Wells Company; Choreographs *Pavane pour une infante défunte* (Maurice Ravel) and *Atalanta of the East*  (Szanto and Seelig) (7 May), giving Laing his first Tudor role

**World**:  Franklin D. Roosevelt inaugurated as president of the United States; institutes New Deal; Hitler named chancellor of Germany

**Dance**:  First Fred Astaire and Ginger Rogers movie, *Flying Down to Rio*; The Rockettes are founded; Denishawn disbands and Shawn forms Men Dancers, the first all-male troupe in the United States; Adolph Bohm forms troupe in San Francisco, forerunner of the San Francisco Ballet; George Balanchine arrives in the United States; Ballets Russes de Monte Carlo tours United States; Ashton choreographs *Les Rendez-vous* (Auber); Fan dancer Sally Rand is arrested when she lifts her fan to reveal herself

**Other Culture**:  "Unit One" group of English painters founded; André Malraux writes *La Condition humaine*

## 1934

**Tudor**:  Choreographs *Paramour* (William Boyce), *The Legend of Dick Whittington* (Martin Shaw), and second major ballet, *The Planets* (Gustav Holst) (28 October)

**Dance**:  Ashton collaborates with Gertrude Stein and Virgil Thomson on opera *Four Saints in Three Acts*; Andrée Howard choreographs *The Mermaid* (Ravel); Bennington School of Dance founded; Catherine Littlefield Ballet begins in Philadelphia; Ballet Jooss flees Germany and is welcomed at Dartington Hall in England; the School of American Ballet opens

**Other Culture**:  James Joyce's *Ulysses* on trial for obscenity

# 1935

**Tudor**: Choreographs *Descent of Hebe* (Ernest Bloch) (7? February); Performs in operas for the open air theater in Regent's Park and choreographs for Covent Garden, Beecham conducting; visits Finland and meets with Sibelius

**World**: Social Security Act passes in the United States; Italy annexes Ethiopia

**Dance**: Balanchine choreographs *Serenade* (Peter Ilyich Tchaikovsky); Lincoln Kirstein's American Ballet debuts; Ashton choreographs *Le Baiser de la fée* (Stravinsky); Shirley Temple and Bojangles Robinson star in *The Little Colonel*

# 1936

**Tudor**: Choreographs *Jardin aux lilas* (Ernest Chausson) (26 January) and much musical theater

**World**: Spanish Civil War begins

**Dance**: Ballet Caravan debuts at Bennington College; Balanchine choreographs *On Your Toes*; Both Colonel de Basil's Ballet Russe de Monte Carlo starring Massine and René Blum's Ballets Russes de Monte Carlo with Fokine as ballet master play London; Humphrey choreographs *With My Red Fires* (Wallingford Riegger); Martha Graham choreographs *Chronicle* (Wallingford Riegger); Charles Weidman choreographs *Lynchtown* (Lehman Engel); Fred Astaire and Ginger Rogers star in *Top Hat* with choreography by Astaire and Hermes Pan

**Other Culture**: Federico García Lorca is shot in Spanish Civil War

# 1937

**Tudor**: More music theater and opera; Begins choreographing for television, highlight is *Fugue for Four Cameras* (Johann Sebastian Bach) (2 March); *Dark Elegies* (Gustav Mahler) premieres 19 February; Leaves Rambert; Tudor and de Mille form Dance Theatre; *Gallant Assembly* (Giuseppe Tartini) premieres 14 June

**World**: Japan invades China

**Dance**: Massine's spectacle ballets are the rage in London; Ashton choreographs *Les Patineurs* (Meyerbeer) and *Wedding Bouquet* (Lord Berners); Andrée Howard choreographs *Death and the Maiden* (Schubert); Hanya Holm choreographs *Trend* (Wallingford Riegger); Littlefield Ballet is first American company to tour Europe; *Dance Magazine* begins publishing; Isadora Duncan dies

**Other Culture**: Orson Welles and John Houseman found Mercury Theatre; Picasso paints *Guernica,* Nazis condemn painting of Oscar Kokoshka, Kandinsky, and others in exhibition of  Degenerate Art; Guggenheim Foundation begins a museum of non-objective art; Margaret Mitchell's *Gone with the Wind* receives Pulitzer Prize

# 1938

**Tudor**: More opera, film, theater, and television choreography; *Judgment of Paris* (Kurt Weill) premieres, *Soirée musicale* (Gioacchino Rossini/Benjamin Britten) for Cecchetti Society (26 November); Dance Theatre ends; Laing and Tudor move to British Grove; Tudor teaches and lectures at Morley College and Toynbee Hall; The London Ballet is born; Choreographs *Gala Performance* (Sergei Prokofiev) (5 December)

**World**: Munich pact permits Hitler to occupy Sudetenland

**Dance**: Performances by Vic-Wells Company, Massine's Ballet Russe de Monte Carlo and Colonel de Basil's Educational Ballet appear in London; Ballet Russe de Monte Carlo begins annual tours of the United States lasting until 1961; Walter Gore choreographs first ballets for Rambert *Valse Finale* (Ravel) and *Paris Soir* (Poulenc); Eugene Loring choreographs *Billy the Kid* (Aaron Copland); Lew Christensen choreographs *Filling Station* (Virgil Thomson); Willam Christensen joins San Francisco Opera Ballet as ballet master; Ruth Page choreographs *Frankie and Johnny* (Jerome Moross) with Bentley Stone for Page-Stone Ballet

**Other Culture**: Sergei Eisenstein produces *Aleksandr Nevsky*

# 1939

**Tudor**: Choreographs for Royal Opera using dancers from London Ballet; continues work in television and theater; Travels to the United States on 12 October to work with Ballet Theatre

**World**: Germany invades Poland; England and France declare war on Germany on 3 September; Russia invades Finland

**Dance**: London Ballet continues performing at Toynbee Hall through 26 April under direction of Maude Lloyd and Peggy van Praagh; Andrée Howard choreographs *Lady into Fox* (Arthur Honegger) for Rambert and *La Fête étrange* (Gabriel Fauré) for London Ballet; In U.S. vaudeville is waning; Mordkin Ballet is transformed into Ballet Theatre; Graham choreographs *Every Soul Is a Circus* (Paul Nordoff); Ballet Russe de Monte Carlo dances at the Metropolitan Opera House in New York ; American Guild of Musical Artists (AGMA) unionizes professional dance; Littlefield Ballet performs; both Colonel de Basil's Ballet Russe de Monte Carlo starring Massine and René Blum's Monte Carlo Ballets Russes with Fokine as ballet master perform in London

**Other Culture**: William Butler Yeats dies; W. H. Auden emigrates to the United States; John Steinbeck's *The Grapes of Wrath* wins Pulitzer Prize; José Clemente Orazco finishes frescos in Guadalajara; British theaters close for two weeks, then reopen with *For Me and My Gal;* Hit tune us "Lili Marlene"

# 1940

**Tudor**: Stages *Jardin aux lilas* for Ballet Theatre (BT) opening night; *Judgment of Paris* and *Dark Elegies* later in season; Dances in Loring's *Great American Goof* (Henry Brant) and other BT productions; Choreographs *Goya Pastoral* (Enrique Granados) (1 August)

**World**: Air attacks on London begin; the United States institutes its first peacetime conscription; Japan joins the Axis; Roosevelt elected to third term; Churchill becomes prime minister

**Dance**: Ballet Theatre premieres; Summer: Ballet Theatre tours Mexico; Humphrey choreographs *Song of the West* (Lionel Nowak, Roy Harris); Graham choreographs *El Penitente* (Louis Horst) and *Letter to*

*the World* (Hunter Johnson); Katherine Dunham plays at the Windsor Theatre and Carmen Miranda at the Versailles Club; Erick Hawkins gives solo debut at Bennington College

**Other Culture**: Carl Sandburg receives his second Pulitzer Prize; Ernest Hemingway writes *For Whom the Bell Tolls*; Jitterbug Championship held; Big bands include: in the United States Glenn Miller, Woody Herman, Duke Ellington, Count Basie; in England, Billy Ternent, George Melachrino, Ted Heath; All-girl bands appear; Vera Lamb is sweetheart of British forces; Charlie Chaplin plays in *The Great Dictator*; Irving Novello's *Lights Up,* with some choreography by Tudor, premieres; Eames chair is designed

# 1941

**Tudor**: Choreographs *Time Table* (Aaron Copland) (29 May) for Kirstein's Ballet Caravan; Begins working with Nora Kaye; Teaches at Jacob's Pillow and begins work on *Pillar of Fire*

**World**: Japanese bomb Pearl Harbor and the United States declares war

**Dance**: Balanchine choreographs *Concerto Barocco* (Johann Sebastian Bach); de Mille choreographs *Three Virgins and a Devil* (Ottorino Respighi); Jacob's Pillow Dance Festival begins; Colonel de Basil's Original Ballet Russe plays Los Angeles; Charles Weidman choreographs *Flickers* (Traditional arranged by Lionel Nowak)

**Other Culture**: Picasso forbidden by Nazis to exhibit his work; Francis Langford is sweetheart of American forces; Bob Hope entertains the troops; Pop tune: "The White Cliffs of Dover"; Movie: *The Maltese Falcon*; In England many performances are moved to 5:00 p.m. because of Blitz; Noel Coward's *Blithe Spirit* premieres; James Joyce dies; Virginia Woolf commits suicide

# 1942

**Tudor**: *Pillar of Fire* (Arnold Schoenberg) premieres 8 April

**Dance**:  Richard Pleasant leaves and Hurok takes over Ballet Theatre; Agnes de Mille choreographs *Rodeo* (Aaron Copland) for Ballet Russe de Monte Carlo

**Other Culture**:  Stefan Wolpe composes *The Man from Median*; Dmitri Shostakovich writes *Seventh Symphony*; Black singers Dinah Shore and Lena Horne appear; Peggy Lee sings with Benny Goodman band, Doris Day with Les Brown, and Ella Fitzgerald, Judy Garland, Jo Stafford, and Perry Como are popular; Bing Crosby sings "White Christmas"; The Zoot suit is in style;  Movies: *In Which We Serve* (Noel Coward)

# 1943

**Tudor**:  Tudor choreographs *The Tragedy of Romeo and Juliet* (Frederick Delius) (partial premiere 6 April, full ballet 10 April) and *Dim Lustre* (20 October)

**World**:  Italy surrenders

**Dance**:  Katherine Dunham troupe performs as part of African Dance Festival; Diana Adams joins Ballet Theatre; Agnes de Mille choreographs *Oklahoma*

**Other Culture**:  Carl Orff composes *Carmina Burana*; Pop tune: "Mairzy Doats," "As Time Goes By"; Alan Lomax collects folk songs; Calypso music comes to the United States from West Indies; Dame Myra Hess organizes lunchtime concerts at National Gallery, London; London Symphony and Halle Orchestras tour factories in England; Leonard Bernstein substitutes for an ailing Bruno Walter beginning his meteoric career; F. Scott Fitzgerald writes *The Last Tycoon*; Movies: *Bataan, Casablanca;* Writers: Betty Smith, *A Tree Grows in Brooklyn*, John P. Marquand, *The Robe*, Sholem Asch, *The Apostle*

# 1944–1945

**Tudor**:  *Undertow* (William Schuman) premieres 10 April, 1945; Choreographs for Broadway *Hollywood Pinafore* (Arthur Sullivan) and *Day Before Spring* (Frederick Loewe); Becomes increasingly disenchanted with Ballet Theatre

**World**: Allied forces invade Europe; Germany surrenders; Atomic bomb is dropped on Japan; Japan surrenders; Yalta talks among Allies lead to partition of Europe into "spheres of influence"; Nuremberg trials begin; HUAC (House UnAmerican Activities Committee) made into a standing committee; Roosevelt dies

**Dance**: Ballet Theatre tours coast to coast; Company on lay-off for part of 1945; Lucia Chase and Sol Hurok feud and part company; Oliver Smith joins Chase at BT; Jerome Robbins choreographs his first ballet, *Fancy Free* (Leonard Bernstein); Graham choreographs *Appalachian Spring* to a commissioned score by Aaron Copland; Merce Cunningham gives solo recital; Pearl Primus plays the Belasco Theatre

**Other Culture**: Benjamin Britten composes *Peter Grimes*; Evelyn Waugh writes *Brideshead Revisited;* Wallace Stevens writes *Esthetique du Mal;* Abstract Expressionism becomes the dominant trend in American art typified by Arshile Gorky, Willem de Kooning, Mark Rothko, Robert Motherwell, and Jackson Pollock; First television set reaches home market; Bobby soxers swoon over Frank Sinatra; Pop tunes: "Don't Get Around Much Anymore"; Frank Loesser's "Praise the Lord and Pass the Ammunition" and Noel Coward's "Don't Let's Be Beastly to the Germans"; Movie: *The Seventh Veil*; Maurice Evans stars in *Hamlet*; *Carousel* on Broadway; Tennessee Williams *The Glass Menagerie* plays; Billy Rose produces *The Seven Lively Arts*; Kathleen Windsor's *Forever Amber* is banned in Boston; John Hersey writes *A Bell for Adano*; Frank Lloyd Wright designs a Modern Gallery of Non-Objective Painting, which is not built until fourteen years later (the Guggenheim Museum)

# 1946–1947

**Tudor**: Teaches at Jacob's Pillow; Appointed artistic administrator of BT; Hugh and Diana marry

**World**: Labor unrest in the United States leads to passage of Taft-Harley Law; Churchill announces that an Iron Curtain has fallen; the United States adopts Truman Doctrine "to support free people resisting subjugation"; Marshall Plan of economic aid; House UnAmerican Activities Committee investigates the entertainment industry; CIA founded; India gains independence; Pakistan created

**Dance**: Ballet Theatre performs in London; Tours the United States and visits Cuba; Balanchine and Kirstein form Ballet Society, precursor of New York City Ballet; Balanchine choreographs *Four Temperaments* (Paul Hindemith) and *Theme and Variations* (Tchaikovsky); Ashton choreographs *Symphonic Variations* (César Franck); Bolshoi Ballet mounts *Cinderella* with newly composed score by Prokofiev; Covent Garden reopens with Sadler's Wells Ballet in residence, ballets performed during season include Robert Helpmann's *Miracle in the Gorbals* (Arthur Bliss), Massine's *Clock Symphony* (Franz Joseph Haydn); Graham choreographs *Cave of the Heart* (Samuel Barber), *Errand into the Maze* (Gian Carlo Menotti) and *Night Journey* (William Schuman); Humphrey choreographs *Day on Earth* (Aaron Copland); Lester Horton and Bella Lewitsky form Dance Theater in Los Angeles; S. Hurok's Original Ballet Russe and Sergei Denham's Ballet Russe de Monte Carlo tour the United States

**Other Culture**: Jackie Robinson breaks the color line in American sports; Robert Lowell wins Pulitzer Prize in poetry; Bertold Brecht writes *Galileo*, George Orwell writes *Animal Farm*, and Mickey Spillane writes *I the Jury*; Pierre Bonnard produces *Still Life*; Lawrence Olivier plays *King Lear*; Movies: *The Road to Rio* staring Bing Crosby, Bob Hope, and Dorothy Lamour, *Dumbo, Fantasia, Citizen Kane, The Best Years of Our Lives, Monsieur Verdoux, Open City, The Bicycle Thief*; Arthur Miller's *Death of a Salesman* is produced; Primitive painter Grandma Moses is discovered; United Nations Building, RCA Building, and Chrysler Tower are built

# 1948

**Tudor**: Choreographs *Shadow of the Wind* (Gustav Mahler) (14 April); Visits Barbados and Paris; Resigns as artistic administrator of BT

**World**: *Coup d'état* in Czechoslovakia; Postwar period of economic prosperity in the United States; Russia blockades Berlin; Southern Democrats leave the party over civil rights issues; Gandhi is assassinated; Israel is established as a nation

**Dance**: Rosella Hightower and Margot Fonteyn captivate Paris audiences; New York City Ballet (NYCB) founded; Balanchine choreographs *Orpheus* (Igor Stravinsky) and *Symphony in C* (Georges Bizet);

de Mille choreographs *Fall River Legend* (Morton Gould); Holm choreographs *Kiss Me Kate*; American Dance Festival begins at Connecticut College featuring Graham, Limón, and Dudley/Maslow/Bales trio; Ashton choreographs *Cinderella* (Prokofiev); NYCB finds a home at City Center Theater; *The Red Shoes* starring Moira Shearer. Léonide Massine and the Sadler's Wells Company are popular favorites

**Other Culture**: Olivier Messien composes Turangalîla *Symphonie*; Matisse begins designing Dominican Chapel in Vence; Spike Jones band records spoofs such as "All I Want for Christmas" and "Der Fuehrer's Face"; The New Look becomes fashionable; Movies: *The Snake Pit* with Olivia De Havilland and *Mrs Miniver* starring Greer Garson; Hollywood figures named as communist sympathizers include Fredric March, Humphrey Bogart, James Cagney, Franchot Tone, and playwrights Clifford Odets and Budd Schulberg, all of whom deny charges; Danny Kaye stars in *Lady in the Dark*; Irwin Shaw's *The Young Lions* is published; W. H. Auden wins Pulitzer Prize for his poem *Age of Anxiety;* New writers emerge after war: Karl Shapiro, Richard Wilbur, Howard Nemirov, John Ciardi, Dylan Thomas

# 1949

**Tudor**: At Jacob's Pillow teaches and choreographs *Dear Departed* (Maurice Ravel); First stay in Sweden where he stages *Giselle* (Adolphe Adam), *Petroushka* (Igor Stravinsky), *Les Sylphides*, (Frédéric Chopin), *Jardin aux lilas,* and *Gala Performance*

**World**: NATO founded; Mao seizes power in China; Russia explodes atomic device; British pound is devalued

**Dance**: Royal Ballet comes to New York with Margot Fonteyn dancing Aurora in *Sleeping Beauty*; Maria Tallchief dances Balanchine's *Firebird* (Stravinsky) with NYCB; Roland Petit's Ballets de Paris plays London; José Limón choreographs *Moor's Pavane* (Henry Purcell)

**Other Culture**: George Rochberg composes *Night Music;* Leonard Bernstein composes *Age of Anxiety; The Olympians* with music by Arthur Bliss, libretto by J. B. Priestley, directed by Peter Brook, premieres; Brook also directs Richard Strauss's *Salome* with set by Salvador Dali; T. S. Eliot's *The Cocktail Party* published and he wins the Nobel Prize; Norman Mailer writes *The Naked and the Dead* and John

O'Hara writes *A Rage to Live*; First "Nightmares" exhibit of Francis Bacon; Major exhibit of Jackson Pollock's work; Pop tunes: "Why Don't We Do This More Often," "As Time Goes By," "When the Lights Go On Again"; The Trapp Family Singers and Edith Piaf gain popularity; Movies: *Kind Hearts and Coronets, The Third Man; South Pacific;* Mary Chase's *Harvey* and William Saroyan's *The Skin of Our Teeth* on Broadway

# 1950

**Tudor**: Returns from Sweden in March; Choreographs *Nimbus* (Louis Gruenberg) (3 May); Accepts directorship of Metropolitan Opera Ballet (briefly) and School; Choreographs several operas during 1950s; Begins to work with Sallie Wilson; Teaches in Philadelphia

**World**: North Korea crosses 39th parallel and war begins; Alger Hiss convicted of perjury; MacArthur is relieved of his command; MacCarthy gains national recognition by alleging he has a list of 250 known communists in the State Department; Karl Fuchs spy scandal in England; India, granted independence in 1947, declares itself an independent republic within the British Commonwealth; Kefauver hearings on organized crime

**Dance**: Tenth anniversary celebration of BT; BT allies with Metropolitan Opera; Nijinsky dies; Jerome Robbins choreographs *Age of Anxiety* (Leonard Bernstein); London Festival Ballet founded; Martha Graham choreographs *Judith* (William Schuman); June Taylor Dancers join *The Jackie Gleason Show* on TV; Jack Cole and Gwenneth (*sic*) Verdon dance in *Alive and Kicking*; Leslie Caron joins Gene Kelly in *An American in Paris*

**Other Culture**: Beat Generation challenges conventionality of the majority; Jack Kerouac publishes *On the Road*; Poet Allen Ginsberg fights obscenity case; Jackson Pollock is throwing paint at canvases; Duck-tail haircuts are in style; Era of the Edsel, Cadillac tail-fins, hot rods, Sid Caesar, TV; Intellectuals of the period include Jacques Barzun, Lionel Trillin, and Arthur J. Schlesinger Jr., and T. S. Eliot; Others writing are Norman Mailer, Dwight MacDonald, Erich Fromm, Ezra Pound, Archibald MacLeish, John Dos Passos; Academy award for best picture goes to *All About Eve*; Pop records are "Goodnight Irene," and "Third Man Theme"; During the 1950s Progressive Jazz

(Stan Kenton, Miles Davis, Thelonius Monk, Ronnie Scott) and Be-Bop (Charlie Parker, Dizzy Gillespie) were born

## 1951

**Tudor**: Leaves Ballet Theatre and joins New York City Ballet; Choreographs *Lady of the Camellias* (Giuseppe Verdi) (28 February) and stages *Lilac Garden* for NYCB; Teaches and choreographes *Les Mains Gauches* (Jacques Ibert) (20 July) and *Ronde de Printemps* (Erik Satie) (1 August) at Jacob's Pillow; Joins Juilliard faculty

**World**: Truce talks with Korea begin; Spies Burgess and Maclean flee to Russia

**Dance**: New works: *La Valse* (Balanchine/Ravel), *Cakewalk* (Ruthanna Boris/Louis Gottschalk), *The Cage* (Robbins/Stravinsky) *Games* (Donald McKayle/Traditional); Michael Kidd wins Tony Award for choreography of *Guys and Dolls*

**Other Culture**: Willie Mays is Rookie of the Year; Academy Award to *An American in Paris*; Other films: *African Queen, Rashomon*; Best-selling books: *The Catcher in the Rye* (J. D. Salinger), *From Here to Eternity* (James Jones), *Lie Down in Darkness* (William Styron); Pop records: Patti Page singing "Tennessee Waltz," Les and Mary Ford singing "How High the Moon," Nat King Cole singing "Too Young;" Music: *Landscapes* (John Cage), *Marginal Intersection* (Morton Feldman), *Amahl and the Night Visitors* (Gian Carlo Menotti); Rock and Roll becomes vastly popular in the 1950s and 1960s

## 1952

**Tudor**: Choreographs *La Gloire* (Ludwig van Beethoven) (26 February); Rehearses *Jardin aux Lilas* with Ballet Rambert

**World**: Eisenhower elected President under slogan "I like Ike"; Nixon gives "Checkers" speech

**Dance**: NYCB tours Europe; Gene Kelly dances in *Singin' in the Rain*

**Other Culture**: Ralph Ellison writes *The Invisible Man;* Hudson, Kenyon, and Partisan Reviews are published; Books: John Kenneth

Galbraith *American Capitalism*, Bernard Malmud *The Natural*; Rocky
Marciano KOs Joe Walcott; Liberace makes TV debut; *I Love Lucy* and
*Dragnet* are popular TV shows; Walt Kelly's comic strip character
Pogo runs for president; Films: *The Greatest Show on Earth, High
Noon, Mr. Hulot's Holiday*; Music: *4'33"* (John Cage); Marianne
Moore wins Pulitzer Prize in poetry; Herman Wouk's *The Caine Mu-
tiny* wins Pulitzer Prize in Fiction

# 1953

**Tudor**: Choreographs and stages works for Juilliard students; Teaches
at Jacob's Pillow; Stages *Les Syphides* and *L'Apres Midi D'un Faune*
(Claude Debussy) in Philadelphia and creates *Offenbach in the Underworld* (Jacques Offenbach) (8 May); Mother dies in December

**World**: Rosenberg's executed for treason; Stalin dies; Elizabeth II is
crowned; Korean War Ends

**Dance**: New works: *Septet* (Merce Cunningham/Erik Satie), *Masks,
Props and Mobiles* (Alwin Nikolais/Jean Sibelius), *Afternoon of a
Faun* (Robbins/Debussy), *Lyric Suite* (Anna Sokolow/Alban Berg);
Jack Cole choreographs Broadway show *Kismet* (Alexander Borodin)

**Other Culture**: Charlie Chaplin refuses to return to America after
being harassed for his political beliefs; Kinsey Report published; Academy Award to *From Here to Eternity*; Music: *Triptych* (Alan
Hovhaness), *Kontra-Punkte* (Karlheinz Stockhausen);

# 1954–1955

**Tudor**: Visits Japan and stages *Lilac Garden, Café Bar du can-can
(Offenbach in the Underworld)*; Begins association with First Zen Institute

**World**: French forces ousted from Indo-China (Vietnam) at Dien Bien
Phu; Rosa Parks sits in the front section of a bus in Montgomery, Alabama; Martin Luther King Jr. becomes spokesman for black protestors;
In *Brown v. Board of Education* Supreme Court orders desegregation
of schools; Senate finally condemns McCarthy; SEATO formed; Alge-
rians revolt against the French; Salk discovers anti-polio vaccine

**Dance:** Martha Graham troupe performs in London; Robert Joffrey Theater Ballet formed; Royal Danish Ballet first appears in U. S. at Jacob's Pillow; NYCB stages Balanchine's *The Nutcracker*; National Ballet of Canada presents full-length *Swan Lake* at Brooklyn Academy; Limón choreographs *The Traitor* (Gunther Schuller); Graham choreographs *Seraphic Dialogue* (Norman Dello Joio); Sokolow choreographs *Rooms* (Kenyon Hopkins); Paul Taylor presents first professional choreography in a shared concert; Jerome Robbins choreographs *The King and I* for Hollywood; *Seven Brides for Seven Bothers* with choreography by Michael Kidd is last great Hollywood musical

**Other Culture:** 1954: Nabokov's *Lolita* published in France; Ernest Hemingway wins Nobel Prize for literature; Clifford Odets *The Flowering Peach* on Broadway; Academy Award for Best Film: *On the Waterfront*; Other films: *Rebel without a Cause, The Wild One, La Strada, Smiles of a Summer Night;* 1955: "Rock Around the Clock" popular record; Books: Anne Morrow Lindbergh *Gift From the Sea*, Sloan Wilson *The Man in the Grey Flannel Suit*; Films: *The Blackboard Jungle, Marty, The Rose Tattoo, The Man with the Golden Arm*; Peanuts comic strip published; Marian Anderson sings at the Metropolitan Opera; Music: *Concerto for Orchestra* (Witold Lutoslawski), *The Bewitched* (Harry Partch); Menotti wins Pulitzer Prize for *The Saint of Bleeker Street*, Wallace Stevens for *Collected Poems*

# 1956–1957

**Tudor:** Tudor dances with ABT to celebrate twenty-fifth anniversary of association; Again accepts directorship of Metropolitan Opera Ballet Company (until 1963)

**World:** Attack on Suez Canal by French, British, and Israeli forces; Hungarian rebellion; Israeli captures Sinai Peninsula; Largest public works in U.S. history: 38,400 miles of roads are funded; Black students turned away from school in Little Rock, Arkansas and Eisenhower calls out the National Guard; Lyndon B. Johnson leads fight to pass first Civil Rights Act in eighty-two years; Russians launch Sputnik; Anticolonial resentment builds in Third World countries; Republic of Ghana formed; Ban the Bomb activity begins

**Dance:** Bolshoi Ballet plays London; Jerome Robbins choreographs and directs *West Side Story* (Leonard Bernstein); Gene Kelly stars in *Invitation to the Dance*; New works: *There Is a Time* (Limón/Dello

Joio), *Suite for Five* (Cunningham/John Cage), *The Concert* (Rob-
bins/Chopin); *Agon* (Balanchine/Stravinsky); *Here and Now with the
Watchers* (Erick Hawkins); Sadler's Wells Ballet becomes the Royal
Ballet; Hanya Holm choreographs *My Fair Lady*

**Other Culture**:   Allen Ginsberg's *Howl* published and confiscated by
police; Elvis Presley records "Hound Dog," "Love Me Tender"; Films:
*Arond the World in 80 Days* (Academy Award), *Bus Stop, The Seventh
Seal, The Ten Commandment*; Books: Grace Metalious *Peyton Place*,
Linus Pauling *No More War*, Williams H. White Jr. *The Organization
Man*; Marilyn Monroe and Arthur Miller are wed;  Films: *Bridge over
the River Kwai, Three Faces of Eve, Twelve Angry Men*; Music: *New
England Triptych* (William Schuman), *Requiem for Strings* (Toru
Takemitsu); Robert Rauschenberg exhibits

# 1958

**Tudor**: Tours South America with ABT; Stages *Pillar of Fire* and
creates *La Leyenda de José*  (Richard Strauss) (19 August) for Teatro
Colon Resident Company in Argentina

**World**: United States unemployment rate is 7.7 perccent; SANE
founded; John Birch Society founded; NASA created

**Dance**: Doris Humphrey dies; New works: *Clytemnestra* (Graham/
Halim El-Dabh), *Summerspace* (Cunningham/Morton Feldman), *Missa
Brevis* (Limón/Zoltán Kodály)

**Other Culture**: Pop records: "Volare," "Rockin' Robin"; Books:
John Kenneth Galbraith *The Affluent Society*, Boris Pasternak *Doctor
Zhivago*, Vladimir Nabokov *Lolita* published in U.S.; Hula hoop fad
reaches peak; Films: *Gigi, Cat on a Hot Tin Roof, Black Orpheus, The
400 Blows*

# 1959

**Tudor**:  First all ballet evening at Metropolitan Opera which includes
new Tudor work *Hail and Farewell* (Richard Strauss) (22 March)

**World:** Growth of the suburbs, Levittowns and shopping malls;  Fidel
Castro captures Cuba; Alaska becomes forty-ninth State and Hawaii

fiftieth; Dalai Lama flees to India when Chinese crush Tibetan revolt; Charles De Gaulle inaugurated

**Dance**: Bolshoi Ballet comes to New York; Alicia Alonso's Ballet de Cuba wins subsidy from Castro government; Donald McKayle choreographs *Rainbow Round My Shoulder* (Traditional); NYCB presents *Episodes* (Anton Webern) part I by Martha Graham and part II by George Balanchine—Sallie Wilson dances in part I and Paul Taylor in part II; Ford Foundation establishes a national ballet scholarship program

**Other Culture**: Three-quarters of U.S. families own television sets; Popular programs are *I Love Lucy, Father Knows Best, Howdy Doody,* and *Mickey Mouse Club;* D.H. Lawrence's *Lady Chatterley's Lover* banned from the mails; Charles Van Doren admits quiz show was rigged; Pop tunes: Bobby Darin "Mack the Knife," Frankie Avalon "Venus," Ray Charles "What'd I Say?"; Films: *Ben Hur, Some Like It Hot, Room at the Top, Hiroshima, Mon Amour;* Books: Leon Uris *Exodus,* Vance Packard *The Status Seekers;* Saul Bellow *Henderson the Rain King,* Philip Roth *Portnoy's Complaint,* William Burroughs *Naked Lunch,* Norman Mailer *Advertisements for Myself;* Music: *Seven Studies on Themes of Paul Klee* (Gunther Schuller); Solomon R. Guggenheim museum opens

# 1960

**Tudor**: Choreographs *A Choreographer Comments* (Franz Schubert) for Juilliard students; *Alcestis* (Christoph Willibald Gluck) and *Tannhäuser* (Richard Wagner) for the Metropolitan Opera

**World**: Sit-in movement is born; U2 Spy plane shot down by Soviets; Oral contraceptive pill for women approved by FDA; seventeen African nations gain independence; SDS (Students for a Democratic Society) and SNCC (Student Non-violent Coordinating Committee) are founded; First voting rights bill enacted

**Dance:** ABT tours Russia; Michael Smuin choreographs for San Francisco Ballet; Robert Dunn teaches a composition class which begins the post-modern avant-garde dance movement; Anna Halprin choreographs *Parades and Change*s which includes nudity, New York police raid her concert; Alvin Ailey and Company premiere *Revelations* (Traditional); Balanchine choreographs *Liebeslieder Waltzer* (Johannes Brahms); Graham choreographs *Acrobats of God* (Carlos Surinach)

**Other Culture**: Films: *On the Beach, Psycho, Elmer Gantry; Camelot* on Broadway; Music: *Time Cycle* (Lucas Foss), *To the Victims of Hiroshima-Threnody* (Krzysztof Penderecki), Summer music school at Darmstadt, Germany, begins; Pop Art begins with Roy Lichtenstein, Andy Warhol, and Claes Oldenberg major proponents; New Realism exhibition in Paris; Half the population is under sixty

## 1961–1962

**Tudor**: Returns to Sweden and mounts *Pillar of Fire, The Tragedy of Romeo and Juliet,* and *Little Improvisations* (Robert Schumann); Becomes president of First Zen Institute of America and moves into Institute; Continues choreographing for Juilliard students; Teaches in Israel; Summers in Athens

**World:** John Fitzgerald Kennedy inaugurated as president of the United States; Bay of Pigs invasion fails; Cuban blockade; Peace Corps initiated; Yuri Gagarin first man in space

**Dance**: Judson Dance Theater founded; George Balanchine is one of the first official guests invited to the White House by the new Kennedy administration; Nureyev defects; Glen Tetley's *Pierrot Lunaire* (Arnold Schoenberg) premieres; Sokolow creates *Dreams* (Collage); Paul Taylor choreographs *Aureole* (George Frideric Handel)

**Other Culture**: Rachel Carson publishes *The Silent Spring* precipitating the Environmental Movement; Other books: Eugene Burdick *Fail Safe*, Joseph Heller *Catch 22*, Truman Capote *In Cold Blood*, Jessica Mitford *The American Way of Death*; Eselen founded as a center for innovative and experimental courses; Psychedelic Op Art introduced by Peter Max; Comic books regain popularity: *Spider Man, Captain America, Batman, Superman; Peanuts* cartoon by Charles Schulz gains wide popularity; Films: *Judgment at Nuremberg, Exodus. Lawrence of Arabia, West Side Story, To Kill a Mockingbird, Miracle Worker*; Ernest Hemingway commits suicide; Music: *Double Concerto* (Elliott Carter), *Aventures* (Gyorgy Ligeti); Le Roy Jones (Amiri Baraka) publishes first book of poetry

# 1963

**Tudor**:  Tudor choreographs *Fandango* (Antonio Soler) (26 March) for Metropolitan Opera dancers; Relinquishes post as director of Opera Ballet;  Becomes director of the Royal Swedish Ballet and choreographs *Echoing of Trumpets* (Bohuslav Martinu) (28 September); Rehearses *Jardin aux lilas* with Ballet Rambert

**World**:  U.S. Civil Rights Act passed; JFK assassinated; Medicare and Medicaid created; First Limited Atomic Test Ban negotiated; 200,000 people march in Washington to protest Vietnam War; Betty Friedan publishes *The Feminine Mystique*; Medgar Evers is shot; Martin Luther King gives "I have a dream" speech; Resurgence of student activism; SDS (Students for a Democratic Society) and SNCC (Student Nonviolent Coordinating Committee) become active; 300 "Freedom Riders" go to South to register black voters; Black church in Birmingham, Alabama, bombed, killing four children

**Dance**:  Alicia Markova assumes directorship of Metropolitan Opera Ballet; Harkness Ballet presents "A Panorama of Theatrical Dancing in America: 1900–63"; Ruth St. Denis returns to stage to perform  *Incense*; Ford Foundation gives $4.5 million to NYCB and School of American Ballet; New works: *Bugaku* (Balanchine/Toshiro Mayazumi), *Imago* (Nikolais/Nikolais), *Scuderama* (Taylor/Clarence Jackson)

**Other Culture**:  Films: *Dr. Strangelove, Lilies of the Field, Dr. No, Bye, Bye Birdie*; Mary McCarthy writes *The Group,* which breaks the code about portraying lesbianism;  Music: *Kaddish* (Leonard Bernstein)

# 1964

**Tudor**:  Revives *Dim Lustre* for New York City Ballet; Continues teaching at Juilliard

**World**:  The United States passes Gulf of Tonkin resolution empowering Lyndon B. Johnson to take all necessary measures in Vietnam; New Civil Rights Law outlaws segregation in all public places; Schwerner, Chaney, and Goodman murdered by Ku Klux Klan (KKK); War resistance movement is born in Berkeley

**Dance**:  Martha Graham troupe returns to London; Merce Cunningham Company visits London, tours Europe; National Association of Regional Ballet chartered; Cunningham choreographs *Winterbranch* (La Monte Young); Ashton choreographs *The Dream* (Felix Mendelssohn/ John Lanchbery)

**Other Culture:**  Robert Rauschenberg and Jasper Johns exhibit in London; Living Theater founded; Andy Warhol exhibits his Brillo Boxes; Music: *Philomel* (Milton Babbitt); *In C* (Terry Riley—first appearence of minimalism); Beatles take the United States by storm

# 1965

**Tudor**:  Returns to Japan and stages *Undertow, Dark Elegies, Pillar of Fire,* and *Jardin aux lilas*

**World**: President Lyndon B. Johnson "declares war" on the KKK; Malcolm X assassinated; Black Panthers founded; Yippie movement begins in order to discredit the government and all authority by means of mockery; First walk in space; Alabama Civil Rights March; Race riot in Watts

**Dance**:  In mid 1960s Ford Foundation grants, to five ballet companies chosen by Balanchine, causes uproar in the United States dance community; National Endowment for the Arts established and begins supporting dance; New York State Council on the Arts becomes permanent agency; New works: *Viva Vivaldi* (Gerald Arpino/Antonio Vivaldi), *Don Quixote* (Balanchine/Ludwig Minkus), *Les Noces* (Robbins/Stravinsky),

**Other Culture**:  Films: *Mary Poppins, The Sound of Music*; "Amos and Andy" taken off air as offensive to blacks; Music: *Punch and Judy* (Harrison Birtwistle); "Make love not war" becomes motto of the "hippies"; Mohammed Ali resists draft on religious grounds; *The Autobiography of Malcolm X* is published posthumously

# 1966

**Tudor**:  Ballet program at Metropolitan Opera includes Tudor's *Concerning Oracles* (Jacques Ibert) (27 March) and the United States premiere of *Echoing of Trumpets*; Leaves Metropolitan Opera Ballet School

**World**: Race riots spread throughout the United States; National Organization of Women founded; FBI infiltrates KKK; Carl B. Stokes is

first black to be elected to the Senate in eighty-five years; Indira Gandhi becomes prime minister of India; Cultural Revolution begins in China

**Dance**: Ballet Rambert becomes a modern dance company and a professional contemporary dance tradition begins in England; Robin Howard founds London School of Contemporary Dance; Merce Cunningham returns to London; Joffrey Ballet becomes resident company of City Center Theater and begins reviving ballet classics by Massine, Jooss, Fokine, and Ashton

**Other Culture**: Films: *The Russians Are Coming, The Russians Are Coming, Dr. Zhivago;* TV: "The Man From U.N.C.L.E."; "Sesame Street" premieres; *Saturday Evening Post, Life,* and *Look* magazines all fold because of competition from TV; Music: *Antony and Cleopatra* (Samuel Barber); Painters: Al Held, Larry Poons, Frank Stella, Kenneth Noland, Ellsworth Kelly; "Black is beautiful" becomes a motto

# 1967

**Tudor**: Choreographs *Shadowplay* (Charles Koechlin) (25 January) for England's Royal Ballet

**World**: Thurgood Marshall is appointed to Supreme Court; First be-in in the Haight-Ashbury section of San Francisco attracts 20,000 "flower children" to hear speeches by Timothy Leary (of LSD fame) and "Beat" poet Allen Ginsberg; In summer there are riots in 162 cities resulting in 83 killed and 250 million dollars damage; McNamara resigns over Vietnam War; Arab–Israeli Six-Day War

**Dance**: London Contemporary Dance Theatre founded; Robert Joffrey's *Astarte* (Chrome Syrcus) a psychedelic ballet, premieres; New York City Ballet visits Edinburgh; Eliot Feld creates first ballet, *Harbinger* (Prokofiev)

**Other Culture**: La Mama and Open Theater founded; Smothers Brothers on TV invite black-listed singers Joan Baez and Pete Seeger to appear; *Rolling Stone* magazine is founded; Films: *The Man for All Seasons, Bonnie and Clyde*; Musical *Hair* premieres; Books: Norman Mailer, *Why We Are in Vietnam* and *Armies of the Night*, William Shirer, *The Rise and Fall of the Third Reich*, Aleksandr Solzhenitsyn, *Cancer Ward*; Music: *Silver Apples of the Moon* (Morton Subotnick)

## 1968

**Tudor**: Stages three ballets in Israel: *Fandango, Little Improvisations,* and *Judgment of Paris*; Choreographs *Knight Errant* (Richard Strauss) for English National Ballet (25 November)

**World:** Anti-war sentiment grows in the United States; Tet Offensive successfully pushes back U.S. forces; Mai Lai massacre; Robert Kennedy and Martin Luther King Jr. assassinated; Mayor Daley orders brutal crack-down on demonstrators at Chicago Democratic Convention; United States in economic decline; stock market falls 36 percent and unemployment reaches 6.6 percent; Nixon reelected; Eugene McCarthy wins New Hampshire primary on peace platform; Student uprising in Paris

**Dance**: Congress cuts NEA arts funding from 20.5 million dollars to 11.2; Arthur Mitchell announces plans to form Dance Theatre of Harlem; Paul Taylor Company is barricaded in Odéon Theatre in Paris by student marchers; New works: *Rainforest* (Cunningham/David Tudor), *At Midnight* (Feld/Mahler), *Tent* (Nikolais/Nikolais), *Public Domain* (Taylor/John Herbert McDowell); *Enigma Variations* (Ashton/Elgar)

**Other Culture**: Beatles, Rolling Stones, and Bob Dylan are popular; *2001: A Space Odyssey* screens; *Boys in the Band* deals with homosexuality; Joe McGinnis writes *The Selling of a President*; Masters and Johnson publish *Human Sexual Response*; Music: *Sinfonia* (Luciano Berio), *Echos of Time and the River* (George Crumb wins Pulitzer Prize); Feminists protest Miss America beauty pageant; Kinetic Art begins

## 1969

**Tudor**: Stages *Pillar of Fire* and choreographs *The Divine Horseman* (Werner Egk) (8 August), for Australian Ballet; Visits family in New Zealand

**World**: Neil Armstrong walks on the moon; Student protest now concerns itself with challenging and reshaping university policies—two out of every three campuses are in revolt; Woodstock Festival; Edward

Kennedy involved in accident at Chappaquidick; Radical group Weathermen becomes active; Feminists burn their bras

**Dance**: Charles Reinhart presents Yvonne Rainer, Twyla Tharp, Don Redlich, Deborah Hay, and Meredith Monk on Broadway; Houston Ballet founded; Suzanne Farrell leaves New York City Ballet and joins the Béjart Company (Ballet du XXième Siècle); New works: *Dances at a Gathering* (Robbins/Chopin), *Intermezzo* (Feld/Brahms), *Private Domain* (Taylor/Yannis Xenakis)

**Other Culture**: Robert Wilson's *The Life and Times of Sigmund Freud* plays; Comic strip "Doonesbury" is syndicated; Films: *Funny Girl, Butch Cassidy and the Sundance Kid, Easy Rider, M\*A\*S\*H;* Jack Paar breaks TV taboo with frank sexual discussion on the "Tonight Show"; Diahann Carroll and Bill Cosby break color line on TV; Shows on TV: "Laugh-In," "The Untouchables," "Hogan's Heroes," "Star Trek," "The Twilight Zone"; *Oh! Calcutta!* premieres; Music: *Eight Songs for a Mad King* (Peter Maxwell Davies), *String Quartet no. 3* (Karel Husa, Pulitzer Prize)

# 1970–1971

**Tudor**: Honorary doctorate from St. Andrews College; Stages *The Tragedy of Romeo and Juliet* for American Ballet Theatre, *Jardin aux lilas* for Royal (English) Ballet, *Dark Elegies* for Norwegian National Ballet and *Jardin aux lilas* in Geneva, *Gala Performance* for Royal Danish Ballet; Choreographs three chamber ballets: *Continuo, Sunflowers,* and *Cereus*; Retires from Juilliard; Lectures at York University in Canada; Stages *Echoing of Trumpets* for London Festival Ballet

**World:** Public learns of U.S. bombing of Cambodia; Nixon visits China; SALT talks culminate in arms control agreement; Congress creates Environmental Protection Agency; Ohio National Guard fires on student demonstrators at Kent State College killing four; Daniel Ellsberg turns Pentagon Papers over to press; eighteen-year-olds given right to vote by twenty-sixth Amendment to the United States Constitution

**Dance**: Makarova defects; Kenneth MacMillan becomes director of Royal Ballet; Dance Theatre of Harlem debuts; Twyla Tharp choreographs *The Fugue*; Robbins choreographs *The Goldberg Variations* (J. S. Bach); Pilobolus Dance Theater founded in 1971; Public Broadcasting System (PBS) begins broadcasting dance

**Other Culture**: Movies: *American Graffiti; The Last Picture Show; The Way We Were;* Music: *Drumming* (Steve Reich); *Synchronism no. 6* (Mario Davidovsky, Pulitzer Prize); Aleksandr Solzhenitsyn wins Nobel Prize; Hyper-realist painters exhibit in New York; The counter-culture affects beards, beads, blue jeans

## 1972–1973

**Tudor**: Begins teaching at the Unversity of California, Irvine; Stages *Gala Performance* for Deutsche Oper am Rhein; Awarded Swedish Carina Ari Gold Medal; Visits Amsterdam; Operated on for hernia in 1973

**World**: Cease-fire in Vietnam; Resistance Movement winds down; OPEC nations join Saudi Arabia in oil embargo; Watergate; *Roe v. Wade* establishes women's constitutional right to abortion in the United States; Spiro Agnew resigns as vice president; Existence of Nixon's enemies list revealed; Alexander Butler accidentally reveals existence of white house tapes; Yom Kippur War; Pinochet displaces Allende in bloody Chilean coup

**Dance**: José Limón and John Cranko die; Joffrey Ballet premieres Twyla Tharp's *Deuce Coupe* (Beach Boys); Musicians' strike at City Center forces New York City Ballet to cancel opening of its twenty-fifth anniversary season; Pina Bausch heads company in Wuppertal; Robbins choreographs *Watermill* (Teiji Ito)

**Other Culture**: Music: *Windows* (Jacob Druckman, Pulitzer Prize 1972), *String Quartet no. 3* (Elliott Carter, Pulitzer Prize 1973); Pablo Neruda and Picasso die in 1973; *MS Magazine* founded

## 1974–1976

**Tudor**: Receives *Dance Magazine* Award; Stages *Shadowplay* for American Ballet Theatre; Becomes associate director of ABT; Turns down invitation to help Ballet Rambert celebrate fiftieth anniversary citing decreased energy; Choreographs *The Leaves Are Fading* (Antonin Dvorak) (17 July,1975)

**World**: United States troops leave Vietnam in disarray; Nixon resigns; Inflation and unemployment in the United States both reach 12 percent; Franco dies; Khmer Rouge seizes power in Cambodia; Viking

spacecraft lands on Mars; Mao Zedong dies; Israel gives up part of
Golan Heights to Syria

**Dance**: Thirty-fifth anniversary of American Ballet Theatre; Eliot Feld
Ballet debuts; Baryshnikov defects, joins ABT and forms partnership
with Gelsey Kirkland; Makarova and Baryshnikov dance *Giselle* as do
Veronica Tennant and Rudolf Nureyev; Fernando Bujones is first
American to win top prize at Varna International Competition; San
Francisco Ballet dancers take to the streets to save their company
helping raise $410,797; Cleveland Ballet debuts; Bruce Marks directs
Ballet West; *Chorus Line* comes to Broadway; Ballet Trocadéro de
Monte Carlo and  Trockadero Gloxinia, two *en travestie* companies,
perform; Public Broadcasting System begins "Dance in America" se-
ries; New works: *Esplanade* (Taylor/J. S. Bach), *Push Comes to Shove*
(Tharp/Franz Joseph Haydn and Joseph Lamb)

**Other Culture**:  Music: *Notturno* (Donald Martino, Pulitzer Prize
1974), *The Flower Fed Buffaloes* (John Harbison), *Einstein on the
Beach* (Philip Glass); First home computers sold; Solzhenitsyn emigrates to the United States

## 1977–1978

**Tudor**: Choreographs *Tiller in the Fields* (Antonin Dvorak) (17 July)

**World**: Carter is president; the United States officially recognizes
People's Republic of China; Panama Canal Treaty signed

**Dance**: The movie *The Turning Point,* directed by Herbert Ross with
Nora Kaye assisting, is released; Baryshnikov joins NYCB

**Other Culture**: Music: *Visions of Terror and Wonder* (Richard Wer-
nick, Pulitzer Prize, 1977), *Wild Angels of the Open Hills* (Joseph
Schwantner)

## 1979

**Tudor**: Suffers massive heart attack; Ceases teaching at UCI

**World**: Camp David accords between Israel and Egypt; USSR invades
Afghanistan; Shah of Iran deposed; Iranians seize American Embassy
and take fifty-four hostages; Margaret Thatcher elected Prime Minister
of England; Three-Mile Island nuclear accident

**Dance**:  Léonide Massine dies

## 1980–1981

**Tudor**:  Returns to work at ABT; Appointed choreographer emeritus

**World**:  AIDS identified; Reagan elected president ushering in supply side economics; Russia represses Polish labor movement "Solidarity"; First woman appointed to Supreme Court; Egyptian president Anwar Sadat assassinated

**Dance:**  Royal Ballet performs *Dark Elegies* (Gustav Mahler); Pacific Northwest Ballet mounts full-length *Swan Lake*; Twyla Tharp collaborates with David Byrne on *The Catherine Wheel* for Broadway; David Parsons joins Paul Taylor Company; Oliver Smith and Lucia Chase leave ABT and Mikhail Baryshnikov  becomes director

**Other Culture**:  Richard Sierra's "Tilted Arc" sculpture installed in Federal Plaza in New York City, causes citywide controversy; Music: *Three Hallucinations* (John Corigliano)

## 1982–1984

**Tudor**:  Stages *Pillar of Fire* for ABT's celebration of the ballet's fortieth anniversary

**World**:  Recession in the United States; Gross National Product falls precipitately; First woman astronaut voyages in space; The United States invades Grenada; Bishop Desmond Tutu wins Nobel Peace Prize

**Dance**: Marie Rambert and George Balanchine die; Joyce Theater opens; ABT dancers picket the management accusing them of a lockout; New artistic directors are Erik Bruhn with National Ballet of Canada, Maina Gielgud with Australian Ballet, Rudolf Nureyev with Paris Opera Ballet, Peter Martins and Jerome Robbins with NYCB (bearing the title of ballet-masters-in-chief); William Forsythe's *Ways: A Piece about Ballet (Gänge 1—Ein Stüxk Über Ballett)* scandalizes audience in Frankfurt; Dance Theater Workshop establishes Bessie Awards; Mark Morris debuts as choreographer; Trisha Brown choreographs *Set and Reset*

**Other Culture**: *Time* Magazine votes the computer as Machine of the Year; Ellen Taaffe Zwilich wins Pulitzer Prize in music (1983); New York Philharmonic begins the Horizons Festivals of new music with The New Romanticism; *Cats* (Gillian Lynne/Andrew Lloyd Webber, based on poems by T. S. Eliot) opens in London

# 1985

**Tudor**: Nureyev presents "Homage à Tudor," a full evening of Tudor ballets with the Paris Opera Ballet; Receives Royal Academy of Dance's Queen Elizabeth II Coronation Award
United States economy rebounds; Reagan–Gorbachev summit

**Dance**: Newly appointed company directors are Helgi Tomasson, San Francisco Ballet; Frank Andersen, Royal Danish Ballet; Anthony Dowell, Royal Ballet (England)

# 1986

**Tudor**: Receives Capezio Award, Dance/USA Award, and the City of New York's Handel Medallion, Kennedy Center Honors

**World**: Iran-Contra scandal revealed; Space shuttle Challenger explodes; AIDS epidemic identified

**Dance**: Full evening work, *The Eternal Triangle,* performed by Bill T. Jones and Arnie Zane Company

**Other Culture**: Music: *Silver Ladders* (Joan Tower)

# 1987

**Tudor**: Dies

**Dance:** Nora Kaye dies a few months before Tudor; Martha Clarke's "The Hunger Artist" premieres; Mark Morris replaces Maurice Béjart at theThéâtre Royal de la Monnaie in Belgium; Bob Fosse dies; "Dancing for Life" benefit raises money to fight AIDS

# Selected Bibliography

Anderson, Jack. *Ballet and Modern Dance*. Princeton, N.J.: Princeton Book Company, 1986.

Archer, Jules. *The Incredible Sixties*. San Diego, Calif.: Harcourt, Brace, Jovanovich, 1986.

Balanchine, George, and Frances Mason. *101 Stories of the Great Ballets*. New York: Doubleday, 1975.

———. *Balanchine's Complete Stories of Great Ballets*. New York: Doubleday, 1954.

Chafe, William H. *America Since World War II*. New York: Oxford University Press, 1986.

Chazin-Bennahum, Judith. *The Ballets of Antony Tudor*. New York: Oxford University Press, 1994.

Clarke, Mary. *Dancers of Mercury,* London: Adam and Charles Black. 1962.

Clarke, Peter. *Hope and Glory: Britain 1900–1990*. London: Penguin Books, 1996.

Cohen, Selma Jeanne, and John Percival. *Dance Perspectives* 17. Brooklyn, N.Y.: Dance Perspectives, Inc., 1963.

*Compton's Encyclopedia On Line*. The Learning Company, 1999. http://www.bartleby.com/65/co/Compton.html

Dallek, Robert. *Lone Star Rising*. New York: Oxford University Press, 1991.

De Mille, Agnes. *Dance to the Piper*. New York: Little Brown, 1952.

Denby, Edwin. *Looking at Dance*. New York: Pellegrini and Cudahy, 1949.

Dunbar, June, ed. *José Limón: The Artist Re-Viewed*. London: Harwood Academic Publishers, 2000.

Evans, Harold. *The American Century*. New York: Alfred A. Knopf, 1998.

Fitzgerald, Gerald, ed. *Annals of the Metropolitan Opera 1883–1985*. Boston: Metropolitan Opera Guild and G. K. Hall, 1989.

Friedman, Francis, Dr. Wood Gray, and Dr. Richard Holstadler. *A Hypertext on American History,* from USIA publications: An Outline of American History, An Outline of American Economy, An Outline of American Government, An Outline of American Literature; American History in the Modern World, Magazine Branch, International Publications Division 011, U.S. Department of State, Washington, D.C., Internet, 1964, 90, 94 updated 2/1/2000  http://www.state.gov/.

Garafola, Lynn. *Diaghilev's Ballets Russes.* London: Oxford University Press, 1989.

Getz, Leslie. *Dancers and Choreographers: A Selected Bibliography.* Wakefield, R.I., London: Moyer Bell, 1995.

Grant, Gail. *Technical Manual and Dictionary of Classical Ballet.* New York: Dover Publications, 1982.

Hall, Fernau. *An Anatomy of Ballet.* London: Andrew Melrose, 1953.

—————. Antony Tudor. unpublished manuscript.

Harris, José. *Private Lives, Public Spirit: Britain 1870–1914.* London: Penguin Books, 1993.

Heuvel, Katrina Vanden, ed. *The Nation 1865/1990.* New York: Thunder Mouth's Press, 1990.

Jenkins, Alan. *The Forties.* New York: Universe Books, 1977.

Kane, Angela. "A Catalogue of Works Choreographed by Paul Taylor." Richard Ralph, ed. *Dance Research* XIV no. 2 (Winter, 1996): 72–75.

Kavanagh, Julie. *Secret Muses,* London: Faber and Faber, 1996.

Kirstein, Lincoln. *Movement and Metaphor.* New York: Praeger, 1970.

Koegler, Horst. *The Concise Oxford Dictionary of Ballet.* London: Oxford University Press, 1977.

Lloyd, Margaret. *The Borzoi Book of Modern Dance.* New York: Dance Horizons, 1974.

Machlin, Lisa Siegel. *Notated Theatrical Dance.* New York: Dance Notation Bureau, 1992.

Machlis, Joseph, and Kristine Forney. *The Enjoyment of Music.* New York: W. W. Norton, 1999.

Markova, Alicia. *Markova Remembers.* London: Hamish Hamilton, 1986.

McDonagh, Don. *The Rise and Fall and Rise of Modern Dance.* New York: New American Library, 1970.

Miller, Douglas T., and Marion Nowak. *The Fifties.* Garden City, New York: Doubleday & Co.,1977.

Noble, Peter. *British Ballet.* London: S. Robinson, 1949.

Payne, Charles. *American Ballet Theatre.* New York: Alfred A. Knopf, 1978.

Philp, Richard, ed. *Dance Magazine,* New York: Roslyne Paige Stern and Robert Stern, January–November 1999.

Picon, Gäryton. *Modern Painting.* New York: Newsweek Books, 1974.

Rambert, Marie. *Quicksilver.* London: Macmillan, 1972.

Randel, Don Michael. *Harvard Concise Dictionary of Music.* Cambridge, Mass.: Belknap Press of Harvard University, 1978.

Sawyer, Elizabeth. "That Englishman Abroad." *Dance Chronicle* 20, no. 3 (1977): 227–273.

Siegel, Marcia B. *The Shapes of Change.* New York: Avon Books, 1979.

Sowell, Debra Hickenlooper. *The Christensen Brothers: An American Dance Epic.* London: Harwood Academic Publishers, 1998.

Taylor, Paul. *Private Domain.* New York: Afred Knopf, 1984.

Tharp, Twyla. *Push Comes to Shove.* New York: Bantam Books, 1992.

Topaz, Muriel, ed. *Choreography and Dance* vol.1 part 2. London: Harwood Academic Publishers, 1989.

Tracy, Robert. *Goddess.* New York: Limelight Editions, 1997.

# Index

# About the Author

At age eleven Muriel Topaz saw Martha Graham perform and decided to devote her life to dance. After a short career as a performer, Topaz began restaging ballets including Tudor's *Jardin aux lilas* for the Milwaukee Ballet and *Continuo* for the Paris Conservatory. Later she served as a senior editor for *Dance Magazine* and executive editor of the journal *Choreography and Dance* and the book series *Choreography and Dance Studies.* She also authored *A Guide to Performing Arts Education.*

A world authority on Labanotation, Topaz organized and co-chaired two International Congresses on Movement Notation, in Israel and Hong Kong. As a professional notator, she has written dance scores of some of the most notable choreographers of our time: Humphrey, Jooss, Robbins, Sokolow, Taylor, Tudor, and Limón. She has authored a standard text, *Elementary Labanotation,* and has taught throughout the United States and in Argentina, Mexico, France, and England. From 1996 to 1999 she was chair of the International Council of Kinetography Laban.

From 1985 until 1993 Topaz directed the dance division of the Juilliard School and, from 1977 to 1985, was executive director of the Dance Notation Bureau. Topaz served on the advisory board and as adjudicator for Regional Dance America, chaired the dance panel of the New York State Council on the Arts, and evaluated dance companies for the Canada Council, the National Endowment for the Arts, Ballet Builders, the New Jersey State Council on the Arts, and the Massachusetts Cultural Council.

In 1998 she was awarded a John Simon Guggenheim Foundation Fellowship to pursue research for *Undimmed Lustre: The Life of Antony Tudor.*

Topaz was married to the distinguished American composer Jacob Druckman until his untimely death in 1996. She has two children, Karen Jeanneret-Druckman, an attorney, and Daniel Druckman, percussionist for the New York Philharmonic Orchestra.